The Big Book of Weekend Woodworking

150 Easy Projects

John A. and Joyce C. Nelson

LARK BOOKS

A Division of Sterling Publishing Co., Inc.
New York

Editor: Paige Gilchrist
Art Director: Shannon Yokeley
Photographers: Evan Bracken, Steve Mann, Deborah Porter-Hayes
Cover Designer: Barbara Zaretsky
Assistant Editor: Susan Kieffer
Art Production Assistance: Lance Wille
Editorial Assistance: Delores Gosnell
Art Intern: Melanie Cooper
Editorial Interns: Meghan McGuire, Janna Norton, Amanda Wheeler

Published by Lark Books, A Division of
Sterling Publishing Co., Inc.
387 Park Avenue South, New York, N.Y. 10016

This book is composed of the following title published by Rodale Press:
The Weekend Woodworker © 1990 by John A. Nelson
and the following titles published by Sterling Publishing Co., Inc.:
52 Weekend Woodworking Projects © 1991 by John A. Nelson
52 Country Projects for the Weekend Woodworker © 1992 by John A. Nelson
52 Decorative Weekend Woodworking Projects © 1993 by John A. Nelson
52 Toys & Puzzles for the Weekend Woodworker © 1994 by John A. Nelson

Text, project designs, and illustrations © 2005, John & Joyce Nelson
Photography © 2005, Lark Books

Contents

Stools, Stands & Shelves

Children's Furniture & Accessories

Toys, Games & Puzzles

Folk Art Projects

Fretsaw Projects

Wall Boxes

Antique Projects

Introduction

Years ago, my wife, Joyce, and I restored a 200-year-old Vermont farmhouse. We wanted to furnish it with antique furniture, but since many of the pieces we saw were way out of our price range, we decided to work together to make copies of antiques we liked instead. Back in those days I had only basic woodworking experience, but I put it to use. Meanwhile, Joyce taught herself all kinds of painting and faux-finishing techniques she used to make our new pieces look centuries old. We had a great time, and we were quite successful at furnishing our home with beautiful replicas.

Soon, woodworking magazines started asking us to write about our woodworking and finishing techniques. They published our instructions, along with how-to illustrations I drew of all the reproductions we had created. Eventually, we had enough material to write a book, and then another, and another. By this time, we had not only perfected our techniques, but we had branched out from antiques to everything from toys and clocks to folk art and household and garden items. At last count, we had contributed more than 500 woodworking articles to many different magazines, and this is our 60th book.

The Big Book of Weekend Woodworking is our chance to fill a single book with 150 of our favorite and most popular projects. We chose them so that there would be plenty of projects for woodworkers at every level. There are many simple items, such as a wooden basket, a candleholder, and a toy train, that require only basic woodworking tools. There are also some more elaborate ones, such as a four-drawer storage unit and an Adirondack chair. All are designed to be made over a weekend. Some can be finished entirely in that time. For others, you might need an extra day or so after you've assembled the project to apply a stain or paint finish. But every one of the projects lets you complete a weekend of woodworking with a sense of accomplishment—and something to show for it.

Part of what makes these projects so weekend friendly is the way we've presented the information. Every project includes a materials list that spells out how much wood you need in what dimensions, step-by-step instructions, and clearly labeled, exploded views that show how to put each project together. The easy-to-follow format gives you all the details and plans, so you can get right to the woodworking.

We've divided the projects into a dozen chapters, covering all the categories readers have asked for most often over the years. In the Kitchen Projects chapter, for example, you'll find salad forks, a classic cutting board, and a wall spice box. In Yard & Garden Projects, there are planters, a trellis, and a couple of birdhouses. And in Children's Furniture & Accessories, projects range from a piggy bank to a doll cradle modeled after a vintage 1900s design. Nine other chapters round out the offerings.

I've built the book's projects and developed the instructions and illustrations. Joyce has done the finishing work on all the projects and helped behind the scenes in countless ways. It gives us great satisfaction to pass along the detailed plans for 150 of our best and most requested projects. We hope you get just as much satisfaction out of using them to make your own handcrafted keepsakes and gifts. Here's to many enjoyable weekends of woodworking.

John A. Nelson

Basics

Using the Drawings for Each Project

With each project there is at least a two-view drawing provided. One is almost always called the front view, and the other is either the side view or the top view. The front view is always the most important view and the place you should start in studying the drawings. At times a section view is used to further illustrate some particular feature of the project. The section view is sometimes a partial view that illustrates only a portion of the project, such as a particular molding detail or way of joining parts.

Most of the projects also have an exploded view, which fully illustrates how the project goes together. Make sure that you fully understand how the project is to be assembled before you begin any work on it.

There is a Materials List of supplies needed for each project, and the part numbers in the lists correspond to the numbers in the illustrated views that accompany each project. This will enable you to see exactly where each part is located and how it fits together with other parts in the design. Note: all measurements are in inches unless otherwise noted.

Multiple parts should be made exactly the same size and shape. Every now and then a project requires a pair of parts—that is, a right-hand piece and a left-hand piece. In such a case, take care not to make duplicate pieces, but rather a left-hand and right-hand pair. In most projects requiring a pair, this is noted, but for any multiple parts double-check if in doubt.

Throughout, when practical, I numbered all the parts of a project in the order that I would suggest you make and assemble them. You might want to make and assemble your project some other way, but this is what worked best for me.

Making a Project

After you thoroughly study the project, start by carefully making each individual part. Take care to make each piece exactly to the correct size and exactly square—that is, each cut at 90° to the face, as required.

Sand each individual piece, but take care to keep all the edges sharp. Do not round the edges at this time; some will be rounded after assembly.

After all the pieces have been made with great care, dry-fit the pieces—that is, cautiously put together the entire project to check for correct fit throughout before final assembly. If anything needs refitting, this is the time to correct it.

When the pieces all fit correctly, glue and/or nail the project together, again taking care that all fits are tight and square. Sand the project all over; it is at this time that edges can be rounded, if necessary. The project is then ready for finishing.

Enlarging a Pattern or Design

Many of the drawings are reduced relative to the actual size of the parts so that all of the information can be presented on the page. In some projects the patterns for irregular parts or irregular portions of parts must be enlarged to full size. A grid of squares is drawn over these parts, and the original size of the grid is noted on the drawing.

There are four ways a design or shape of the irregular part or parts can be enlarged to full size.

METHOD ONE

One of the simplest and least expensive ways is to use a photocopy machine with an enlarging/reducing feature. Simply put the book page on the machine, choose the enlargement mode you need (usually expressed as a percentage of the original), and make a copy. In a few cases, you may have to make another copy of the enlargement copy in order to get the required size. Once in awhile you will not be able to get the exact size required, but the result will be close enough for most work, perhaps requiring a little touching up, at most.

METHOD TWO

A very quick and extremely accurate method is to ask a local commercial printer to make a P.M.T. (photomechanical transfer) of the area needed to be enlarged or reduced. This is a photographic method that yields an exact size without any difficulty. This method will cost a little money, depending on the size of the final P.M.T., but if your time is valuable, it might be worth it.

METHOD THREE

Another simple, quick method is to use a drawing tool called the pantograph. It is an inexpensive tool that is very simple to use for enlarging or reducing to almost any required size. If you do a lot of enlarging or reducing, the cost of this tool may be well worth the price.

METHOD FOUR

Most authors assume woodworkers will use the grid and dot-to-dot method. It is very simple; you do not have to be an artist to use the method. It can be used to enlarge or reduce to any size or scale and requires just eight simple steps:

1. Note what size the full-size grid should be. This is usually indicated on the drawing near the grid. Most of the grids used with the project drawings must be redrawn so that each square is ½ inch or 1 inch per side.

2. Calculate the overall required width and height. If it is not given, simply count the squares across and down and multiply by the size of each square. For example, a ½-inch grid with 15 squares across requires an overall width of 7½ inches.

The paper size needed to draw the pattern full size should be a little larger than the overall size of the part.

3. It will be helpful, but not necessary, if you have a few basic drafting tools. Tools suggested are: a drafting board, a scale (ruler), a T-square, a 45° triangle, masking tape, and a sheet of paper a little larger than the required overall size of the pattern. Tape the paper to the drafting board or other surface, and carefully draw the required grid on the paper, using the drafting tools or whatever tools you have.

4. On the original, reduced drawing in the book, start from the upper left corner and add letters across the top of the grid from left to right, A through whatever letter it takes to get to the other side of the grid. From the same starting point, add numbers down, from 1 to whatever number it takes to get to the bottom of the grid.

5. On your full-size grid, add letters and numbers in exactly the same way you did on the original.

6. On the original reduced drawing, draw dots along the pattern outline wherever it crosses the grid.

7. On your full-size grid, locate and draw the same dots on the grid. It is helpful to locate each dot by using the letters across the top and the numbers along the side. For example, a dot at B-6 can easily be found on the new, full-size grid by coming down from line B and over on line 6.

8. All that is left to do is to connect the dots. Note: you do not have to be exact, all you have to do is to sketch a line between the dots using your eye to approximate the shape of the original, reduced drawing.

Transferring the Pattern from Paper to Wood

Tape the full-size pattern to the wood with carbon paper in between for transferring the pattern, and use a pen to trace over the pattern. If you are going to copy the pattern many times, make a template instead. Simply transfer the pattern onto a sheet of heavy cardboard or ⅛-inch-thick hardboard or plywood and cut out the pattern. This template can then be used over and over by simply tracing around the template to lay out the pattern for each copy.

If the pattern is symmetrical—that is, exactly the same size and shape on both sides of an imaginary line—make only a half-pattern and trace it twice, once on each side of the midline. This will ensure the perfect symmetry of the finished part.

For small patterns—8½ inches x 11 inches or smaller at full size— make a photocopy of the full-size pattern using any copy machine. Tape the copy, printed side down, and using a hot flatiron or hot wood-burning set, heat the back side of the copy. The pattern will transfer from the paper directly to the wood. This method is very good for very small or complicated patterns.

Another method for small patterns—8½ inches x 11 inches or smaller at full size—is to make a photocopy of the pattern, and, using rubber cement or spray-mount adhesive, lightly glue the copy directly to the wood. Cut out the piece with the copy glued directly to the wood. Simply peel the copy away from the wood after you cut out the piece. Then sand all over.

Selecting Material for Your Project

As lumber will probably be the most expensive material you will purchase for each project, it is a good idea that you have some basic knowledge about lumber so that you can make wise choices and save a little money here and there on your purchases.

All lumber is divided into two kinds, hardwood and softwood. Hardwoods are deciduous trees, trees that flower and lose their leaves seasonally; softwoods are the coniferous trees, which are cone-bearing and usually evergreen. In actuality, a few hardwoods are softer than some softwoods—but on the whole, hardwoods are harder, closer grained, much more durable, tougher to work, and take a stain beautifully. Hardwood typically costs more than softwood, but it is well worth it.

All wood contains pores—open spaces that serve as water-conducting vessels—that are more noticeable in some kinds of wood than in others. Woods such as oak and mahogany have pores that are very noticeable and probably should be filled, for the best-finished appearance. Maple and birch are what are called close-grained woods, which provide a beautiful, smooth finish.

The grain of wood is the result of each year's growth of new cells. Around the tree's circumference each year, annular growth forms a new and hard fibrous layer called a ring. Growth in most trees is seasonal but somewhat regular so that these rings are evenly spaced. In other trees this annular growth is not very regular, thus creating uneven spacing and thickness. The pattern formed by the rings when the tree is cut into lumber is what we see as the grain pattern.

The softwoods I used for most of the projects are pine, spruce, and fir. Pine was the favorite since it is the easiest to work, especially for simple accessories such as those found in this book. The hardwoods I used most were maple, walnut, oak, cherry, poplar, and birch.

Always buy dried lumber, as green lumber will shrink, twist, and warp while drying. Purchase the best lumber you can find for these projects since none of them require a great deal of material. Your work will go more easily, and the finished project will be so much better for the superior-quality wood. The actual cost difference between an inexpensive piece of wood and the best you can find will be quite small since the overall cost of any of these projects is very low to begin with.

A few projects call for wide boards. I believe the projects would look best if you could find the correct width. The correct width also adds to the authenticity. If this is not possible, glue narrower boards together by edge-joining them to produce the necessary width. Try to match grain patterns with great care so that each joint will not be so noticeable. Even though I prefer the look of the single, wide board, I should point out that a glued joint is as strong as a single piece of wood and probably will not warp.

Lumber is sold by the board foot. A board foot is a piece of wood that is 1 foot wide, 1 inch thick, and 1 foot long. A piece of wood 4 inches wide ($\frac{1}{3}$ foot), 1 inch thick, and 12 feet long contains 4 board feet of wood. The formula is: width in feet x thickness in inches x length in feet = board feet (in the example, $\frac{1}{3}$ x 1 x 12 = 4 board feet).

In the Materials Lists, the dimensions given of the wood needed for each project are listed in inches, first thickness, then width, and then length. For example: Body - $\frac{1}{2}$ x 6$\frac{1}{2}$ — 14 LONG.

FINDING BOARD FEET USING A FACTOR

Using the table below to find the appropriate factor, we can easily calculate that a board 1 inch thick, 5 inches wide, and 12 feet long can be converted to board feet by multiplying 12 (linear length) times 0.417 (factor) to give 5.004 board feet of lumber. (The term linear length refers to the actual length of any board as it is measured.)

Dressed lumber comes in actual sizes other than the nominal size would indicate because of the finishing process. For example, a 1 x 6 measures about ³⁄₄ inch by 5⁵⁄₈ inches in actual size. The chart below indicates what some of the actual sizes may be. Note: today, the actual width may vary—in some areas a 1 x 6 might be 5¹⁄₂ inches wide rather than 5⁵⁄₈ inches wide. Check around in your area before buying wood.

BOARD FEET USING LINEAR LENGTH

1/2" THICK BOARD		1" THICK BOARD	
WIDTH	FACTOR	WIDTH	FACTOR
2	.083	2	.167
3	.125	3	.250
4	.166	4	.333
5	.209	5	.417
6	.250	6	.500
8	.333	8	.666

ROUGH SIZE	FINISHED SIZE
1 x 2	³⁄₄ x 1⁵⁄₈
1 x 3	³⁄₄ x 2⁵⁄₈
1 x 4	³⁄₄ x 3⁵⁄₈
1 x 5	³⁄₄ x 4⁵⁄₈
1 x 6	³⁄₄ x 5⁵⁄₈
1 x 8	³⁄₄ x 7⁵⁄₈
1 x 10	³⁄₄ x 9¹⁄₂
1 x 12	³⁄₄ x 11¹⁄₂

HARDWARE FOR YOUR PROJECT

The extra money spent on hardware of high quality versus that saved on low-cost hardware is—as noted in purchasing lumber—a very small difference since the overall cost of your project is already quite low. Don't forget, the hardware is usually what is most visible, so the little extra spent will be well worth the increased look of quality for many years to come.

Kinds of Joints

The projects require four kinds of joints—and, for the most part, only three. These basic joints are the butt joint, the rabbet joint, the dado joint and, in a few instances, the dovetail joint. These can be made by hand without power tools. If you do have power tools, use them; early crafters would have used them if they had had them.

Most of the simpler projects use the butt joint. This is the simplest of all joints and, as its name implies, is simply two boards that are butted up against each other and joined together, perhaps with glue and nails or screws. The major disadvantage of the butt joint is that there is less surface area available for gluing or nailing than for other joints. Nails sometimes back out of the joint over time, which also makes an opening at the joint. A rabbet joint is an L-shaped cutout made along the edge or end of one board to overlap the edge or end of the mating board. This joint can also be nailed and/or glued together. Because rabbet joints are often cut into side pieces, the nails—put in from the sides—may be hidden somewhat from view. Dado joints are similar to rabbet joints, except that the cut is made leaving wood shoulders on both sides. A drawer side is an excellent example of the use of both a dado joint and a rabbet joint. The most difficult joint is the dovetail joint, but with a little thought and careful layout, they can be easily made. Dovetail joints are made by interlocking ends of boards that have had notches cut into them.

Gluing

Glue was not in general use until after 1750. Therefore, most of the antique projects featured in this book probably were simply nailed together. If by chance they were glued together, they were probably glued together with hot animal, or hide, glue.

Wood glues are either hot or cold glue, depending on whether or not heat is used to prepare them. Hot glue is made from animal parts and is very strong and quick-setting. Until very recently, old-fashioned hide glue was considered the only true, satisfactory kind of glue to use in cabinetmaking. Recent developments in new and better cold glues have made this generalization debatable. Cold glues are all derived from synthetic material of one kind or another. They vary in durability and strength. For the simpler projects cold glue is, by far, the easiest to use, and I recommend its use. In using cold glue, always follow the instructions given on the label.

When gluing, always take care to clean all excess glue from around the joint. This is a must if you are going to stain the project. The excess glue will not take the stain and will appear white. I find that by waiting for 10 to 15 minutes, just until the glue is almost set, I can carefully remove most of it with a sharp wood chisel. Do not wipe off the excessive glue with a wet cloth as the water will weaken the glue joint and possibly spread glue irretrievably into the pore space, staining the wood.

For the few projects that are a little difficult to hold together properly while gluing, the new hot-glue guns can be very helpful. Hot-glue guns use solid glue sticks that are inserted, heated to their melting point, and then liquid glue is pushed through the tip while very hot. This kind of glue dries very quickly and sets in about 10 seconds without clamping. Take care if you use this kind of glue as it is difficult to get good tight-fitting joints every time. The glue sets up so quickly that you have to work very fast. This kind of glue is good to use for special applications but not for everything; the slower-drying cold glue is still better to use for most of the projects.

Finishing

Once you have completed assembling your project, you are then ready to apply a finish. This is an important part and should not be rushed. Remember, this is the part that will make the biggest impression for many years to come. No matter how good the wood and hardware you use, regardless of how good the joints are, a poor finish will ruin your project. If it takes eight hours to make the project, plan on eight hours to finish it correctly.

PREPARING
1. All joints should be checked for tight fits. If necessary, apply water putty to all joints, and allow ample time for drying. Apply water putty to fill those nail heads also.

2. Sand the project all over in the direction of the wood grain. If sanding is done by hand, use a sanding block, and be careful to keep all corners still sharp. Use 100-grit sandpaper. Resand all over, using a 180-grit sandpaper, and, if necessary, sand once more with 250-grit sandpaper. Take care not to round edges at this time.

3. If you do want any of the edges rounded, use the 180-grit sandpaper, and later the 250-grit sandpaper, specifically to round the edges.

4. A copy of an antique that looks new seems somehow to be a direct contradiction. Distressing—making the piece look old—can be done in many ways. Using a piece of coral stone about 3 inches in diameter, or a similar object, roll the stone across the various surfaces. Don't be afraid to add a few random scratches here and there, especially on the bottom or back, where an object would have been worn the most. Carefully study the object, and try to imagine how it would have been used through the years. Using a rasp, judiciously round the edges where you think wear would have occurred. Resand the entire project and the newly worn edges with 180-grit paper.

5. Clean all surfaces with a damp rag to remove all dust.

FILLERS

A paste filler should be used for porous wood such as oak, ash, or mahogany. Purchase paste filler that is slightly darker than the color of your wood as the new wood you used will turn darker with age. Before using paste filler, thin it with turpentine so it can be applied with a brush. Use a stiff brush, and brush with the grain in order to fill the pores. Wipe off with a piece of burlap across the grain after 15 or 20 minutes, taking care to leave filler in the pores. Apply a second coat if necessary; let it dry for 24 hours.

STAINING

There are two major kinds of stain: water-base stain and oil-base stain. Water stains are commonly purchased in powder form and mixed as needed by dissolving the powder in hot water. Premixed water-base stains have recently become available. Water stain has a tendency to raise the grain of the wood, so that after it dries, the surface should be lightly sanded with fine sandpaper. Oil stain is made from pigments ground in linseed oil and does not raise the grain.

1. Test the stain color on a scrap piece of the same kind of lumber you are using to make certain it will be the color you wish.

2. Wipe or brush on the stain as quickly and as evenly as possible to avoid overlapping streaks. If a darker finish is desired, apply more than one coat of stain. Try not to apply too much stain on the end grain. Allow to dry in a dust-free area for at least 24 hours.

FINISHES

Shellac is a hard, easy-to-apply finish and dries in a few hours. For best results, thin slightly with alcohol and apply an extra coat or two. Several coats of thin shellac are much better than one or two thick coats. Sand lightly with extra-fine sandpaper between coats, but be sure to rub the entire surface with a dampened cloth. Strive for a smooth, satin finish—not a high-gloss finish coat—for an antique effect.

Varnish is easy to brush on and dries to a smooth, hard finish within 24 hours. It makes an excellent finish that is transparent and will give a deep-finish look to your project. Be sure to apply varnish in a completely dust-free area. Apply one or two coats directly from the can with long, even strokes. Rub between each coat, and after the last coat, with 0000 steel wool.

Oil finishes are especially easy to use for projects such as those in this book. Oil finish is easy to apply, long-lasting, never needs resanding, and actually improves wood permanently. Apply a heavy, wet coat uniformly to all surfaces, and let set for 20 or 30 minutes. Wipe completely dry until you have a pleasing finish.

PAINTED PROJECTS

Use a high-quality paint, either oil- or water-base. Today, the trend is towards water-base paint. Prime your project, and lightly sand after it dries. Apply two light coats of paint rather than one thick coat. We like to add some water to thin water-base paint since we feel that water-base paint tends to be a little thick. On all projects for children, and for all toys, always be sure to use a non-toxic paint.

Note: for a very satisfying feel to the finish and professional touch to your project, apply a topcoat of paste wax as the final step.

Achieving an Aged Look

Follow the five steps outlined for preparing your project as described under Finishing. Then follow these steps to distress your project.

1. Seal the wood with a light coat of shellac with 50% alcohol. After the shellac is dry, rub lightly with 0000 steel wool. Wipe clean.

2. Apply an even coat of oil-base paint, taking care to use an antique color paint. Let dry for 48 hours. Do not paint the backs or bottoms—these were seldom painted on the original pieces.

3. Sand with 120-grit sandpaper all the rounded edges you prepared for wear marks in step 4 of Preparing. Remember, if these edges were worn, the paint surely would have been removed also. Sand away paint from all sharp edges and corners since edges and corners would wear through the years.

4. Lightly sand all over to remove any paint gloss, using 180-grit sandpaper. Wipe clean.

5. Wipe on a wash coat of oil-base black paint with a cloth directly from the can. Take care to get the black paint in all corners, and in all distress marks and scratches. Don't forget the unpainted back and bottoms. Wipe all paint off immediately before it dries, but leave black paint in all corners, joints, scratches, and distress marks, If you apply too much, wipe off using a cloth with turpentine on it. Let dry for 24 hours. Apply a light coat of paste wax.

ALTERNATIVE ONE

For a really aged look, apply two coats of paint, each a totally different color (for example, first coat, a powder blue; second coat, antique brick red). Allow 24 hours between coats. After the second coat has dried for 48 hours or more, follow steps 3 and 4 above, but sand the topcoat off so that the first color shows through here and there at worn areas. Finish up with step 5 as outlined above. This is especially good on projects such as footstools or large painted wall boxes.

ALTERNATIVE TWO

If you want your painted project to have a crackled finish, follow these additional steps. After step 1, page 20, apply a coat of liquid hide glue over the intended painted surfaces. Let dry four to 12 hours. Then paint on a coat of gesso (a form of base paint in use since the sixteenth century). Paint lightly and do not go over any strokes. In 10 to 15 seconds, the gesso will start to crackle. Let dry for 24 hours in a very dry area. After 24 hours or more, continue on to step 2. (It would be a good idea to experiment on scrap wood before applying any of this to your finished project. Some crafters combine step 2 with the crackling by mixing their paint with the gesso, two parts gesso to one part paint.)

Visits to museums, antique shops, and flea markets will help you develop an eye for exactly what an original antique looks like. This will give you an excellent idea of how antiques have been worn through the years. With this firsthand experience, you will have a much clearer idea of what kind of finish you are after, so that your careful reproduction will realistically look hundreds of years old.

Hardware

Some of the projects in this book require special hardware—special parts such as hangers, hooks, clock quartz movements, hands, bezels, wheels, axles, hinges, latches, etc. If you are going to do any woodworking at all you should acquaint yourself with the various companies that specialize in handling these special items. You should write for as many woodworking supply and clock component catalogs as possible, in order to have a large choice of parts. This also gives you the opportunity to compare prices and to save a little money.

Before starting any project it is a good idea to obtain the parts ahead of time, in order to modify your projects to fit the parts, if necessary.

To get a good selection of catalogs, go to a local library and check out a woodworking magazine or two, to find companies to contact for catalogs.

You also could check for hardware on the Internet.

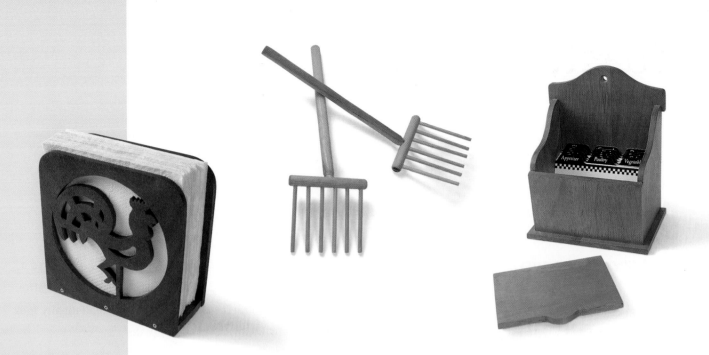

Kitchen Projects

Here's a collection of practical projects that are not only easy to make, but that add a handcrafted look of cozy charm to any kitchen. All you need now is a loaf of warm bread for the breadbasket.

Toaster Tongs

If you're like most folks, you start off the day in frustration. You can't get the darn toast out of the toaster! Once you make this simple, handy kitchen implement you'll be ready to face each morning—at least after a cup of coffee.

1. Select the wood. There are several ways to make a pair of toaster tongs. My approach is to start with a piece of oversized stock—¾ inch thick x 1⅛ inches wide x 9 inches long—and then work it down to the finished dimensions. Use a hardwood such as maple or cherry.

2. Lay out the tongs. Draw a line down the center of the wide side of the stock. At a point on the line roughly 1½ inches from one end, mark the center of a ⅝ inch-diameter hole and draw the hole. To lay out the insides of the legs, draw two lines: each one is tangent to the hole and parallel to the sides of the stock, as shown.

To lay out the outside of the tongs, locate a second point on the center line, ⅝ inch above the center of the hole. Swing a ⁷⁄₁₆-inch arc from that point, as shown in the top view. Extend a line from the bottom of the arc to lay out the outside of the legs. If you've measured correctly, the outside lines are ⅛ inch from the inside lines.

3. Cut out the tongs. Drill out the hole and cut along the layout lines with a band saw. Saw just outside the lines and sand down to the final leg thickness of ⅛ inch, taking care to make the legs as nearly identical as possible.

4. Finish the tongs. Either leave the wood unfinished, or apply a coat of vegetable oil or salad-bowl finish.

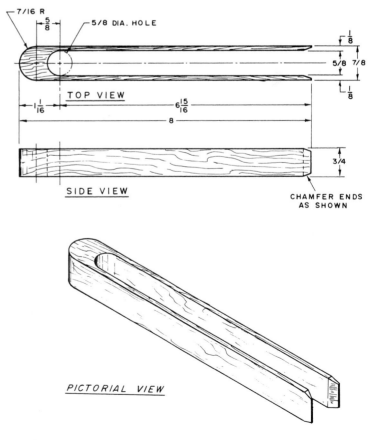

PICTORIAL VIEW

Classic Cutting Board

*Cutting boards come in
all shapes and sizes. There are
pigs, chickens, turkeys, and even rabbits
as cutting boards. This design is a simple rectangle
with a round handle. Most any kind of hardwood and most
any thickness of wood can be used. I used 1-inch-thick ash for the
one pictured. As cutting boards are very popular, keep your full-size pattern. You'll probably be making more than one cutting board, especially
after everyone sees the first one.*

1. Carefully lay out the full-size pattern on a piece of cardboard about 12 x 22 inches in size. Cut out the full-size pattern, and transfer the shape to the wood. If you have to glue up material to get the full 11-inch-wide board, be sure to use waterproof glue.

2. Carefully cut out the cutting board, and sand all edges and surfaces. Using a ⅜-inch-radius router bit with a ball-bearing follower, rout the top and bottom edges, and then resand all over.

3. Be sure to use a finish that is non-toxic, such as one labeled as salad-bowl finish.

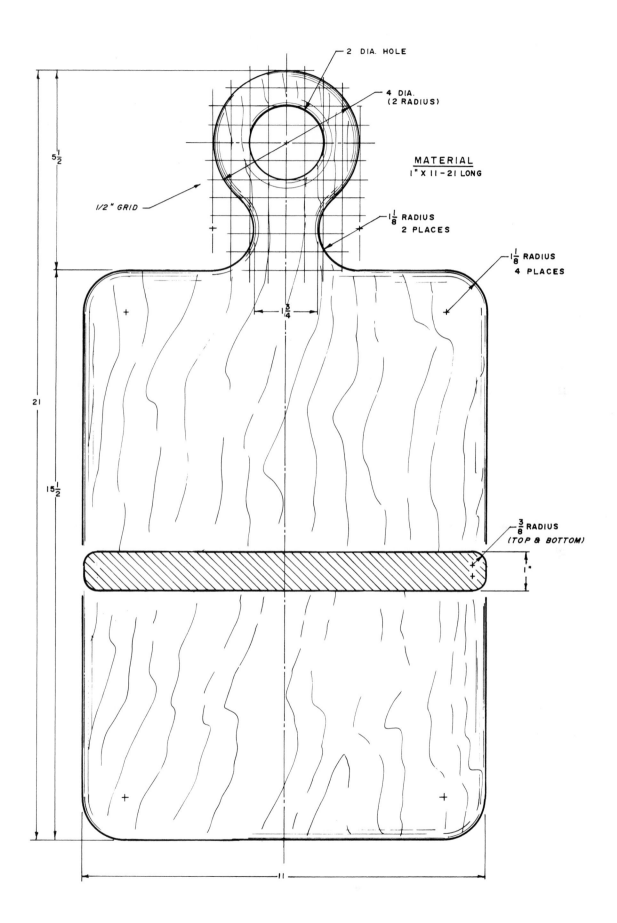

2 DIA. HOLE

4 DIA.
(2 RADIUS)

MATERIAL
1" X 11-21 LONG

$5\frac{1}{2}$

1/2" GRID

$1\frac{1}{8}$ RADIUS
2 PLACES

$1\frac{1}{8}$ RADIUS
4 PLACES

$1\frac{3}{4}$

21

$15\frac{1}{2}$

$\frac{3}{8}$ RADIUS
(TOP & BOTTOM)

1"

11

Pasta and Salad Forks

Our daughter, Joy, bought an electric pasta maker that makes all shapes and sizes of pasta, but I was more impressed with her new pasta forks. I went right home and made a similar pair. They also make good salad forks.

EXPLODED VIEW

MATERIALS LIST

NO.	NAME	SIZE	REQ'D.
1	SUPPORT	½ DIA. – 3⅞ LONG	2
2	TEETH	3/16 DIA. – 3 5/16 LONG	12
3	HANDLE	½ DIA. – 9 LONG	2

1. Select the stock and cut the dowels. All you need is dowel stock in two diameters. Cut the dowels to the lengths given in the Materials List.

This project will progress more easily if you have a drill press. To keep the dowel from turning as you drill, put it into a long V-shaped groove that you've cut into a block of wood. Clamp the block to the drill press table. Locate and drill the six 1/16-inch-diameter holes in the support (part 1), making them 1/16 inch deep. Keep the holes all in a line and drill them at the same angle. Locate and drill the ¼-inch-diameter handle

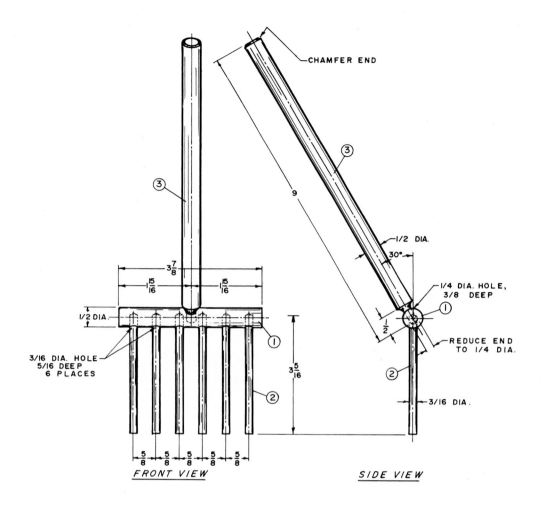

CHAMFER END

3

9

1/2 DIA.

30°

3/8

7
3—
8

1
5
—
16

1
5
—
16

1/4 DIA. HOLE,
3/8 DEEP

1/2 DIA.

3/16 DIA. HOLE
5/16 DEEP
6 PLACES

1

5
3—
16

1
—
2

REDUCE END
TO 1/4 DIA.

2

3/16 DIA.

5
—
8

5
—
8

5
—
8

5
—
8

5
—
8

FRONT VIEW

SIDE VIEW

hole ⅜ inch deep. With the support placed so that the
six smaller holes are facing downward, this hole will
be roughly 30° from vertical, as shown in the side view.

2. Shape the handle. Use a sharp knife to chamfer
one end of the handle (part 3) and taper the other end
down to a diameter of ¼ inch. The taper should start
½ inch from the end.

3. Assemble the fork. Glue the teeth (part 2) in place.
When the glue sets, trim the ends to the same length
with a backsaw. Glue the handle in place.

4. Finish the fork. Sand lightly, taking care to remove
any sharp edges. Either leave the wood as it is or apply
a light coat of salad-bowl finish.

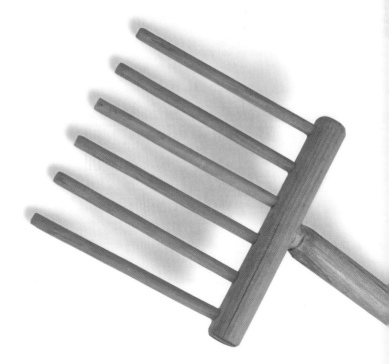

Bread Basket

This project has all kind of uses and can be made of any softwood. Stained or painted, it will make an appealing addition wherever it is used.

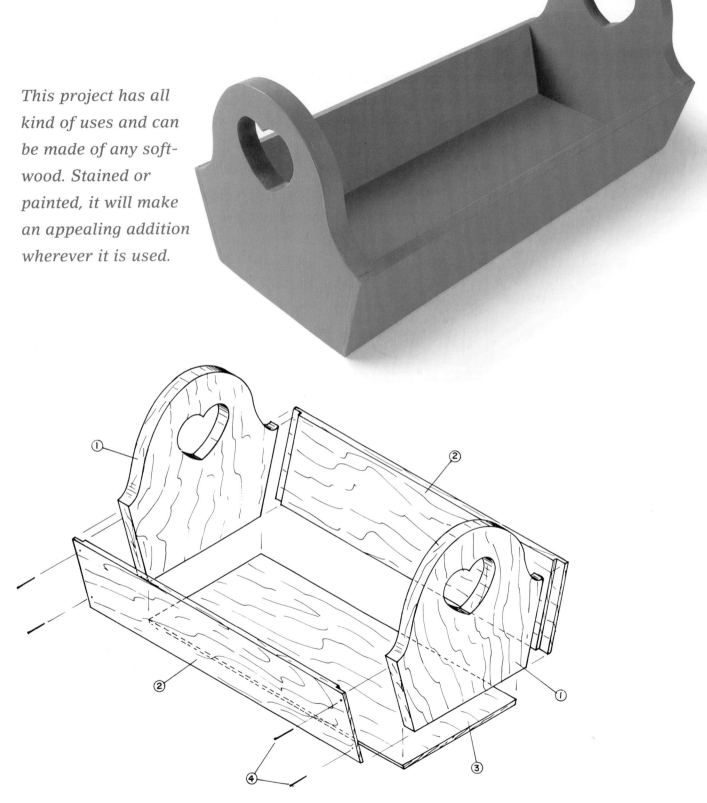

EXPLODED VIEW

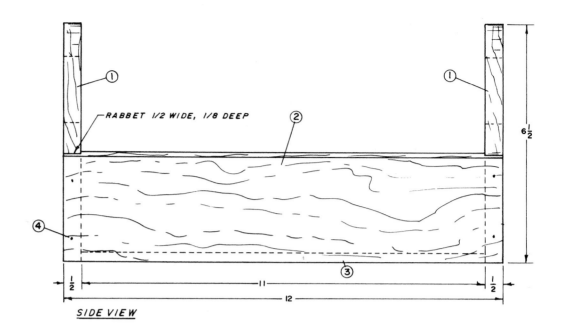

RABBET 1/2 WIDE, 1/8 DEEP

6½

½   11   ½

12

SIDE VIEW

MATERIALS LIST			
NO.	NAME	SIZE	REQ'D.
1	END	½ x 6½ – 6½ LONG	2
2	SIDE	¼ x 3 – 12 LONG	2
3	BOTTOM	¼ x 4¹³⁄₁₆ – 11 LONG	1
4	BRAD	½ LONG	8

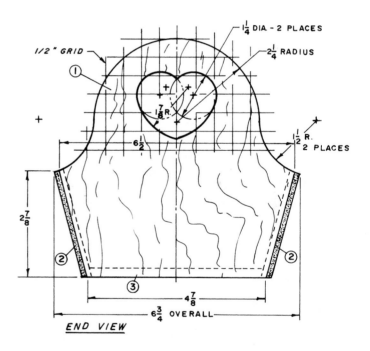

1¼ DIA - 2 PLACES

1/2" GRID

2¼ RADIUS

7⁄8 R.

6½

1½ R.
2 PLACES

2⁷⁄₈

4⁷⁄₈

6¾ OVERALL

END VIEW

1. Cut all the parts to size per the cutting list. Make a full-size pattern for the ends, and transfer the pattern to the wood. Tape two pieces of stock together with the pattern in place and cut out both end pieces at once. Sand all edges while they are still taped together so that the two ends will match exactly.

2. Cut a ½-inch-wide, ⅛-inch-deep rabbet on both ends of the side pieces. Set your saw at 15°, and cut the bottom edge of the sides at this setting so that the inclined edge will be flush with the bottom piece when assembled.

Also, cut the two side edges of the bottom piece at 15°. It is a good idea to fit the bottom piece after the ends and sides are assembled to allow for some adjustments due to variation in construction.

3. Glue and nail the complete assembly, and finish to your liking.

Wooden Trivet

This is a quick project with a practical purpose. These trivets look especially good in traditionally decorated kitchens.

MATERIALS LIST

NO.	NAME	SIZE	REQ'D.
1	LEG	½ x 1⅛ – 10 LONG	2
2	TOP BOARD	½ x 1 – 10 LONG	7
3	NAIL – FINISH	6 d	AS REQ'D.

1. Select the stock and cut the parts. The entire piece is made out of ½-inch-thick stock. I used pine, but almost any kind of wood will do. Cut the parts to the sizes given in the Materials List. Sand them with a sanding block or an electric palm sander. Make sure you keep the edges sharp.

2. Make a paper pattern and cut the legs to shape. Draw a grid with ¼-inch squares and enlarge the outline of the legs (part 1) onto it. Transfer the enlargement to one of the legs. To get identical legs, tape or rubber cement the legs together with the pattern facing out. Cut out both and sand them together.

3. Assemble the trivet. Glue and nail the top boards (part 2) to the legs, taking care that everything is square. Sand thoroughly

4. Finish the trivet. This project can be finished clear or painted if it is to be a display item.

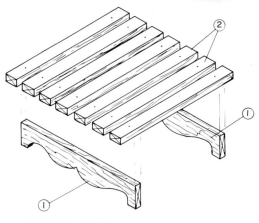

EXPLODED VIEW

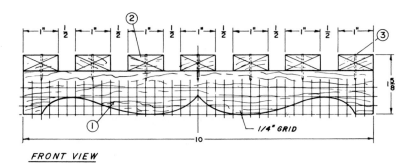

FRONT VIEW

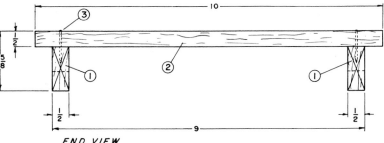

END VIEW

Serving Tray

This project is easy to make. The handle can be cut out quickly, and the rest of the parts go together with little trouble. These trays make great gifts, so consider making two or three of them.

1. Select the stock. I suggest using hardwood and applying a clear finish. The tray is made of ½-inch-thick boards. If you can't find a board wide enough for the bottom (part 1), glue it from smaller pieces.

2. Cut out the parts. Cut out the ends (part 2), sides (part 3), and bottom rails (part 4) to the dimensions given in the Materials List. Cut the bottom later, so that you can cut it to fit the tray exactly.

3. Cut out the handles. Before cutting out the handles, place one end on top of the other. Join them temporarily with tape or rubber cement. On the top piece, draw the outline of the two ¾-inch-diameter holes and the two ⅜-inch-radius arcs. Note the ⅛-inch space between the arcs allows a saw blade to enter and cut the handle in one pass. Draw the 9¼-inch and 6-inch-radius arcs, as shown. While the ends are still attached to one another, cut the arcs with a band saw, coping saw, or jigsaw. Sand the edges and separate the ends.

MATERIALS LIST			
NO.	NAME	SIZE	REQ'D.
1	BOTTOM	½ x 11½ – 20½ LONG	1
2	END	½ x 3 – 11½ LONG	2
3	SIDE	½ x 1¾ – 21 LONG	2
4	BOTTOM RAIL	⅛ x ½ – 20¾ LONG	4
5	BRAD	¾ LONG	AS REQ'D.
6	BRAD	½ LONG	AS REQ'D.

4. Cut the rabbets. The rabbets all are ½ inch wide and ¼ inch deep. Cut them where shown in the drawing.

5. Assemble the tray. Glue and tack the sides together with ¾-inch brads. If the piece is made of hardwood, drill pilot holes for the brads. The best bit for drilling pilot holes is an actual brad. Cut off the head with some wire cutters and tighten the brad in the drill chuck. Drill the hole and drive in a full-length brad. Check that the tray is square.

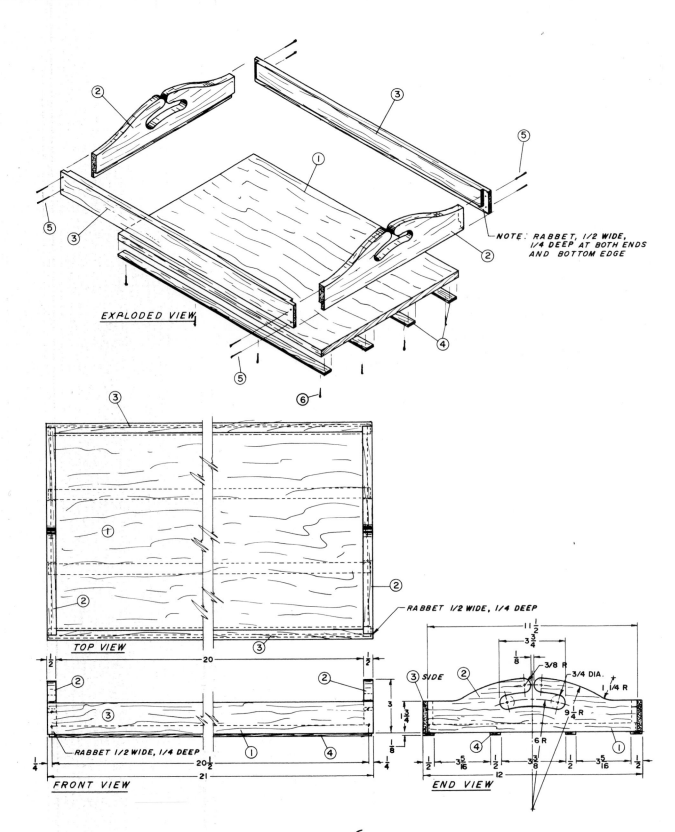

② ③ ⑤ ① ⑤ ③ ⑤ ②

NOTE: RABBET, I/2 WIDE, I/4 DEEP AT BOTH ENDS AND BOTTOM EDGE

EXPLODED VIEW

④ ⑤ ⑥

③ ① ② ② ③

TOP VIEW

RABBET 1/2 WIDE, 1/4 DEEP

② ② ① ④

RABBET 1/2 WIDE, 1/4 DEEP

20
20½
21

FRONT VIEW

③ SIDE ②

11½
3¾
⅛
3/8 R
3/4 DIA.
1 1/4 R
9¼ R
6 R

④ ①

½ 3 5/16 ½ 3⅜ ½ 3 5/16 ½
12

END VIEW

When the glue has set, measure the opening for the bottom. Cut the bottom to fit, and glue and tack it in place as above. Tack the four bottom rails to the bottom with ½-inch brads, spacing the rails, as shown in the end view.

6. Apply finish. Sand the entire piece. Stain the tray if you choose, and apply two or three coats of varnish. If food is to come in contact with the tray, apply a non-toxic salad bowl finish instead of varnish.

Napkin Holder

The pattern for this piece was taken from an antique New England weather vane. Weather vanes are a great design resource for many woodworking projects. If you have a favorite pattern, try using it in place of the crowing rooster shown here.

MATERIALS LIST			
NO.	**NAME**	**SIZE**	**REQ'D.**
1	FRONT/BACK	¼ x 6¼ – 6½ LONG	1 EA.
2	BASE	⅜ x 2 – 6¼ LONG	1
3	PIN	⅛ DIA. – ¾ LONG	6

1. Select the stock and cut out the parts. You'll need ¼-inch and ⅛-inch-thick stock. I used ash for the piece in the photograph. Cut the parts to the sizes given in the Materials List.

2. Make a paper pattern and cut out the rooster. Draw a grid with ½-inch squares and enlarge the rooster onto it. Transfer the drawing to the front piece (part 1). Note that the holder is slightly taller than it is wide. Orient the grain, as shown. Glue the front and back together with rubber cement so that the pattern faces out.

Drill holes in each of the areas that will be cut out so you can begin the cuts that will remove them. Cut out the design with a jigsaw or a scroll saw and sand the edges.

Cut a 1-inch radius in the top corners of each piece, as shown. Sand what will be the inside of the holder before assembling the pieces.

3. Assemble the holder. Glue the front and back to the base (part 2). Make sure that the front and back are square to the base and parallel to one another.

After the glue sets, lay out and drill the six ⅛-inch-diameter holes that hold the pins (part 3). Place a small amount of glue on each pin and tap them into the holes. Once the glue has dried thoroughly, sand the front and back.

4. Apply finish. Use a clear finish or paint. Another alternative is to paint only the outline of the rooster and then varnish the entire piece.

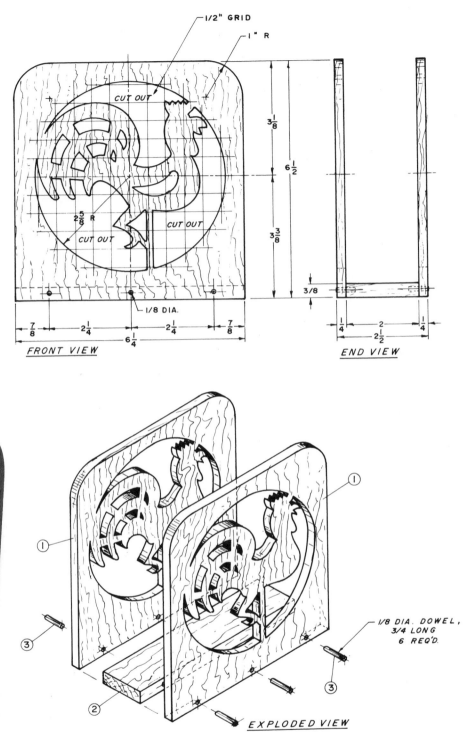

1/2" GRID

1" R

CUT OUT

CUT OUT

$2\frac{5}{8}$ R

CUT OUT

$3\frac{1}{8}$

$6\frac{1}{2}$

$3\frac{3}{8}$

3/8

1/8 DIA.

$\frac{7}{8}$ $2\frac{1}{4}$ $2\frac{1}{4}$ $\frac{7}{8}$

$6\frac{1}{4}$

FRONT VIEW

$\frac{1}{4}$ 2 $\frac{1}{4}$

$2\frac{1}{2}$

END VIEW

1/8 DIA. DOWEL,
3/4 LONG
6 REQ'D.

EXPLODED VIEW

Grocery List Holder

This holder hangs on a wall so that it's always handy when someone wants to jot down an item. The printed grocery list pad shown in the photo is purchased, as are the carriage bolts.

1. Select the stock and cut the parts. I used ash for this piece, but choose any wood you happen to have on hand. Pick out a piece of 1/4-inch-thick stock with an eye to the grain, unless you'll be painting the holder to match accessories or trim in the kitchen. Cut the parts to the sizes given in the Materials List.

2. Layout the backboard and cut the parts to shape. Use the given radii to lay out the curves and the handle. Locate the centers of the two 1/16-inch-diameter holes for the carriage bolts that hold the locking bar. Cut out the backboard (part 1) and drill the two holes.

   Cut the locking bar (part 2) to the dimensions given, and drill 3/16-inch-diameter holes through it for the carriage bolts (part 3).

3. Finish the holder. Sand thoroughly, and either varnish or paint the piece. Use the locking bar and carriage bolts to clamp a pad of paper in place.

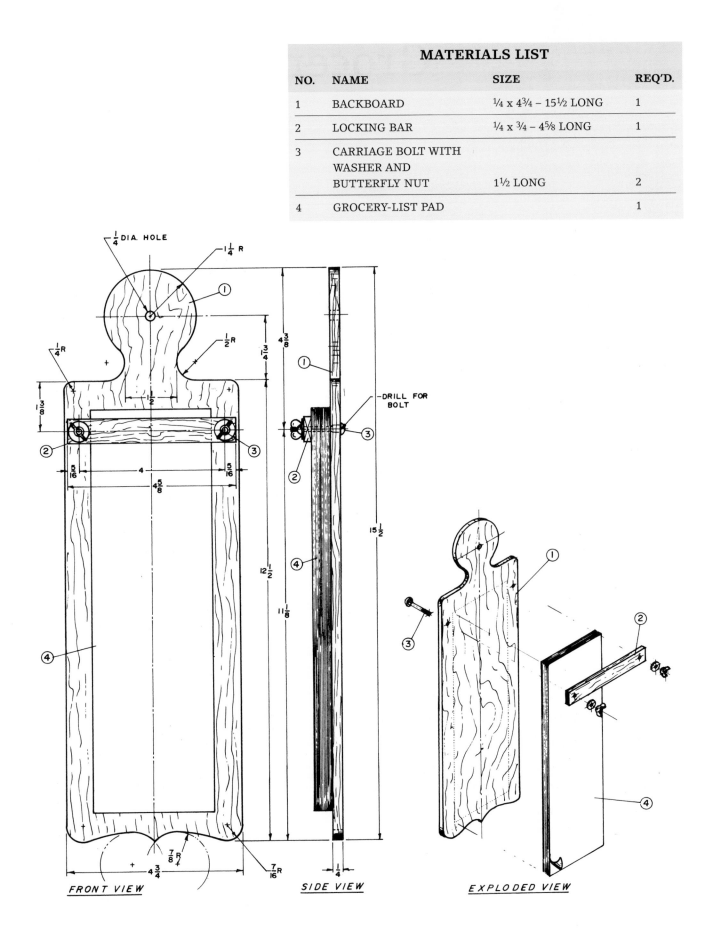

MATERIALS LIST			
NO.	NAME	SIZE	REQ'D.
1	BACKBOARD	¼ x 4¾ – 15½ LONG	1
2	LOCKING BAR	¼ x ¾ – 4⅝ LONG	1
3	CARRIAGE BOLT WITH WASHER AND BUTTERFLY NUT	1½ LONG	2
4	GROCERY-LIST PAD		1

FRONT VIEW

SIDE VIEW

EXPLODED VIEW

Recipe Box

Here is a handy place to store the recipe cards that tend to end up in the back of kitchen drawers.

1. Select the stock and cut the parts. You can use almost any kind of wood for this project. I made the holder shown here out of pieces of ¼-inch mahogany from my scrap pile. The holder is made entirely with simple butt joints. Cut the parts to the sizes given in the Materials List.

2. Make a paper pattern and cut the parts to shape. Draw a grid with ½-inch squares and enlarge the back (part 1) and a side (part 2) onto it. Transfer the enlargements to the wood. Lay out the outline of the lid (part 5), establishing the curve in the front edge by drawing the ⅝-inch radius.

   Cut the pieces to shape. You can save time and ensure accuracy by cutting the two sides out together. Note the 20° cuts on the lid, front (part 3), and stop (part 6), as shown.

   Drill the ¼ inch-diameter hole in the back.

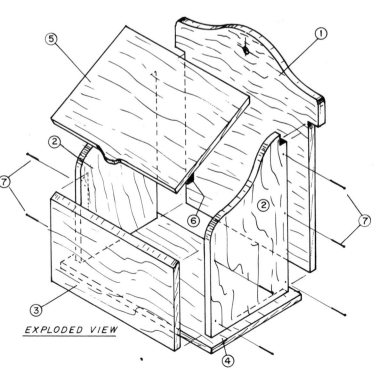

EXPLODED VIEW

3. Assemble the holder. Using the 4d finishing nails (part 7), nail the sides to the back and front, aligning their bottom edges on a flat surface. Sand the bottom edges of this subassembly as necessary so that it will sit flat.

Turn the assembly upside down. Hold the lid in place and scribe a line on it to locate the front edge of the stop. Glue the stop in place.

Nail the bottom (part 4) in place, keeping it centered and flush with the back as shown.

4. Apply finish. Sand thoroughly, rounding the edges slightly. Apply clear varnish.

MATERIALS LIST			
NO.	**NAME**	**SIZE**	**REQ'D.**
1	BACK	¼ x 7½ – 6 LONG	1
2	SIDE	¼ x 3¾ – 5¾ LONG	2
3	FRONT	¼ x 3¼ – 5⅛ LONG	1
4	BOTTOM	¼ x 3¹⁵⁄₁₆ – 6 LONG	1
5	LID	¼ x 4½ – 5¹⁄₁₆ LONG	1
6	STOP	¼ x ¼ – 5¹⁄₁₆ LONG	1
7	NAIL – FINISH	4 d	16

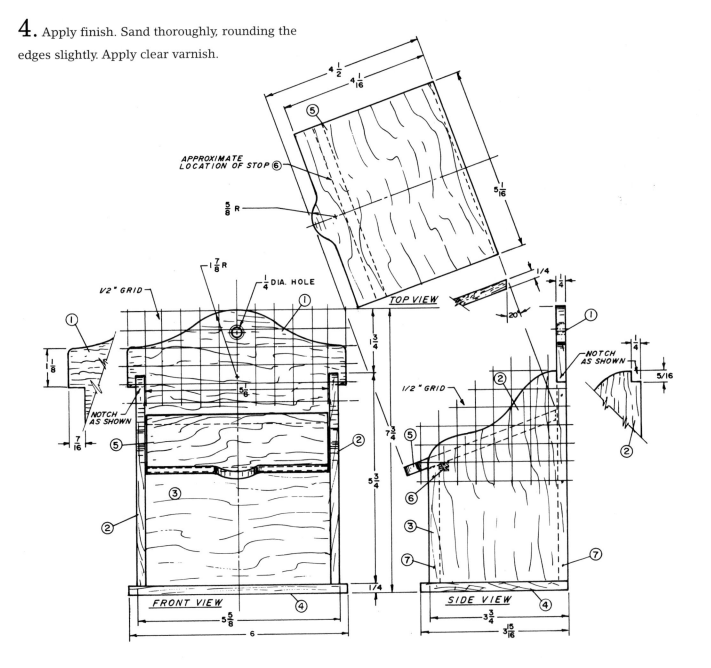

Wall Spice Box

This box can be mounted on an empty bit of wall area to give you a place to tuck all sorts of odds and ends. The drawers are all small and simple, making it a good piece for practicing your drawer making.

1. Select the stock and cut the parts. I used ash for the box shown here simply because that's what I had on hand at the time. Use whatever wood you'd like. The pulls are white glass with brass centers.

Cut the back (part 1), the side (part 2), and the dividers (part 3) to the dimensions given in the Materials List.

2. Cut the back and sides to shape. Lay out and cut the back as shown. Drill the ¼-inch-diameter hole for hanging the box.

Draw a grid with ½-inch squares and enlarge the drawing of the sides (part 2) onto the grid. Transfer the enlargement to the actual side. Tape the sides together and cut the sides to shape. Sand the edges while the pieces are still joined.

MATERIALS LIST

NO.	NAME	SIZE	REQ'D.
1	BACK	½ x 5 – 30 LONG	1
2	SIDE	½ x 4½ – 28½ LONG	2
3	DIVIDER	½ x 4 – 5½ LONG	9
4	DRAWER FRONT	½ x 2¼ – 5 LONG	8
5	DRAWER SIDE	¼ x 2 – 3⅝ LONG	16
6	DRAWER BACK	¼ x 1 – 4½ LONG	8
7	DRAWER BOTTOM	¼ x 3⅝ – 5 LONG	8
8	DRAWER PULL	⅝ DIA.	8
9	BRAD	1 LONG	AS REQ'D.

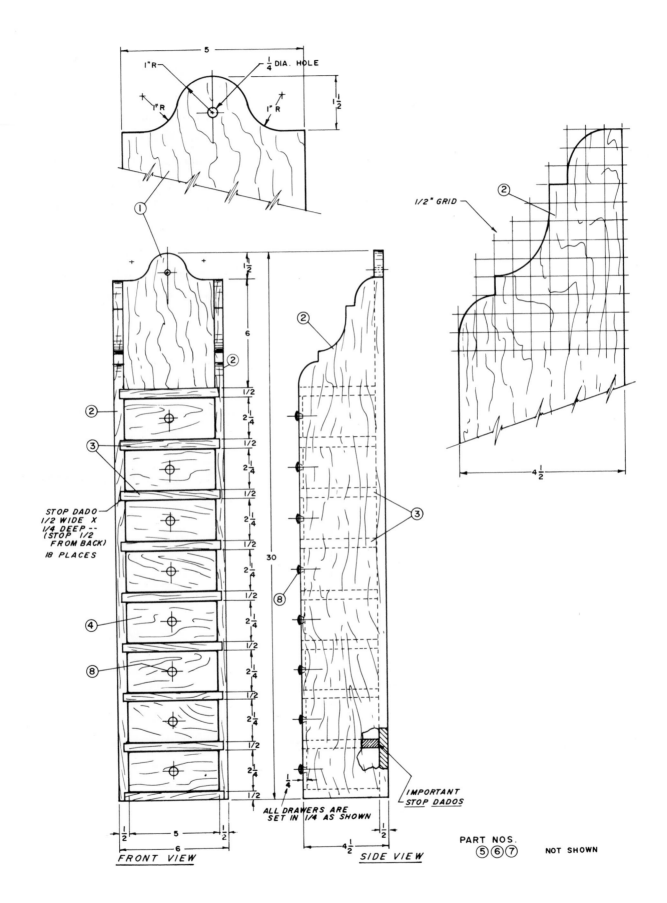

5

1"R.

¼ DIA. HOLE

1"R

1"R

1½

1

1/2" GRID

2

4½

2

1½

6

½
2¼
½
2¼
½
2¼
½
2¼
½
2¼
½
2¼
½
2¼
½

30

2

3

8

STOP DADO
1/2 WIDE X
1/4 DEEP --
(STOP 1/2
FROM BACK)
18 PLACES

2

3

4

8

½   5   ½

6

FRONT VIEW

¼

ALL DRAWERS ARE
SET IN 1/4 AS SHOWN

4½

½

SIDE VIEW

IMPORTANT
STOP DADOS

PART NOS.
5 6 7   NOT SHOWN

Separate the sides and lay out the dadoes for the dividers. The sides are not identical: they are mirror images of each other. Rout the dadoes with a ½-inch straight bit. Clamp a straight edge to the side and guide the router against it. Stop all the dadoes ½ inch from the back edge.

3. Dry-assemble the case. Without using glue, test-fit the back, sides, and dividers (part 3) to make sure that everything comes together properly. Make any necessary adjustments and glue up the parts. Make sure the case is square before the glue sets. Sand the case and dividers when the glue dries.

4. Make the drawers. In drawer making, the Materials List is only a guide. Always fit a drawer to its opening.

Cut eight drawer fronts (part 4) to fit snugly in the drawer openings and rabbet them to accept the drawer sides (part 5). Measure the distance between the rabbets and cut the drawer back (part 6) to that length.

Cut the sides to fit next. In this case, measure the depth of the opening and subtract ½ inch. Rabbet the front to accept the drawer bottom (part 7). Temporarily assemble the drawers and cut bottoms to match.

Glue the drawers together, leaving the bottoms off for now. Use rubber bands as clamps and make sure that all sides are square. After the glue has set, tack the drawer bottom in place with 1-inch wire brads. Sand all surfaces until the drawer slides smoothly in the opening.

Drill a hole for the pull (part 8) in the center of each drawer front.

5. Apply finish. Varnish or paint the case and drawers. Attach the drawer pulls.

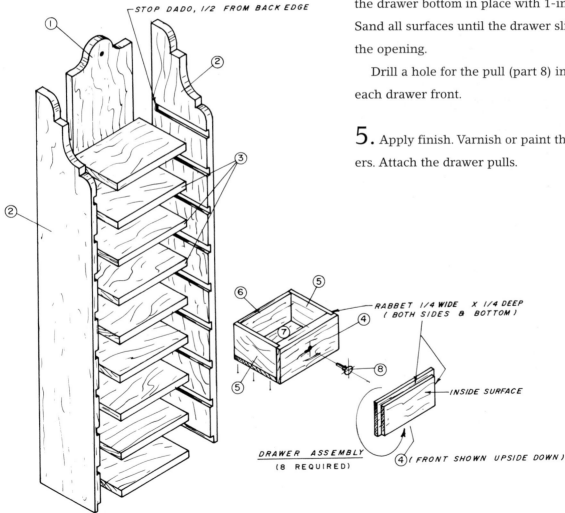

STOP DADO, 1/2 FROM BACK EDGE

RABBET 1/4 WIDE X 1/4 DEEP
(BOTH SIDES & BOTTOM)

INSIDE SURFACE

DRAWER ASSEMBLY
(8 REQUIRED)

④(FRONT SHOWN UPSIDE DOWN)

EXPLODED VIEW

Office Projects

A place for everything, and everything in its place. Projects ranging from an in/out mail basket to a storage unit will have you organized in no time. Office work has never been this fun.

Clipboard

You can buy clipboards made of cheap pressboard, but any self-respecting woodworker needs a clipboard made of real wood, perhaps even exotic wood. I made this one out of scrap pieces of mahogany that I had around and just hated to burn up. Now this is a woodworker's clipboard!

MATERIALS LIST			
NO.	NAME	SIZE	REQ'D.
1	BOARD	¼ (⅜) x 9 – 13 LONG	1
2	CLIP	6 SIZE	1
3	SCREW POST		2
4	FOOT W/NO. 10 SC.	421/20	4
5	SCREW FOR FOOT		4

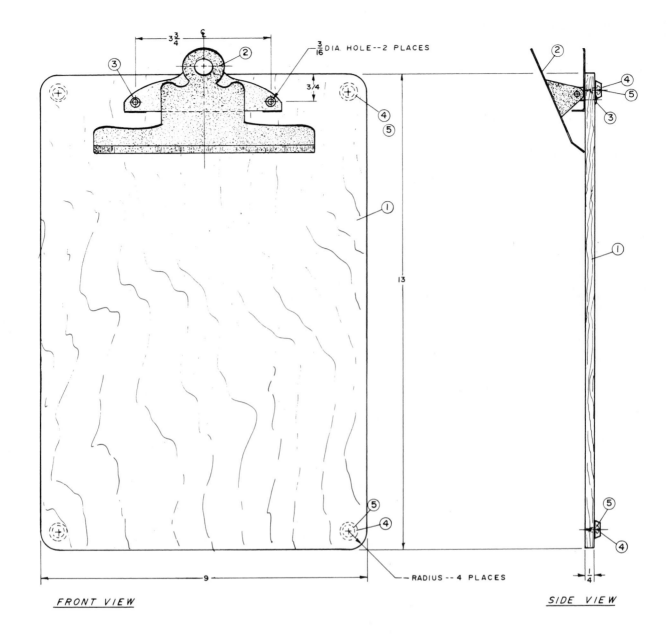

FRONT VIEW   SIDE VIEW

1. Glue material to make up the 9 x 13-inch board, if necessary. Use pieces of wood with pleasing grain patterns. Plane the wood to $\frac{1}{4}$ inch or $\frac{5}{16}$ inch thick. (It is okay to leave the wood a little thick.) Sand all over.

2. Cut to exact size, and round the four corners. Locate and drill the two $\frac{3}{16}$-inch-diameter holes for the screws to hold the clip in place. Locate and drill from the bottom surface for the screws to hold the four feet in place. Take care not to drill through.

3. Sand all over with fine grit sandpaper. Do not round the edges. Apply two or three coats of a clear, hard finish on top, bottom, and edges. Lightly sand between coats. Assemble the clip and four feet.

Paperweight

This is an interesting project that can be used as a paperweight or simply a conversation piece. If you have 1-inch and 2-inch-diameter Forstner bits and a 1/2-inch-diameter drill, it's very simple. It's a project that no one can leave alone. Put it on your desk and watch how people pick it up—they'll wonder how you made it. Most will think you carved out the inner blocks, and they will never realize how easy it really was to make—unless you tell them.

1. Start with a solid 2½-inch cube. If you have a solid piece of wood large enough, use it. If not, glue together scraps slightly larger than the 2½ inches needed—that's what I did with scrap pieces of ash. You might want to make two or three blocks to start with in case you set a drill depth incorrectly later on.

The only tricky part of the project is that your block must be exactly 2½ inches on all sides, and it must be square. If not, then the rest of the steps will not come out correctly. Sand all six surfaces using a sanding block, keeping all edges sharp.

2. Using a sharp pencil, draw light diagonal lines from corner to corner, as shown in the drawing, to locate the exact center of each surface. Using a pointed punch, prick-punch the exact center of each surface.

3. The drilling must be done on a drill press with an adjustable depth stop. With a 2-inch-diameter Forstner bit, drill a ¹⁵/₃₂-inch-deep hole in the center of all six surfaces. If your work has been precise, you should end up with a new block inside the outer block, hanging on by its corners, as shown in the drawings.

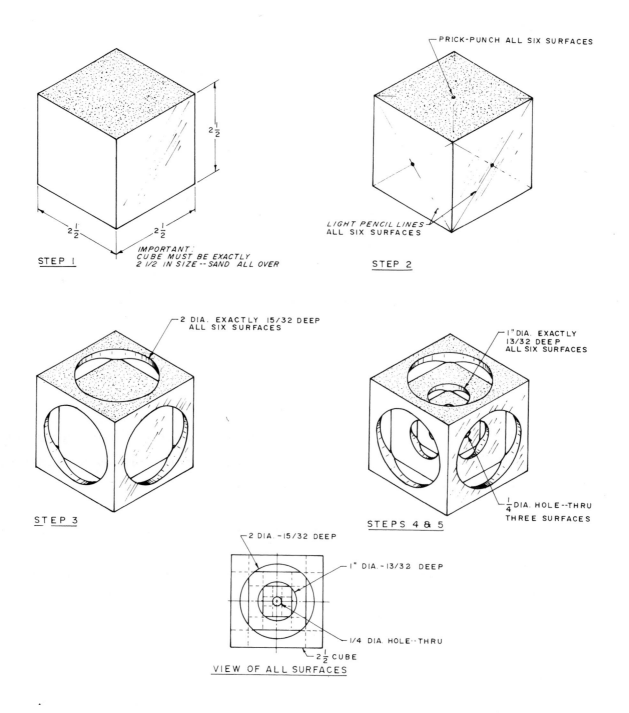

STEP 1

2 1/2

2 1/2

2 1/2

IMPORTANT:
CUBE MUST BE EXACTLY
2 1/2 IN SIZE -- SAND ALL OVER

STEP 2

PRICK-PUNCH ALL SIX SURFACES

LIGHT PENCIL LINES
ALL SIX SURFACES

STEP 3

2 DIA. EXACTLY 15/32 DEEP
ALL SIX SURFACES

STEPS 4 & 5

1" DIA. EXACTLY
13/32 DEEP
ALL SIX SURFACES

1/4 DIA. HOLE--THRU
THREE SURFACES

2 DIA. -15/32 DEEP

1" DIA. -13/32 DEEP

1/4 DIA. HOLE--THRU

2 1/2 CUBE

VIEW OF ALL SURFACES

4. Using the indent left by the tip of the 2-inch-diameter bit, drill a 1-inch-diameter hole exactly $^{13}/_{16}$ inches deep using a Forstner bit, centered inside each of the six 2-inch-diameter holes. The depth must be exact. You will find that you have created another block inside the two outer blocks.

5. Finish up by drilling a ¼-inch-diameter hole in the indent left by the tip of the 1-inch-diameter bit.

6. If the wood grain is interesting, leave the cube unfinished. If you like color, interesting patterns can be achieved by painting the blocks or their side surfaces different colors.

Key Rack

This is one project you really should make if you always seem to be losing your keys.

1. Select the stock and cut the wood to the overall dimensions. I suggest using an attractive hardwood and finishing it clear. You'll need a ¼-inch-thick piece of wood, measuring roughly 4 x 11 inches. The brass hooks can be picked up at a hardware store.

2. Make a paper pattern. Draw a grid with ½-inch squares and enlarge the drawing of the key onto it. Include the location of the five brass hooks and the centers of all four holes. Transfer the pattern to the wood.

3. Drill the holes and cut the rack to shape. Drill the holes. Countersink the ⅛-inch-diameter holes to take flathead screws for mounting the rack. Cut out the key rack. Use an awl to make indentations at the five points where the hooks will be placed. Sand the rack.

4. Finish the rack. Stain the rack, if you wish, and apply a clear finish. Screw the hooks in place.

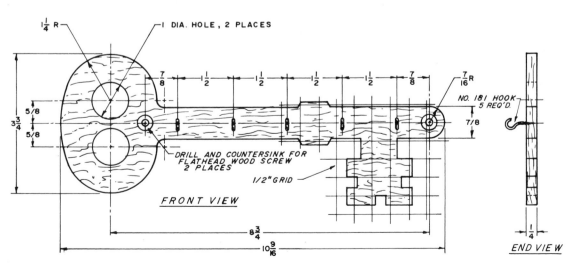

In/Out Mail Basket

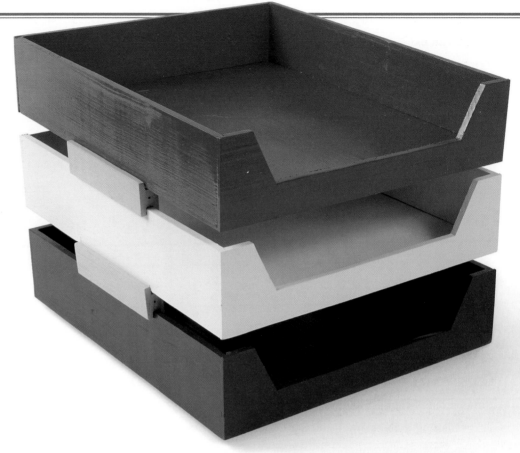

To add a little class and color to your desk, replace your plastic in/out basket with this good-looking substitute for the standard office supply.

1. Select the stock and cut the parts. Any hardwood will do, but oak and ash strike me as appropriate for an office. I chose ash for the basket in the photo. The entire piece is made from ¼-inch stock.

Decide how many units the basket will have. The Materials List gives the number of parts required to make one unit. With a couple of simple spacers, you can stack two units on top of each other; four spacers will let you stack three units, as shown here.

Cut all pieces to the sizes listed in the Materials List. Lay out the notch in the front (part 1) and cut it out on a band saw or jigsaw. If you are making more than one basket, tape the fronts together in a pile and cut out all the notches at once. Sand the edges of the notches while the fronts are still together

2. Rabbet the front and back to accept the sides (part 2). Cut a groove for the bottom in the front, back, and sides, as shown in the side view.

Cut a piece of ⅝-inch stock for the spacers (part 4), making it about an inch longer than the combined lengths of the individual spacers you'll need. Rout or cut grooves along both the top and bottom edges of this piece, as shown in the spacer detail. Cut the piece into the individual 4-inch-long spacers.

MATERIALS LIST			
NO.	NAME	SIZE	REQ'D.
1	FRONT/BACK	¼ x 2½ – 10 LONG	1 EA.
2	SIDE	¼ x 2½ – 11¾ LONG	2
3	BOTTOM	¼ x 9¹¹⁄₁₆ – 11¾ LONG	1
4	SPACER	⅝ x 1⅛ – 4 LONG	AS REQ'D.

3. Assemble the basket. Dry-fit the parts. Trim as necessary and glue up the parts, keeping everything square. Do not glue the bottom (part 3) in place, so that it can expand and contract with the weather. Sand the basket and spacers.

4. Finish the basket. The basket in the photo has a coat of light stain and two coats of varnish, but the distinctive grains of ash and oak look equally good without stain.

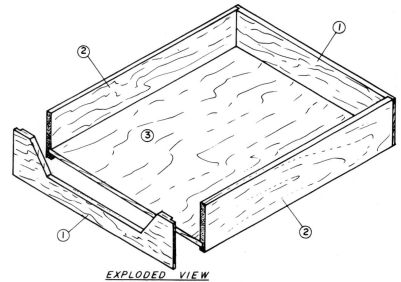

EXPLODED VIEW

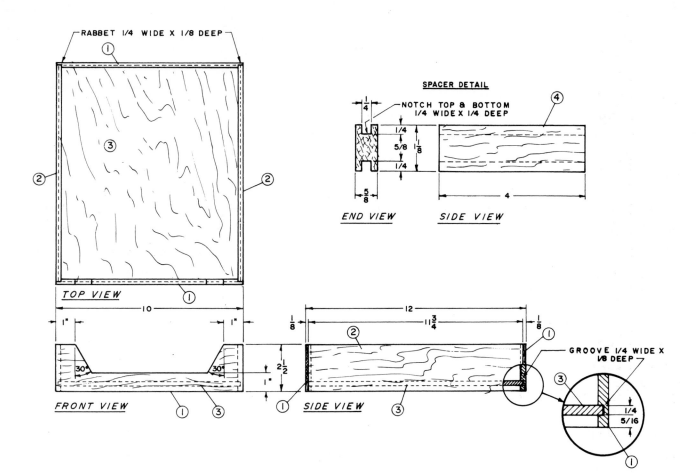

Four-Drawer Storage Unit

You never have enough storage areas, especially if you're a collector. Here is a drawer unit that can be used vertically or horizontally, or both (the photo shows two stacked together). It doesn't take up much space and can fit most anywhere. Don't let the four drawers intimidate you. A drawer is nothing more than a box with the top missing. The drawer construction for this project is a little different from most drawer construction; it is a simplified drawer and easy to make.

1. Cut all pieces per the Materials List, keeping all cuts at 90°. Carefully locate and make the three ½-inch-wide, ¼-inch-deep dado cuts and the two ½-inch-wide, ¼-inch-deep rabbets in the two sides. Take care as these cuts must be accurate. You must maintain the four-inch dimension between each drawer divider. Cut the ¼-inch-wide, ¼-inch-deep rabbet along the inner back edge of the sides as shown. Take care to make a left and right-hand pair of sides.

2. Glue the drawer dividers and backboard in place, taking care that everything is square. Add the drawer supports. Apply glue to only the front half of each support to allow for expansion. This is a good tip whenever you are gluing wood together and the grain of one piece is running at 90° to the grain of the other. Check that each drawer opening is exactly four inches square.

3. Cut the pieces for the drawers using a saw stop on your saw. Each matching piece must be exactly the same size and shape; the saw stop will ensure that they are. Carefully cut the ¼-inch-wide, ¼-inch-deep rabbet on both the inner side and bottom edge of each drawer front; see the exploded view.

4. Dry-fit all of the drawer parts, and check that the drawer fronts are just a little under four inches square. Fit one drawer into the opening to make sure that it fits correctly. Make adjustments on the parts if necessary. Glue and nail the drawer units together. Carefully find the middle of the drawer fronts by drawing two lines diagonally from corner to corner. Drill a hole in each front for the screw to secure the ¾-inch-diameter knobs.

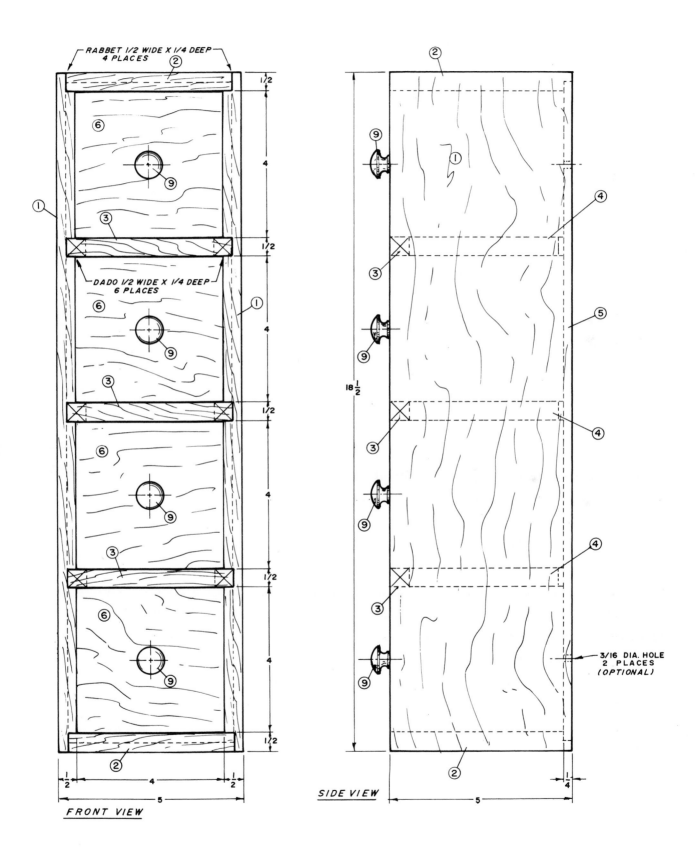

RABBET 1/2 WIDE X 1/4 DEEP
4 PLACES

② ① ⑥ ⑨ ③

DADO 1/2 WIDE X 1/4 DEEP
6 PLACES

1/2 4 1/2 4 1/2 4 1/2 4 1/2

1/2 4 1/2

5

FRONT VIEW

② ① ⑨ ③ ④ ⑤

18 1/2

3/16 DIA. HOLE
2 PLACES
(OPTIONAL)

1/4

5

SIDE VIEW

MATERIALS LIST

NO.	NAME	SIZE	REQ'D.
1	SIDE	½ x 5 – 18½ LONG	2
2	TOP/BOTTOM	½ x 4½ – 4½ LONG	2
3	DIVIDER	½ x ½ – 4½ LONG	3
4	SUPPORT	½ x ½ – 4 LONG	6
5	BACK	¼ x 4½ – 14 LONG	1
6	FRONT/BACK DRAWER	½ x 4 – 4 LONG	8
7	SIDE DRAWER	¼ x 4 – 4¼ LONG	8
8	BOTTOM DRAWER	¼ x 3½ – 4¼ LONG	4
9	PULL (WOOD)	¾ DIA.	4
10	NAIL – FINISH	6 d	48

5. After everything is assembled, sand the case and each drawer with medium and then fine-grit sandpaper. Clean off all dust with a tack rag.

6. Prime and paint all outer surfaces. Now you have a place for all those important things you just can't bear to throw away.

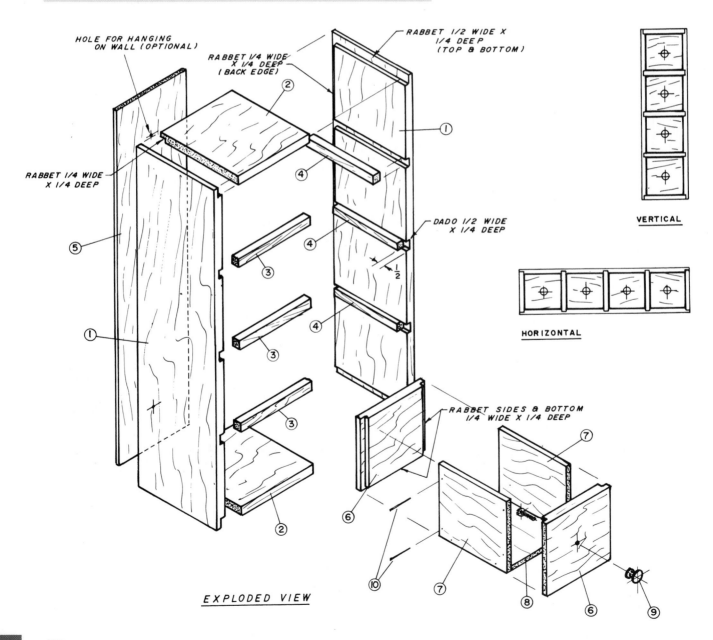

EXPLODED VIEW

Yard & Garden Projects

Complete a few of the projects in this chapter, and your plants and birds will be happier, your garden tools will have their own home, and you'll always have the soothing sound of chimes in your garden. What better way to enjoy the outdoors?

Garden Caddy

This is a project that can be used for all kinds of things. It can be made of any kind of wood, but it looks best in oak or ash. If you have never worked with oak or ash, this project is the perfect time to try it.

MATERIALS LIST			
NO.	NAME	SIZE	REQ'D.
1	END	½ x 7 – 12 LONG	2
2	SIDE	½ x 5⅜ – 10 LONG	2
3	BOTTOM	½ x 7 – 10 LONG	1
4	HANDLE (DOWEL)	⅞ DIA. – 11¼ LONG	1
5	FINISH NAIL	6 d	16

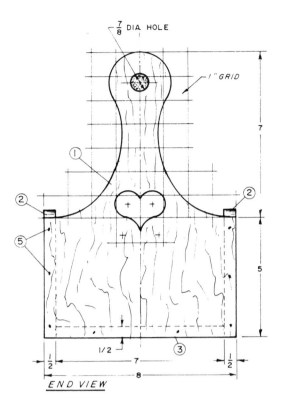

$\frac{7}{8}$ DIA HOLE

1" GRID

7

5

1/2

$\frac{1}{2}$

7

$\frac{1}{2}$

8

 END VIEW

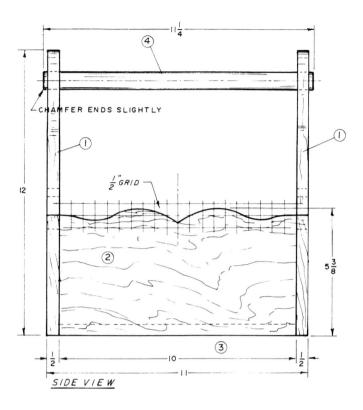

$11\frac{1}{4}$

CHAMFER ENDS SLIGHTLY

$\frac{1}{2}$" GRID

12

$5\frac{3}{8}$

$\frac{1}{2}$

10

$\frac{1}{2}$

11

SIDE VIEW

1. Make full-size patterns for the ends and sides on a piece of cardboard. Tape or tack two pieces of stock together, and cut both ends out together. Drill the ⅞-inch-diameter hole at this time. Sand the edges while the end pieces are still taped or tacked together to ensure that the two ends are exactly the same size. Do the same for the two sides.

2. To finish, glue and nail the caddy together, and sand all over. The caddy can be stained or painted. If you used oak or ash, you can finish your caddy by simply applying a topcoat of tough, clear finish.

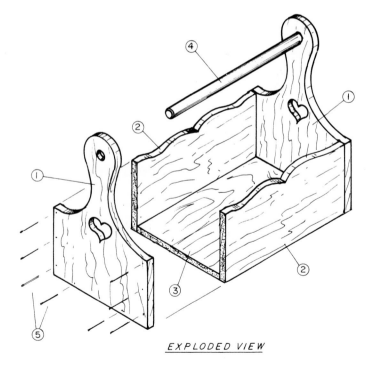

EXPLODED VIEW

Rabbit Plant Holder

Now here's a plant holder that's different! Usually, you want to keep the rabbits away from your plants. This project actually calls for two of them. But, don't make them too realistic; you might attract the real thing.

MATERIALS LIST			
NO.	NAME	SIZE	REQ'D.
1	SIDE	½ x 11¾ – 11 LONG	2
2	SHELF	¾ x 4¾ – LONG	1
2	FINISH NAIL	8 d	4

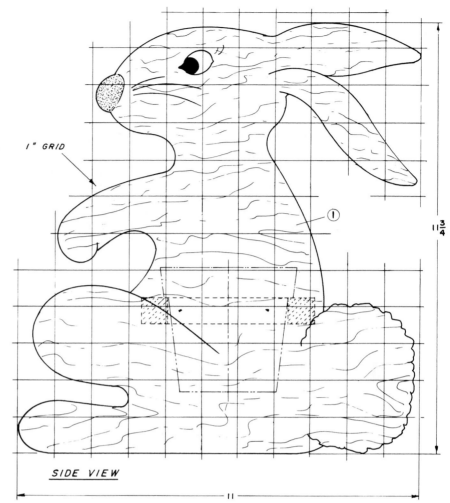

1" GRID

11¾

SIDE VIEW

11

1. On a 1-inch grid lay out the profile of the side (part 1).

2. Tack or tape two pieces of wood together. Transfer the profile to the wood, and cut both sides at the same time. Sand all edges. Cut the shelf (part 2) to size, and drill two or three holes to fit your potted plants. Sand all over to remove all sharp edges.

3. Glue and nail together.

4. Paint to suit.

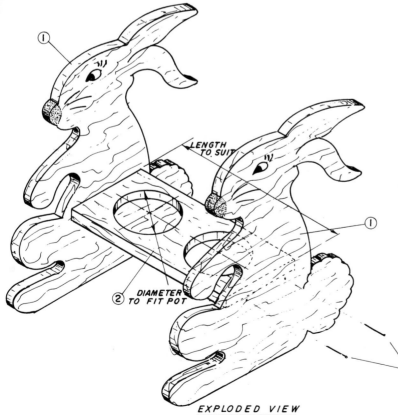

LENGTH TO SUIT

DIAMETER TO FIT POT

EXPLODED VIEW

Rail Planter

You can build this project out of scraps. It is designed to fit over the rail of a patio or deck where it will help keep plants from falling over the edge. You will have to make the width to fit your deck rail. Note: the white bottom piece in the photograph represents your rail.

1. Select the stock. Use whatever wood you have on hand. The length of the short boards (part 3) depends on how wide the rail happens to be. Measure the width of the rail and add 5 inches. The drawings give a length of 10½ inches for a planter that will fit over a 2 x 6 rail.

If you will be making the planter from new wood, note that you can rip ten ¾-inch-wide pieces from a knot-free 1 x 10. The base board (part 1) is cut from a 2 x 4.

2. Cut the parts. Rip your scraps to ¾ x ¾ inch. Get the long boards out of the longer scraps, and the short boards from the leftovers. Cut the eight spacers (part 4). Cut the base boards and chamfer, as shown. Sand all parts.

3. Assemble the planter. The planter will hold together well enough with finishing nails (part 5), but for greater durability you may want to use a waterproof glue as well, or even screw the parts together.

Put the base boards on the bench with the chamfer down and nail a long board into them, flush with the top and ends. Space the base boards as far apart as the width of the rail. Nail the first two short boards in place. They should overhang the long boards by one-quarter at each end. Keep everything square. Before going on, make sure the piece will fit over the rail without binding. Then continue stacking long boards and short boards, nailing them in place and using spacers, as indicated in the drawings. Check for squareness as you build.

4. Apply finish. Stain or paint the planter if you wish. Be sure to use products intended for exterior use. Screw the planter to the rails.

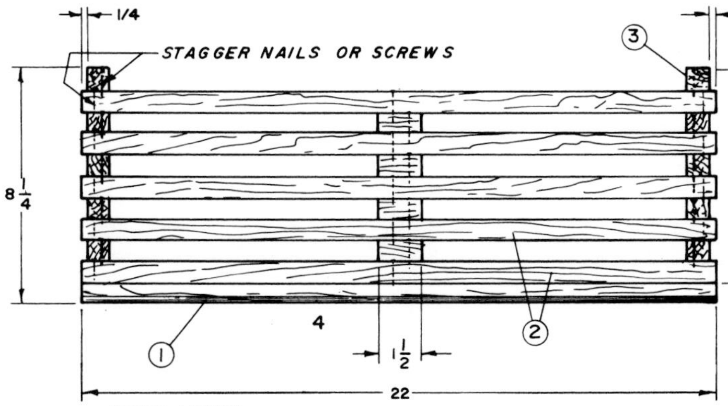

1/4
STAGGER NAILS OR SCREWS
3
1/4
8 1/4
7 1/2
4
1 1/2
2
1
22

SIDE VIEW

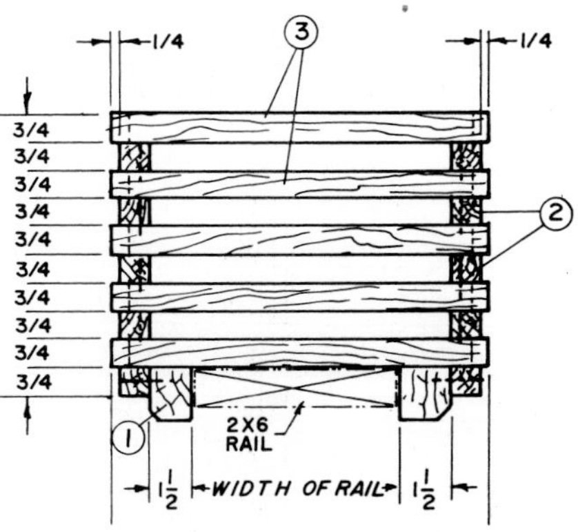

1/4
3
1/4
3/4
3/4
3/4
3/4
3/4
3/4
3/4
3/4
3/4
3/4
2
2X6 RAIL
1
1 1/2
WIDTH OF RAIL
1 1/2

END VIEW

MATERIALS LIST			
NO.	NAME	SIZE	REQ'D.
1	BASE BOARD	1½ x 1½ LONG	2
2	LONG BOARD	¾ x ¾ LONG	10
3	SHORT BOARD	¾ x ¾ LONG	10
4	SPACER	¾ x ¾ – 1½ LONG	8
5	NAIL – FINISH	4 d	48

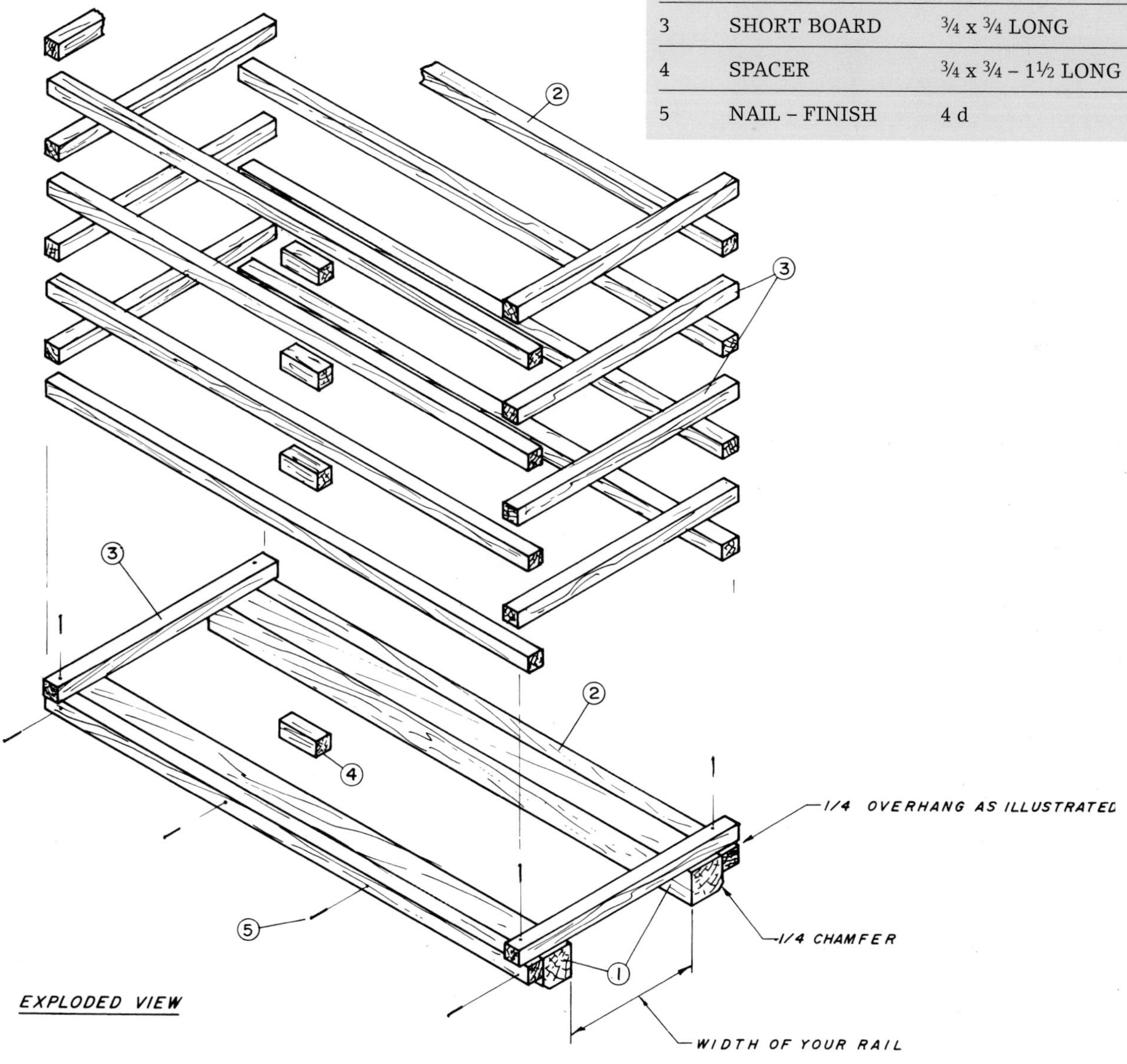

2
3
3
2
4
1/4 OVERHANG AS ILLUSTRATED
1/4 CHAMFER
5
1
WIDTH OF YOUR RAIL

EXPLODED VIEW

Quaint Birdhouse

I have designed and built many birdhouses. This is the most elaborate one I've made. It's a takeoff of a Victorian house. I designed it based on an earlier, somewhat plain-Jane bird house of mine combined with one I saw in a magazine. This is a simple project, but it will require a little fitting. Now, wait for spring; I'm sure you'll soon have it full of happy birds, especially if they appreciate Victorian architecture.

1. Cut all parts to overall size. It is a good idea to cut the front and back (part 1) to shape while the parts are either tacked or taped together, to ensure an exact pair. (Only the front will have the 1¼-inch-diameter hole).

2. Assemble the front, back, two sides, bottom, roof, and perch (parts 1, 2, 3, 4, and 5). Note: if you glue it together, use waterproof glue.

MATERIALS LIST

NO.	NAME	SIZE	REQ'D.
1	FRONT/BACK	½ x 7 – 10½ LONG	2
2	SIDE – RIGHT	½ x 4⅛ – 4¾ LONG	1
3	SIDE – LEFT	½ x 4⅞ – 4¾ LONG	1
4	BOTTOM	½ x 4¾ – 6 LONG	1
5	PERCH	¾ x 1¼ – 3⅛ LONG	1
6	TRIM	¼ x ¼ – 6½ LONG	1
7	TRIM	¼ x ¼ – 6¼ LONG	1
8	TRIM	¼ x ¼ – 4 LONG	1
9	TRIM	¼ x ¼ – 1⅜ LONG	1
10	TRIM	¼ x ¼ – 4⅜ LONG	1
11	TRIM	¼ x ¼ – 3½ LONG	1
12	TRIM	¼ x ¼ – 3¾ LONG	1
13	TRIM	¼ x ¼ – 2¾ LONG	1
14	TRIM	¼ x ¼ – 3½ LONG	1
15	ROOF	¼ x 1¾ – 7½ LONG	14

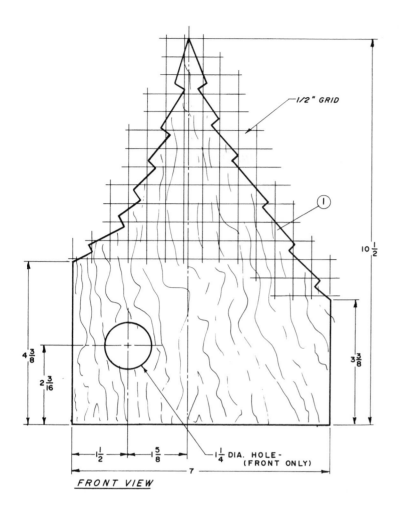

1/2" GRID

①

10 1/2

3 3/8

4 3/8

2 3/16

1 1/2

5/8

1 1/4 DIA. HOLE-
(FRONT ONLY)

7

FRONT VIEW

3. Carefully add the trim as shown in the drawings. Add the pieces in the order they are listed, that is: 6 first, 7 second, 8 third, etc. Glue and use small headless brads for the trim. Test if your wood tends to split. If so, predrill for the nails.

4. Prime and paint using an exterior paint. Here comes the fun part; paint the trim boards as you wish. I painted mine forest green, but you could match your house color.

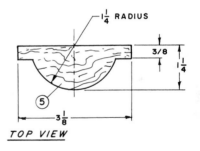

1 1/4 RADIUS

3/8

1 1/4

⑤

3 1/8

TOP VIEW

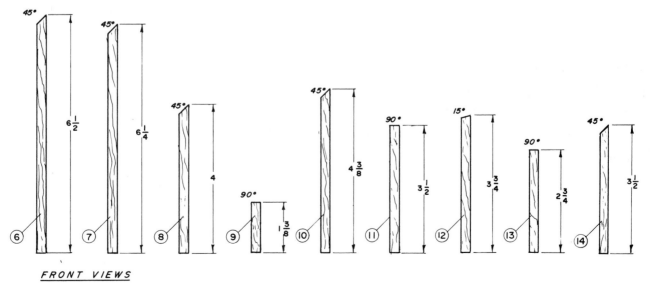

45°

45°

6 1/2

6 1/4

45°

4

90°

1 3/8

45°

4 3/8

90°

3 1/2

15°

3 3/4

90°

2 3/4

45°

3 1/2

⑥ ⑦ ⑧ ⑨ ⑩ ⑪ ⑫ ⑬ ⑭

FRONT VIEWS

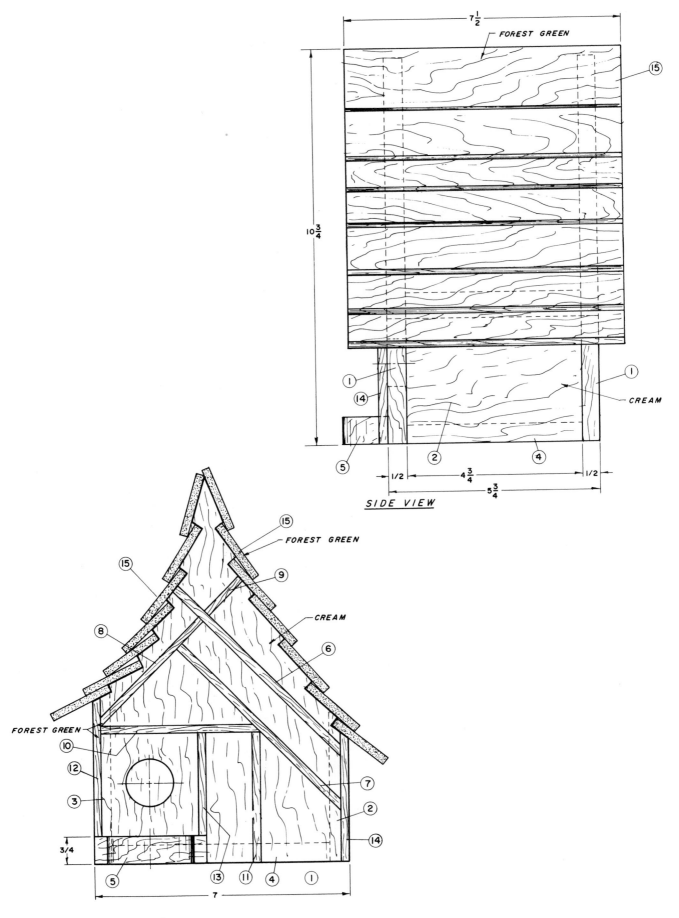

7½

FOREST GREEN

⑮

10¾

①

⑭

CREAM

②

④

⑤

1/2   4¾   1/2

5¾

SIDE VIEW

⑮

FOREST GREEN

⑮

⑨

⑧

CREAM

⑥

FOREST GREEN

⑩

⑫

⑦

③

②

⑭

3/4

⑤   ⑬   ⑪   ④   ①

7

FRONT VIEW

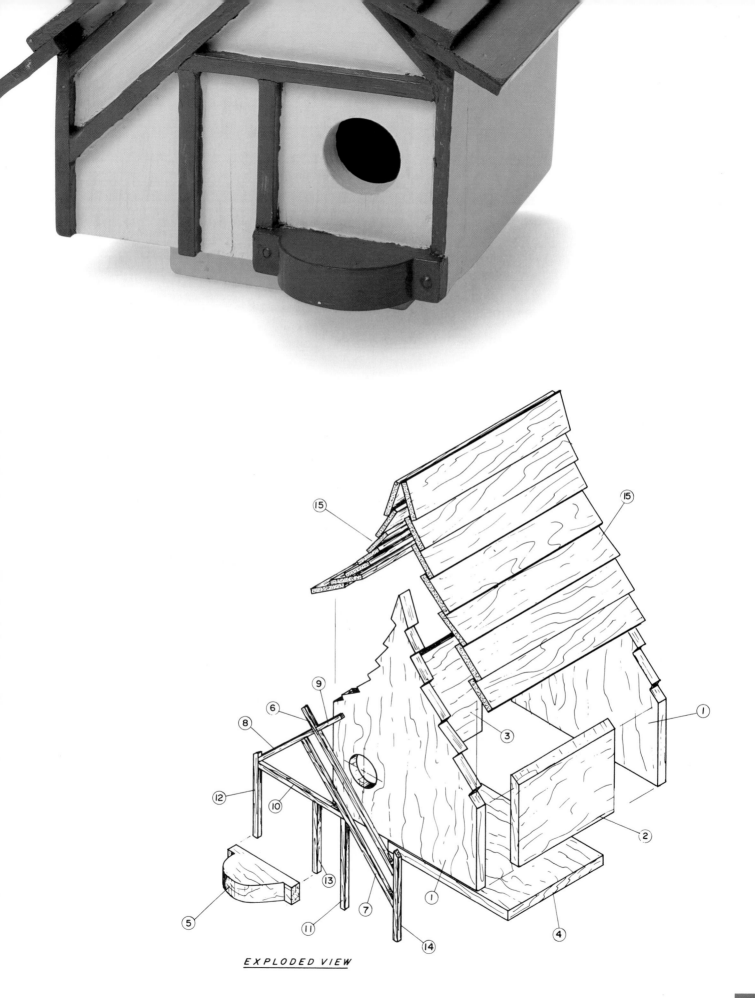

EXPLODED VIEW

Bluebird Nesting Box

Bluebirds were once a common sight in eastern North America, but their numbers have diminished by some 90 percent over the past half-century. The reasons include irresponsible use of pesticides, loss of habitat, and competition with sparrows and starlings. You can give bluebirds an edge by building a nesting box designed especially for them. The back is attached with screws so that it can be removed for cleaning.

Bluebirds are particular about their nesting sites; you'll increase your chances of attracting them by hanging the boxes on posts or trees in clearings and no more than four or five feet above the ground.

NO.	NAME	SIZE	REQ'D.
	MATERIALS LIST		
1	BACK	3/4 x 4 1/2 – 24 LONG	1
2	SIDE	3/4 x 6 1/4 – 15 1/16 LONG	2
3	FRONT	3/4 x 4 1/2 – 9 3/4 LONG	1
4	BOTTOM	3/4 x 4 1/2 – 2 LONG	1
5	TOP	3/4 x 7 1/2 – 11 LONG	1
6	PERCH	1/4 DIA. – 2 1/2 LONG	1
7	SCREW – FL. HD.	NO. 8 – 1 1/2 LONG	6

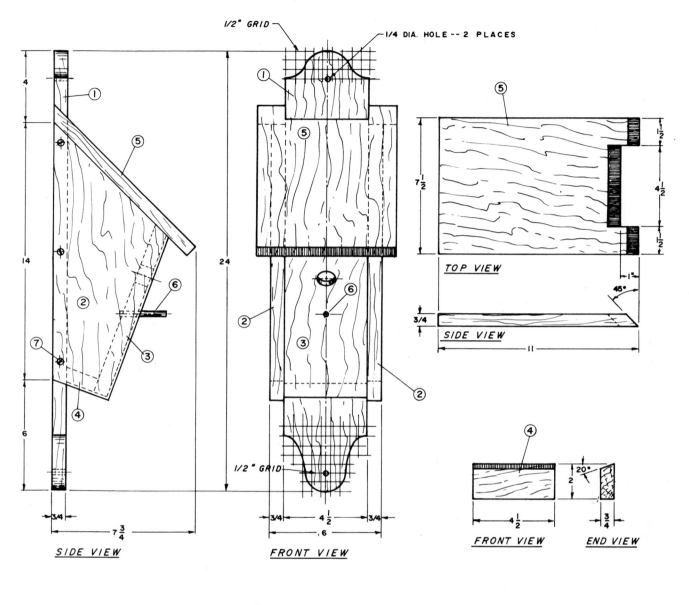

1/2" GRID

1/4 DIA. HOLE -- 2 PLACES

4

14

6

3/4

7 3/4

SIDE VIEW

24

1/2" GRID

3/4 4 1/2 3/4

6

FRONT VIEW

5

7 1/2

3/4

TOP VIEW

SIDE VIEW

11

1 1/2

4 1/2

1 1/2

1"

45°

4

20°

2

FRONT VIEW

4 1/2

END VIEW

3/4

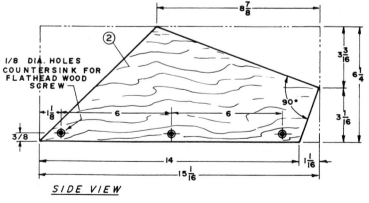

8 7/8

1/8 DIA. HOLES
COUNTERSINK FOR
FLATHEAD WOOD
SCREW

1 1/8

6

6

3/8

14

15 1/16

90°

3 3/16

6 1/4

3 1/16

1 1/16

SIDE VIEW

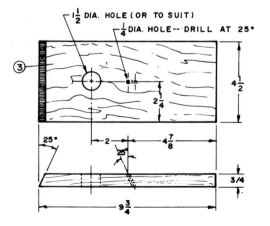

1 1/2 DIA. HOLE (OR TO SUIT)

1/4 DIA. HOLE -- DRILL AT 25°

4 1/2

2 1/4

25°

2

4 7/8

25°

9 3/4

3/4

1. Select the stock and cut the parts; you can use any sort of wood for this project. You might be able to make several boxes out of the ¼-inch-thick scraps in your workshop. Cut out the parts to the sizes given in the Materials List.

2. Make a paper pattern and cut the back to shape. Draw a grid with ½-inch squares and enlarge the back (part 1) onto it. Transfer the enlargement to the wood and cut out the back. Locate and drill the two ¼-inch-diameter hanging holes in the back.

The two sides (part 2) can be cut to shape and drilled at the same time. Place one on top of the other, attaching them with rubber cement.

Lay out the shape on the top piece, as shown in the side view of part 2. Maintain the 90° angle between the front and bottom. Cut the sides to shape on the band saw. While the pieces are still together, drill the ⅛-inch-diameter screw holes and countersink them on both sides for a #8 flathead screw (part 7). Sand the edges and take the sides apart.

3. Cut the front (part 3) and bottom (part 4) to shape, as shown in the details for those parts. Note the bevel on each. Locate and drill holes for the entrance and the perch in the front. The 1½-inch-diameter entrance may seem small, but it discourages other species from taking up residence. Note that the perch hole is drilled at a 25° angle so that the perch will project horizontally from the assembled birdhouse.

4. Cut the top (part 5) to shape, beveling both the edge and the back of the notch at 45°, as shown. I cut the bevels with a band saw, but a saber saw set at 45° would also work.

5. Assemble the nesting boxes. Screw the sides to the back—do not use glue. Glue the front, bottom, top, and sides together Note that the sides overhang the front and bottom by ⅛ inch, as shown in the side and exploded views. Do not glue any of these parts to the back, or you won't be able to take the nesting box apart for cleaning. Glue the perch (part 6) in place.

6. Apply finish. Remove the back from the sides, brush on an oil-base primer, and then an oil-base exterior paint inside and out. The example in the photograph has a two-tone paint job. When dry, put the box together with the six flathead screws.

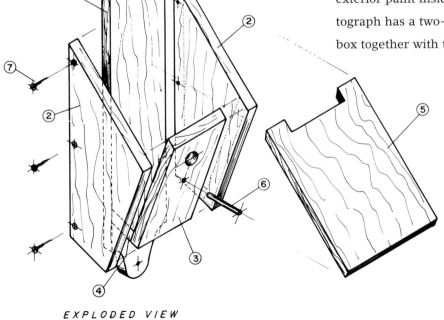

E X P L O D E D   V I E W

Garden Toolbox

This is one of my favorite projects. It is easy to make, has beautiful lines, can be made from scrap wood, and the finished project is extremely useful. But perhaps I like it most of all because it becomes a hot item at craft shows.

These plans are based exactly on an original tool-box, but I scaled it down to three-quarters of the origi-nal size. The original was painted, but you can either stain or paint yours.

1. Study the plans carefully. Note how each part is to be shaped. As you study the plans, try to visualize how you will make each part, and then how the project will be assembled. Note which parts you will put together first, second, and so on.

The ends and handle (parts 1 and 4) are irregular in shape and will have to be laid out on ½-inch grids to make full-size patterns. Lay out the full-size grids on heavy paper or cardboard, and transfer the shape of each piece to the grids, point by point.

2. Transfer the full-size patterns to the wood, and carefully cut out the pieces. Check all dimensions for accuracy. Sand all over with fine grit sandpaper, keep-ing all edges sharp.

3. Carefully cut the other parts to size according to the Materials List. Take care to cut all of the parts to

exact size, keeping them precisely square. Stop and recheck all dimensions before going on.

4. The sides (part 2) have a molded top edge. If you have a router, rout a shape as close as you can to the one shown.

5. Lightly sand all surfaces and edges with medium sandpaper to remove tool marks. Take care to keep all edges square and sharp.

6. After all of the pieces have been carefully made, dry-fit the parts. If anything needs refitting, now is the time to correct it. Once all of the parts fit together cor-rectly, assemble the project, keeping everything square as you go. Check that all fits are tight.

Finish to suit, following the general finishing instructions given in the introduction.

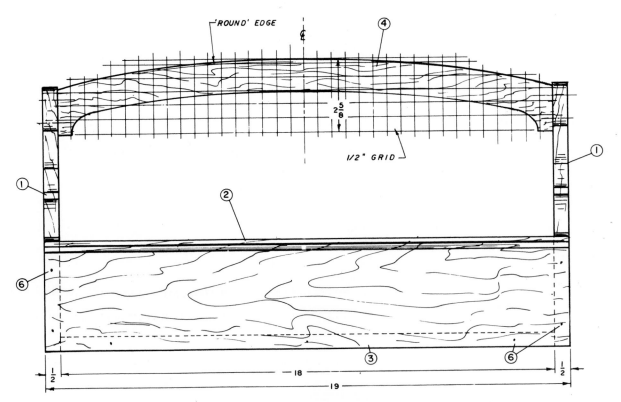

'ROUND' EDGE

1/2" GRID

$2\frac{5}{8}$

18

19

$\frac{1}{2}$

$\frac{1}{2}$

SIDE VIEW

MATERIALS LIST			
NO.	NAME	SIZE	REQ'D.
1	END	$\frac{1}{2}$ x $7\frac{1}{8}$ – $9\frac{1}{2}$ LONG	2
2	SIDE	$\frac{1}{2}$ x 4 – 19 LONG	2
3	BOTTOM	$\frac{1}{2}$ x $7\frac{1}{8}$ – 18 LONG	1
4	HANDLE	$\frac{5}{8}$ x $2\frac{5}{8}$ - 18 LONG	1
5	SCREW – FL. HD.	NO. 6 x $1\frac{1}{4}$ LONG	4
6	NAIL – FINISH	6 d	18

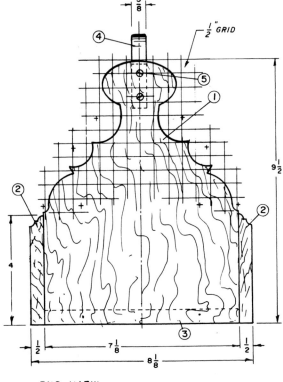

$\frac{5}{8}$

$\frac{1}{2}$" GRID

$9\frac{1}{2}$

4

$\frac{1}{2}$

$7\frac{1}{8}$

$\frac{1}{2}$

$8\frac{1}{8}$

END VIEW

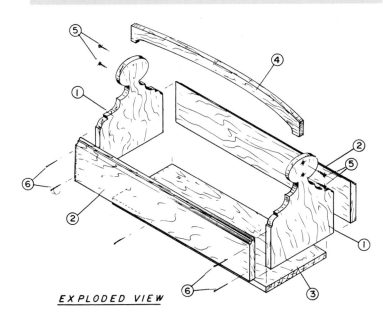

EXPLODED VIEW

Wind Chimes

With this project, you can turn your workshop scraps and the wind into music.

$1.$ Select the stock and cut the parts. Almost any wood will do, although especially weatherproof choices include redwood, cedar, and teak. I used leftover ash.

Cut the wooden parts—the supports, spacers, and clanger (parts 1, 2, 3, and 11)—to their overall sizes, as given in the Materials List. Turn the clanger to the profile shown or leave it unadorned. Drill a 1/16-inch-diameter hole in the exact center.

Cut out the sail (part 13) from any scrap metal or wood, following the pattern shown in the detail.

MATERIALS LIST			
NO.	**NAME**	**SIZE**	**REQ'D.**
1	MAIN SUPPORT	¾ x 6 – 6 LONG	1
2	TOP SUPPORT	½ x 3 – 3 LONG	1
3	SPACER	¼ DIA. – 2½ LONG	5
4	EYEBOLT	⅛ DIA. – 1 LONG	2
5	HEX NUT	FOR EYEBOLTS	2
6	CHIME	⅝ DIA. – 15½ LONG	1
7	CHIME	⅝ DIA. – 14½ LONG	1
8	CHIME	⅝ DIA. – 13½ LONG	1
9	CHIME	⅝ DIA. – 12½ LONG	1
10	CHIME	⅝ DIA. – 11½ LONG	1
11	CLANGER	½ x 2½ DIA.	1
12	BEAD	TO SUIT	2
13	SAIL	1/16 x 2½ – 3½ LONG	1
14	FISH LINE	60 LB. TEST	1

2. Make the metal chimes from either ⅝-inch-diameter copper pipe or electrical conduit. Cut the chimes (parts 6, 7, 8, 9, and 10) with a pipe cutter or hack saw to get five different tones: 11½ inches, 12½ inches, 13½ inches, 14½ inches, and 15½ inches (the tones will be close to a pentatonic scale, and you can further tune a chime to your liking by grinding it to raise the pitch).

Drill ⅛-inch-diameter holes ⅜ inch down from the top of the chimes and the sail. Lightly sand the sharp edges of the metal parts.

3. Make a paper pattern and cut the supports to shape. Draw a grid with ½-inch squares, and enlarge the main support and the top support onto it. Transfer the enlargement to the wood. Locate and drill the holes, as shown. Cut the parts to shape. Sand thoroughly.

4. Add the spacers. Glue the five spacers (part 3) in the holes in the main and top supports, leaving a space of 1 inch between the supports. Unless you have used teak, brush two or three coats of an exterior sealer on this subassembly and on the clanger.

5. Assemble the chimes. Study the top and exploded views to see how the chimes are put together. Thread a continuous length of fishing line (part 14) through the pipes and supports, as shown in the exploded view. The chimes should be about 1½ inches below the main support. Once you've gotten back to the starting point, tie a square knot in the end of the line and put a dab of glue on the knot to secure it. (Note: cord was used here for the project so that it would show up in the photo.)

Next, install the eyebolts (part 4) in the main support. Tie a new piece of fishing line to it, then run the line through a small wooden bead (part 12)

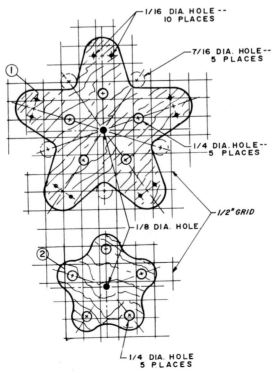

1/16 DIA. HOLE --
10 PLACES

7/16 DIA. HOLE --
5 PLACES

1/4 DIA. HOLE --
5 PLACES

1/2" GRID

1/8 DIA. HOLE

1/4 DIA. HOLE
5 PLACES

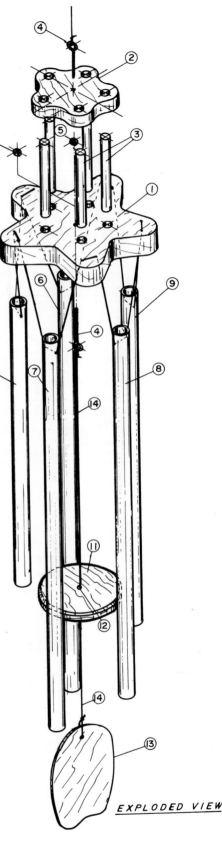

EXPLODED VIEW

and the clanger. Feed the line through the second bead, and then bring it back up and through the bead a second time to hold the clanger in place. The clanger should be about 7¼ inches from the main support. Thread the fish line through the hole in the sail and knot it. Place a bit of epoxy glue on the knots and at both beads.

To hang up the chimes, place the eyebolt in the top support and attach fishing line to it.

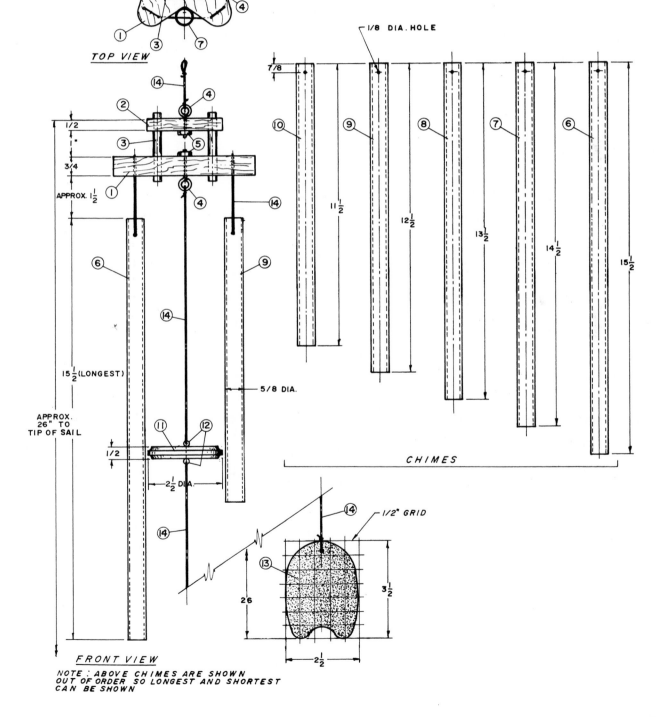

TOP VIEW

FRONT VIEW

NOTE: ABOVE CHIMES ARE SHOWN
OUT OF ORDER SO LONGEST AND SHORTEST
CAN BE SHOWN

CHIMES

1/8 DIA. HOLE

Trellis

This is a copy of a simple trellis that was popular in the late 1930s and early 1940s. It is suited for roses and other climbing plants.

1. Select the stock. It is important to use knot-free, straight-grained wood for this project. Spruce and hemlock are good choices, although nearly any wood should serve.

2. Cut the parts and saw the kerfs. Cut the parts to the sizes given in the Materials List. Locate and draw the position of the four kerfs along the length of the body (part 1). Take the width of the saw blade into consideration when laying out the kerfs. Drill a $3/16$-inch-diameter hole at what will be the end of each kerf and rip the stock until you reach the hole, as illustrated in detail A. The hole keeps the kerf from splitting the body. If the wood seems likely to split even with this precaution, you can run a $1/4$-inch-diameter hex-head bolt through the width of the body, about 2 inches below the ends of the kerfs. Keep the bolt in place with a washer and nut.

3. Spread the fingers. Lay out the position of the top and bottom bars (parts 2 and 3) on the body. Drill a $1/16$-inch-diameter pilot hole in each finger for the 6d

MATERIALS LIST

NO.	NAME	SIZE	REQ'D.
1	BODY	1 x 3⅛ – 72 LONG	1
2	TOP BOARD	⅝ x 1 – 47 LONG	2
3	BOTTOM BOARD	⅝ x 1 – 18 LONG	2
4	NAIL – FINISH	6 d	20

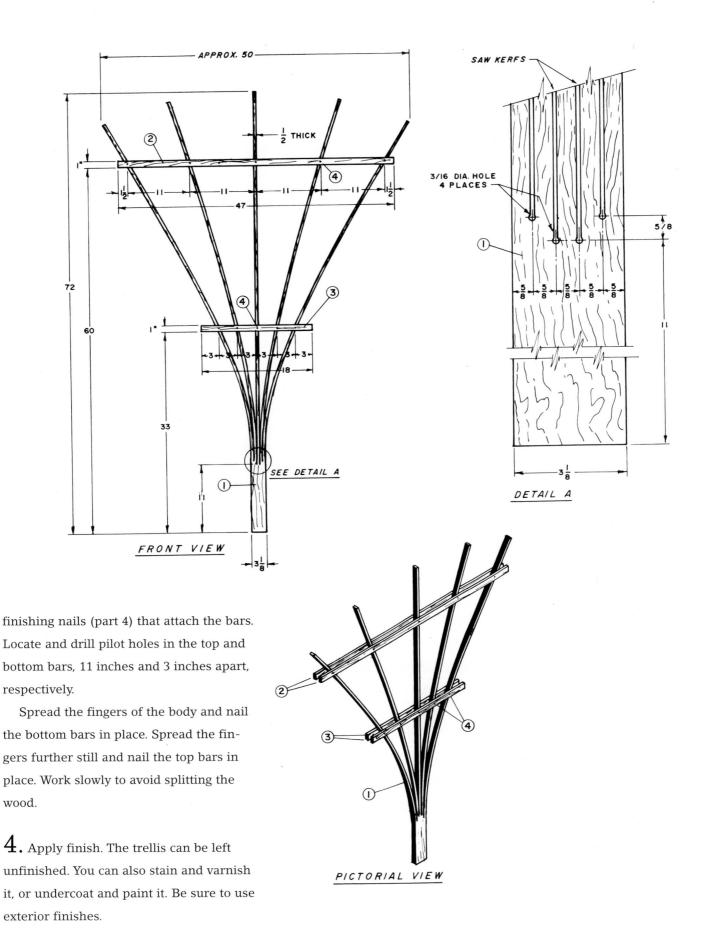

FRONT VIEW

SAW KERFS

3/16 DIA. HOLE
4 PLACES

DETAIL A

SEE DETAIL A

finishing nails (part 4) that attach the bars. Locate and drill pilot holes in the top and bottom bars, 11 inches and 3 inches apart, respectively.

Spread the fingers of the body and nail the bottom bars in place. Spread the fingers further still and nail the top bars in place. Work slowly to avoid splitting the wood.

4. Apply finish. The trellis can be left unfinished. You can also stain and varnish it, or undercoat and paint it. Be sure to use exterior finishes.

PICTORIAL VIEW

Full-Size & Child's Adirondack Chair

The design for the original Adirondack chair is credited to H. C. Bunnel. He received a patent for his straight, boxy version in 1905. The chair was named for the region in upstate New York where it was designed and first used.

Over the years, Bunnel's design has been modified by others to make it more accommodating to the body. Backs have been rounded, and the seats contoured. But the chairs you see here stay quite close to the early chairs. They are exact copies of one made by my grandfather around 1918, when he was living in the Adirondacks. As a very young woodworker, I copied one of my grandfather's rotted chairs in 1949. You can see that the design is unpretentious—no frills, no curved back or seat. And yet it is quite comfortable. The chair is roomy enough for you to prop yourself on a pillow or two. You can lay a book or a drink on the wide arms.

On becoming a grandfather myself, I made a child's version, scaled down about a quarter. Either it or the full-size chair can be made with these plans and instructions. The Materials List gives two sets of overall dimensions. Note that even the thickness of the stock has been reduced for the child's chair—⁹⁄₁₆ inch, rather than ³⁄₄ inch.

The chair can be put together with either brass-plated flathead screws or waterproof glue and finishing nails. You may want to countersink the screws ³⁄₁₆ inch or so and cover them with plugs cut from dowels; nails should be set and puttied.

1. Select the stock and cut the parts. In New England, knot-free pine or spruce are common choices for making lawn furniture. If primed and kept painted, the wood should last 20 years or more. Woods especially suited for outdoor furniture include Honduran mahogany, oak, redwood, and teak.

Decide which chair model you are going to make. Cut the parts to the thickness and width given in the Materials List, but leave pieces with curved or angled ends an inch or so long.

2. Make the seat. An Adirondack chair begins with the seat. You can save time when cutting details in the seat rail and other paired parts by joining the pieces temporarily with double-sided tape. Lay out the details on one board, and then cut both boards at once.

Cut a notch in each seat rail (part 2) to accept the back support (part 3). Round-over one end of the seat rail, following the pattern given and cut the other end at a 66° angle, as shown. Cut the seat rail to the proper length in the process.

After you've cut the seat rails to the proper profile, nail or screw the slats (part 5) to them. Attach the back support. Rip a 24° bevel on one edge of the front brace (part 4) and nail or screw it in place.

Round-over the front slat, as shown, with a router and the appropriately sized round-over bit.

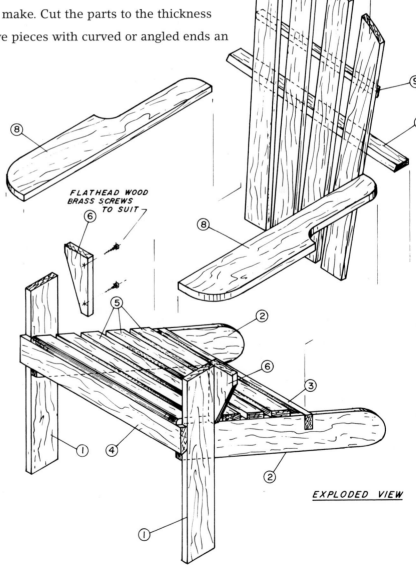

FLATHEAD WOOD
BRASS SCREWS
TO SUIT

EXPLODED VIEW

3. Make the back subassembly. I found that the best way to assemble the back is to lay it out on a full-size pattern drawn on a large sheet of paper.

Draw a box 30 inches high and 16¾ inches wide on the paper. Lay out in pencil the location of the parts, as shown in the front view of the back.

Carefully position the back slats (part 10) on the drawing.

Rip a 24° bevel on the lower cross base (part 7) and chamfer the corner of the upper cross brace (part 9), as shown in the view at A-A. Position the upper and lower cross braces on the back slats. Check that the cross braces are parallel to the bottom of the box and then attach the slats to them with screws or nails and glue.

To lay out the cut for the curved top of the back, draw a 15-inch-radius arc from the center of the upper cross brace. Cut the curve with a saber saw and sand the cut edges.

Clamp the assembled back to the back support and glue or nail it in place. The back will be somewhat flimsy until you attach the arms, so treat it with respect.

4. Attach the legs and arms. Attach the legs (part 1) to the seat rail, as shown in the side view. Cut the arm braces (part 6) to the profile shown in the top view of part 6, and attach the braces to the legs so the top surfaces are flush with each other. Cut the arms (part 8) to the profile shown. Position the arms so the front extends about 1 inch beyond the legs. The arms' inner edges should be parallel to each other and flush with the inner face of the legs. Nail or screw them to the leg and arm brace. Clamp the back end of the arm to the upper cross brace and nail or screw the two together. Nail or screw the back slats to the lower brace.

5. Apply finish. If you've used nails, set them all over the chair, then putty and sand the holes. If you decided to countersink the screws, glue the plugs in place now.

NO.	NAME	SIZE	REQ'D.
MATERIALS LIST			
ADULT'S CHAIR			
1	FRONT LEG	¾ x 3½ – 20 LONG	2
2	SEAT RAIL	¾ x 3½ – 30½ LONG	2
3	BACK SUPPORT	¾ x 1½ – 19 LONG	1
4	FRONT BRACE	¾ x 3½ – 20½ LONG	1
5	SEAT SLAT	¾ x 2½ – 19 LONG	5
6	ARM BRACE	¾ x 3 – 6½ LONG	2
7	LOWER CROSS BRACE	¾ x 1¾ – 22 LONG	1
8	ARM	¾ x 4¾ – 24 LONG	2
9	UPPER CROSS BRACE	¾ x 1 – 15¼ LONG	1
10	BACK SLAT	½ x 2½ – 30 LONG	4
11	NAIL – FINISH	6 d and 8 d	AS REQ'D.
12	SCREW – FL. HD.	NO. 6 - 1 LONG NO. 8 - 1½ LONG	AS REQ'D.
CHILD'S CHAIR			
1	FRONT LEG	9/16 x 2⅝ – 15 LONG	2
2	SEAT RAIL	9/16 x 2⅝ – 22½ LONG	2
3	BACK SUPPORT	9/16 x 1⅛ – 14¼ LONG	1
4	FRONT BRACE	9/16 x 2⅝ – 15⅜ LONG	1
5	SEAT SLAT	9/16 x 1⅞ – 14¼ LONG	5
6	ARM BRACE	9/16 x 2¼ – 4⅞ LONG	2
7	LOWER CROSS BRACE	9/16 x 1¼ – 22½ LONG	1
8	ARM	9/16 x 3½ – 18 LONG	2
9	UPPER CROSS BRACE	9/16 x ¾ – 11½ LONG	1
10	BACK SLAT	⅜ x 1⅞ – 22½ LONG	4
11	NAIL – FINISH	6 d and 8 d	AS REQ'D.
12	NAIL – FL. HD.	NO. 6 - 1 LONG NO. 8 - 1½ LONG	AS REQ'D

Sand the chair all over. If you used a weather-resist-ant wood, your work is done. For added protection, you might add a coat or two of marine spar varnish. Other woods should be primed and finished with two coats of exterior paint. Don't forget to cover the bottom surfaces of the legs. You can expect to apply another coat of paint every two or three years.

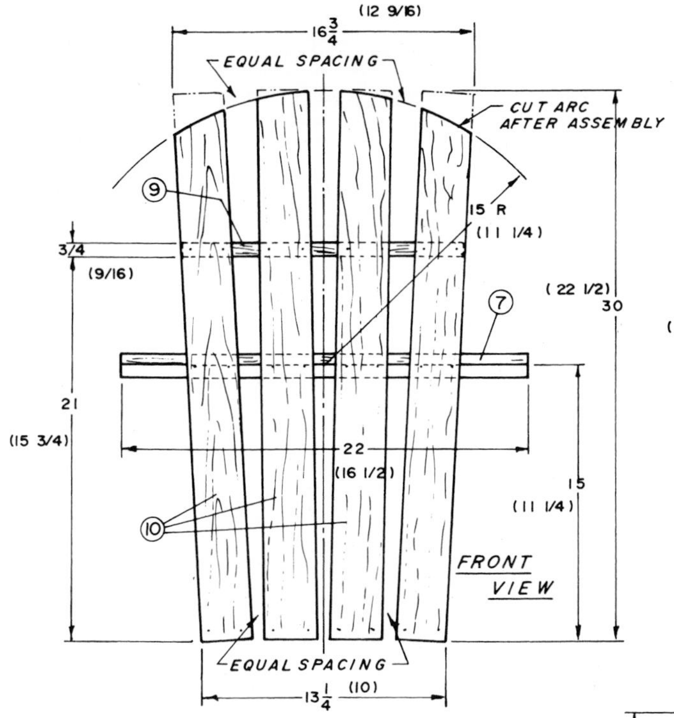

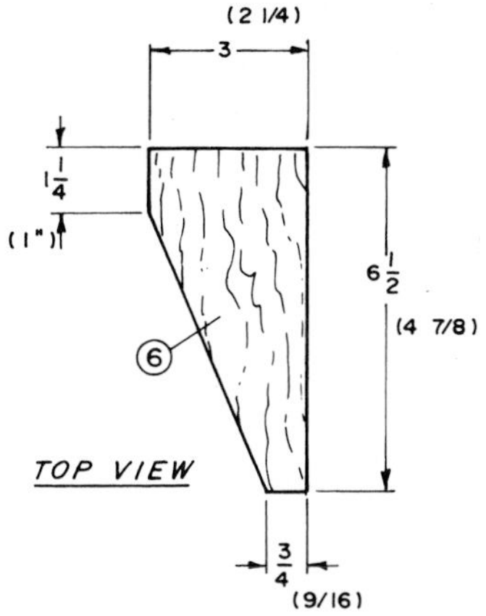

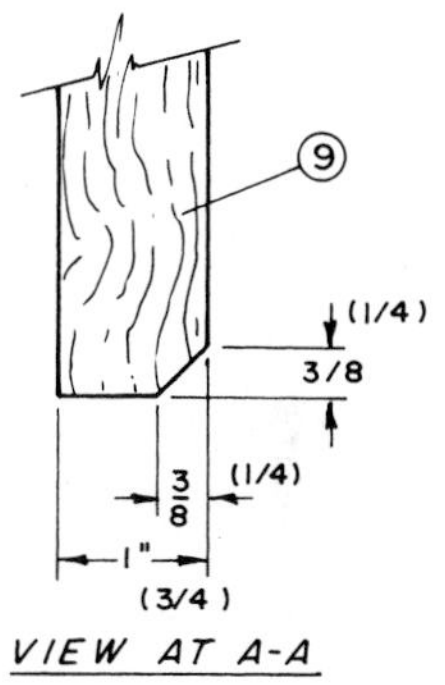

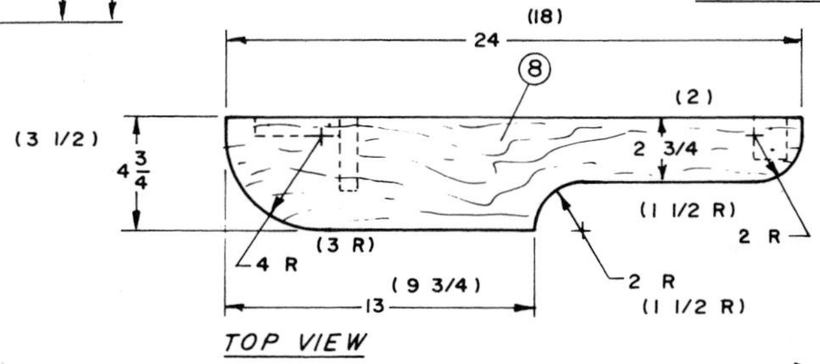

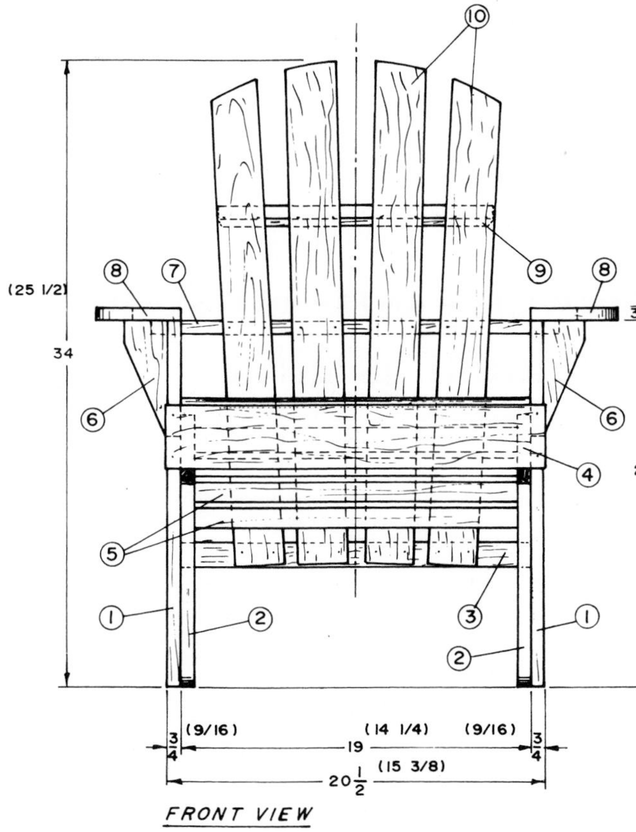

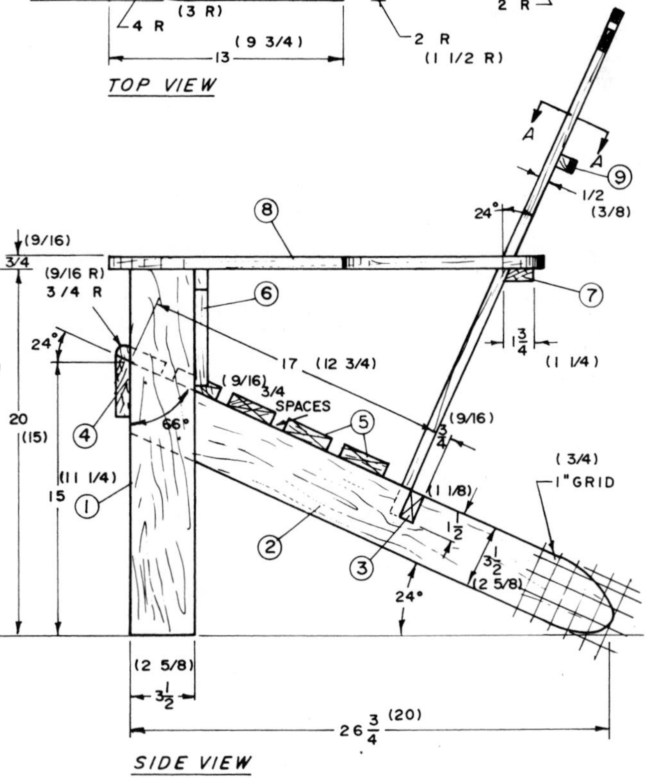

FRONT VIEW

TOP VIEW

VIEW AT A-A

TOP VIEW

FRONT VIEW

SIDE VIEW

Useful Household Projects

This delightful mix of contemporary and traditional designs is guaranteed to perk up any room in your home. You'll find everything from a picture frame and a candleholder to a jewelry box. Most of the projects are also ideal as gifts.

Tulips on a Stand

In New Hampshire we have very short summers, and these bright wooden flowers can help make winter bearable.

MATERIALS LIST

NO.	NAME	SIZE	REQ'D.
1	BASE	¾ x 4 – 16 LONG	1
2	LEAF	¾ x 4½ – 3½ LONG	5
3	FLOWER	¾ x 2½ – 2½ LONG	5
4	STEM	¼ DIA. – 7¾ LONG	5

1. Select the stock and cut the parts. Except for the ¼-inch dowel used for the stems, all you need are ¾-inch-thick scraps of any wood.

2. Make a paper pattern. Draw a grid with ¼-inch squares and enlarge the drawing of the leaves (part 2) and flowers (part 3) onto the grid. Transfer the enlargements to the wood and cut them to shape. You can save time by drawing the patterns on just one flower and one leaf and cutting out several of the same pieces at once. Stack similar pieces and attach them to each other with either double-sided tape or rubber cement.

Draw curves at both ends of the base (part 1) and cut them out. Locate and drill the ¼-inch-diameter holes in the flowers, leaves, and base, as directed on the drawings. Sand each part entirely.

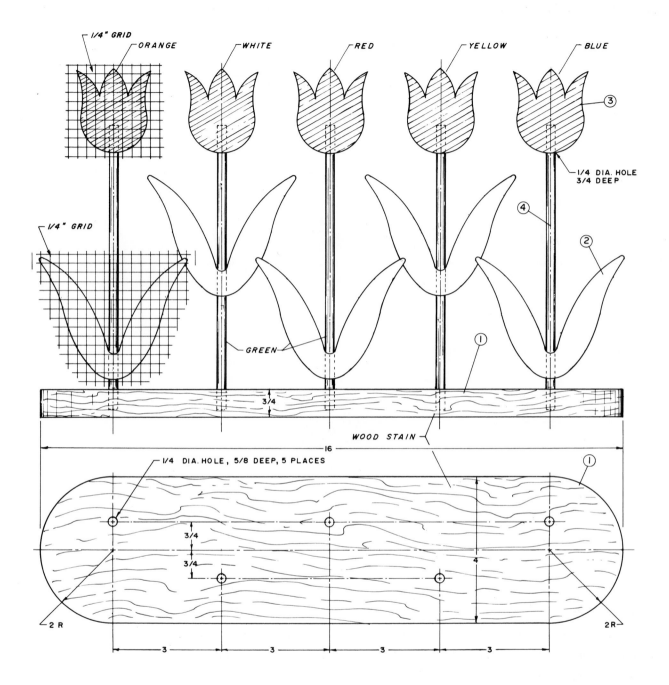

3. Assemble the tulips. Apply glue to each stem at the location of the leaf. Slide the leaves over the dowel stems (part 4). Spread glue on the tops of the stems and insert them into the flower blossoms. Spread glue on the bottoms of the stems and insert them into the base. Wipe off any excess glue.

4. Finish the tulips. Paint as you choose. The front view suggests colors for the various parts, along with stain for the base to represent soil. To make the piece more interesting, try varying the shade of green you use on the leaves and stems.

Simple Wooden Basket

Baskets don't come much simpler than this, and yet its lines are pleasing. We've found that these baskets sell well at craft shows.

1. Select the stock and cut the parts. You can make this basket out of workshop scraps. Cut the parts to the sizes given in the Materials List.

2. Cut the parts to shape. Make two 45° cuts in both ends (part 1). Drill a ⅜-inch-diameter handle hole in the handle supports (part 3). Trim the top ends of the supports, as shown in the end view, by making 45° cuts that begin about ³⁄₁₆ inch from the corners. Chamfer the ends of the handle (part 4) slightly with sandpaper.

3. Assemble the basket. I recommend gluing the pieces together and then nailing them with roundhead brass nails (part 5), but any ½-inch-long nail will do.

Start assembly by putting the ends upside-down on the bench and attaching the two bottom slats (part 2). Leave ¾ inch between the slats; the handle support fits into this space, as shown in the end view.

Turn the basket on one side and attach the three slats to the opposite side. Turn the basket over to attach the remaining slats.

Attach the handle supports. When attaching the second support, align it with the first support by temporarily putting the handle in place. After you've attached the supports, glue the handle in place.

4. Apply finish. You can leave the basket unfinished or stain and varnish it. If you plan to store food in the basket, finish it with a salad-bowl finish.

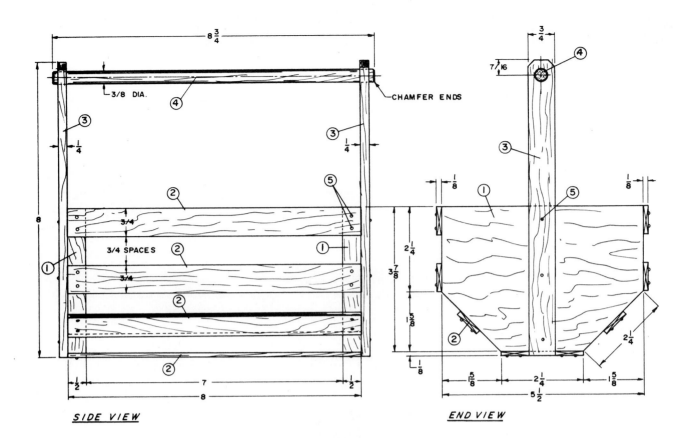

SIDE VIEW

END VIEW

MATERIALS LIST

NO.	NAME	SIZE	REQ'D.
1	END	½ x 3⅞ - 5½ LONG	2
2	SLAT	⅛ x ¾ – 8 LONG	8
3	HANDLE SUPPORT	¼ x ¾ - 8 LONG	2
4	HANDLE	⅜ DIA. - 8¾ LONG	1
5	BRASS NAIL – RD. HD.	½ LONG	AS REQ'D.

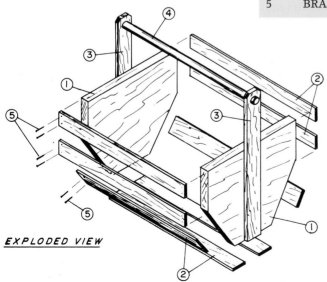

EXPLODED VIEW

Modern Picture Frame

This is a design by a good friend of mine. It's very easy to make, attractive, and truly functional.

1. Cut all pieces to overall size.

2. Cut the ends (part 1) to shape. Locate and drill the three ³/₁₆-inch-diameter holes. Do not drill through; drill only ³/₁₆ inch deep. Make the ³/₁₆-inch-wide x ¹/₈-inch-deep dado. The width should be the width of two pieces of glass, plus a photo. Be sure to make a right-hand and a left-hand pair.

3. Cut the three dowels (part 2) to length.

4. Carefully glue the ends (part 1) to the three dowels (part 2). It is a good idea to have the glass temporarily in place so that the ends will be square.

MATERIALS LIST			
NO.	NAME	SIZE	REQ'D.
1	END	¼ x 3⅛ – 6 LONG	2
2	DOWEL	³/₁₆ DIA. – 6½ LONG	3
3	STOP	⅛ x ³/₁₆ – ³/₁₆ LONG	2
4	GLASS	³/₃₂ x 4¾ – 6½	2
5	PHOTOGRAPH	4¾ x 6½	1

5. Add the small stops (part 3) as shown.

6. Remove the glass; finish to suit. Add clean glass and a photo; now you have a beautiful, modern picture stand.

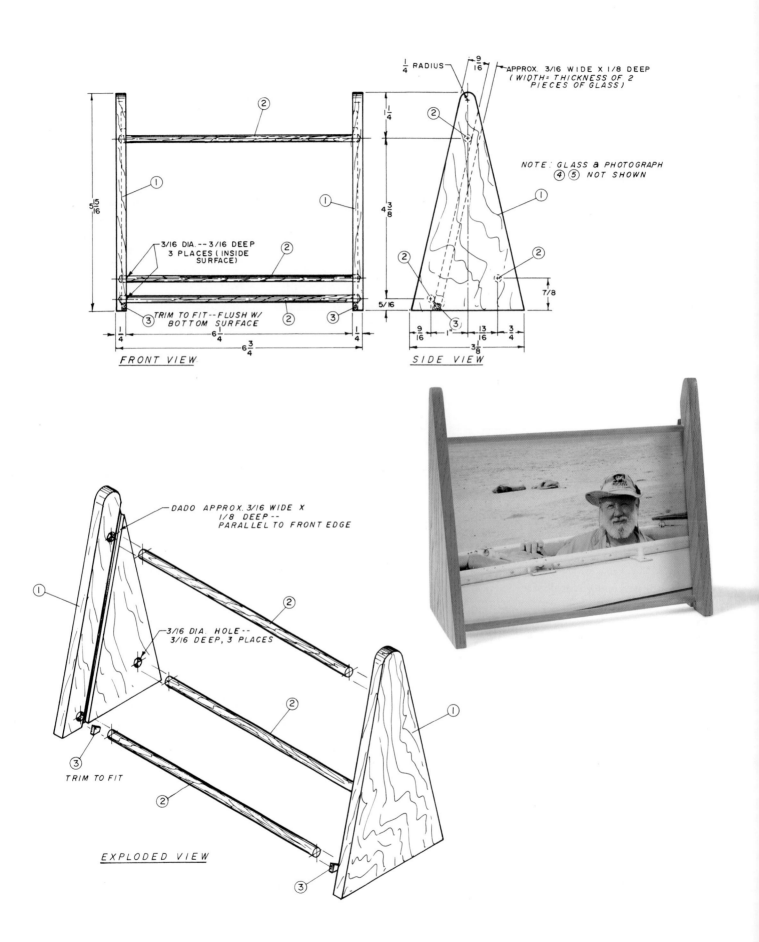

Tie Rack

This handy project could be a good one to try if you are interested in selling your work at craft shows. Otherwise, if you're like me, you'll have to go out and buy some ties to justify making the rack!

MATERIALS LIST			
NO.	NAME	SIZE	REQ'D.
1	BASE	¾ x 2 - 16⅛ LONG	1
2	PEG	3/16 DIA. (TENON) – 2⅜ LONG	31

1. Select the stock. Use any kind of wood for the base. Purchase the pegs before starting on the project.

2. Cut the base. Before cutting out the base (part 1), drill the detail at each corner with a ¾-inch drill bit. Then cut the base to its overall dimensions. Rout a cove around the edge of the base with a ¼-inch-radius cove bit with a ball-bearing guide.

3. Lay out the peg positions. With a soft pencil, draw two lines parallel to the long sides of the base and ⅝ inch from these sides. Along each line, lay out the centers of the peg holes. Mark the centers by dimpling the wood with an awl; this will keep the bit from wandering when you drill the holes. Start 1½ inches from either end on the top line and make a mark every ⅞ inch. Make 16 marks, leaving a margin of 1½ inches at the far end. Next, make 15 marks along the lower line. The two rows of pegs are staggered, so start this row 1¹⁵/₁₆ inches from either end. Make a mark every ⅞ inch. If you've done everything correctly, you'll have 1¹⁵/₁₆ inches left when you reach the other end.

Lay out the centers of the two holes that will be used to hang the rack.

4. Drill the holes. Drill a 3/16-inch-diameter hole ⅝ inch deep at each peg mark. Set the depth gauge on the drill press to make sure that the holes will be exactly the same depth. If you're using a hand drill, buy a commercially available drill-bit stop. Drill the two 3/16-inch-diameter hanging holes and countersink them to take flathead screws.

Sand the face of the rack with a flat-sanding block or an electric palm sander. Sand the edges by hand.

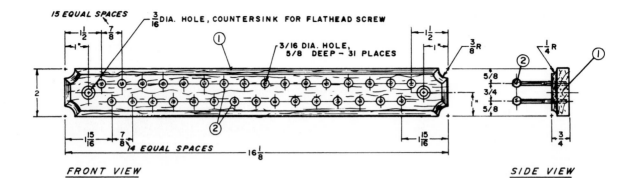

15 EQUAL SPACES
3/16 DIA. HOLE, COUNTERSINK FOR FLATHEAD SCREW
3/16 DIA. HOLE,
5/8 DEEP – 31 PLACES
①
②
3/8 R
1/4 R
①
②

FRONT VIEW

14 EQUAL SPACES

SIDE VIEW

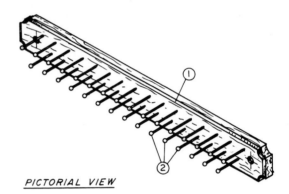

PICTORIAL VIEW

5. Assemble the rack. Place a small amount of glue in each peg hole. (Be careful to keep glue off the surface of the rack.) Put the pegs in the holes. To drive them all the same depth, press down on them simultaneously with a piece of wood. Tap the wood lightly to drive the pegs home. Make a final check to see that all of the pegs extend the same distance. Let the glue dry.

6. Apply finish. Apply a coat of stain, if you wish, and follow with two or three coats of a high-gloss varnish.

Shoeshine Box

Here's my version of a store-bought shoeshine box. It's a bit higher so that you don't have to bend over quite so far to shine your shoes. Note that only simple butt joints are used throughout.

1. Select the stock. The box is made entirely from ¾-inch stock. I made mine out of ash. The hinges and hasp are purchased items, as are the feet.

2. Build the box. Rather than build a lid to match an open box, I built a closed box and cut it open to create a perfectly matching lid. Dimensions for building a box with this technique are given in the Materials List. Make sure that all cuts are exactly 90°. Butt joints that do not meet squarely are weak. Dry-fit the two sides (part 1), the two ends (part 2), and the top and bottom (part 3). If necessary, trim the parts to fit and then glue up the box, keeping everything square.

3. Cut the lid. Draw a line 8 inches from the bottom all the way around the box. Set the table-saw fence to make an 8-inch-wide cut and set the blade slightly more than ¾ inch above the table. Run the box through the saw to cut the two ends, keeping the box

MATERIALS LIST			
NO.	NAME	SIZE	REQ'D.
1	SIDE	¾ x 8⅝ – 11 LONG	2
2	END	¾ x 8⅝ – 6½ LONG	2
3	TOP/BOTTOM	¾ x 8 – 11 LONG	1 EA.
4	SUPPORT	¾ x 3 – 9¾ LONG	3
5	SHOE REST	¾ x 3¼ – 7 LONG	1
6	HING	1½ x 1½	2
7	HASP		1
8	FOOT		4
9	NAIL – FINISH	6 d	AS REQ'D.

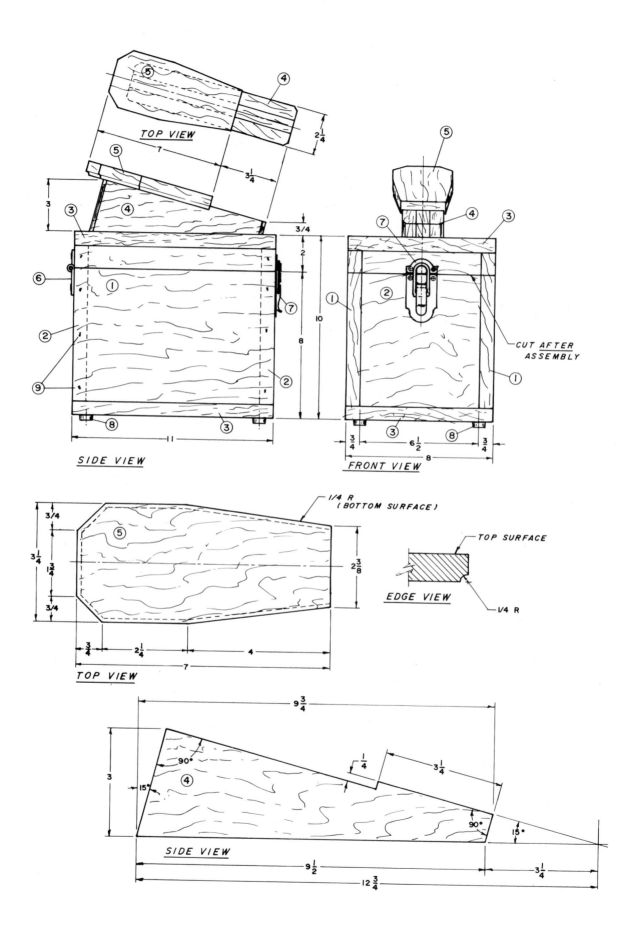

TOP VIEW

7

3 1/4

2 1/4

3/4

3

2

8

10

SIDE VIEW

11

FRONT VIEW

3/4

6 1/2

3/4

8

CUT AFTER
ASSEMBLY

1/4 R
(BOTTOM SURFACE)

TOP SURFACE

EDGE VIEW

1/4 R

3/4

3 1/4

1 3/4

3/4

2 3/8

3/4

2 1/4

4

7

TOP VIEW

9 3/4

90°

1/4

3 1/4

3

15°

90°

15°

9 1/2

3 1/4

12 3/4

SIDE VIEW

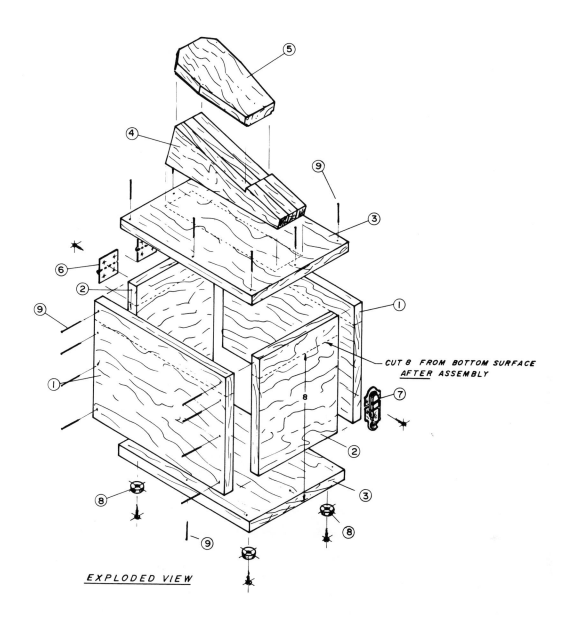

EXPLODED VIEW

CUT 8 FROM BOTTOM SURFACE
AFTER ASSEMBLY

firmly against the fence. To keep the kerfs open when running the remaining two sides through the saw, place scraps of wood the width of the kerf into each cut and tape them in place. Cut the sides, again keeping the box firmly against the fence. Reinforce the butt joints with 6d finishing nails (part 9) and fill the holes. Sand the box well.

4. Cut the shoe rest and support. Band-saw the shoe rest (part 5) to the shape shown in the illustration and sand off the saw marks. Rout a cove with a ¼-inch-radius cove bit around the perimeter, except at the end which meets the heel.

Glue up three pieces of ¾-inch stock to make the 2¼-inch-thick support (part 4). After the glue sets, band-saw the support to the shape, as shown.

5. Assemble the box. Glue the support to the shoe rest. Center the support and shoe rest assembly on the top of the lid and glue it in place. Temporarily attach the two hinges (part 6), hasp (part 7), and four rubber feet (part 8). If everything works as it should, remove them and proceed to the next step.

6. Finish the box. Brush on two coats of varnish. Reattach the hardware.

Folding Candleholder

While visiting a craft shop during a recent summer, we saw a simple candleholder similar to this one and found it very interesting. If you have a band saw it's very easy to make, although it can be made with a handsaw. It folds up easily for storage, but you'll probably want to have this elegant display piece out all the time.

1. Select a board with a pleasing grain pattern, preferably hardwood, and cut part 1 to ³⁄₄ x 2⁷⁄₈ x 8¹⁄₂ inches long.

2. Sand all over with coarse sandpaper down to a fine grit. Apply a coat of stain and one light top-coat. Lightly sand.

3. Locate and drill a ¼-inch-diameter hole through, at the right end, as shown.

4. Carefully locate and drill the six ½-inch-diameter holes ⁹⁄₁₆ inch deep, as shown. Lightly resand.

5. Being precise, and using a small square, draw the cuts on the side of the wood.

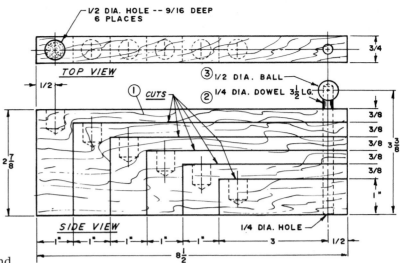

1/2 DIA. HOLE -- 9/16 DEEP
6 PLACES

TOP VIEW

3/4

1/2

③ 1/2 DIA. BALL
① *CUTS*
② 1/4 DIA. DOWEL 3½ LG.

3/8
3/8
3/8
3/8
3/8

3⅜

1"

2⅞

SIDE VIEW

1/4 DIA. HOLE

1" 1" 1" 1" 1" 3 1/2

8½

6. With great care, make the cuts as shown. Sand all fresh cuts and stain all surfaces again.

7. Apply two to three more topcoats of a high-gloss finish.

8. Temporarily add the ¼-inch-diameter dowel (part 2) with a ½-inch-diameter ball (part 3) on top.

9. Fan out the fingers to check that the pieces clear each other. Trim lightly, as necessary.

10. Again, attach the dowel (part 2) and ball (part 3). Glue to the bottom board only. Add candles, and open out the fingers in a fan-like position.

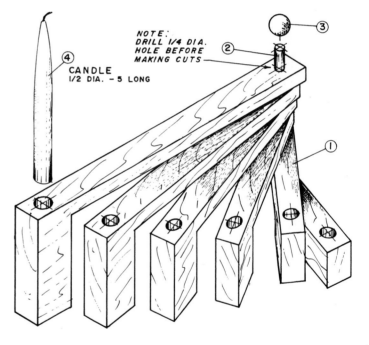

④ CANDLE
1/2 DIA. - 5 LONG

NOTE:
DRILL 1/4 DIA.
HOLE BEFORE
MAKING CUTS

③
②
①

EXPLODED VIEW

Simple Toolbox

This box can be made of any kind of wood, but a hardwood is recommended. It's a simple item that can be used for all kinds of things, but it's perfect for tools. If it's necessary to fit a particular need, you can make it longer than 14 inches. Now you can collect all your tools or other gadgets in one place, so you know just where to find them.

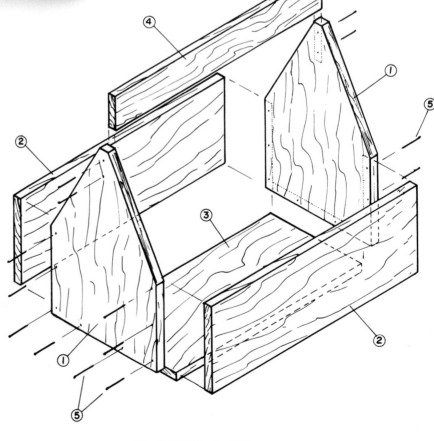

EXPLODED VIEW

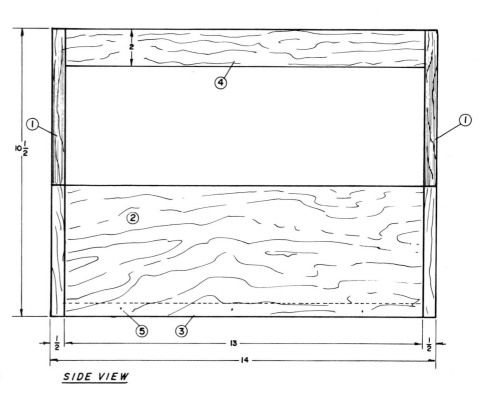

SIDE VIEW

1. Cut parts to size per the Materials List. Take care to make all cuts at 90°. Sand all surfaces with medium-grit sandpaper.

2. Cut the two ends to shape according to the plans. It is a good idea to tape two pieces of stock together to cut both ends at the same time. This way both will be exactly the same size and shape.

3. If a hard wood is used, it is a good idea to pre-drill for all the nails, so that the wood does not split. All joints are simple butt joints making this tool box easy to put together. Glue and nail all joints, taking care to keep everything square as you assemble the box. Add the handle last.

4. After assembly, resand all over, but keep all the edges sharp. This project can be finished with either a stain and clear top coat or painted.

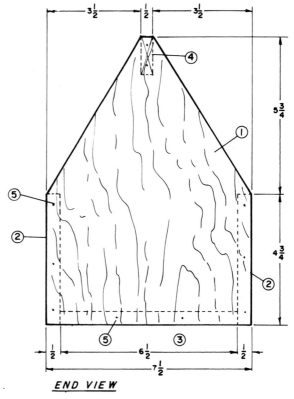

END VIEW

MATERIALS LIST

NO.	NAME	SIZE	REQ'D.
1	END	½ x 7½ – 10½ LONG	2
2	SIDE	½ x 4¾ – 13 LONG	2
3	BOTTOM	½ x 6½ – 13 LONG	1
4	HANDLE	½ x 2 – 13 LONG	1
5	NAIL – FINISH	6 d	28

Eight-Sided Jewelry Box

This box makes an excellent gift. In addition to jewelry, it can be used for anything from a clock case to a music box.

As with other projects in this book, I made a lid that matches the box perfectly by first making a completely sealed box. Then I cut the box open to form the lid. Unlike most other projects, this box has a dust lip: a lip on the box fits inside a rabbet in the lid.

A friend of mine, Jerry Ernce, showed me how to cut the lip and rabbet in the process of cutting the box apart. I call it the Jerry joint in his honor and now use this lid on nearly all the boxes I make.

Before jumping into this project, take the time to study how the box fits together and how the Jerry joint is made.

MATERIALS LIST			
NO.	NAME	SIZE	REQ'D.
1	SIDE	1/2 x 4 3/4 – 2 5/8 LONG	8
2	TOP/BOTTOM	1/4 x 6 – 6 LONG	1 EA.
3	HINGED CATCH		1
4	HINGE		1
5	RUBBER F00T	1/2 LONG	4

1. Select the wood and cut the board for the sides. I suggest using a hardwood. If you choose to make it out of an undistinguished wood, you can make it resemble rosewood with the directions at the end of the project. I used bird's-eye maple in this version.

Begin the box by cutting a ½-inch-thick board 4¾ inches wide and at least 24 inches long. In step 2, you will cut the eight sides (part 1) from this board.

Cutting the Jerry joint involves cutting a groove on what will be the inside of the box before assembly. Later, an adjoining groove on the outside will create the dust lip. For now, cut a groove ¼ inch wide and ³⁄₁₆ inch deep on the inside, as shown in figure 1, page 96.

2. Cut the sides. Set the blade of a table saw at 22½°. Cut some sample joints to make sure the pieces will come together in an octagon without leaving gaps at the joints. Adjust as necessary and then cut the 24-inch-long piece into the eight sides, each exactly 2⅝ inches long, as shown in figure 2, page 96. Dry-fit the eight sides to make sure they come together as they should.

Glue the octagon with the help of masking tape. Here's how: put a long strip of tape on the bench, sticky side up. Place the outside face of one side on the tape with the top edge parallel to the tape. Put an adjoining side on the tape next to the first side. The toes of the miters—the long narrow edge that you will see from the outside of the assembled box—must touch along their entire lengths. Position the sides so that the grooves are in line with each other. Continue the process, side by side, until you've taped all eight pieces to form a long line.

Put glue in the miters, fold the pieces together to form an octagon, and clamp with a band clamp or heavy rubber band.

3. Cut the top and bottom. Cut the octagonal top and bottom (part 2) slightly oversized. Sand the edges flush with the box after you've assembled it. Glue the top and bottom to the box, as shown in figure 3, page 97.

4. Measure for the lid cut. The sealed box should now look as shown in the drawing for figure 4, page 97. When the glue has dried, sand the top and bottom edges flush with the sides. Draw a line around the box, 1½ inches down from the top surface and parallel to it. This will be the top of a groove that separates the lid from the box.

5. Cut the lid. To free the lid, cut a groove along the line, ¼ inch wide and ³⁄₁₆ inch deep, as shown in figure 5, page 97. It should meet the inside groove to form a lipped lid. Follow a sequence of cuts as indicated by the letters A through H. If the lid fits too tightly, sand the lower of the two lips.

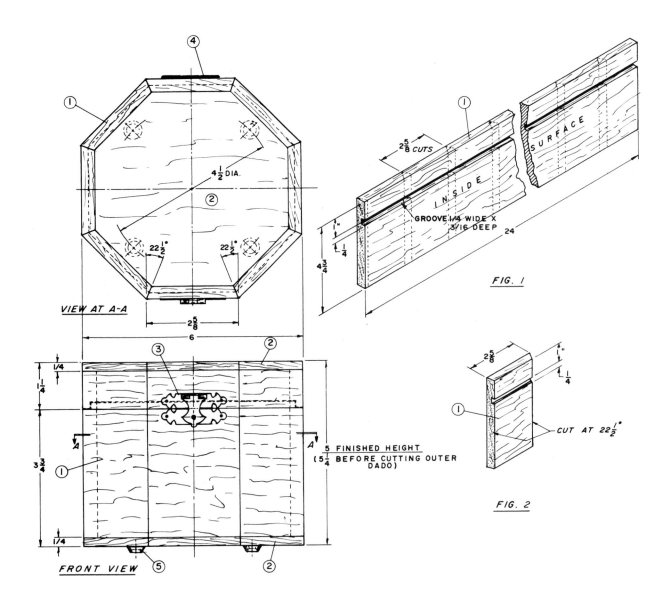

VIEW AT A-A

FIG. 1

FIG. 2

FRONT VIEW

6. Attach the hardware. Temporarily add the hardware (parts 3, 4, and 5), as shown in the drawing for figure 6. Remove it to apply the finish.

7. Apply finish. Varnish the piece if you like the look of the wood as is. Or, use one of the following methods to suggest the appearance of rosewood.

Apply two coats of oil-based orange or red paint, sanding between coats. Next apply two coats of varnish or shellac, rubbing with steel wool between coats.

Or, dilute oil-base, black paint with paint thinner until it is the consistency of milk. You will make a design in a coat of wet black paint with a goose or turkey feather, but first dip the feather in thinner and run your thumb over the edge from tip to base in order to separate the individual hairs. Apply a coat of black paint to the box; then, drag the thinner-dampened feather over it to suggest the swirling grain of rosewood.

8. When the finish has dried, reinstall the hardware.

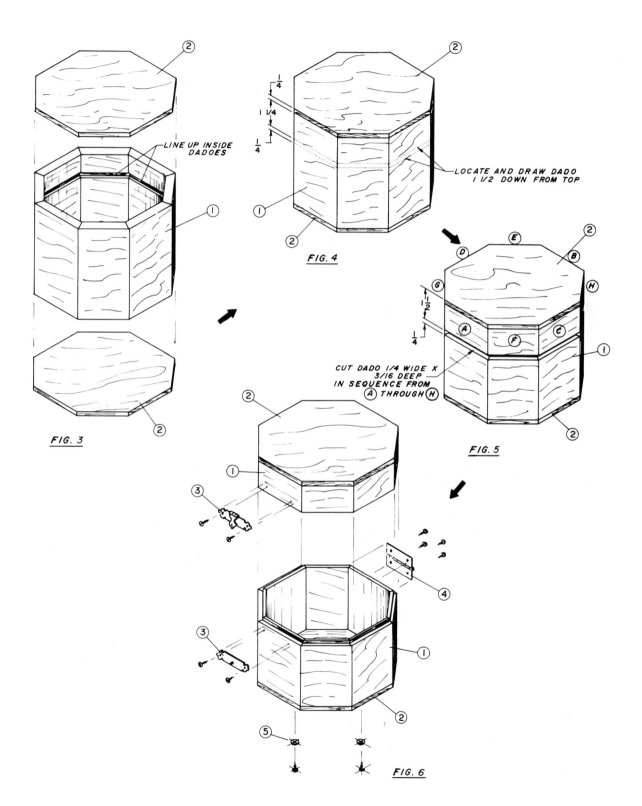

LINE UP INSIDE DADOES

FIG. 3

LOCATE AND DRAW DADO 1 1/2 DOWN FROM TOP

FIG. 4

CUT DADO 1/4 WIDE X 3/16 DEEP IN SEQUENCE FROM Ⓐ THROUGH Ⓗ

FIG. 5

FIG. 6

Duck Basket

Baskets come in all shapes and sizes, but this is the first one I've seen posing as a duck. A lot of folks must love these baskets because I have a friend who has built and sold 2,000 of them. When his baskets were featured on a regional television show, they were referred to as New Hampshire baskets. Whatever you want to call them, they make great holders for potted plants, among other things.

MATERIALS LIST			
NO.	NAME	SIZE	REQ'D.
1	FRONT/BACK	¾ x 6 – 4¾ LONG	1 EA.
2	HEAD	¾ x 4 – 10⅝ LONG	1
3	BOTTOM	⅜ x 1⁵⁄₁₆ – 9⅝ LONG	4
4	SIDE BOARD	⅜ x 1¼ – 14¼ LONG	8
5	TAIL FEATHER	⅜ x 1½ – 6 LONG	3
6	SCREW – FL. HD.	NO. 6 – 1½ LONG	2
7	TACK	¾ LONG	AS REQ'D.

1. Select the stock and cut the parts. The front, back, and head are made of ¾-inch-thick stock; the rest of the pieces are ⅜-inch-thick slats. Use any wood you have on hand. Cut the parts to the dimensions given in the Materials List.

2. Lay out the parts. Lay out the front and back (part 1), as shown in the front view.

Make a paper pattern to lay out the head. Draw a grid with ½-inch squares and enlarge the drawing of the duck's head (part 2) onto the grid. Transfer the enlarged drawing to ¾-inch-thick wood.

3. Cut the parts to shape, except for the side boards. Stack and tape the front and back together. Cut them at the same time to make certain they are identical. Cut out the head. Don't overlook the ⅜-inch notch in the head where it is attached to the front board; the notch is labeled on the side view. To drill the ¼-inch-diameter eye hole cleanly, bore through the head until the point of the bit just pokes through. Turn the head over and finish drilling from the other side. Do not attach the head to the body yet.

Cut the tail feathers to shape. A grid is provided for them, as shown in the top view, but there is no need to bother with a pattern unless you will be turning out dozens of these baskets. Simply sketch the shape directly on the wood.

4. Assemble the basket. Assemble the parts with ¾-inch tacks (part 7), preferably brass. Begin by tacking the bottom slats (part 3) to the front and back. Make sure that the front and back are perpendicular to the bottom.

Attach the side boards (part 4); they should extend 1⅝ inches beyond the front and 2⅞ inches beyond the

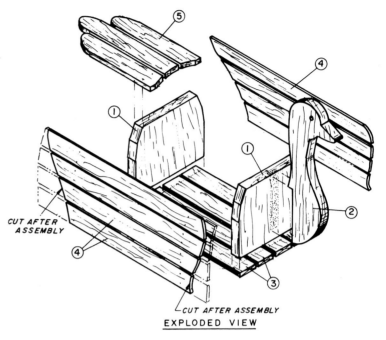

CUT AFTER ASSEMBLY

CUT AFTER ASSEMBLY
EXPLODED VIEW

back, as shown in the side view. Sketching directly on the side boards, lay out the duck's front and back profile, which are labeled Cut After Assembly in the side view. As with the tail feathers (part 5) a ½-inch grid is given for guidance, but you don't have to take the trouble to make a pattern. Cut along the sketched line. The cut can be made most easily on the band saw by laying the duck on its side.

5. Apply finish and add the head and tail. Stain the duck's body and paint the head and tail feathers a matte black. When the parts are dry, attach the head with two flathead screws (part 6). To prevent splitting, pre-drill a clearance hole through the front that is slightly larger than the diameter of the screw shank. Drill a pilot hole slightly smaller than the shank diameter into the head. Tack the three tail feathers to the back. Apply a coat or two of stain over the entire

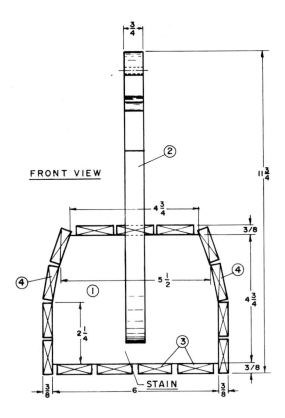

FRONT VIEW

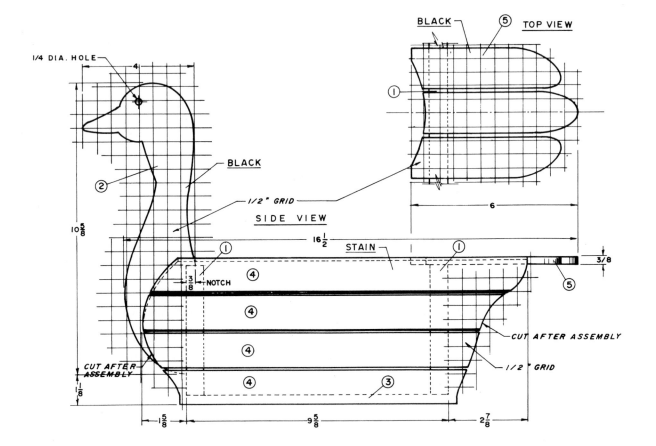

TOP VIEW

SIDE VIEW

1/4 DIA. HOLE

BLACK

1/2" GRID

STAIN

NOTCH

CUT AFTER ASSEMBLY

CUT AFTER ASSEMBLY

1/2" GRID

Candle Sconce with Drawer

Here's a woodworking project that will add a lot to any Early American setting. It's very functional, since the drawer is a great place to store matches. Before I made this project, every time the power went out, I could never find matches. With this candle sconce you, too, will be ready with a candle and matches all in one place.

NO.	NAME	SIZE	REQ'D.
1	BACK	½ x 4 - 16 LONG	1
2	SIDE	½ x 2¾ - 12⅛ LONG	2
3	SHELF	½ x 3¼ - 2¾ LONG	2
4	HOLDER	TO SUIT	1
5	SCREW - FL. HD.	NO. 6 - 1 LONG	1
6	FRONT	½ x 2½ - 3 LONG	1
7	SIDE	¼ x 2½ - 2½ LONG	2
8	BACK	¼ x 2½ - 2¾ LONG	1
9	BOTTOM	¼ x 2⅛ - 2¾ LONG	1
10	PULL	½ DIA.	1
11	FINISH NAIL	6d	14
12	CANDLE	TO SUIT	1

MATERIALS LIST

1. Study the drawing of the exploded view so that you know how it all goes together.

2. Cut all of the pieces to size according to the Materials List.

3. Lay out the shape of the back (part 1) and the two sides (part 2), using a ½-inch grid. Transfer the shapes to the wood, and cut them out. Be sure to make an exact pair of sides.

4. Carefully make the two stop dadoes, ½ inch wide and ⅛ inch deep on the inside surfaces of the sides. Be sure to stop the dadoes ¼ inch from the back edge. (See the exploded view below.)

5. After all of the pieces have been made, assemble the case. Check that everything is square. Be sure to screw the holder (part 4) to the shelf (part 3) before assembly.

6. Fit the drawer assembly to the case. Add the knob (part 10).

7. This project looks great either stained or painted. Add a candle, and don't forget to put matches in the drawer.

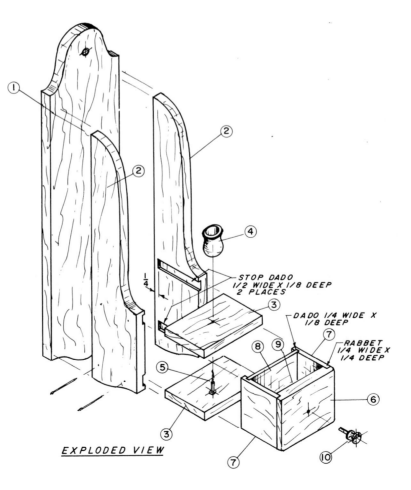

EXPLODED VIEW

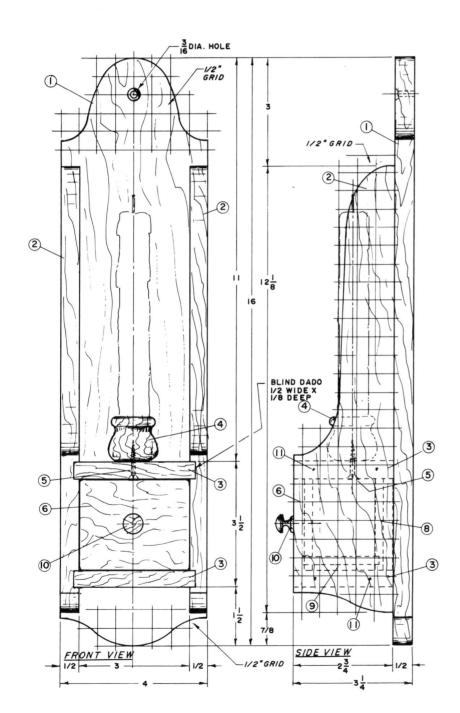

③/₁₆ DIA. HOLE

1/2" GRID

1/2" GRID

BLIND DADO
1/2 WIDE X
1/8 DEEP

3

12 ⅛

16

11

3 ½

1 ½

7/8

FRONT VIEW

1/2 3 1/2

4

1/2" GRID

SIDE VIEW

2 ¾ 1/2

3 ¼

Box for Forstner Bits

I've always wanted a complete set of Forstner bits. When I recently received a set, my delight was dampened just a bit by the packaging—they were simply wrapped in paper. I hated the thought of their banging around and getting dull. This box is my solution.

You can change the overall dimensions to make a box for other items that need a home. I made a slightly larger box to store router bits. If you pick a handsome wood like walnut, you'll have a box suited for jewelry or important documents.

Like other boxes in this book, I built a sealed box and then cut it open to create the lid. This box has a lipped lid that I created as I cut open the box. I did this by cutting two adjoining grooves. Before assembly, I cut a groove inside the box. After assembly, I cut the second groove on the outside, creating the lip, as shown in figure 1, page 106.

1. Select the stock and cut the parts. Choose any appropriate wood, but I suggest hardwood for the exterior of a box that will see rough use in a workshop. Tempered hardboard works well for the bit supports.

Before you build this box, measure the length of your bits. I've designed the storage box for bits that are no longer than 3¾ inches overall with a shank no longer than 2⅝ inches. If your bits are different, adjust the dimensions accordingly.

A piece of wood ½ inch thick and 5½ inches wide x 60 inches long will be enough to make the top, bottom, and all four sides, as shown in figure 2. Cut it to form the parts, as described in the next step.

2. Cut the parts and assemble the box. Square up the edges of the board and cut off pieces for the top and bottom (part 3) of the box. Before cutting the remaining piece into four sides, rip a groove ⅜ inch wide and ¼ inch deep, as shown in figure 2, page 106. This is the first of two cuts that form the dust lip. Once you've cut the groove, saw the board into the front, back, and ends (parts 1 and 2).

Rabbet the front and back pieces to accept the sides, as shown in figure 3, page 106. Then glue and nail the four sides together, keeping the groove for the dust lip inside the box.

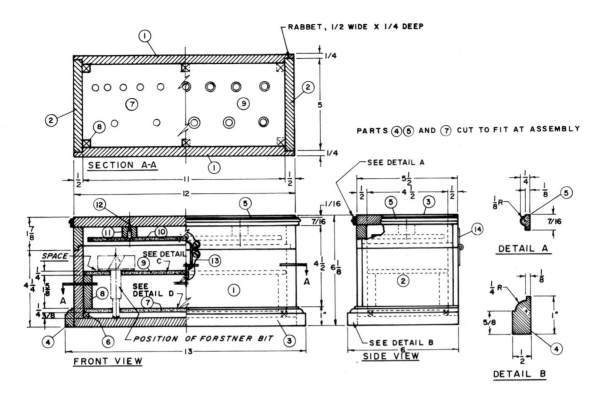

RABBET, 1/2 WIDE X 1/4 DEEP

SECTION A-A

PARTS ④⑤ AND ⑦ CUT TO FIT AT ASSEMBLY

DETAIL A

FRONT VIEW

POSITION OF FORSTNER BIT

SIDE VIEW

SEE DETAIL B

DETAIL B

3. Cut off the lid. Nail the top and bottom in place. After the glue sets, fill the nail holes with wood putty and sand the box smooth, taking care to keep all edges sharp and square.

Cut the second groove that separates the lid from the rest of the box and forms the dust lip. Set the table saw fence to position the cut, as shown in figure 1, and cut a groove ¼ inch deep and ⅜ inch wide on the two long sides of the box. To keep the lid from wobbling while cutting the ends of the box, tape ⅜ inch-wide spacers in the kerf before cutting the end grooves, as shown in figure 5, page 107.

4. Add the molding. Cut the molding (parts 4 and 5) with a router or shaper; there is no need to reproduce the moldings illustrated as long as you keep within the overall dimensions. Miter and attach the molding with glue and nails, as shown in figure 6, page 107.

5. Make the inside parts. Cut the inside parts to fit the box. To ensure that the holes will be in the same positions in both the lower base and upper support, tape the two parts together, one on top of the other.

MATERIALS LIST

NO.	NAME	SIZE	REQ'D.
1	FRONT/BACK	½ x 5½ – 12 LONG	1 EA.
2	END	½ x 5½ – 5 LONG	2
3	TOP/BOTTOM	½ x 5½ – 12 LONG	1 EA.
4	SKIRT MOLDING	½ x 1 – 36 LONG	1
5	TOP MOLDING	¼ x ⁷⁄₁₆ – 36 LONG	1
6	BASE SUPPORT	⅜ x ⅜ – 36 LONG	1
7	LOWER BASE	¼ x 4½ – 11 LONG	1
8	LOWER SPACER	¾ x ¾ – 1⅝ LONG	4
9	UPPER SUPPORT	¼ x 4½ – 11 LONG	1
10	UPPER BOARD	¼ x 4 – 10 LONG	1
11	UPPER SPACER	2 x 2 – 1¼ LONG	2
12	SCREW – FL. HD.	NO. 8 – 2 LONG	2
13	LATCH	TO SUIT	1
14	HINGE	¾ x 2 LONG	2
15	NAIL – FINISH	4 d	AS REQ'D.

Lay out the centers for the 14 holes on either support, as shown in detail C. (Note that these dimensions are for a 14-piece set of Forstner bits, ranging in diameter from ⅜ inch to 2 inches; if your set is different, you

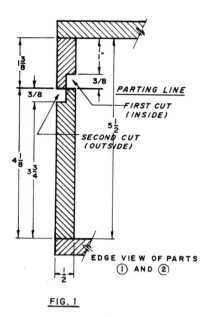

FIG. 1

will have to move the holes to suit.) Using a ¹⁄₁₆-inch-diameter bit, drill the holes through both parts. Separate them.

Use the ¹⁄₁₆-inch holes as layout marks. In the lower base, drill and countersink ³⁄₈ inch-diameter holes centered on the marks, as shown in detail D. In the upper support, drill holes to match your bits.

6. Complete the assembly. Dry-fit the remaining parts and put the bits in their places to make sure that everything goes together as it should. The bits should fit rather loosely so that moisture doesn't get trapped against them.

Glue the base support (part 6), lower spacers (part 8), lower base (part 7), and upper support (part 9) in place. The upper board (part 10) and upper spacers (part 11) are also in place with screws, as shown. The upper board holds the bits in place in case the box is turned upside down.

7. Finish the box as you choose. Attach the hardware.

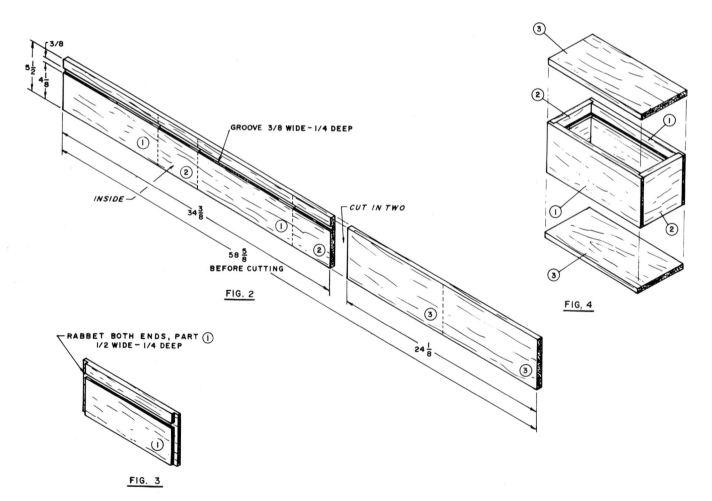

FIG. 2

FIG. 3

FIG. 4

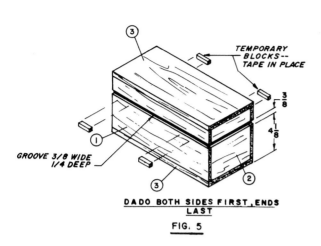

TEMPORARY
BLOCKS--
TAPE IN PLACE

③

①

GROOVE 3/8 WIDE
1/4 DEEP

③

②

3/8

4 1/8

DADO BOTH SIDES FIRST, ENDS
LAST

FIG. 5

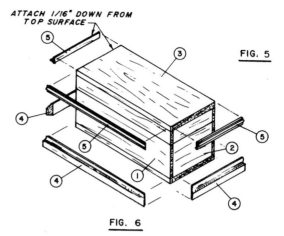

ATTACH 1/16" DOWN FROM
TOP SURFACE

FIG. 5

⑤

③

④

⑤

⑤

④

②

①

④

FIG. 6

⑨

3/8   1/2   5/8   3/4   7/8   1   1 1/8   1 1/4   1 3/8

1 1/4

2   4 1/2

2   1 7/8   1 3/4   1 5/8   1 1/2

1 1/4

DETAIL C

OUTLINE OF FORSTNER BITS

11

1/2 DIA.   ⑨

3/8 DIA.

SECTION B-B

3/8 DIA. HOLE -- COUNTERSINK
TO 1/2 DIA., SEE SECTION B-B

⑦

B   B

1 1/4

11/16 11/16 13/16 15/16 1 1/16 1 3/16 1 5/16 1 7/16 1 9/16 1 1/4

2   4 1/2

11/16   2 1/4   2 1/16   1 15/16   1 13/16   1 5/16

1 1/4

DETAIL D

HOLE SPACING, SAME AS ABOVE

11

Wall Barometer

This wall-mounted weather station tells the barometric pressure, temperature, and relative humidity. The barometer was invented by an Italian physicist in the mid-1600s, and by the end of the century, the British were framing them in elegant cases similar to this one. The project involves a little inlay work and some very simple carving of the molding.

1. Select the stock and cut the parts. Purchase the instruments before you start building to make sure your instruments will fit the case. Build the case from a hardwood such as cherry, walnut, mahogany, maple, or birch. Cut the parts ½ inch longer and wider than called for and cut them to the dimensions given in the Materials List as you shape them.

2. Draw a pattern directly on the stock. The most challenging job in this project is laying out the body (part 1). To avoid errors, it's best to lay out the pattern directly on the wood. Draw a grid with 1-inch squares on the stock for the base. The series of center points and diameters shown in the drawing will help you lay out the circles and arcs that form the base. Transfer the center points to the grid and lay out the curves with a compass. The enlarged detail of the top will help you lay out the curves for the pediment. Lay out the area for the thermometer and barometer by putting them in place on the body. Double-check all dimensions.

3. Cut the body to shape. Before I begin cutting the body to shape on the band saw, I head for the drill press. I've found that rather than saw curves, it's sometimes easier to drill them out. The results are perfect, symmetrical, and repeatable. With large enough bits, you can even produce the four 1½-inch-radius curves required here. Drill all the holes, except for the two at the pediment. On the band saw, cut out the rest of the body except for the pediment. Sand the edges smooth.

MATERIALS LIST

NO.	NAME	SIZE	REQ'D.
1	BODY	1½ x 9½ – 31 LONG	1
2	BAROMETER FLANGE	¼ x 9⅛ DIA.	1
3	FRONT TOP MOLDING	⅜ x 2⅛ – 4¾ LONG	1
4	SIDE TOP MOLDING	⅜ x 2⅛ – 2 LONG	2
5	GOOSENECK MOLDING	¼ x 1¼ – 4¾ LONG	2
6	SIDE MOLDINGS	CUT FROM PART 5	2
7	INLAY	2 DIA	1
8	PEDIMENT CAP	⅛ x 1⅜ – 1⅝ LONG	1
9	HYGROMETER		1
10	BAROMETER		1
11	THERMOMETER		1
12	BRASS FINIAL		1
13	HANGER	1½ LONG	1

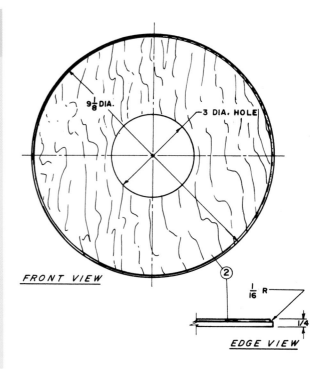

9⅛ DIA.

3 DIA. HOLE

FRONT VIEW

2

1/16 R

1/4

EDGE VIEW

4. Cut out the pediment. The pediment topping the barometer is built from several pieces: a top molding wraps around the case. Two carved gooseneck moldings are applied over it. A brass finial tops off the piece.

First, cut a piece of stock for the top molding (parts 3 and 4). It should be as wide and thick as the molding and at least 12 inches long. Rout a cove in it, as shown, with a ¼-inch-core box bit. Core box bits are like cove bits, except that they come in smaller sizes and don't have ball-bearing guides. Put the router in a router table and guide the cut against the fence.

Once you've cut the cove, cut the ⅛-inch x 1⅝-inch step above it on the table saw. First, clamp a piece of wood to the saw's fence and move the fence so the wood just touches the blade. Raise the blade to 1⅝ inches. Stand the molding on its top edge and put its outside face against the fence to make the cut. Feed the stock against the blade with a push stick.

Cut the stock into three pieces, each about an inch longer than needed to make the molding. Miter the corners, cut the molding to fit, and glue the molding in place.

When the glue dries, drill holes through the top molding and body to define the arches. Band-saw the pediment to its final shape and sand smooth.

5. Make and attach the gooseneck molding. The front gooseneck moldings (part 5) are not identical; they are mirror images of each other. Two side moldings (part 6) miter into the gooseneck. All four moldings must be carved by hand.

Put the stock for the gooseneck on the bench and trace the shape of the pediment onto it. Use this as a guide to lay out the entire molding, as shown in the drawing. Cut the molding to shape and sand the curves smooth.

The cove around the bottom of the gooseneck is too small to rout, so you will have to carve it. A 9-sweep, 2 mm carving gouge is almost perfect for the job, but any small carving gouge will do the trick. Carve both goose-necks and the side moldings that fit into them. Miter and glue all four in place.

Drill a pilot hole in the pediment cap (part 8) to accept the brass finial (part 12). Glue the cap in place but don't mount the finial until after you've applied finish.

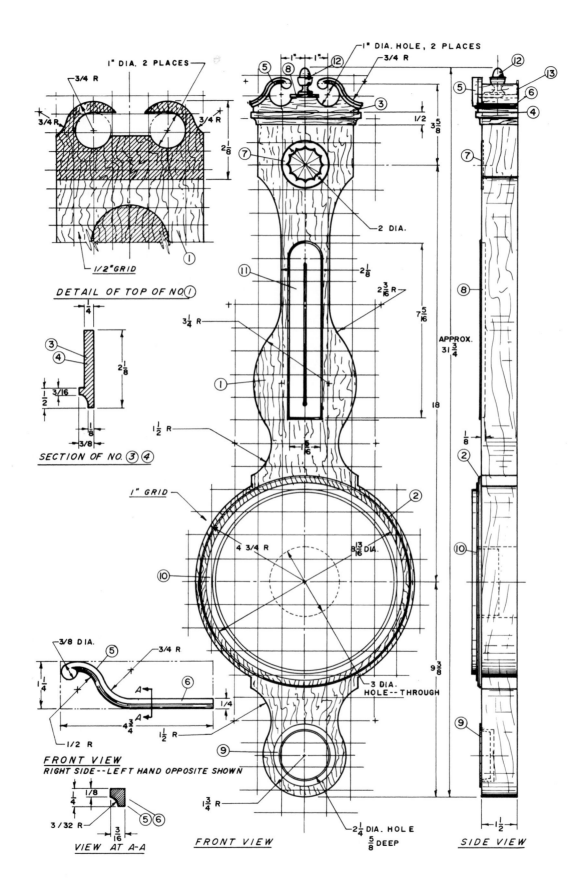

1" DIA. 2 PLACES

3/4 R

3/4 R

3/4 R

2 1/8

1/2" GRID

DETAIL OF TOP OF NO.①

1/4

2 1/8

3/16

1/2

1/8

3/8

SECTION OF NO. ③ ④

1" GRID

3/8 DIA.

3/4 R

1 1/4

A

A

4 3/4

1/2 R

1/4

FRONT VIEW

RIGHT SIDE--LEFT HAND OPPOSITE SHOWN

1/8

1/4

3/32 R

3/16

VIEW AT A-A

FRONT VIEW

1" DIA. HOLE, 2 PLACES

3/4 R

1" DIA. HOLE, 2 PLACES

1/2

3 5/8

2 DIA.

2 1/8

2 3/16 R

3/4 R

7 5/16

1 1/2 R

5/6

18

4 3/4 R

8 13/16 DIA.

3 DIA. HOLE--THROUGH

9 3/8

1 3/4 R

2 1/4 DIA. HOLE
5/8 DEEP

3/4 R

APPROX. 31 3/4

1/8

1 1/2

SIDE VIEW

6. Make the recess and holes for the instruments. To cut the recess for the thermometer (part 11), drill a series of overlapping holes with the appropriate Forstner bit. The width will depend on the thermometer you buy. With Forstner bits, the overlap can be quite large: The center for one hole need be no more than about ⅛ inch from the next. Clean up the edges of the recess with a sharp chisel.

Drill a hole large enough to accommodate the back of the barometer (part 10). If you don't have a bit large enough, use a circle cutter, coping saw, or jigsaw.

Drill a 2¼-inch hole to accommodate the hygrometer (part 9).

7. Drill the recess for the inlay. The inlay (part 7) is made by gluing pieces of veneer to a piece of paper. When purchased ready-made, inlay comes with the paper still attached. Leave it attached.

Drill a hole in the body for the inlay. Put a Forstner bit in your drill press and drill a 2-inch-diameter hole, not quite as deep as the inlay is thick.

Glue the inlay in place with the paper side up. When the glue dries, sand the paper off, and sand the inlay flush. If there are any gaps, fill them with wood filler.

8. Make the barometer flange. Cut the circular flange (part 2) on a band saw. The easiest way to cut a circle is to make a simple jig. Screw the center of a square piece of stock to a piece of scrap. Position the jig so that you can cut the circle by rotating the square into the blade. Clamp the jig in place and cut the circle. Cut a cove in the edge with a ⅛-inch-diameter core box bit. (Core box bits this small are also sold as veining bits.) Remember, these bits don't have ball-bearing guides, so you'll have to rout this in a table against a fence. Routing curved surfaces is easier if you band-saw a hollow in a wooden fence to match the curve.

Cut or drill a hole in the center of the flange to match the one in the body and glue the flange to the base.

9. Apply finish. Sand thoroughly. Temporarily install the three instruments and drill for all screws. The brass screws that come with the instruments may break off, unless pilot holes are drilled for them.

Remove the instruments and varnish the piece. Install the instruments with screws and add the brass hanger (part 13) and brass finial.

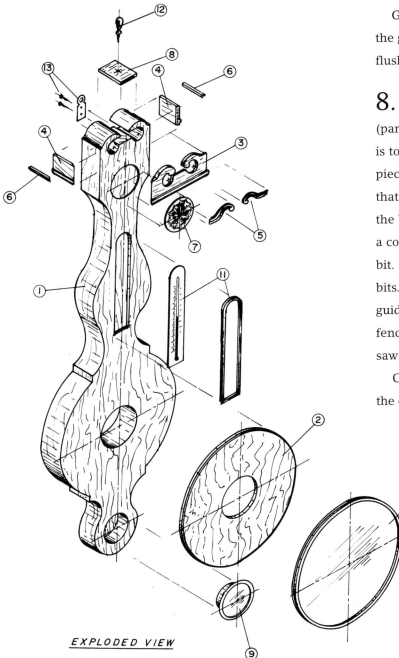

EXPLODED VIEW

Clocks

Some of the designs in this chapter are sleek and modern, such as the Triangle Clock and the always-useful Notepad Clock. Others date back to the 1800s—reproductions that will look as handsome today in a contemporary setting as the originals looked back then.

Triangle Clock

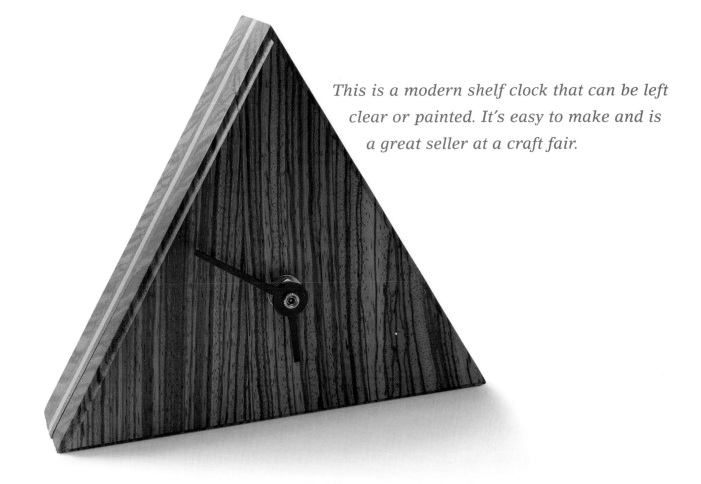

This is a modern shelf clock that can be left clear or painted. It's easy to make and is a great seller at a craft fair.

| \multicolumn{4}{c}{**MATERIALS LIST**} |
NO.	NAME	SIZE	REQ'D.
1	BODY	1¾ x 5¾ – 6⅝ LONG	1
2	QUARTZ MOVEMENT	LONG STEM	1
3	HANDS (1½ SIZE)	MODERN STYLE	1 PR.
4	FOOT	½ SIZE	4

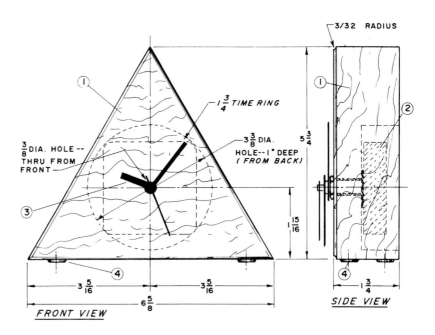

3/32 RADIUS

1¾ TIME RING

3/8 DIA. HOLE-- THRU FROM FRONT

3⅜ DIA. HOLE--1" DEEP (FROM BACK)

5¾

1 15/16

3 5/16

3 5/16

6 5/8

FRONT VIEW

1¾

SIDE VIEW

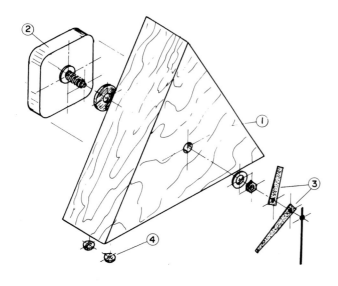

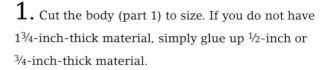

EXPLODED VIEW

1. Cut the body (part 1) to size. If you do not have 1¾-inch-thick material, simply glue up ½-inch or ¾-inch-thick material.

2. Locate and drill a 3⅜-inch-diameter hole.

3. Cut to shape, and sand all surfaces with fine sandpaper.

4. Using a 3/32-inch-radius cove cutter with a ball-bearing follower, cut a radius around the outer edge as shown.

5. Drill a hole for the center shaft of the movement.

6. Finish to suit. Add feet (part 4).

7. Add a battery to the clock movement, and add to the body.

8. Add hands, and set the correct time.

Tambour Clock

This is the smallest clock project and the easiest to make. It is a scaled-down version of a clock that was popular from 1820 right through the middle of the last century. All major clock makers once offered two or three models of the tambour clock. The clock got its name, by the way, from the similarity of its shape to a tambour drum.

MATERIALS LIST			
NO.	NAME	SIZE	REQ'D.
1	BODY	1½ x 3¼ – 6½ LONG	1
2	BASE	¼ x 1^{11}/$_{16}$ – 6⅞ LONG	1
3	FOOT	^{1}/$_{16}$ x ⅝ – ⅝ LONG	4
4	MOVEMENT		1

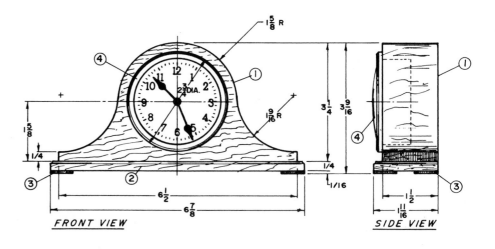

FRONT VIEW   SIDE VIEW

1. Select the wood and cut the parts. Walnut, oak, and cherry are the more obvious choices of woods for this project. Cut the parts to the sizes given in the Materials List. Purchase the movement before starting on the project.

2. Lay out the clock. Lay out the pattern on the body (part 1), and locate the center of the hole for the clock face. Drill the hole about ⅝ inch deep. Cut just outside the outline of the body with a jigsaw or band saw, then sand down to the layout line.

Rout the front and sides of the base (part 2) to the profile shown, with a ⅛-inch-radius cove bit with a ball-bearing guide.

3. Assemble the clock. Locate and glue the body to the base, making sure that the back of the base and body align. Glue the feet (part 3) to the bottom of the base. Sand thoroughly.

4. Apply finish. Apply a thin coat of stain, if you wish, and two or three coats of varnish. Let the finish dry and install the movement.

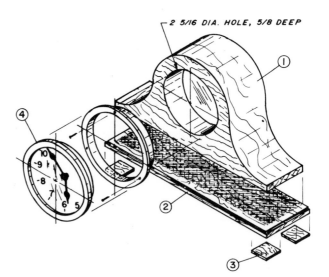

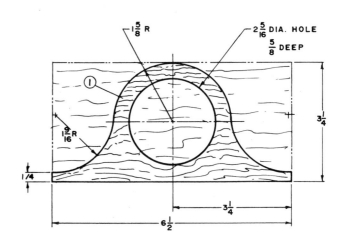

Notepad Clock

This is a handy clock. It's great placed next to a telephone, because you can keep notepaper in it for taking messages.

1. Cut all of the pieces to overall size. Sand all surfaces, keeping all of the edges sharp.

2. Locate and drill the 2⅛-inch-diameter hole for the insert. Cut the two 45° top edges.

3. Assemble the back board, front, and sides together (parts 1, 2, and 3).

4. Cut a ¼-inch-wide x ¼-inch-deep dado around the bottom inside surface as shown at view A-A, page 118.

5. Cut the bottom (part 4) to size, and tack it in place. Do not glue. Make a loose fit to allow for expansion.

6. Finish to suit.

7. Add a battery to the clock movement, and insert it into the hole.

8. Add the feet and paper (parts 7 and 8).

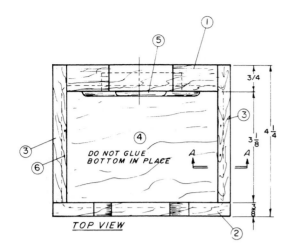

TOP VIEW

DO NOT GLUE
BOTTOM IN PLACE

3/4

4 1/4

3 1/8

3/8

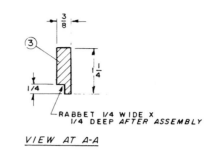

3/8

1 1/4

1/4

RABBET 1/4 WIDE X
1/4 DEEP AFTER ASSEMBLY

VIEW AT A-A

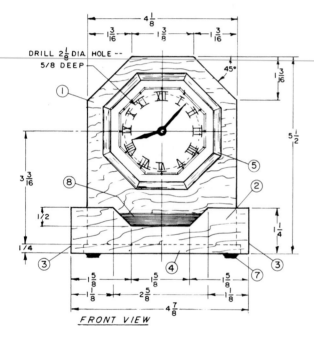

DRILL 2 1/8 DIA HOLE --
5/8 DEEP

4 1/8

1 3/16   1 3/8   1 3/16

45°

1 3/16

5 1/2

3 3/16

1/2

1/4

1 1/4

1 5/8
1 1/8

2 5/8

1 5/8
1 1/8

4 7/8

FRONT VIEW

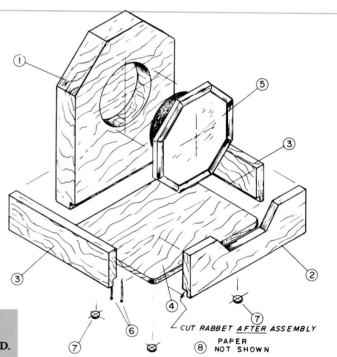

CUT RABBET *AFTER* ASSEMBLY

PAPER
NOT SHOWN

EXPLODED VIEW

NO.	NAME	SIZE	REQ'D.
\multicolumn{4}{c|}{**MATERIALS LIST**}			
1	BACK BOARD	3/4 x 5 1/2 – 4 1/8 LONG	1
2	FRONT	3/8 x 1 1/4 – 4 7/8 LONG	1
3	SIDE	3/8 x 1 1/4 – 3 7/8 LONG	2
4	BOTTOM	1/4 x 3 5/8 – 4 5/8 LONG	1
5	CLOCK – OCTAGON		1
6	BRAD	3/4 LONG	4
7	FOOT OR PAD	1/2 DIA.	4
8	PAPER	3 x 4	

Galley Wall Clock

This clock acquired its name specifically because it was designed for use in a ship's galley. This is a copy of a Waterbury galley clock, circa 1830. It was made of oak and had an eight-day brass movement. Note the two hangers; this is to stop the clock from swinging back and forth in rough seas. The original movement did not have a pendulum—it instead had a special balance-wheel escapement. Since a pendulum clock cannot work on a moving, rocking ship, the balance wheel escapement was designed to allow ships to have an accurate, dependable clock on board. This, in conjunction with other instruments, gave early navigators the ability to calculate exactly where they were at all times.

You will need a lathe to make this clock—and perhaps a 48-foot sailboat to display it!

MATERIALS LIST			
NO.	NAME	SIZE	REQ'D.
1	SIDE	¾ x 2 – 3¾ LONG	8
2	FRONT	¾ x 2³⁄₁₆ – 3⁹⁄₁₆ LONG	8
3	BRACE	⁹⁄₁₆ x 1⅛ – 2⅝ LONG	8
4	BACK	¼ x 8¼ SQUARE	1
5	BEZEL SUPPORT	¼ x 7 SQUARE	1
6	BEZEL	6¼ DIA.	1
7	MOVEMENT		1
8	SCREW – FL. HD.	NO. 6 – ⅝ LONG	8
9	HANGER – BRASS	½ x 1⅛ LONG	2
10	HANDS	2¾ LONG	2

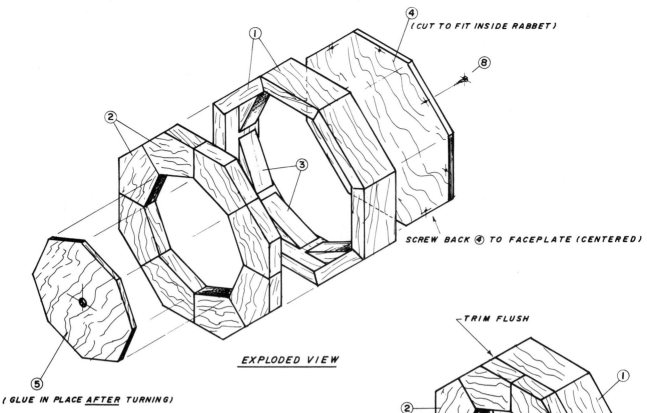

① (CUT TO FIT INSIDE RABBET)

⑧

SCREW BACK ④ TO FACEPLATE (CENTERED)

EXPLODED VIEW

(GLUE IN PLACE AFTER TURNING)

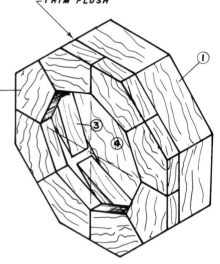

TRIM FLUSH

AS GLUED -- READY FOR TURNING

1. Study the exploded view that shows the steps involved in assembling the case. Carefully cut all of the pieces according to the plan, and glue up as shown. Be sure to use a lot of glue and to let the case assembly set for 48 hours or more before turning. You do not want the pieces to come apart while turning on the lathe.

2. Position the assembly on a faceplate. Take extreme care and double-check that it is in the exact center. The case will not come out right if it is not perfectly centered. Carefully turn the case while wearing a face mask and using all safety precautions. Use View at A-A as a guide to get the

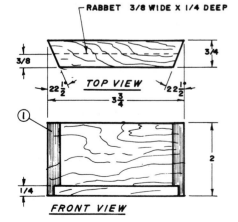

RABBET 3/8 WIDE X 1/4 DEEP

TOP VIEW

FRONT VIEW

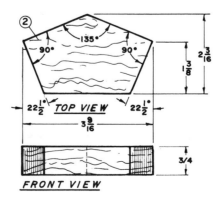

② TOP VIEW

FRONT VIEW

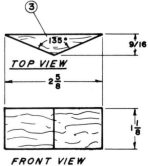

③ TOP VIEW

FRONT VIEW

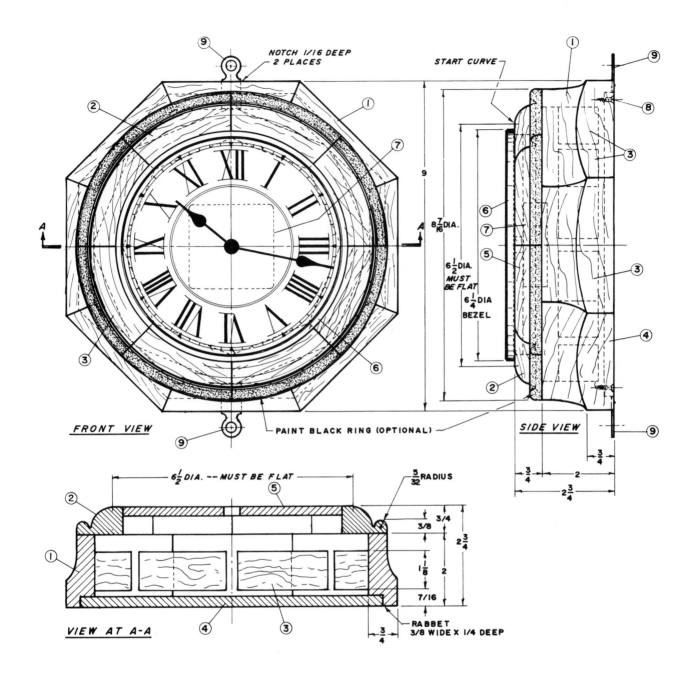

FRONT VIEW

NOTCH 1/16 DEEP — 2 PLACES

PAINT BLACK RING (OPTIONAL)

START CURVE

9

8 7/16 DIA.

6 1/2 DIA. MUST BE FLAT

6 1/4 DIA BEZEL

SIDE VIEW

3/4

3/4

2

2 3/4

VIEW AT A-A

6 1/2 DIA. — MUST BE FLAT

5/32 RADIUS

3/4

3/8

2 3/4

1 1/8

2

7/16

3/4

RABBET 3/8 WIDE X 1/4 DEEP

correct profile. Sand all over while the assembly is still mounted on the lathe.

3. Clean all of the surfaces and apply a stain if you desire. Apply three or four top coats of a clear finish, and lightly sand between coats. Do all of this while the case is still mounted on the lathe.

4. The original galley clock had a 3/8-inch-wide black ring around the case as shown in the front and side views. This is optional; it is rather easy to add while the case is still mounted on the lathe. Remove the case from the faceplate and drill a hole for the shaft of the movement. Add the two hangers, as shown. Mount the dial bezel to the case; add the movement and hands.

Square New England Wall Clock

The original clock on which I based this design is simply a frame with a porcelain dial face. It was made around 1800. Porcelain faces can be purchased today, so this project is very easy to make.

1. Study the plans carefully. Make up material for the frame and trim (parts 1 and 2). The frame's profile is given in the Frame Detail on the plans. Make up about 72 inches of this material.

2. Measure and miter the four frame pieces, cut at 45° and at exactly the same length as given in the plans. Cut a saw kerf along the 45° cut for the spline—this will give the frame a lot of added strength. Glue the frame pieces together with the splines (part 3).

  Note: it is a good idea to buy the porcelain dial face before cutting the frame lengths. Fit the frame to the dial face.

3. Attach the trim pieces (part 2) around the frame. Let them overhang the frame about 3/16 inch, as shown in the View at A-A.

4. Finish to suit, following the general finishing instructions in the introduction. Attach the dial face (part 4) with the four inserts (part 5). Attach the movement (part 6) to the dial. Add the hands and a fresh battery. The movement provides a built-in hanger.

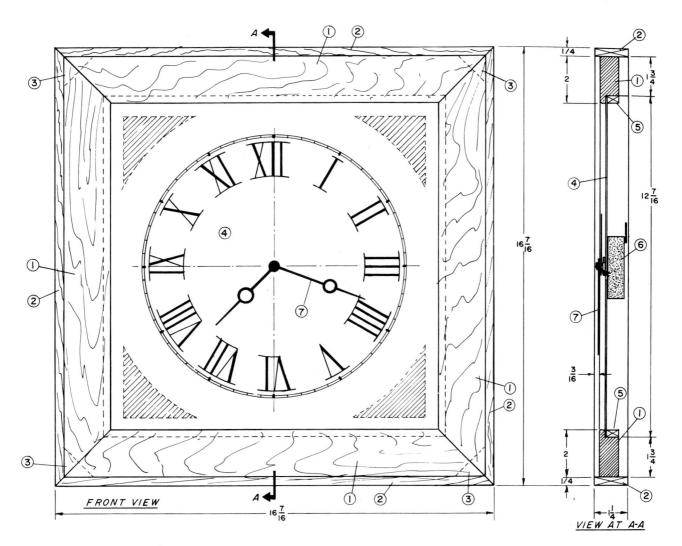

FRONT VIEW

16 7/16

VIEW AT A-A

16 7/16

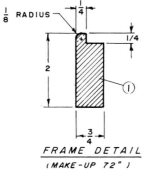

1/8 RADIUS

FRAME DETAIL
(MAKE-UP 72")

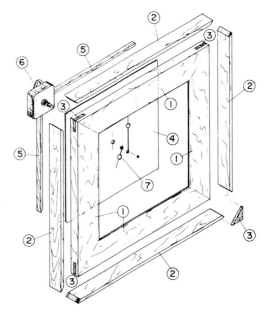

MATERIALS LIST

NO.	NAME	SIZE	REQ'D.
1	FRAME	$3/4$ x 2 – $15^{15}/16$ LONG	4
2	TRIM	$1/4$ x $1^{1}/4$ – $16^{7}/16$ LONG	4
3	SPLINE	$1/8$ x $3/4$ – $1^{1}/4$ LONG	4
4	DIAL FACE (METAL)	$9^{1}/2$ TIME RING	1
5	INSERT	$1/4$ x $1/2$ – $12^{7}/16$ LONG	4
6	MOVEMENT	QUARTZ	1
7	MOON HANDS	$4^{3}/4$ SIZE	1 PR.

Shaker Shelf Clock, c.1850

We have a collection of original clocks, most of which have wooden works. Clocks are among our favorite antiques. Some of the most beautiful ones were made by the Shakers. I don't recall seeing an original Shaker clock for sale; most are found in museums.

The three or four models of Shaker clocks that I especially like were made by Isaac Benjamin Youngs from Watervliet, New York. This is his third model that I have recorded. It has been scaled down to 50 percent of the original. The original was very large— much too large for today's homes. I have kept the same lines and proportions.

1. Study the plans carefully. Note how each part is to be shaped. As you study the plans, try to visualize how you will make each part and how the project will be assembled. Note which parts you will put together first, second, and so on—exactly how you will put it together. I recommend that you make the door assembly first and build the box case around the door.

2. The wood will have to be planed down to ¼ inch thickness, if you can't purchase it at the correct thickness. Because the clock is scaled down, the wood ended up as ¼ inch thick.

3. Carefully cut all of the parts to size according to the Materials List. Take care to cut all parts to exact size and exactly square (90°). Stop and recheck all dimensions before going on.

4. Lightly sand all surfaces and edges with medium sandpaper to remove all tool marks. Take care to keep all edges square and sharp.

5. Make the door following the plans, except make the door solid without the round 5½-inch-diameter cutout. Cut out the hole after the door is made. For strength—even though I doubt the scaled-down version needs it—add splines (part 18) to hold the three door segments (part 7) together. Note: I suggest cutting an extra door segment (part 7) in case you have trouble getting a good fit.

6. Refer to the exploded view—note how the bottom of the door is notched to hold it all together. The panel (part 10) actually adds strength to the bottom section of the door. Carefully make up the door to the approximate sizes given. After the glue sets, sand the top and bottom surfaces—especially the front surface. Locate and cut out the 5½-inch-diameter hole, as shown. Using a router and a rabbet cutter with a follower, make the rabbet cuts on the inside surface, as illustrated on the drawing. Note that the inside view is given. Turn the door over and round the front surface of the 5½-inch-diameter edge, as shown—approximately 1/16 inch or so. Resand all over, and sand the four edges of the door assembly at this time, keeping the edges sharp and square.

7. The hard part is over; all that is left is to make a simple four-piece box to go around the door. Carefully cut the profile of the top, bottom, and sides (parts 1 and 2). Miter the top, bottom, and side pieces to length, cut at exactly 45°. Assemble the box. Cut and fit the back (part 3) to the case.

8. Make the dial supports and the dial face (parts 4 and 5). Locate and glue the dial supports in place, approximately 4 inches apart. Temporarily, attach the dial face to the supports with small screws (part 6).

MATERIALS LIST

NO.	NAME	SIZE	REQ'D.
1	SIDE	¼ x 2 – 10½ LONG	2
2	TOP/BOTTOM	¼ x 2 – 7 LONG	2
3	BACK (PINE)	¼ x 6¾ – 10¼ LONG	1
4	DIAL SUPPORT	¼ x ¾ – 7 LONG	2
5	DIAL FACE	¼ x 6½ x 6½ LONG	1
6	SCREW RD. HD.	NO. 6 – ¾ LONG	4
7	DOOR SEGMENT	⅜ x 1 ¾ – 6¾ LONG	4
8	DOOR SIDE	⅜ x ⅝ – 3½ LONG	2
9	DOOR BOTTOM	⅜ x ⅝ – 5½ LONG	1
10	PANEL	¼ x 3¼ – 6 LONG	1
11	GLASS	6 DIA.	1
12	MOVEMENT	QUARTZ	1
13	HANDS	2¼ SIZE	1 PR.
14	HINGE	¾ W – ⅝ H	2
15	KNOB W/LATCH	MADE FROM SCRAP	1
16	BLOCK FOR LATCH	TO SUIT	1
17	DIAL FACE	3¾ TIME RING	1
18	SPLINE	1/16 x ¼ – 1¾ LONG	4

9. Fit the door assembly to the case with the two brass hinges (part 14). Because the side panel (part 1) is so thin where the hinge is attached, I attached the hinges to the door and then epoxied them to the sides. (This was so quick and easy that I think I will use this technique on more projects.) Use a thin piece of paper between the leaves of the hinges so any epoxy that gets on the other leaf will not glue the hinge together.

10. Make up the latch assembly and the block for the latch (parts 15 and 16) out of scrap wood pieces, as shown. Check that it works correctly, locking the door

shut; adjust as necessary. I fitted these pieces before attaching the backboard in place. Glue the dial face paper (part 17) to the board (part 5) positioning it in the center of the 5½-inch hole in the door—this is important. Remove the dial face and drill the hole for the movement (part 12). Add the glass (part 11) using black putty, if you can find it.

Finish to suit, following the general finishing instructions in the introduction—a clear-satin top coat would be best. Attach the movement to the dial face; add a battery and the hands according to the instructions that came with the movement. Attach the dial face to the supports using the four wood screws.

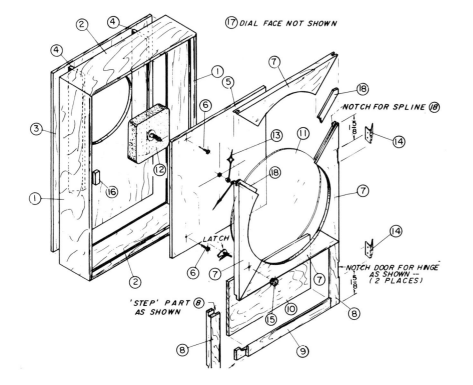

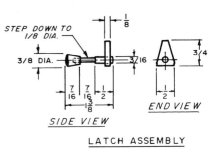

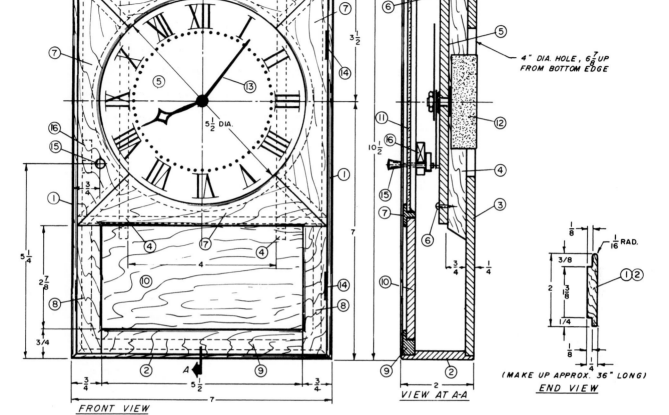

A

3½   3½
⑦   ②

3½

⑭

⑯
⑮

①   ¾

5½ DIA.
⑤   ⑬

⑯
⑮
⑦
⑥

10½

①

7

⑭
⑧

5¼

2⅞

⑧

¾

②   A   ⑨

¾   5½   ¾
7

FRONT VIEW

⑦   ②
⑥

4" DIA. HOLE, 6⅞ UP
FROM BOTTOM EDGE
⑤

⑤

⑪

⑫

④
③

⑦

⑥

¾   ¼
⑩

⑨   ②

VIEW AT A-A

⅛
1/16 RAD.
3/8
2   1⅜   ⑫
¼
⅛
¼

(MAKE UP APPROX. 36" LONG)
END VIEW

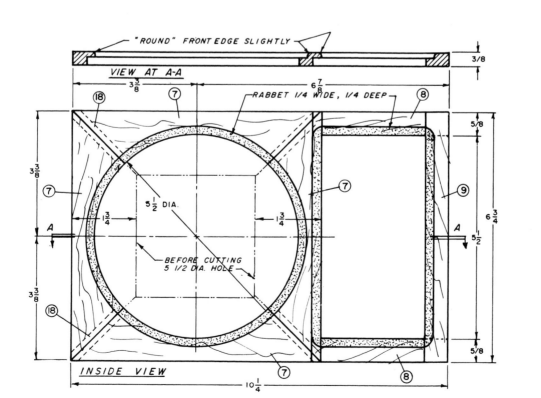

"ROUND" FRONT EDGE SLIGHTLY

3/8
VIEW AT A-A

3⅜   6⅞
⑱   ⑦   RABBET ¼ WIDE, ¼ DEEP   ⑧

5/8

3⅜   ⑦   5½ DIA.   ⑦   ⑨

A   1¾   1¾   A   6¾   5½

BEFORE CUTTING
5 1/2 DIA. HOLE

3⅜   ⑱   5/8

INSIDE VIEW   ⑦   ⑧

10¼

Terry SheIf Clock

Ely Terry was an early clock maker and one of the first in the United States to use mass-production methods. Most of his clocks had wooden gears, and many are still in use today. My research suggests that the original of this small shelf clock was made by Terry around 1860. It caught my eye because the movement has two springs mounted outside of the plates rather than between them—a very unusual feature. Could the clock have been one of Terry's prototypes?

This project is taken precisely from the original; note that the nail heads are left showing. You can use a wind-up movement, but the new quartz movements with operating pendulums are very accurate, never need winding, and look old-fashioned once they're in place. It's a sound practice to read through the steps of any project before getting busy. It's also a sound practice to wait until you have the clock movement in hand before building a clock. This clock is no exception to either rule.

1. Select the stock and order the clockwork. The original was made of walnut, but any good grade of hardwood will do. A friend made this clock out of apple wood and the results were beautiful, if less than

authentic. The back (part 4) and braces (part 12) can be cut from a less-precious wood than the rest of the case. Before getting too far under way, order the manufactured clock parts you will need.

2. Cut the parts. Cut the wooden parts, except for the moldings and skirt, to the sizes given in the Materials List. Lay out the holes for the dial and pendulum in the front (part 3), as shown on the exploded view, and cut them out.

MATERIALS LIST

NO.	NAME	SIZE	REQ'D.
1	SIDE	⅜ x 2½ – 11¼ LONG	2
2	BOTTOM/FALSE TOP	⅜ x 2¼ – 7½ LONG	1 EA.
3	FACE	¼ x 7⅞ – 11¼ LONG	1
4	BACK	¼ x 7½ – 11¼ LONG	1
5	TOP	⅝ x 3⅛ – 8⅜ LONG	1
6	TOP MOLDING	¼ x ½ – 24 LONG	1
7	TOP MOLDING (SIDE)	CUT FROM PART 6	2
8	TOP MOLDING (FRONT)	CUT FROM PART 6	1
9	SKIRT	¾ x 1⁵⁄₁₆ – 24 LONG	1
10	SIDE SKIRT	CUT FROM PART 9 – 3⁷⁄₁₆ LONG	2
11	FRONT SKIRT	CUT FROM PART 9 – 9⅛ LONG	1
12	BRACE	¾ x ¾ – 2⅝ LONG	3
13	VERTICAL MOLDING	¼ x ⅜ – 11¼ LONG	2
14	LARGE BEZEL		1
15	SMALL BEZEL		1
16	DIAL PAN		1
17	SMALL LATCH	¹⁄₁₆ x ¼ – 1 LONG	1
18	LARGE LATCH	¹⁄₁₆ x ⅜ – ⅞ LONG	1
19	HINGE	¾ x ⁵⁄₁₆ LONG	2
20	DIAL FACE		1
21	MOVEMENT		1
22	HANDS		1 PAIR
23	SCREW – FL. HD.	NO. 2 x ⅜ LONG	10
24	BRAD – HEADLESS, SQ. CUT	⅞ LONG	14

3. Cut the joints. Dado the top and bottom of the side panels (part 1) as shown in detail A, page 131. Rabbet the false top and the bottom (part 2) to create a tongue that fits in the dado, as shown in the exploded view. Cut rabbets in the sides to accommodate the back.

4. Make the skirt and moldings. Rout long lengths of the skirt and moldings (parts 9 and 6), and then cut them to make the individual parts (parts 7, 8, 10, 11, and 12). Rout the moldings on the edge of a wide board , and then rip the molding from it; a ¼-inch-wide piece of stock is too difficult to work.

5. Assemble the case. Glue the sides to the bottom and false top, keeping everything square. Drill holes slightly larger than the screw shank in the back for the four screws that hold it in place; drill pilot holes slightly smaller than the screw shank in the case. Temporarily screw the back in place.

Glue the face to the assembled case. Glue the false top to the top so that it is flush with the back and overlaps the sides equally.

Miter the top moldings to fit, and nail them in place with square-cut headless brads (part 24). Keep the top of the molding flush with the top of the piece.

Glue and nail the two vertical moldings (part 13) to the front of the clock. Miter and glue up the skirt separately. The clock rests on the skirt, as shown in the detail. Glue the three braces (part 12) in place, as shown.

6. Prepare the bezels, hinges, and latches. If you order the parts specified in the Materials List, the hinges and latch come with the bezel when you order it. Before you can mount the bezels, however, you must do some simple metal work. Fortunately, brass is easy to work and can be cut and filed to size and shape. First, notch the bezels (parts 14 and 15) for the brass hinges (part 19), as illustrated. Bend and solder the hinges to the bezels;

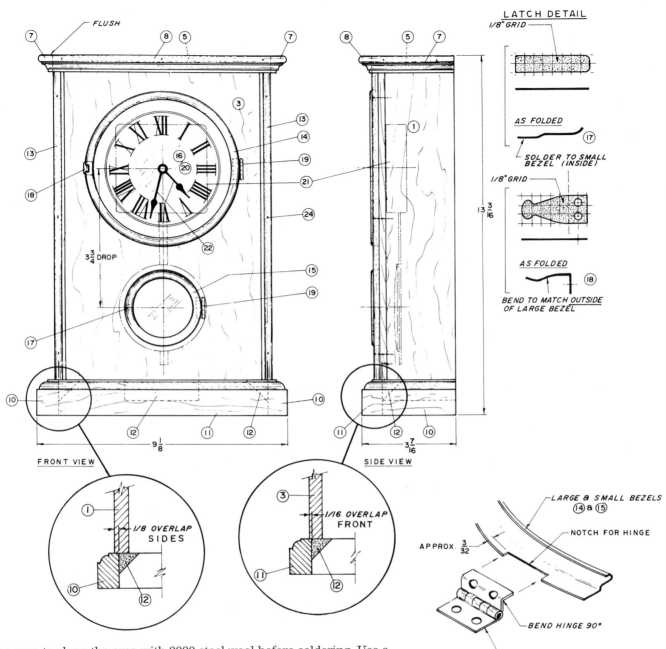

LATCH DETAIL

FRONT VIEW

SIDE VIEW

be sure to clean the area with 0000 steel wool before soldering. Use a 50/50 acid-core solder.

A metal latch (parts 17 and 18) keeps each bezel from opening. The large latch screws to the case and snaps over the large bezel to keep it closed; the small latch is soldered to the small bezel and snaps against the case. Make the latches from 1/16-inch-thick brass that comes with the bezel. The exact profiles are shown in the latch detail. Solder the small latch to the inner edge of the small bezel. Drill holes in the large latch. You'll screw it to the case later. Bend both latches to shape after the final assembly in Step 8.

A series of metal tabs solder to the bezel to hold the glass in place. Position the glass and solder the tabs to the bezel. Polish all brass parts, and set them aside for final assembly

7. Apply finish. Sand thoroughly. Stain, if you choose to, and varnish.

8. Install the clockwork. Cut the dial face (part 20) to size and attach it to the dial pan (part 16) with rubber cement. Be sure the face is centered inside the pan. Attach the dial pan to the case with four screws, 90° apart from one another on the rim of the pan. Check that the dial face is centered. Center the large bezel over the dial pan, slide the hinge under the pan, and screw the hinge in place. Slide the latch under the dial pan and

screw it in place; adjust the latch until it holds the large bezel closed.

Attach the small bezel.

Remove the back and attach the quartz movement (parts 21 and 22) according to the directions that come with it. Cut the pendulum rod so that the pendulum is centered inside its window and swings freely. Attach the pendulum rod and screw the back in place.

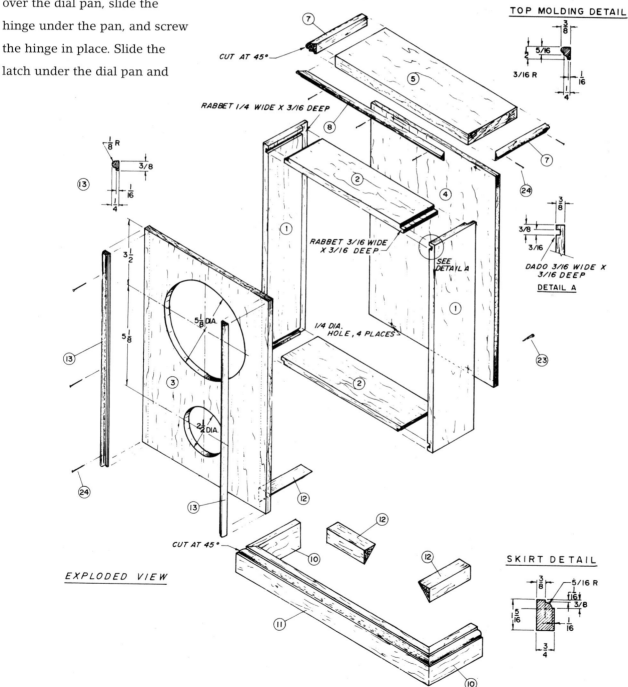

TOP MOLDING DETAIL

CUT AT 45°

RABBET 1/4 WIDE X 3/16 DEEP

3/16 R

3/8

RABBET 3/16 WIDE X 3/16 DEEP

SEE DETAIL A

DADO 3/16 WIDE X 3/16 DEEP

DETAIL A

3½

5⅛ DIA.

5⅛

1/4 DIA. HOLE, 4 PLACES

2½ DIA.

CUT AT 45°

EXPLODED VIEW

SKIRT DETAIL

Schoolhouse Clock

For many years, schoolchildren looked impatiently at the schoolhouse clock hanging on the wall next to Gilbert Stuart's portrait of George Washington. I hate to date myself, but I remember staring at a schoolhouse clock just like this one, waiting for school to end.

The original schoolhouse clock design is credited to the Ansonia Clock Company of Connecticut. Through the second half of the 1800s and up until around 1910, the clocks were made by manufacturers, both here and abroad. Although they are often regarded as prime examples of Americana, many of our antique schoolhouse clocks were actually made in China and Japan.

The clock shown here is a copy of an antique that probably was made overseas around 1895. The original was pine, had a black pinstripe painted on it, and had a low-quality, eight-day brass movement. For accuracy and convenience, I suggest substituting a quartz movement.

1. Select the stock. Use either pine or the more traditional oak. You can buy the bezel assembly, dial face, brass hinges, hanger, door latch, movement, and hands.

2. Lay out and cut the octagon to size. Take your time when laying out the sectors for the octagon (part 8). To avoid problems, cut a test octagon in scrap and dry-fit it together. If there are gaps, adjust the angle at which you cut and try again. When you have a perfect octa-

gon in scrap, cut the octagon for the clock. Cut the octagon to the exact dimensions, or the bezel assembly will not fit.

3. Assemble the octagon. Glue up the octagon in two groups of four sectors each.

Masking tape will help you align the pieces and keep them from collapsing when you clamp. Stretch the masking tape along your bench, sticky side up. Line the four sectors along it with their long edges on the tape and their mitered corners touching each other. Put glue in the joints, and with the tape still in place, fold the pieces together. Put the assembly in a band clamp and tighten gently.

Let the glue set thoroughly, then dry-fit the two subassemblies. If the halves do not come together tightly, trim the miters as necessary. Then glue the halves together. After the glue has set, rout ¼-inch-wide, ⅜-inch-deep grooves in the back of the octagon at each of the eight joints and glue in the splines (part 9).

Round over the outside edge of the octagon after the glue has set. The original profile will require a custom-made bit. The View at A-A, page 134, shows both the original profile and a simpler profile you can cut with a standard router bit.

4. Cut and assemble the case. Cut the sides (part 11), top (part 2), and bottoms (part 3) to size. Cut the joints; dry-fit the pieces together, and make any necessary corrections.

Glue the pieces together, keeping everything square and level. When the glue dries, rout a rabbet in the assembly to accept the back (part 4). Square off the corners with a chisel. Screw the back in place (part 29) so that you can remove it later to change the clock batteries.

Cut the top rail (part 5), the stiles (part 6), and the bottom rails (part 7) to fit the case. Glue them in, one at a time. Make sure you cut the notch for the hinges (part 19) in the right-hand stile before you glue it in place. Keep the rails and stiles flush with the front surface.

MATERIALS LIST

NO.	NAME	SIZE	REQ'D.
1	SIDE	½ x 3¼ – 14⅝ LONG	2
2	TOP	½ x 3¼ – 7⅛ LONG	1
3	BOTTOM	½ x 3¼ – 4⅜ LONG	2
4	BACK	¼ x 7⅛ – 16⅜ LONG	1
5	TOP RAIL	⅜ x 1⅜ – 6⅝ LONG	1
6	STILE	⅜ x 1¼ – 5⅛ LONG	2
7	BOTTOM RAIL	⅜ x 1¼ – 3¹³⁄₁₆ LONG	2
8	SECTOR	¹¹⁄₁₆ x 2½ –5¹⁄₁₆ LONG	8
9	SPLINE	¼ x ⅜ – 2 LONG	8
10	DOOR TOP	⅝ x ⅝ – 4⅜ LONG	1
11	DOOR SIDE	⅝ x ⅝ – 3⅜ LONG	2
12	DOOR BOTTOM	⅝ x ⅝ – 2⁹⁄₁₆ LONG	2
13	MOLDING SIDE	¼ x ⅝ – 6⅛ LONG	2
14	MOLDING BOTTOM	¼ x ⅝ – 4⅜ LONG	2
15	BEZEL ASSEMBLY		1
16	GLASS	CUT TO SIZE	1
17	DIAL FACE	7 DIA.	1
18	HINGE BLOCK	⁵⁄₃₂ x ½ – ¾ LONG	2
19	HINGE		2
20	GLASS	CUT TO SIZE	1
21	GLASS RETAINER	⅛ x ¼ – 20 LONG	1
22	HANGER		1
23	DOOR LATCH		1
24	LATCH LOCK	¼ x ⅜ – 1 LONG	1
25	SCREW – RD. HD.	NO. 6 – ¾ LONG	1
26	MOVEMENT		1
27	HANDS		1 PAIR
28	SPACER	¾ x 3 – 4½ LONG	1
29	SCREW	NO. 4 – ¾ LONG	AS REQ'D

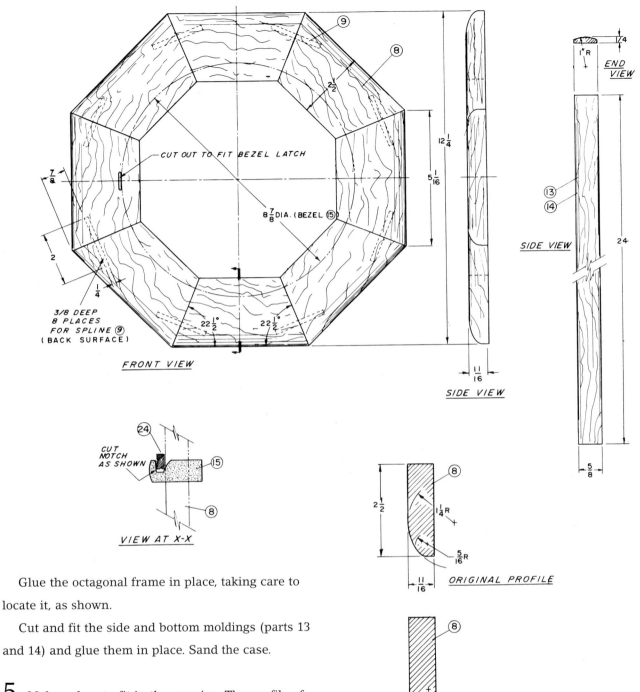

CUT OUT TO FIT BEZEL LATCH

$8\frac{7}{8}$ DIA. (BEZEL ⑮)

3/8 DEEP
8 PLACES
FOR SPLINE ⑨
(BACK SURFACE)

FRONT VIEW

SIDE VIEW

END VIEW

SIDE VIEW

CUT
NOTCH
AS SHOWN

VIEW AT X-X

ORIGINAL PROFILE

SUGGESTED PROFILE

VIEW AT A-A

Glue the octagonal frame in place, taking care to locate it, as shown.

Cut and fit the side and bottom moldings (parts 13 and 14) and glue them in place. Sand the case.

5. Make a door to fit in the opening. The profile of the door is delicate. To avoid injury, cut the molding onto a wide board, and then cut the board to free the molding.

First, rout a roundover on the edge of a board, $\frac{5}{8}$ inch thick, 6 inches wide, and 36 inches long.

Next, cut a groove to help create one of the steps in the door profile, as seen in the door molding end view. Set your dado blades to cut a groove, $\frac{5}{32}$ inch high and $\frac{1}{2}$ inch wide. Set the saw fence to cut in the groove in

one face only. Rout the other step when the door is assembled.

Put a regular blade back in the saw to cut the extra width off the stock. Put the square edge of the stock against the fence and adjust the fence so you can cut a

⅝-inch strip from the other edge of the board. This cutoff will be the door stock. At the moment, it only has one rabbet in it. This makes it easier to glue up the door.

Carefully miter the door stock to form the door top, sides, and bottom (parts 10, 11, and 12). Cut the miters so that the rabbet you have already cut will be the one that holds the glass. Glue the door together with masking tape and band clamps.

Rout the second rabbet in the door when the glue has dried. Rout the rabbet with the door flat on the surface of a table-mounted router. Use push sticks to keep your fingers away from the bit.

Check that the door fits into its opening; sand or plane it to fit if necessary. Attach the door with the two hinge blocks and hinges (parts 18 and 19). Attach the door latch (part 23), and see that it locks the door smoothly.

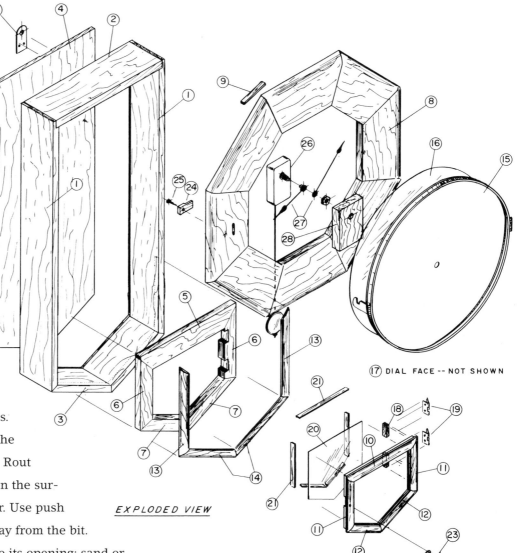

EXPLODED VIEW

(17) DIAL FACE -- NOT SHOWN

6. Attach the hardware. Center the bezel assembly (part 15) on the octagon and lay out a groove to accept the tongue on the bezel, as shown in the exploded view in the octagon. Rout the groove.

Make the latch lock (part 24), and attach it to the back of the clock. File the tongue to fit the latch, as shown in the View X-X.

Attach the dial face (part 17) to the bezel assembly with rubber cement. Apply thin coats to both the bezel and to the back of the dial face. When the cement is

dry, set the face in position. Be sure you remember which direction is up on the bezel—it's easy to glue the face on upside down.

Cut the spacer (part 28); drill a hole in it and put the movement's hand shaft through the hole. Put the hand shaft through the hole in the clock and tighten it in place with a nut that comes with the movement. Screw the bezel to the octagon with #4 x ¾-inch screws (part 29).

The pendulum that comes with the movement is longer than necessary. Cut the pendulum off at about 10 inches so that it is centered in the middle of the lower door.

Notch for and temporarily install the hanger (part 22).

7. Apply finish. Remove the bezel assembly, the door assembly, the hanger, and the hinges.

Sand and apply a stain, if you wish. If you plan to add the pinstripe, apply one coat of shellac or varnish first. Paint the pinstripe with oil-base black paint. When the paint dries, apply two or three more coats of shellac or varnish.

Put the glass (part 16) in the bevel assembly. Small metal tabs come with it to hold the glass in place. Solder the tabs inside the bezel. Put the glass (part 20) in the lower door. Glue the wooden retainer (part 21) in place to hold the glass in the door.

Reassemble the clock; attach the quartz movement (part 26), and put the hands (part 27) in place.

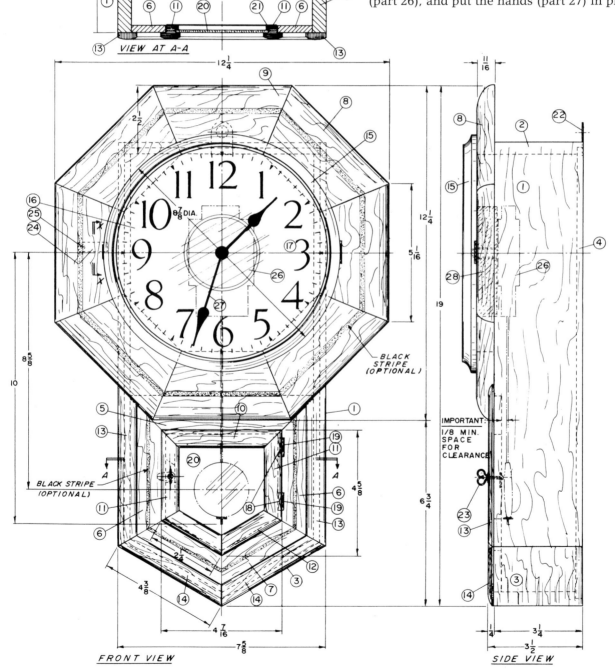

VIEW AT A-A

FRONT VIEW

SIDE VIEW

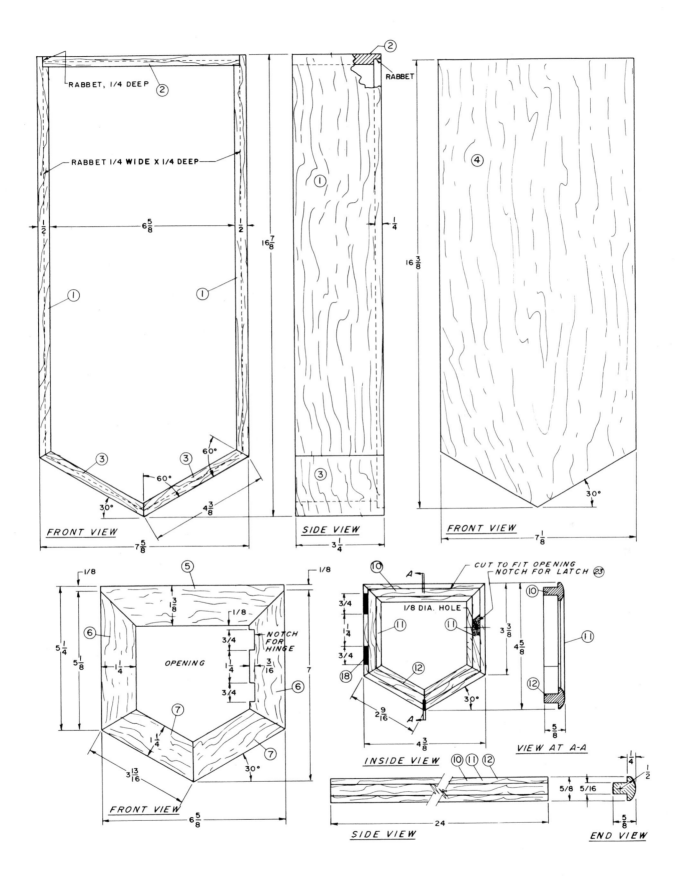

RABBET, 1/4 DEEP ②

RABBET 1/4 WIDE X 1/4 DEEP

1/2   6 5/8   1/2   16 7/8

①   ①   ①

60°

③   ③   60°

30°   4 3/8

FRONT VIEW

7 5/8

RABBET ②

①   1/4

16 3/8

③

SIDE VIEW

3 1/4

④

FRONT VIEW

30°

7 1/8

1/8   ⑤   1/8

3/8

⑥   ⑥

5 1/4   5 1/8

1/4   OPENING   3/16

NOTCH FOR HINGE

1/8   3/4   1/4   3/4

7

⑦   1 1/4   ⑥

⑦

3 13/16   30°

FRONT VIEW

6 5/8

⑩   A   CUT TO FIT OPENING
NOTCH FOR LATCH ㉓

3/4   1/8 DIA. HOLE   ⑩

1/4   ⑪   ⑪   3 3/8

3/4   4 5/8

⑱   ⑫   ⑪

2 9/16   A   30°   ⑫

4 3/8   5/8

INSIDE VIEW

VIEW AT A-A

⑩ ⑪ ⑫

SIDE VIEW

24

5/8   5/16

1/4   1/2

5/8

END VIEW

Shaker Wall Clock, c.1840

This clock is a copy of a clock Isaac Benjamin Youngs made in 1840 at the age of 47. It was made of pine and had a light exterior stain and a dark-walnut stain interior. Youngs also made variations of this wall clock that had double glass panels in the lower door in place of the wood panel.

There were very few Shaker clockmakers—perhaps ten at the most, Youngs was one of the most famous. He became the chief clock maker at the New Lebanon, New York, colony, and although he built tall case clocks, his most well-known clock design is this small wall clock.

1. Study all of the drawings very carefully; be sure you fully understand how the various parts are made and go together before starting. You will see this wall clock is not much more than a simple box with two lids—doors. This project goes together quite quickly, so you might want to order the parts in plenty of time and not be held up waiting for the purchased parts.

Cut all parts to overall size according to the materials list. Sand the surfaces with medium- to fine-grit sandpaper.

2. Locate and cut out the 1¾-inch by 7½-inch windows of the two sides (part 1). Cut the ¼-inch-wide by ¼-inch-deep rabbet along the top, back, and bottom surfaces. Notch for the four hinges on the right side only. Resand all over, keeping all edges sharp.

3. Cut a ⁵⁄₁₆-inch by 5¼-inch notch in the top only (part 4) as shown, and round the front and two sides.

4. Cut to shape the hanger (part 6), divider (part 7), and the dial supports (part 9). Again, resand all parts, keeping all edges sharp. Dry-fit the box assembly using the exploded view as a guide with part numbers 1 through 8. Adjust as necessary. When you are satisfied with the fit, apply very little glue and, for authenticity, use square-cut nails. Temporarily set the divider (part 7) in place, making adjustments later when doors are added, as necessary. Note: the original clock used a completely different dial face support. In the 1840 clock, the back of the movement was actually the back of the case. The dial face was attached to the movement. The two dial supports used in this reproduction are the same design as those used in other, wooden weight-driven clocks of the same era.

If you want to see the movement, cut notches in the two dial supports (part 9) that line up with the two windows in the sides (part 1). Check that the box is square before the glue sets—this is important. Cut the dial board (part 10), to size and sand all over.

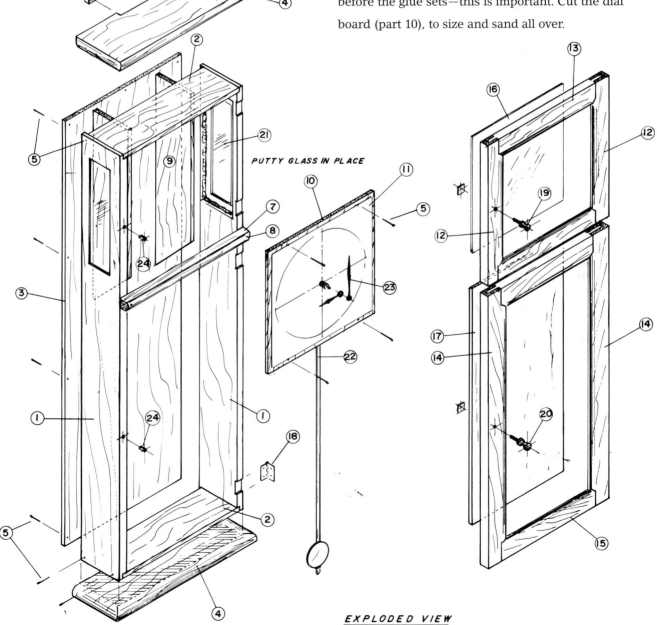

PUTTY GLASS IN PLACE

EXPLODED VIEW

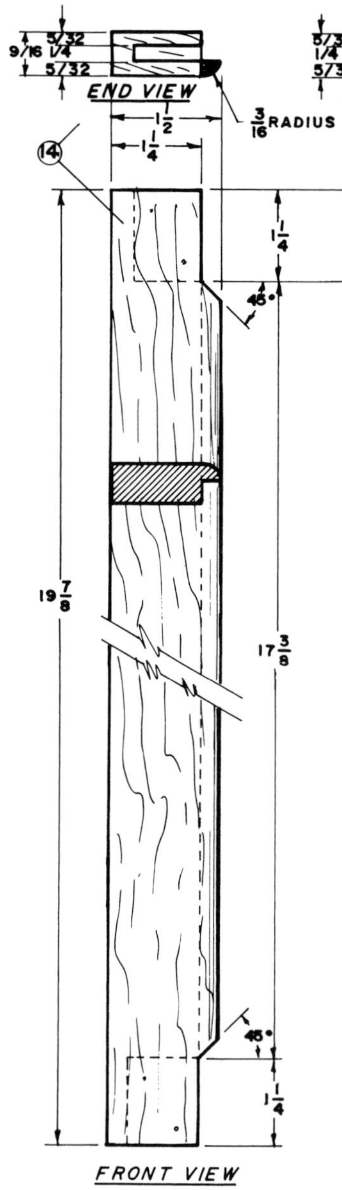

5/32
9/16
1/4
5/32
END VIEW
3/16 RADIUS
1 1/2
1 1/4
14
1 1/4
45°
19 7/8
17 3/8
45°
1 1/4
FRONT VIEW

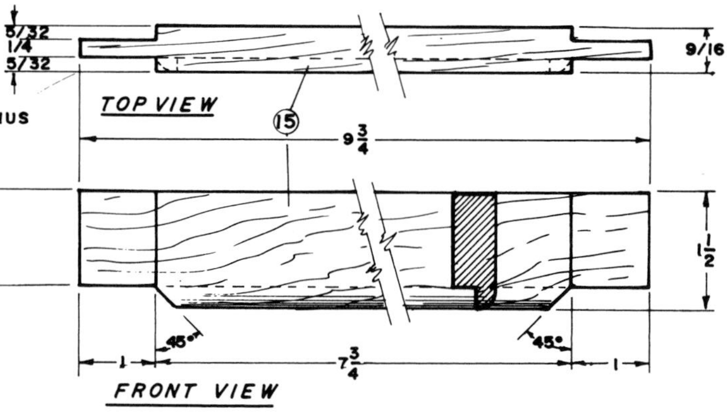

5/32
1/4
5/32
9/16
TOP VIEW
15
9 3/4
1 1/2
45°
45°
1
7 3/4
1
FRONT VIEW

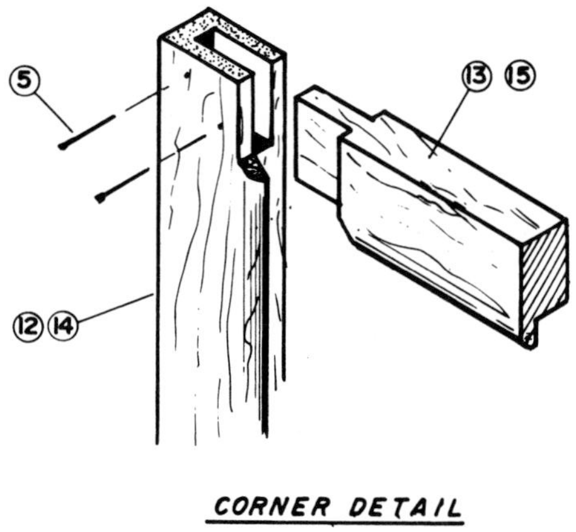

5
13 15
12 14
CORNER DETAIL

MATERIALS LIST

NO.	NAME	SIZE	REQ'D.
1	SIDE	1/2 x 3 1/4 – 30 3/4 LONG	2
2	INSERT	1/4 x 3 – 9 3/4 LONG	2
3	BACK	1/4 x 9 3/4 – 30 3/4 LONG	1
4	TOP/BOTTOM	5/8 x 4 9/16 – 11 1/2 LONG	2
5	NAIL – SQ. CUT FINISH	3/4 LONG	36
6	HANGER	5/8 x 3 – 5 1/4 LONG	1
7	DIVIDER	5/8 x 9/16 – 10 1/4 LONG	1
8	NAIL – SQ. CUT FINISH	1 LONG	4
9	DIAL SUPPORT	1/4 x 2 7/8 – 13 3/4 LONG	2
10	DIAL BOARD	1/4 x 9 SQUARE	1
11	DIAL FACE	7 1/2 DIA. (IVORY)	1
12	STILE – UPPER	9/16 x 1 1/4 – 10 1/4 LONG	2
13	RAIL – UPPER	9/16 x 1 1/4 – 9 3/4 LONG	2
14	STILE – LOWER	9/16 x 1 1/2 – 19 7/8 LONG	2
15	RAIL – LOWER	9/16 x 1 1/2 – 9 3/4 LONG	2
16	GLASS	3/32 x 7 5/8 SQUARE	1
17	PANEL (OR GLASS)	1/4 x 7 5/8 – 17 1/4 LONG	1
18	HINGE – BRASS	1 x 1	4
19	PULL – UPPER	1/2 DIA. – 1 1/4 LONG	1
20	PULL – LOWER	3/4 DIA. – 1 3/8 LONG	1
21	GLASS	3/32 x 2 1/4 – 8 LONG	2
22	MOVEMENT	20 PENDULUM	1
23	HANDS – BLACK	3 3/4 SIZE	1 PR.
24	MAGNETIC CATCH	3/8 DIA.	2

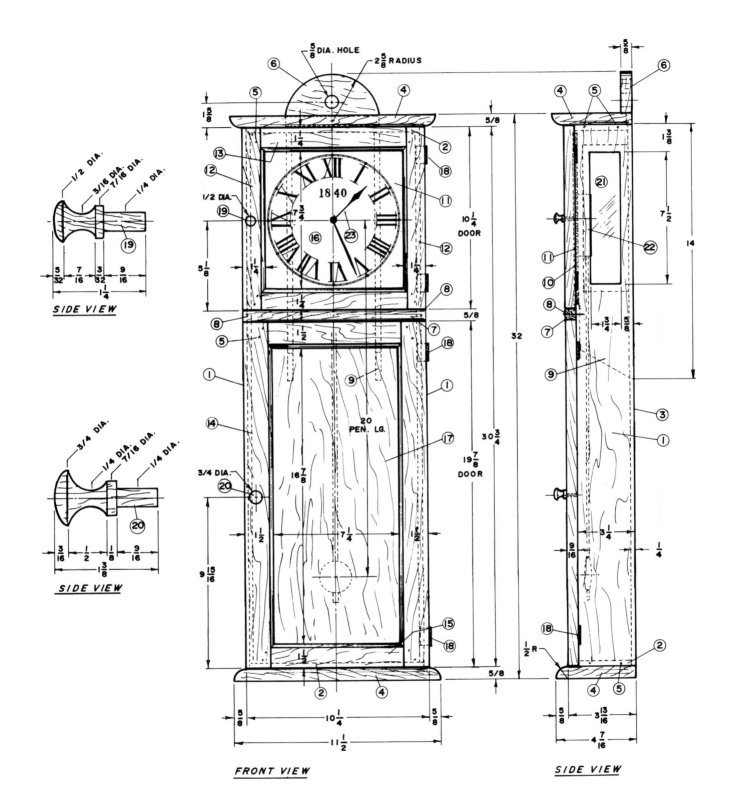

5/8 DIA. HOLE

2 5/8 RADIUS

1/2 DIA.

3/16 DIA.

7/16 DIA.

1/4 DIA.

19

5/32 | 7/16 | 3/32 | 9/16

1 1/4

SIDE VIEW

3/4 DIA.

1/4 DIA.

7/16 DIA.

1/4 DIA.

20

3/16 | 1/2 | 1/8 | 9/16

1 3/8

SIDE VIEW

1/2 DIA.

3/4 DIA.

1 5/8

5/8

6

5

13

12

19

1 1/4

16

7 3/4

23

18 40

11

8

8

5

1

14

1 1/2

9

20 PEN. LG.

16 7/8

17

7 1/4

9 15/16

20

1 1/2

2

4

5/8 | 10 1/4 | 5/8

11 1/2

FRONT VIEW

2

18

11

12

5/8

10 1/4 DOOR

7

18

1

32

30 3/4

19 7/8 DOOR

5/8

15

18

5/8

6

4

5

1 3/8

21

7 1/2

22

14

11

10

8

7

3 1/4

9

18

1/2 R

18

9/16

3 1/4

1/4

2

1

3

5/8 | 3 13/16

4 7/16

4 | 5

SIDE VIEW

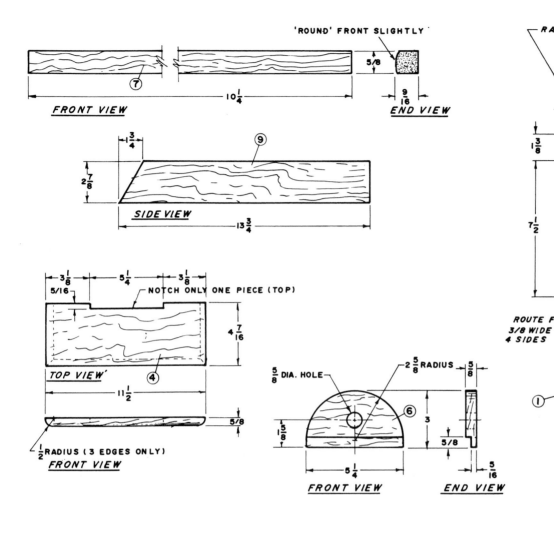

5. The two doors are the only parts of this project that are a little difficult, so take your time and measure as accurately as possible. Plane the material for the door to $^9/_{16}$-inch thickness. Cut the $^3/_{16}$-inch radius on all door parts (parts 12, 13, 14, and 15). Notch for the glass, $^3/_{16}$ inch wide and $^5/_{16}$ inch deep, as shown. Very carefully, cut the door parts to size as indicated in the drawings. Work as accurately as possible so that you have a well-fitted door.

Dry-fit the door parts. Also check that they fit correctly with the case. Adjust as necessary. Glue the doors together; for extra strength and for an old, authentic look, add the square-cut nails, as shown. Do not glue the panel (part 17) in place; let it float.

6. After the glue sets, fill in any loose joints, and touch up as necessary. Sand all over, keeping all edges sharp. Do not try to hide the nails—they were not hidden on the original clocks. Turn the door pulls (part 20), and add them to the doors. Locate and drill for the two round magnetic catches (part 24). Make a final fit of the doors, and temporarily add the hinges. Check again that everything fits correctly. Remove the hinges and doors; sand the doors and case, using very fine-grit sandpaper.

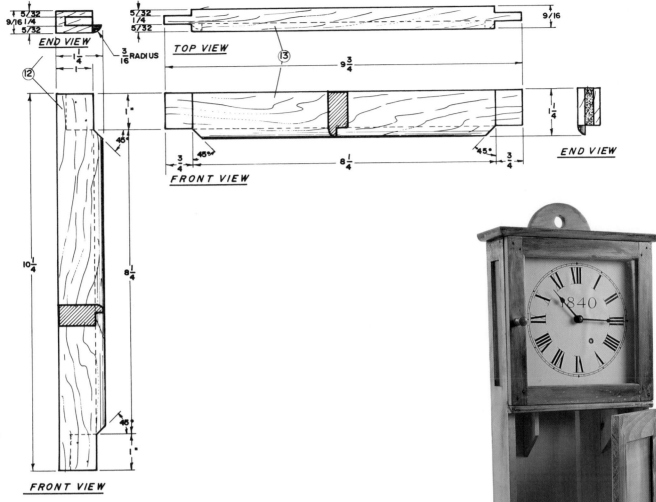

Temporarily attach the two dial supports (part 9). They can be tacked or screwed in place from the back. Temporarily add the dial board (part 10). This is held in place by four square-cut, finished nails or small, round, brass screws.

7. Clean all surfaces with a tack rag and apply a coat of pine stain to the outside of the case and to the inside and outside of the two doors. Add the glass (parts 16 and 21) to the top, using a dark grey putty, if you can find it.

Reattach the dial supports. Glue the dial face to the dial board, taking care that it is centered inside the top door—this is important! Drill a hole in the dial board for the shaft of the movement. Apply two coats of clear shellac; use 0000 steel wool between coats.

Apply a coat of paste wax to all exterior surfaces.

Reattach the two doors. Add a battery to the movement, and attach the movement to the dial face with washer and nut. Screw or nail the dial board, with the movement and hands attached, to the dial supports, with the movement attached to the face.

Add the pendulum; hang the clock on a peg, and give the pendulum a push.

Stools, Stands & Shelves

From a plant stand and an artist's easel to classic stepping stools and knickknack shelves, the projects in this chapter are both clever and handy.

Small Wall Shelf

Our forefathers had a great sense of proportion when it came to designing wall shelves. Their shelves were graceful and beautiful, with lines that computer-assisted design can't improve.

I found the model for this project in Maine, where it was made sometime during the eighteenth century. I was attracted to its smooth lines. It's rather small, but it may be just right for holding a clock or a favorite object.

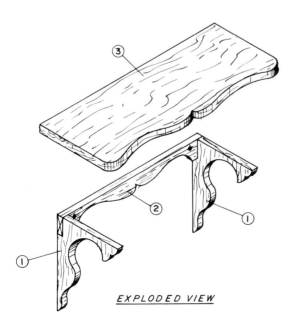

EXPLODED VIEW

NO.	NAME	SIZE	REQ'D.
	MATERIALS LIST		
1	SIDE	³⁄₈ x 4 ³⁄₄ – 7¹⁄₈ LONG	2
2	BRACE	1¹⁄₂ x 2 – 12 LONG	1
3	SHELF	³⁄₈ x 5¹⁄₂ – 14¹⁄₂ LONG	1
4	BRAD – SQ. CUT	⁷⁄₈ LONG	AS REQ'D.

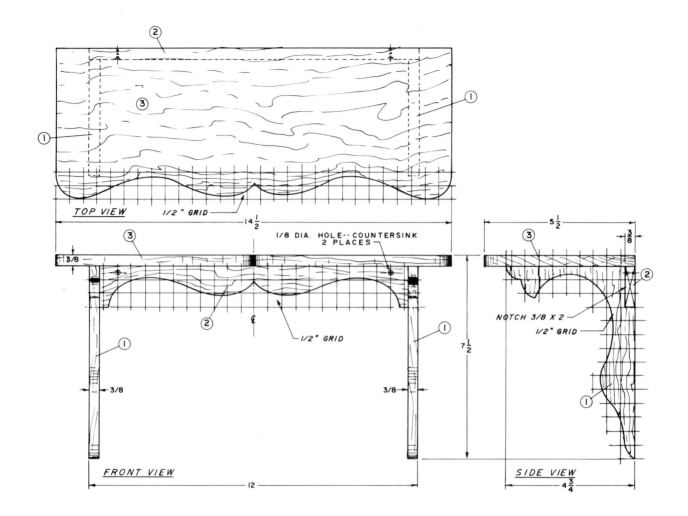

TOP VIEW 1/2" GRID 14½

1/8 DIA. HOLE--COUNTERSINK 2 PLACES

5½ 3/8

3/8

1/2" GRID

7½

NOTCH 3/8 X 2

1/2" GRID

FRONT VIEW 12

3/8 3/8

SIDE VIEW 4¾

1. Select the stock. This shelf can be made of any kind of wood, but I think that hardwood suits it best. There are only four parts: two sides, a brace, and a shelf, all made from 3/8-inch stock. Cut them to the sizes given in the Materials List.

2. Make a paper pattern, and cut the parts to shape. Draw a grid with ½-inch squares, and enlarge the drawing of the parts onto it. Transfer the patterns to the stock, and cut the parts to shape. To ensure that the sides (part 1) are identical, attach one on top of the other with double-sided tape and cut them as a unit.

While the pieces are still together, sand the edges, and cut a notch for the brace.

Drill two ⅛-inch-diameter mounting holes in the brace (part 2), and countersink them from the front.

3. Assemble the shelf. Glue up the parts. Before the glue sets, make sure the sides are square with the brace. To make the shelf look like the original, attach the shelf (part 3) with ⅞-inch square-cut brads (part 4).

4. Apply finish. Sand thoroughly, rounding the edges slightly. Finish with a low-luster varnish.

Folding Plant Stand

We have a lot of plants but limited space to display them. I built this folding plant stand to give us room to pack more plants into a small area. It raises some plants above others and is a nice furniture piece.

Study the plans carefully before starting so that you know how the legs fold together. Note the notch in the support (part 3) to lock the legs in an open position.

NO.	NAME	SIZE	REQ'D.
	MATERIALS LIST		
1	TOP – CENTER	$\frac{1}{4}$ x $\frac{3}{4}$ – $9\frac{1}{4}$ LONG	7
2	TOP – END	$\frac{1}{4}$ x 1 – $9\frac{1}{4}$ LONG	2
3	SUPPORT	$\frac{3}{8}$ x $\frac{3}{4}$ – $8\frac{1}{2}$ LONG	2
4	BRAD	$\frac{5}{8}$ LONG	48
5	LEG	$\frac{3}{8}$ x $\frac{3}{4}$ – $11\frac{3}{4}$ LONG	4
6	BRACE	$\frac{1}{4}$ x $\frac{3}{4}$ – $4\frac{1}{4}$ LONG	1
7	BRACE	$\frac{1}{4}$ x $\frac{3}{4}$ – $5\frac{1}{16}$ LONG	2
8	SCREW FL. MD.	NO. 6 – $\frac{5}{8}$ LONG	4

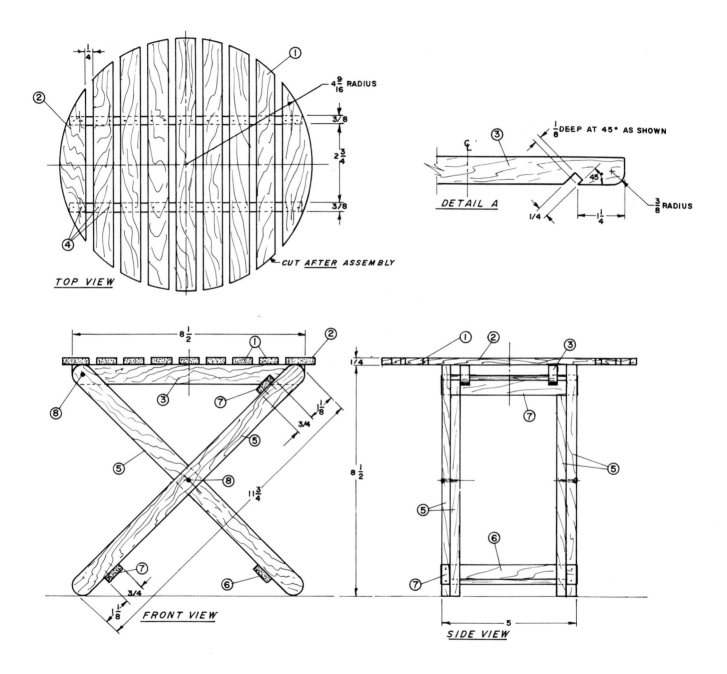

$\frac{1}{4}$

① ②

$4\frac{9}{16}$ RADIUS

$3/8$

$2\frac{3}{4}$

$3/8$

④

TOP VIEW

CUT AFTER ASSEMBLY

DETAIL A

③

$\frac{1}{8}$ DEEP AT 45° AS SHOWN

45°

$\frac{3}{8}$ RADIUS

$1/4$

$1\frac{1}{4}$

$8\frac{1}{2}$

① ②

③

⑦

⑧

⑤ ⑤

⑧

$1\frac{1}{8}$

$3/4$

$11\frac{3}{4}$

$8\frac{1}{2}$

⑤

⑦

$3/4$

$1\frac{1}{8}$

⑥

FRONT VIEW

---

① ② ③

$1/4$

⑦

⑤ ⑤

⑤

⑥

⑦

5

SIDE VIEW

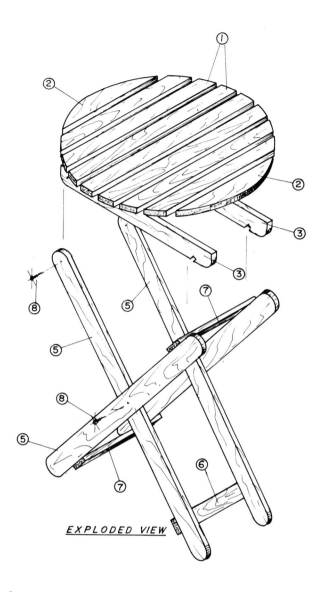

EXPLODED VIEW

1. Cut the top pieces (parts 1 and 2) to rough size. I suggest that you cut the pieces a little long.

2. Cut the two supports (part 3) to size, and make the notch following detail A. Drill a $\frac{1}{16}$-inch-diameter location hole in the opposite end for the screw (part 8).

3. Glue and tack the top pieces (parts 1 and 2) to the two supports (part 3). Leave a $\frac{1}{4}$-inch space between parts. Be sure they are $2\frac{3}{4}$ inches apart and parallel, as shown.

4. Locate the exact center of the top assembly, and swing a $4\frac{9}{16}$-inch radius all of the way around. Sand down to the line so that you have an exactly round top with all of the pieces in place.

5. Carefully locate and drill a $\frac{1}{16}$-inch-diameter hole for the screw (part 8) at the crossover midpoint of the leg.

6. Assemble all of the parts, and check that everything functions correctly. Check that the legs lock in an open position.

7. Finish to suit with either paint or stain.

Knickknack Shelf With Hearts

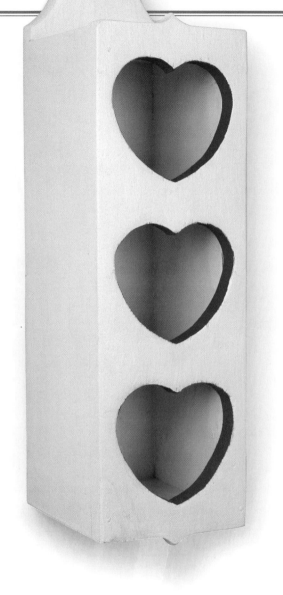

This what-not shelf provides a great place to display a small grouping of tiny collectibles. It looks great either painted or stained.

1. Cut all pieces to overall sizes and sand all surfaces.

2. Lay out and cut the back (part 1) according to the given dimensions.

3. Carefully lay out and cut out three hearts (part 2) following the given dimensions.

4. Dry-fit all of the pieces. If the pieces fit correctly, nail together as shown in the drawings.

5. Sand all over, and round all of the edges slightly.

6. Paint or prime to suit.

MATERIALS LIST

NO.	NAME	SIZE	REQ'D.
1	BACK	½ x 5 – 18 LONG	1
2	FRONT	½ x 5 – 14½ LONG	1
3	SIDE	½ x 4½ – 14½ LONG	2
4	SHELF	½ x 4 – 4 LONG	4
5	FINISH NAIL	6d	22

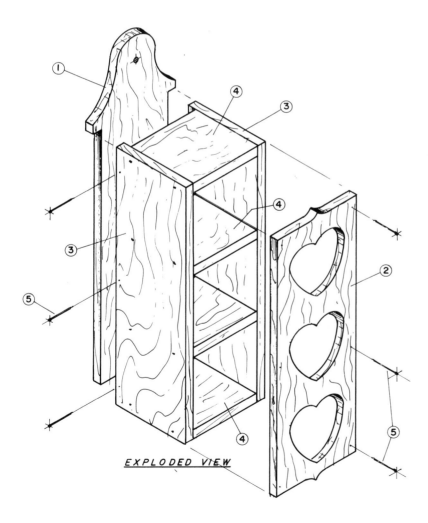

EXPLODED VIEW

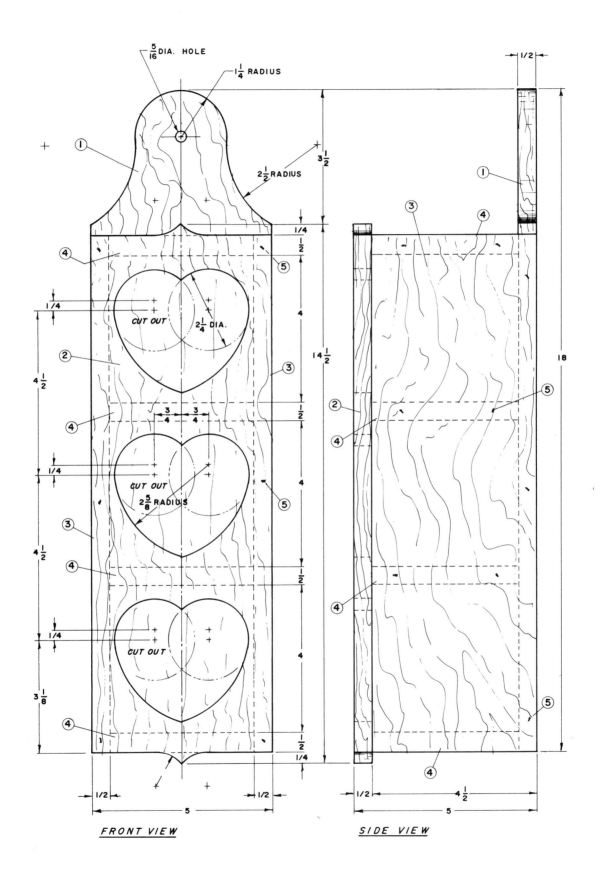

FRONT VIEW

SIDE VIEW

Footstool with Heart

In colonial times, footstools were known as crickets and often could be found before a chair in front of the fireplace. Designs for them vary greatly, because we all have our own ideas about what a footstool should look like. The model for this footstool comes from eighteenth-century New England. This replica is easy to make and very sturdy.

1. Select the stock and cut the parts. Your choice of wood will be influenced by whether or not you plan on painting the footstool. Poplar or pine takes paint well; a clear finish calls for an attractive hardwood. Cut the parts to the sizes given in the Materials List.

2. Lay out the legs and skirts. To save a bit of time, tape the legs (part 1) together with double-sided tape before you lay out the curves with a compass. Make your layout lines on the top piece only, and cut out both pieces at once. Lay out the notch that houses the skirt and cut it with a backsaw.

Draw a grid with ½-inch squares to make a pattern for the skirt (part 2). Enlarge the drawing of the skirt onto the grid. Tape the skirts together and transfer the

MATERIALS LIST			
NO.	NAME	SIZE	REQ'D.
1	LEG	⅝ x 6 – 5⅜ LONG	2
2	SKIRT	½ x 1⅞ – 12 LONG	2
3	TOP	⅝ x 6 – 12 LONG	1
4	NAIL – FINISH	6 d	AS REQ'D.

enlargement to the wood. Lay the hearts out directly on the wood.

Sand the edges while the pieces are still together. Separate the parts and sand the surfaces.

3. Assemble the footstool. Attach the legs to the skirts with glue and finishing nails (part 4). Be sure to keep everything square. Once the glue has set, line up the top (part 3) and attach it with glue and 6d nails.

4. Apply finish. Sand thoroughly, rounding the top edges. The footstool can be either varnished or painted.

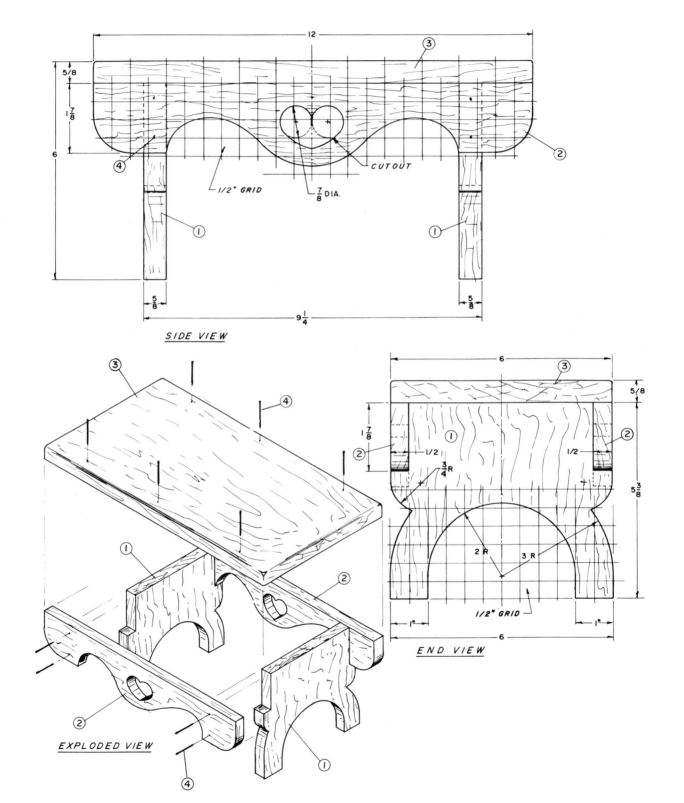

SIDE VIEW

EXPLODED VIEW

END VIEW

Bed Step Stool

One year I built my granddaughter Hilary a colonial pencil-post bed. As with many beds of the period, this one was a little high for a youngster. I knew she had trouble getting in and out of bed, so when I found a bed step stool in an antique shop in Vermont, I knew it would be just perfect for her. This project, based on that antique, can be used for its original purpose, but would also be handy anywhere around the house—especially in the kitchen.

1. Study the plans carefully. Note how each part is to be shaped. As you study the plans, try to visualize how you will make each part and how the project will be assembled. Note which parts you will put together first, second, and so on—exactly how you will put it together.

The two sides (part 1) are 14 inches wide, so if you do not have wood this wide, you will have to glue up wood to make the width. As the sides are irregular in shape, they will have to be laid out. If

MATERIALS LIST			
NO.	NAME	SIZE	REQ'D.
1	END	¾ x 14 – 11¼ LONG	2
2	FRONT BRACE	¾ x 1¾ – 18 LONG	2
3	REAR BRACE	¾ x 1¾ – 18 LONG	1
4	STEP	¾ x 7½ – 19 LONG	2
5	FINISH NAIL	6 d	24

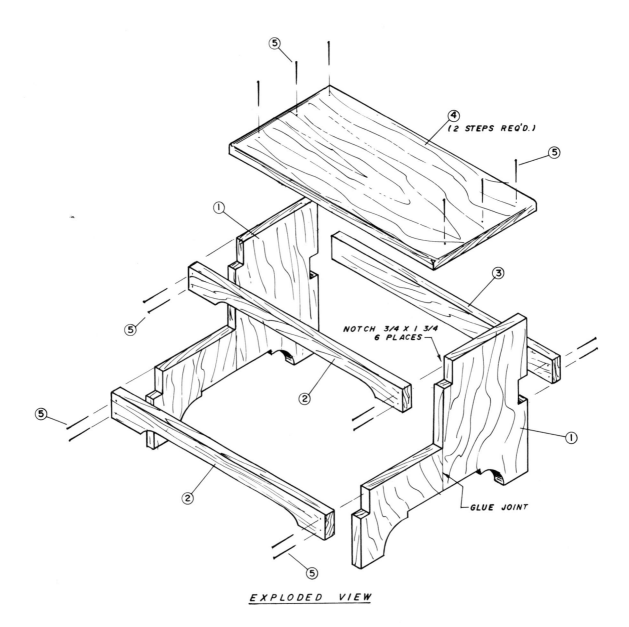

⑤

④ (2 STEPS REQ'D.)

⑤

①

③

NOTCH 3/4 X 1 3/4 6 PLACES

⑤

②

①

⑤

②

GLUE JOINT

⑤

EXPLODED VIEW

you are going to make only one step stool, lay out the shape directly on the wood. To make a perfectly matching pair, tack the two side pieces together. Cut and sand them while they are still tacked together. Locate and cut the two ¾-inch by 1¾-inch notches before separating the parts.

2. Carefully cut the remaining parts to size according to the Materials List. Take care to cut all parts to exact size and exactly square (90°). Stop and recheck all dimensions before going on.

3. Lightly sand all surfaces and edges with medium sandpaper to remove all tool marks. Take care to keep all edges square and sharp.

After all of the pieces have been carefully made, dry-fit the parts—that is, put the complete project together without glue or nails to check for accuracy and good-fitting joints. If anything needs refitting, now is the time to correct it. Once all of the parts fit together correctly, assemble the project, keeping everything square as you go. Check that all fits are tight.

4. Finish to suit, following the general finishing instructions in the introduction.

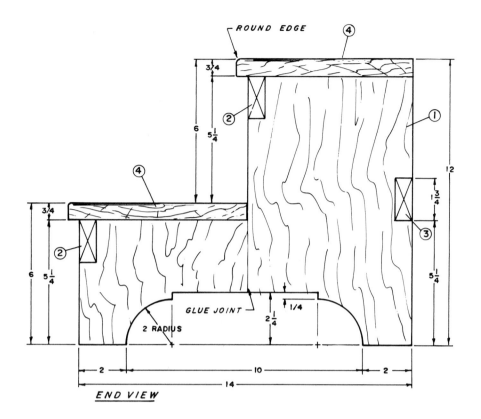

END VIEW

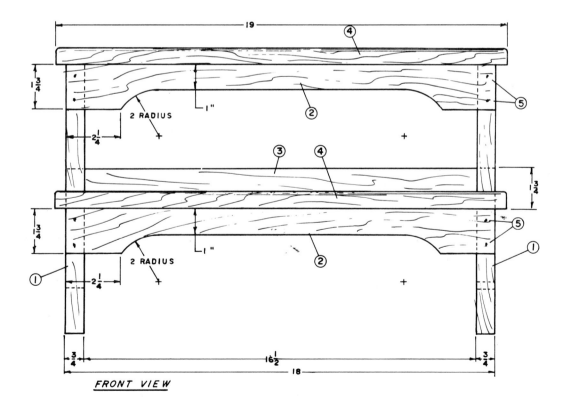

FRONT VIEW

Wall Shelf

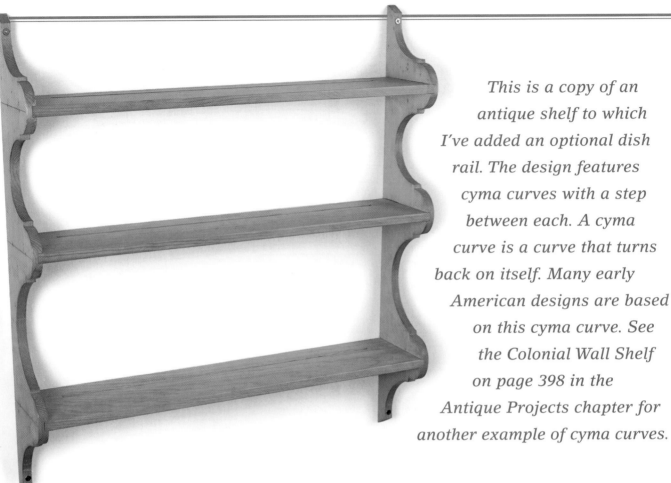

This is a copy of an antique shelf to which I've added an optional dish rail. The design features cyma curves with a step between each. A cyma curve is a curve that turns back on itself. Many early American designs are based on this cyma curve. See the Colonial Wall Shelf on page 398 in the Antique Projects chapter for another example of cyma curves.

1. Select the stock and cut the parts. The original shelf was made of pine. The entire piece is made from 3/4-inch-thick stock. Cut the parts to the sizes given in the Materials List.

2. Make a paper pattern and cut the sides to shape. Draw a grid with 1-inch squares and enlarge the drawing of the sides onto it. Include the dadoes for the shelves in the pattern.

Temporarily tack the two sides (part 1) together. Try placing the tacks in the center of the top and bottom dadoes. Transfer the pattern to the top piece of wood and cut the sides to shape. Sand the edges while they are still together, and then separate them.

Cut the dadoes for the shelves in each side. If you choose, cut a dish-rail groove in each shelf, 1⅝ inches from the back edge.

Drill ½-inch holes ¼ inch deep for the wooden plugs that cover the four hanging holes. Drill the 3/16-inch-diameter hanging holes on the same centers as the ½-inch holes.

MATERIALS LIST

NO.	NAME	SIZE	REQ'D.
1	SIDE	¾ x 5½ – 32 LONG	2
2	SHELF	¾ x 5½ – 22 LONG	3
3	NAIL – SQ. CUT FINISH	6 d	12
4	PLUG	½ DIA.	4

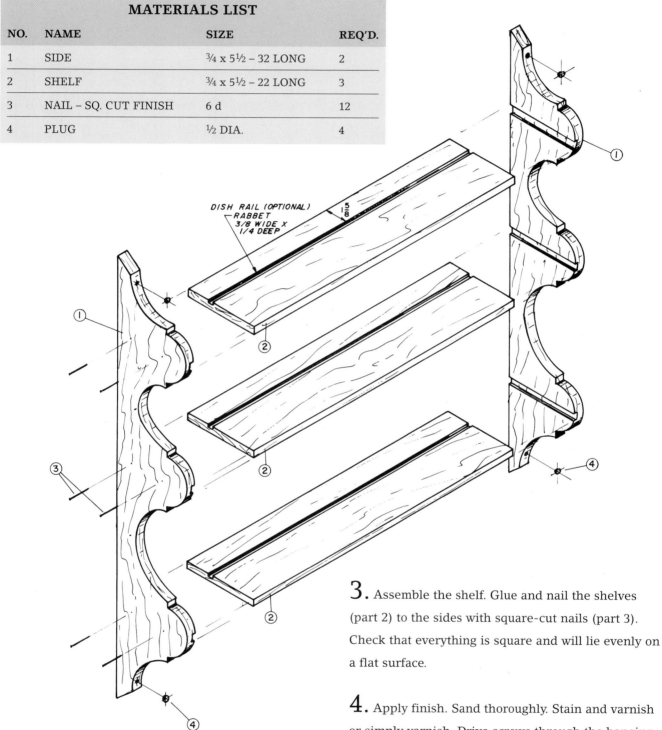

DISH RAIL (OPTIONAL)
RABBET
3/8 WIDE X
1/4 DEEP

$\frac{5}{8}$

3. Assemble the shelf. Glue and nail the shelves (part 2) to the sides with square-cut nails (part 3). Check that everything is square and will lie evenly on a flat surface.

4. Apply finish. Sand thoroughly. Stain and varnish or simply varnish. Drive screws through the hanging holes to hang the shelf. Cover them with the four plugs (part 4).

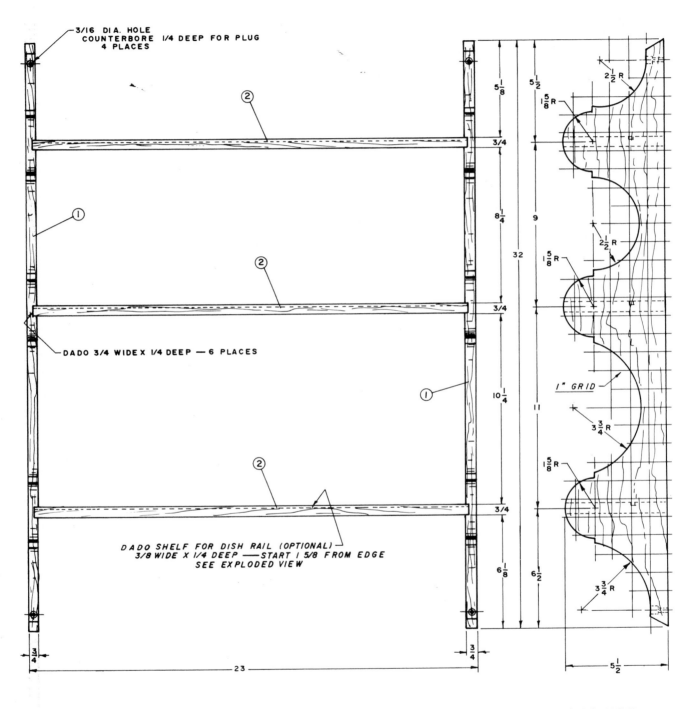

3/16 DIA. HOLE
COUNTERBORE 1/4 DEEP FOR PLUG
4 PLACES

②

①

DADO 3/4 WIDE X 1/4 DEEP — 6 PLACES

②

①

②

DADO SHELF FOR DISH RAIL (OPTIONAL)
3/8 WIDE X 1/4 DEEP — START 1 5/8 FROM EDGE
SEE EXPLODED VIEW

5 1/8

3/4

8 1/4

3/4

10 1/4

3/4

6 1/8

3/4

5 1/2

9

11

6 1/2

32

3/4

23

FRONT VIEW

2 1/2 R

1 5/8 R

2 1/2 R

1 5/8 R

1" GRID

3 3/4 R

1 5/8 R

3 3/4 R

5 1/2

SIDE VIEW

Bathroom Shelf

Use this shelf in the bathroom or anywhere else in the house. You can make it longer by adding spindles on 2½-inch centers. You can buy the spindles if you won't be turning them yourself. A 41-inch-long shelf would have eight more spindles than the project illustrated here.

1. Select the stock and cut the parts. The shelf in the photo was made from ash. I bought the oak spindles. Cut the parts to the sizes given in the Materials List.

2. Cut the parts to shape. Notch the rear edge of the shelf (part 1) to accept whichever metal hangers (part 7) you will use. Brass hangers are a good choice and can be purchased.

Miter the ends of the front rail (part 2) and side rails (part 3) where they will meet. Glue the rails together, making sure that the corners they form are square. After the glue sets, strengthen the joints with splines (part 4). Let the glue dry and then sand the entire rail.

The spindles I bought fit nicely in ³/₁₆-inch-diameter holes that were ⅜ inch deep. Mark the center of each hole on the rail and on the shelf with an awl. Make sure

MATERIALS LIST			
NO.	NAME	SIZE	REQ'D.
1	SHELF	½ x 6 – 21 LONG	1
2	FRONT RAIL	½ x 1 – 21 LONG	1
3	SIDE RAIL	½ x 1 – 6 LONG	2
4	SPLINE	⅛ x 1 – 1 LONG	2
5	SPINDLE		13
6	WALL BRACE	½ x 4 – 5 LONG	2
7	METAL HANGER	AS AVAILABLE	2
8	NAIL	6 d	AS REQ'D.

that the points on the shelf line up exactly with those on the rail and then drill to fit your spindles (part 5).

Draw a grid with ½-inch squares, and enlarge the drawing of the wall brace (part 6) onto it. Transfer the enlarged drawing to the wood. Cut the two braces to shape.

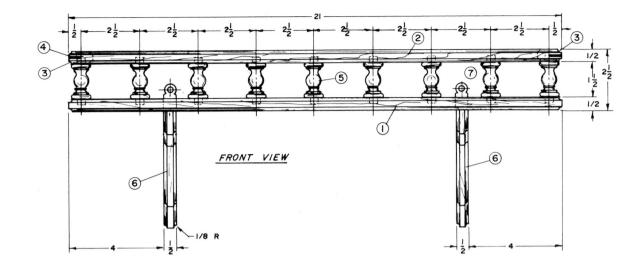

FRONT VIEW

3. Cut the molded edges. Rout coves into the edges of the shelf, the wall braces, and the rail with a ⅛-inch-radius cove bit that has a ball-bearing guide. Clean up the routing on the inside corners of the brace with a gauge. The router may tend to tip when routing the narrow rail. You can steady it by placing a scrap ½ inch thick x 6 inches wide x 18 inches long between the rails while routing.

4. Assemble the shelf; then sand the entire shelf. Dry-assemble the spindles in the holes in the shelf, and then fit the glued-up rail in place. Make any necessary adjustments. Disassemble the parts; apply a little glue to the top and bottom of the spindles, and put the parts back together

When the glue dries, position the wall braces 4 inches from the outer edges of the shelf, and nail them in place with 6d finishing nails (part 8).

5. Apply finish. Sand the entire shelf and paint or varnish it.

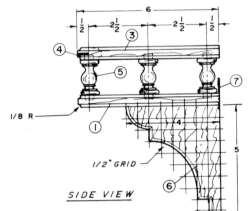

1/2" GRID

SIDE VIEW

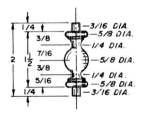

SPINDLE DETAIL

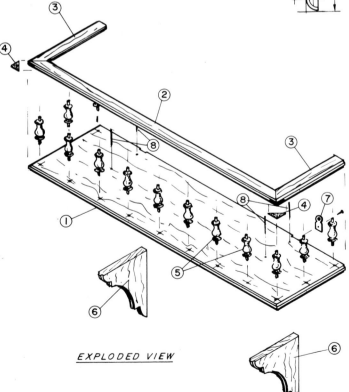

EXPLODED VIEW

Tall Plant Table

Here is an old-style plant stand. I remember my grandmother had one just like it in her parlor. It's simple to build and will make an interesting stand for your plants. A biscuit joiner was used in making my copy, but ¼-inch-diameter dowels would work just as well. Your friends and plants will love this stand.

1. Cut all pieces to size. Sand all over.

2. Cut the bottom taper of the legs (part 1) 3 inches up, as shown, on the two inside surfaces only. Cut two slots with the biscuit joiner on the two inside surfaces as shown in the drawing of the exploded view. Sand all over.

3. Lay out the skirt (part 2). Cut two slots with the biscuit joiner to match the legs. Using a ½-inch-radius cove cutter with a ball-bearing follower, make a cut on the lower inside edge of the skirt to give a thin appearance, as shown in the view at B-B. Sand all over.

4. Following the given dimensions, cut a notch in all four corners of the shelf (part 4). Sand all over.

5. Using a router with a ⅜-inch-radius round cutter, make up the top (part 7).

6. Glue the skirts (part 2) to the legs (part 1) and clamp. Check that everything is square.

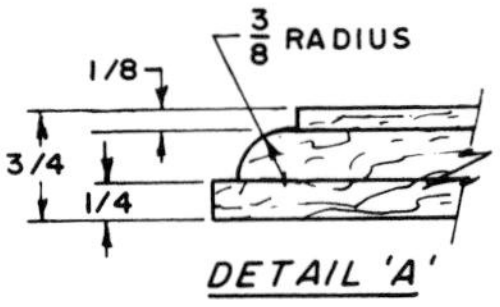

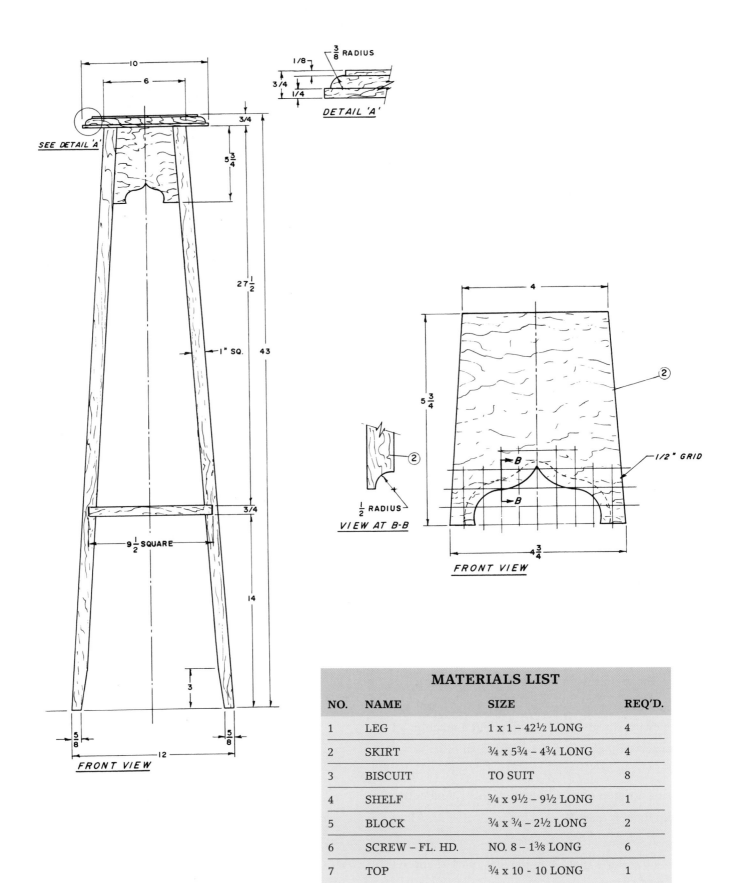

3/8 RADIUS
1/8
3/4
1/4
DETAIL 'A'

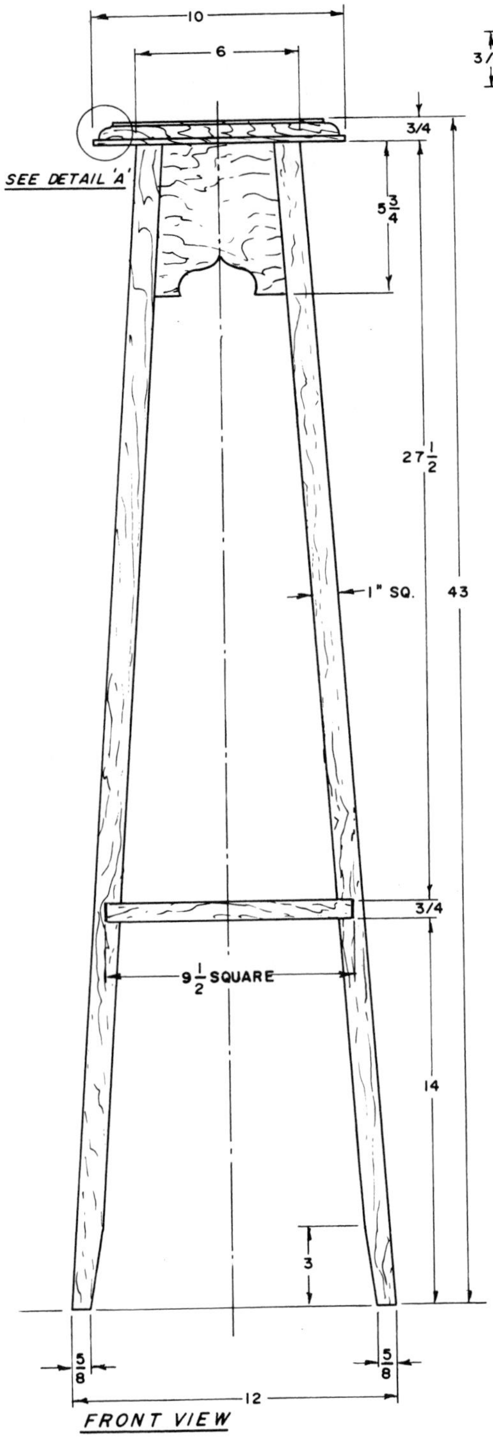

10
6
3/4
SEE DETAIL 'A'
5 3/4
27 1/2
1" SQ.
43
3/4
9 1/2 SQUARE
14
3
5/8
5/8
12
FRONT VIEW

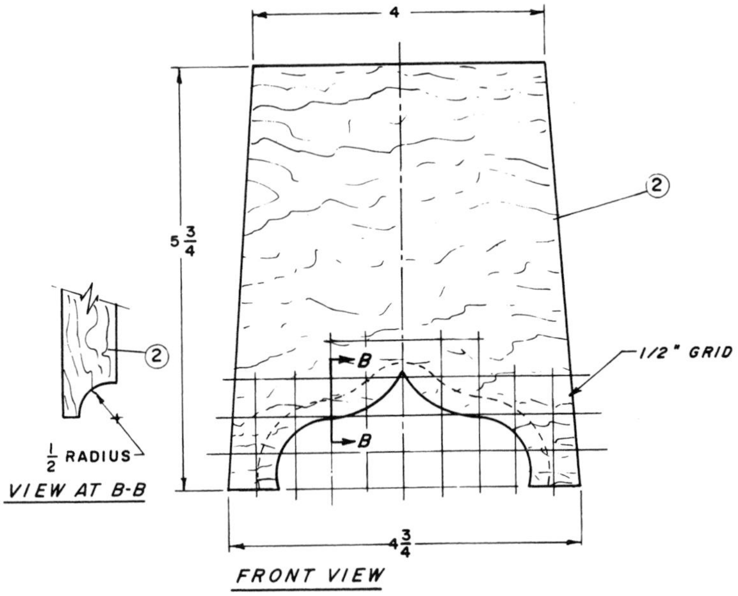

4
5 3/4
2
B
B
1/2" GRID
2
1/2 RADIUS
VIEW AT B-B
4 3/4
FRONT VIEW

MATERIALS LIST

NO.	NAME	SIZE	REQ'D.
1	LEG	1 x 1 – 42½ LONG	4
2	SKIRT	¾ x 5¾ – 4¾ LONG	4
3	BISCUIT	TO SUIT	8
4	SHELF	¾ x 9½ – 9½ LONG	1
5	BLOCK	¾ x ¾ – 2½ LONG	2
6	SCREW – FL. HD.	NO. 8 – 1⅜ LONG	6
7	TOP	¾ x 10 - 10 LONG	1

7. Slide the shelf (part 4) up into place. The top surface should be about 14¾ inches above the floor. If everything is okay, glue it in place. (You might want to drill and nail it in place if you plan to have heavy plants on the shelves.)

8. Add the two blocks (part 5) with the screws (part 6).

9. Screw the top (part 7) to the blocks (part 5). Do not glue in place.

10. This is another project that could be either stained or painted.

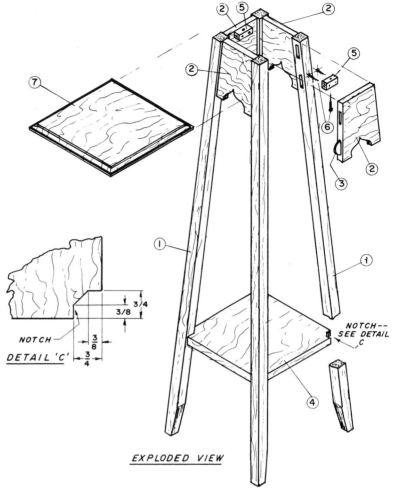

DETAIL 'C'

NOTCH

3/4
3/8
3/8
3/4

NOTCH--
SEE DETAIL
C

EXPLODED VIEW

Artist's Easel

Here's a project that's perfect for the painter in your life. This easel doesn't take long to make, although you do have to be particular when selecting wood for the legs.

1. Select the stock and cut the parts. Because the legs are so long and thin, they should be made out of knot-free stock. I made do with flawed pieces I had on hand and ended up replacing several broken legs. Cut the parts to the sizes given in the Materials List.

2. Cut the parts to shape. Study the drawings and then lay out the shape on the block you've cut for the head. Locate the holes, the notch, and the rabbet. I cut the head (part 1) with a band saw. First, cut the $13/16$ x $1^{11}/_{16}$-inch notch shown in the front view. Then cut the rabbet, $3/4$ inch wide and $1^{5}/_{16}$ inches deep, as shown in the side view.

Drill two $1/4$-inch-diameter holes in the head, as shown in the front view, for the bolts that hold the front legs.

Drill the hole for the bolt that fastens the rear leg in two steps. First, drill a $1/4$-inch-diameter hole all the way through the head, as shown in the side view. Then redrill the hole on the right side to a $1/2$-inch diameter, using the first hole as a guide, as shown in the pictorial view.

The four corners of the legs (part 2) can be left square or shaped with a router, as shown. Drill a hole in each for the bolt that attaches it to the head.

MATERIALS LIST

NO.	NAME	SIZE	REQ'D.
1	HEAD	$1\frac{5}{8}$ x $2\frac{9}{16}$ – 3 LONG	1
2	LEG	$\frac{3}{4}$ x $\frac{3}{4}$ – 60 LONG	3
3	SUPPORT SHELF	$\frac{3}{4}$ x $1\frac{1}{4}$ - 21 LONG	1
4	BRACE	$\frac{3}{4}$ x $\frac{3}{4}$ – 21 LONG	1
5	UPPER SUPPORT	$\frac{3}{4}$ x $2\frac{1}{2}$ – $2\frac{9}{16}$ LONG	1
6	CARRIAGE BOLT	$\frac{3}{16}$ x $2\frac{1}{4}$ LONG	1
7	CARRIAGE BOLT	$\frac{3}{16}$ x 2 LONG	2
8	CARRIAGE BOLT	$\frac{3}{16}$ x $3\frac{1}{4}$ LONG	1
9	WASHER – FLAT	$\frac{3}{16}$ LONG	4
10	NUT – WING	$\frac{3}{16}$ LONG	4
11	SCREW – RD. HD.	NO. 8 – $\frac{3}{4}$ LONG	2
12	RUBBER FOOT	$\frac{1}{2}$ DIA.	3
13	SCREW – RD. HD.	NO. 4 – $\frac{3}{4}$ LONG	3
14	SCREW – EYE		2
15	CHAIN	16 TO 18 LONG	1

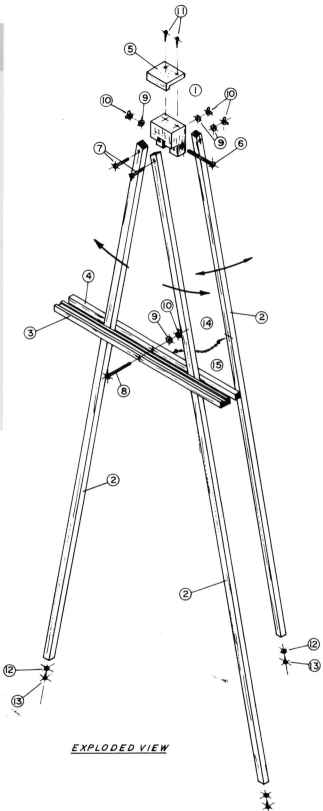

EXPLODED VIEW

Drill the $\frac{1}{4}$-inch-diameter holes in the support shelf (part 3) and brace (part 4). Cut or rout the groove, $\frac{1}{2}$ inch wide and $\frac{3}{16}$ inch deep, in the support shelf.

Drill two $\frac{1}{8}$-inch-diameter screw holes in the upper support (part 5) for the mounting screws (part 11). Put the support in place over the head and transfer the location of the screw holes to the head. Drill $\frac{1}{16}$-inch pilot holes in the head at these locations.

3. Apply finish. Sand thoroughly. Stain the easel if you wish, and apply a coat of varnish.

4. Assemble the easel. The exploded view shows how the pieces come together. The center leg is held in the center slot of the head with the $2\frac{1}{4}$-inch carriage bolt (part 6). The head of the bolt rests in the $\frac{1}{2}$-inch-diameter hole. Attach the other legs to the head with 2-inch carriage bolts (part 7). Attach the support shelf and brace with the $3\frac{1}{4}$-inch carriage bolt (part 8).

Attach the rubber feet (part 12) to the bottom of the legs. The chain (part 15) prevents the back leg from opening so far that it will threaten the stability of the easel. Attach it with eye screws (part 14) in the brace and back leg.

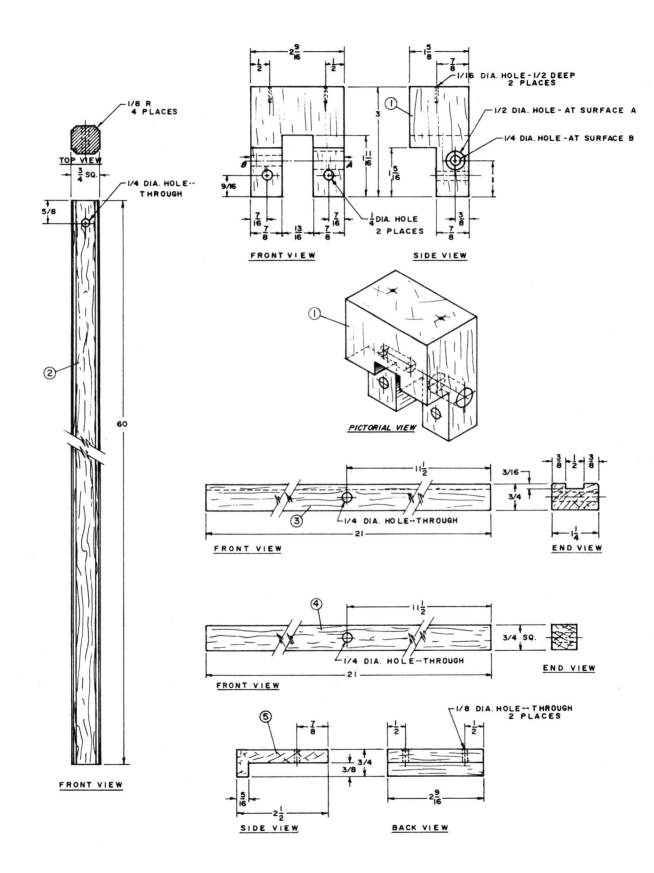

TOP VIEW

1/8 R
4 PLACES

3/4 SQ.

1/4 DIA. HOLE–
THROUGH

5/8

②

60

FRONT VIEW

2 9/16

1/2   1/2

①

3

1 11/16

1 5/16

9/16

B   A

7/16   7/16
7/8   13/16   7/8

1/4 DIA. HOLE
2 PLACES

FRONT VIEW

5/8

7/8

1/16 DIA. HOLE–1/2 DEEP
2 PLACES

1/2 DIA. HOLE – AT SURFACE A

1/4 DIA. HOLE – AT SURFACE B

1 5/16

3/8

7/8

SIDE VIEW

①

PICTORIAL VIEW

11 1/2

③

1/4 DIA. HOLE–THROUGH

21

FRONT VIEW

3/16

3/4

3/8 1/2 3/8

1 1/4

END VIEW

④

11 1/2

1/4 DIA. HOLE–THROUGH

21

FRONT VIEW

3/4 SQ.

END VIEW

⑤

7/8

1/8 DIA. HOLE–THROUGH
2 PLACES

3/4
3/8

1/2   1/2

5/16

2 1/2

SIDE VIEW

2 9/16

BACK VIEW

Children's Furniture & Accessories

What child wouldn't delight in having a chest of drawers or a rocking chair that's just the right height? These and other child-sized projects are sure to please that favorite little person in your life.

Cow Jumping Over Moon

This simple toy gives life to the poem, "Hey diddle, diddle, the cat and the fiddle, The cow jumped over the moon." It makes an interesting toy.

1. Transfer the shapes of the cow, moon, and base to ³⁄₄-inch-thick wood.

2. Cut out the cow, moon, and base, and sand all over.

3. Drill ¼-inch-diameter holes in the cow, moon, and base, as shown.

4. Assemble with a ¼-inch-diameter dowel cut to the lengths indicated. Paint to suit.

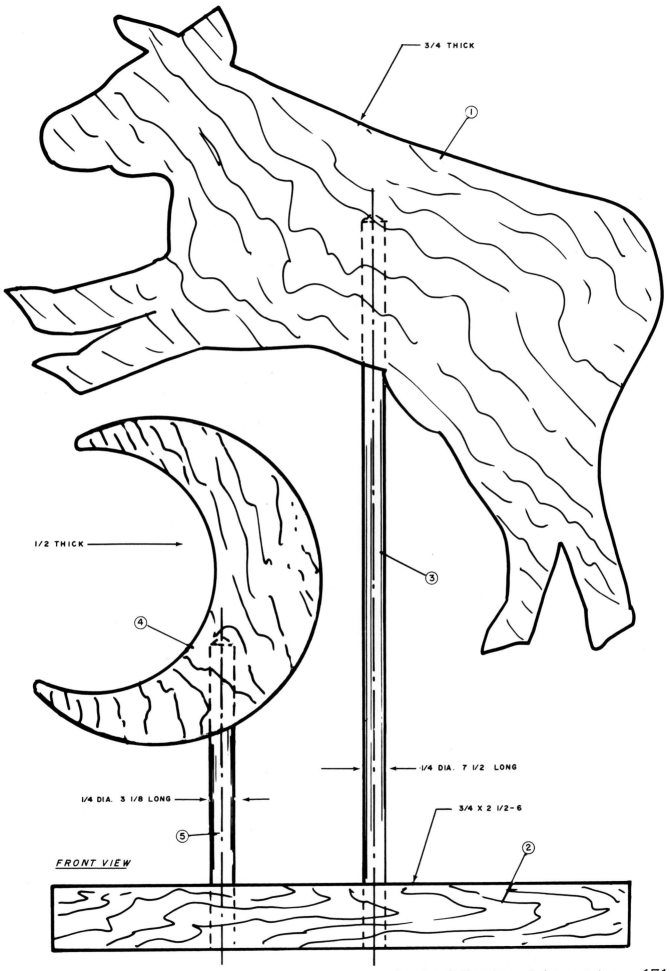

3/4 THICK

①

1/2 THICK →

③

④

1/4 DIA. 7 1/2 LONG

1/4 DIA. 3 1/8 LONG →

3/4 X 2 1/2-6

⑤

②

FRONT VIEW

Children's Furniture & Accessories   171

Dog Bookrack, c.1950

Although it's not an actual toy, this bookrack is a favorite with kids.

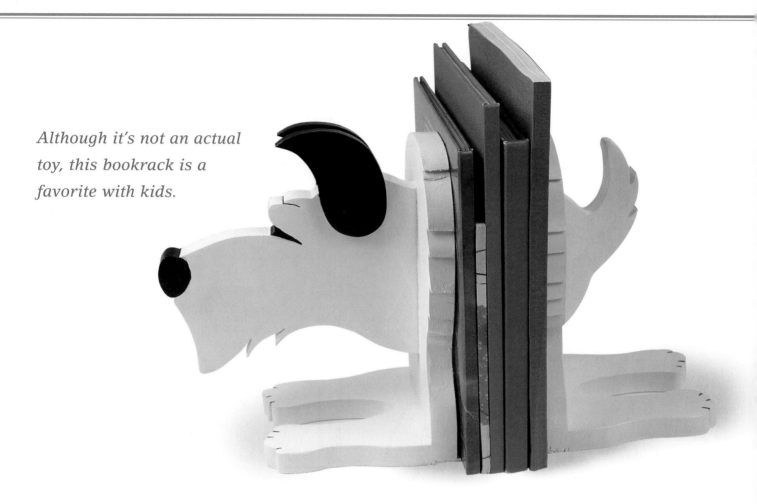

MATERIALS LIST			
NO.	NAME	SIZE	REQ'D.
1	BODY	¾ x 5½ X 10 LONG	2
2	HEAD	¾ x 6 – 8 LONG	1
3	TAIL	¾ x 3¼ – 6½ LONG	1
4	BASE (FOOT)	¾ x 5½ – 5¼ LONG	2
5	EAR	¼ x 2½ – 4¼ LONG	2
6	SUPPORT	¹⁄₁₆ x 5½ – 6 LONG	2
7	SCREW – FL. HD.	NO. 8 – 2 LONG	8

1. Cut all pieces to overall size, according to the cutting list.

2. On a 1-inch grid, lay out the detail of the various pieces.

3. Transfer the patterns to the wood, and carefully cut each piece out.

4. Sand all over.

5. Locate and drill all countersunk holes for the flathead screws (part 7).

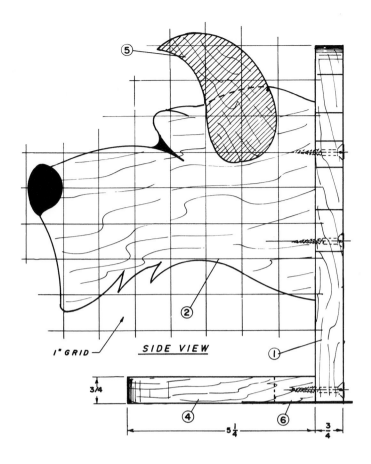

⑤

1" GRID

SIDE VIEW

② ①

3/4

④ ⑥

5¼ 3/4

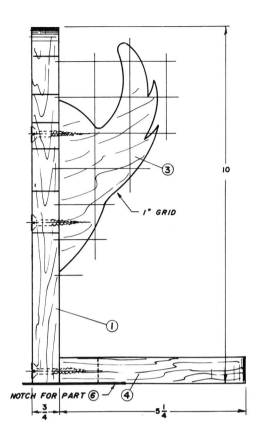

③

1" GRID

①

NOTCH FOR PART ⑥ ④

3/4 5¼

10

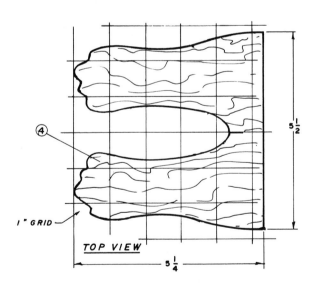

④

1" GRID

TOP VIEW

5½

5¼

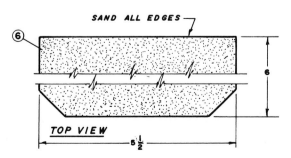

⑥

SAND ALL EDGES

TOP VIEW

6

5½

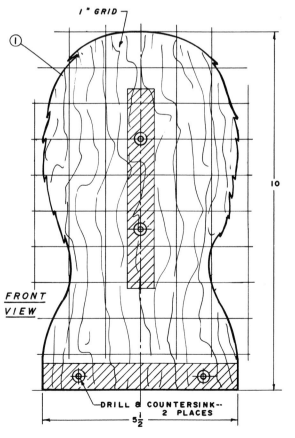

1" GRID

①

FRONT
VIEW

10

DRILL & COUNTERSINK--
2 PLACES

5½

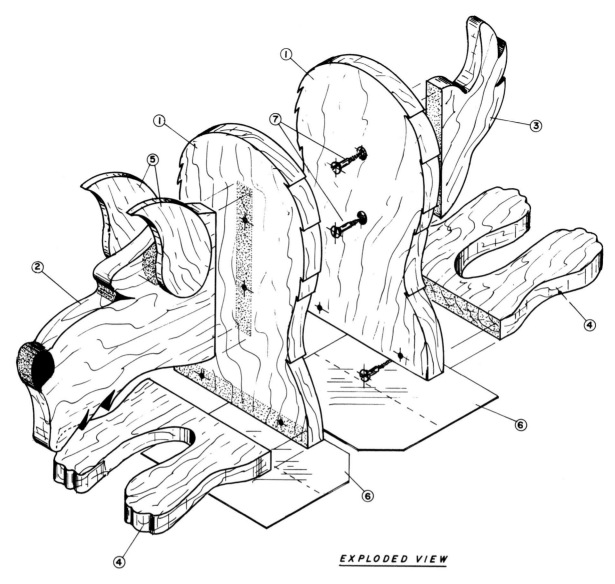

EXPLODED VIEW

6. The supports (part 6) are made from a thin piece of metal, approximately ¹⁄₁₆ inch thick. If you don't have materials or tools to prepare these supports, any sheet-metal shop can cut them for you from pieces of scrap metal.

7. Assemble all pieces, keeping everything square.

8. Epoxy the metal supports to the bottom, as shown.

9. Resand all over and round slightly to remove all sharp edges.

10. Paint to suit.

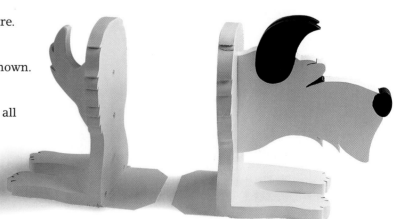

Child's Footstool

This footstool makes a great project for those who like rosemaling or tole painting. It should be made of a hardwood so that it will hold up under all conditions.

1. Draw a ½-inch grid on heavy paper or cardboard, and lay out the patterns for the seat, leg, and brace. On the seat pattern, locate the four screw holes.

Transfer the patterns to the wood, and cut them out. Note the two, parallel 15° cuts on the top and bottom ends of the two legs. Drill holes and countersink in the top and legs for the eight No. 8 screws.

2. Screw the stool together to check all fits, and make adjustments as necessary. When everything is all right, take the assembly completely apart again.

3. Using a router equipped with a ⅛ inch-radius cove-cutter bit that has a ball-bearing follower, cut the outer edge of the top, the lower edge of the brace, and the outside edges of the two legs, as shown in the exploded view.

4. Apply glue and screw the stool together. Check that the stool is sturdy enough for all conditions.

5. Finish this charming footstool as you desire.

MATERIALS LIST			
NO.	NAME	SIZE	REQ'D.
1	SEAT	¾ x 8⅜ – 10 LONG	1
2	LEG	¾ x 6½ – 5⅝ LONG	2
3	BRACE	¾ x 1⅞ – 6⅞ LONG	1
4	SCREW – FL. HD.	NO. 8 – 1¼ LONG	8

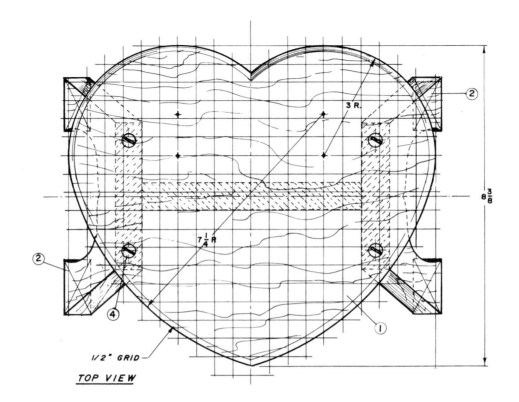

3 R.

7 1/4 R

1/2" GRID

TOP VIEW

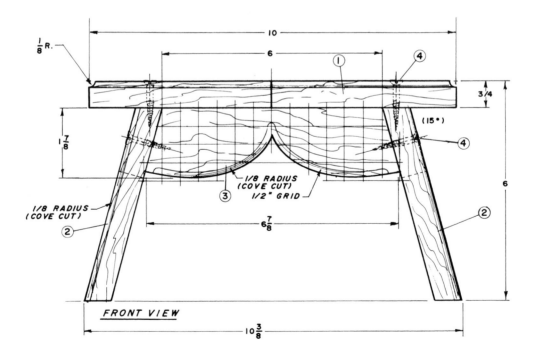

1/8 R.

10

6

3/4

(15°)

1 7/8

6

1/8 RADIUS
(COVE CUT)

1/2" GRID

1/8 RADIUS
(COVE CUT)

6 7/8

FRONT VIEW

10 3/8

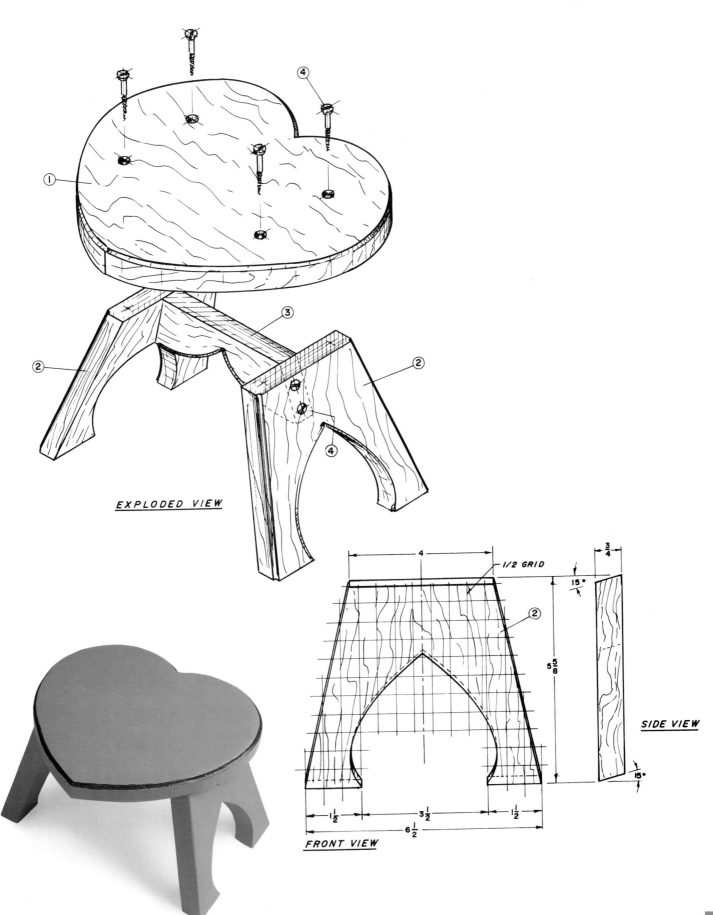

EXPLODED VIEW

④

①

②

③

②

④

1/2 GRID

2

4

3/4

15°

5 5/8

15°

SIDE VIEW

1 1/2

3 1/2

1 1/2

6 1/2

FRONT VIEW

Children's Furniture & Accessories   177

Piggy Bank

Having raised pigs in northern Vermont years ago, I really appreciate them. They are very smart, fun to have around, and, believe it or not, a very clean animal. This is a pig that you can take to the bank. Perhaps, if you're lucky, this project will instill thrift in your little ones.

You can paint it any color you like—I especially like a pink pig. Don't forget to add a new penny for luck!

MATERIALS LIST			
NO.	NAME	SIZE	REQ'D.
1	BODY/LEGS	$3/4$ x $5^1/2$ – $6^3/4$ LONG	2
2	CENTER	$1/2$ x $4^3/4$ – $7^1/4$ LONG	2
3	CENTER/SLOT	$1/4$ x $4^3/4$ – $7^1/4$ LONG	1
4	EAR	$1/8$ x $1^3/4$ – $2^1/2$ LONG	2
5	PLUG	$3/4$ DIA.	1
6	EYE (OVAL)	$5/8$ SIZE	2

1. Cut all parts to overall size, and sand the top and bottom surfaces.

Lay out the pieces on a 1-inch grid. Note: there are five pieces that make up the body; two $3/4$ inch thick, two $1/2$ inch thick, and one $1/4$ inch thick. Don't forget to lay out the interior cut for the center pieces (parts 2 and 3).

Transfer the patterns to the wood.

2. Cut out the center areas of the three center pieces (parts 2 and 3). Cut the tail in part 3 only.

Line up all pieces except the center piece (part 3) and cut away the wood where the tail would be. (Tail is only on center piece.)

Line up the three center pieces (parts 2 and 3) and cut away the wood where the legs would be.

Line up all of the pieces and glue them together.

3. Make the rest of the outer body cutout starting and ending in the tail section. (Don't forget to leave the tail on the center section and the legs on the two outer pieces.)

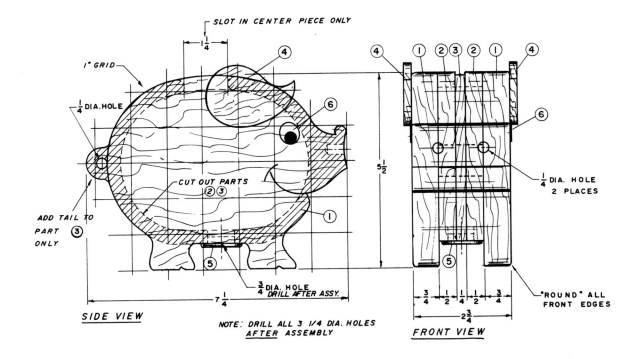

SIDE VIEW

NOTE: DRILL ALL 3 1/4 DIA. HOLES
AFTER ASSEMBLY

FRONT VIEW

4. Drill ¼-inch-diameter holes in the tail and nose.

Drill a ¾-inch-diameter hole up from the bottom for the plug.

Sand all over and round all edges slightly. (I used a ⅛-inch-radius router bit with a ball-bearing follower.)

5. Cut out and add the ears (part 4) as shown.

6. The eyes can either be painted on, or you can use ⅝-inch-diameter jiggling eyes that glue on. If small children might get their hands on this piggy bank, only use non-toxic paint for the eyes.

Add a plug, either a purchased rubber plug or one you make yourself.

Paint to suit.

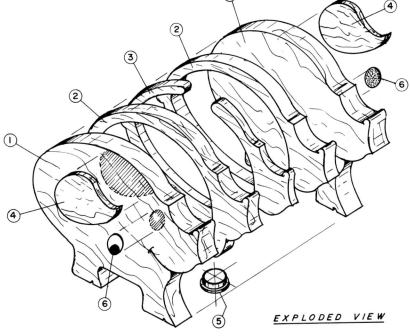

EXPLODED VIEW

Elephant Bank

I'm quite fond of elephants and have designed a number of projects using them as a motif. This particular animal is hollow, to store a child's coins. The bottom is attached with two screws that can be removed without too much trouble when it's time to withdraw the funds.

1. Select the stock. This elephant is something of a sandwich, with a hollowed-out body (part 1) capped by two sides (part 2). Cut the parts to the sizes given in the Materials List but don't glue them together yet.

2. Make a paper pattern. Draw a grid with ½-inch squares and enlarge the elephant, his ears (part 7), and his legs (parts 5 and 6) onto it. Be sure to locate the mortise for the ears, as shown in the side view. Transfer the patterns to the wood. Cut out the ears and legs but not the body or sides.

3. Hollow out the body. Cut the body along the dashed lines shown in the side view. Then cut the mortises for the ears in the side pieces: draw a line down the center of the mortise, and center a series of adjoining 7/16-inch holes along this line. Cut out the edges of the mortise with a sharp chisel. Check the fit of the ears as you chisel.

MATERIALS LIST

NO.	NAME	SIZE	REQ'D.
1	BODY	1 x 6½ – 7¼ LONG	1
2	SIDE	¼ – 6½ – 7¼ LONG	2
3	BOTTOM	¼ x 1 – 3 LONG	1
4	SCREW – RD. HD.	NO. 6 – 5/8 LONG	2
5	FRONT LEG	½ x 1½ – 1¾ LONG	2
6	REAR LEG	½ x 1½ – 2 LONG	2
7	EAR	½ x 2½ – 3¾ LONG	2
8	TAIL	1/8 DIA. – ¾ LONG	1
9	JIGGLE EYE		1 PR.

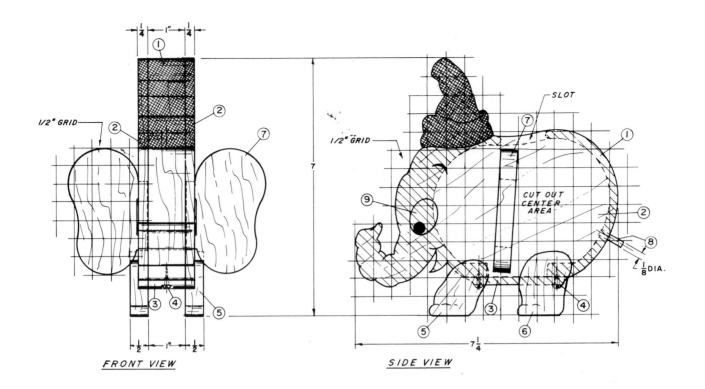

1/4 | 1" | 1/4

1/2" GRID

②

②

⑦

7

③ ④

⑤

1/2 | 1" | 1/2

FRONT VIEW

SLOT

⑦

1/2" GRID

⑨

①

CUT OUT CENTER AREA

②

⑧

1/8 DIA.

③

④

⑤

⑥

7 1/4

SIDE VIEW

4. Glue the sides to the body and cut to shape.

Screw the bottom to the elephant. Drill clearance holes slightly larger than the shank of the screw (part 4) in the bottom, and pilot holes slightly smaller than the screw shank in the body. Screw the bottom in place.

Cut out the outline of the body.

5. Add the ears, legs, and tail. Locate and cut out the slot for coins in the top of the body; you can first drill ⅛-inch-diameter holes at either end of the slot and then saw out the portion in between.

The legs are notched and then attached to the body as shown in the exploded view. To lay out the notch, place a ¾-inch piece of wood between the bottom of the elephant and the workbench. This puts the elephant at the height it will be when the legs are attached. Hold a leg in place with the foot flat on the bench, and trace the outline of the bottom and sides on the leg. Use a fine-tooth saw or chisel to cut the notches. Repeat for the remaining legs. Glue the legs in place.

Drill a ⅛-inch-diameter hole at an angle for the tail (part 8), as shown in the side view, and glue the tail in

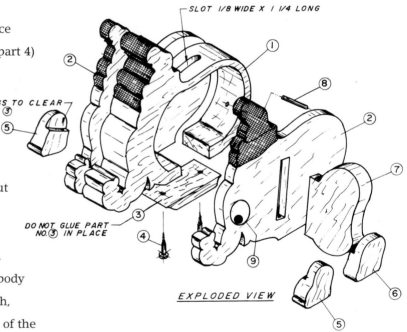

SLOT 1/8 WIDE X 1 1/4 LONG

②

NOTCH LEGS TO CLEAR PART NO. ③

⑤

DO NOT GLUE PART NO. ③ IN PLACE

③

④

⑨

①

⑧

②

⑦

⑥

⑤

EXPLODED VIEW

place. Glue the ears in place, making sure they are in line with each other.

Sand thoroughly.

6. Apply finish. Remove the bottom. Decorate the elephant with nontoxic paints. Reattach the bottom. Attach the jiggle eyes (part 9).

Child's Wall Clock

Here's another favorite elephant project of mine. You'll note that the basic pattern is the same as the previous one for the Elephant Bank.

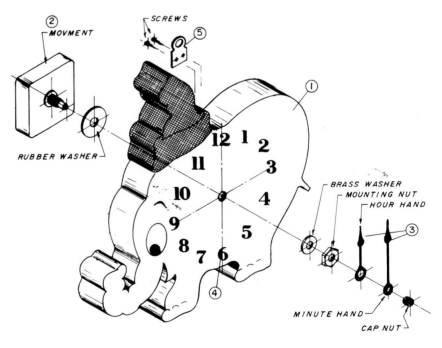

MATERIALS LIST

NO.	NAME	SIZE	REQ'D.
1	BODY	¾ x 9½ – 9½ LONG	1
2	QUARTZ MOVEMENT		1
3	HANDS		1 PR.
4	NUMBERS		1 SET
5	HANGER		1

1. Select the stock and transfer the pattern. Pine is a good choice for this project. If you haven't already made a paper pattern, make one now. Draw a grid with ½-inch squares and enlarge the elephant's body onto it. Transfer the pattern to the stock and cut the elephant (part 1) to shape.

The hole for the clock's hand shaft must be centered in the hole for the movement. Locate the center of the hand shaft on the clock and drill a ¹⁄₁₆ inch-diameter hole through the body This establishes the center of both the hand shaft and movement holes. From the back, drill or rout a ⅝-inch x 3-inch-diameter hole centered on this mark.

Drill a ⁵⁄₁₆-inch-diameter hole from the front, using the ¹⁄₁₆-inch-diameter hole as a guide.

Sand thoroughly.

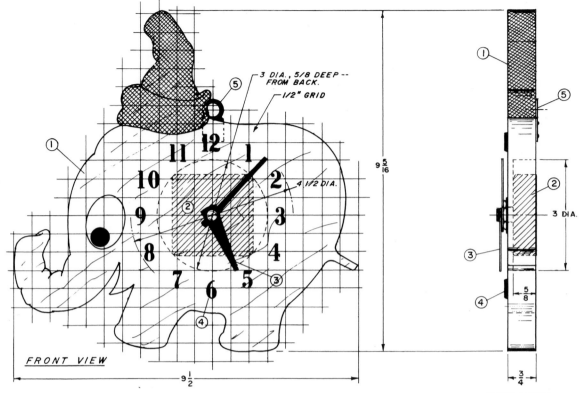

3 DIA., 5/8 DEEP -- FROM BACK.

1/2" GRID

4 1/2 DIA.

$9\frac{5}{16}$

$9\frac{1}{2}$

FRONT VIEW

3 DIA.

$\frac{5}{8}$

$\frac{3}{4}$

SIDE VIEW

2. Apply finish. Paint the clock any colors that appeal to you. Attach the hanger, as shown.

3. Add the numbers. Lay out the numbers (part 4) of the clock so that they all fall within a 4½ inch circle, as shown. Enlarge the dial face template on a photocopier to help you position the numbers. Mark the location of the numbers, remove the template, and glue the numbers just inside the circle. Keep the numbers upright, as shown on the elephant drawings, so that they can be read more easily

4. As directed by the instructions that come with the clock movement, install it, put the hands in place, and add the battery.

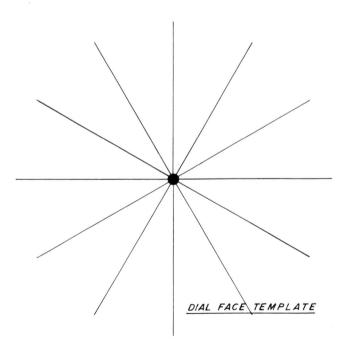

DIAL FACE TEMPLATE

Doll Chair

Here's a replica of a small chair I saw hanging on a wall outside an antique shop in New Hope, Pennsylvania. I especially liked the dovetail joint holding the sides together. The original was painted and very weathered. I'm not sure how the original chair was used, but this one will make a great doll's chair.

Don't worry about making the dovetail joints; they are really quite easy to make. If you've never cut a dovetail joint before, this is just the project to practice on.

1. Study the plans carefully. Note how each part is to be shaped. As you study the plans, try to visualize how you will make each part.

The two sides, back, and brace (parts 1, 2, and 3) are irregular in shape and will have to be laid out on ½-inch grids to make full-size patterns. Lay out the grids on heavy paper or cardboard, and transfer the shape of each piece to the appropriate grid, point by point.

2. Carefully cut all of the parts to overall size according to the Materials List. Take care to cut all parts to exact size and exactly square (90°). Stop and recheck all dimensions before going on.

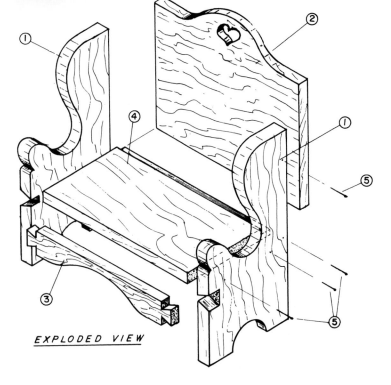

EXPLODED VIEW

MATERIALS LIST			
NO.	NAME	SIZE	REQ'D.
1	SIDE	¾ x 5⅜ – 10½ LONG	2
2	BACK	¾ x 9¼ – 8 LONG	1
3	BRACE	¾ x 1⅝ – 10¾ LONG	1
4	SEAT	¾ x 5½ – 9¼ LONG	1
5	NAIL - FINISH	6 d	14

3. Lightly sand all surfaces and edges with medium sandpaper to remove any burrs and all tool marks. Take care to keep all edges square and sharp at this time.

4. Transfer the full-size patterns to the wood, and cut out. Check all dimensions for accuracy. Resand all over with fine grit sandpaper, still keeping all edges sharp. It is a good idea to make the two sides (part 1) while they are either tacked or taped together so that you have a pair of exactly matching sides.

5. Carefully lay out and cut out the tail and pin of the dovetails in the side and brace pieces (parts 1 and 3).

6. After all of the pieces have been carefully made, dry-fit all of the parts; that is, put the complete project together without glue or nails to check for accuracy and good-fitting joints. If anything needs refitting, now is the time to correct it. Once all of the parts fit together correctly, assemble the project starting with the two sides and brace. Then, fit the other parts to these pieces. Keep everything square as you go. Check that all fits are tight.

7. Finish to suit, following the general finishing instructions given in the introduction.

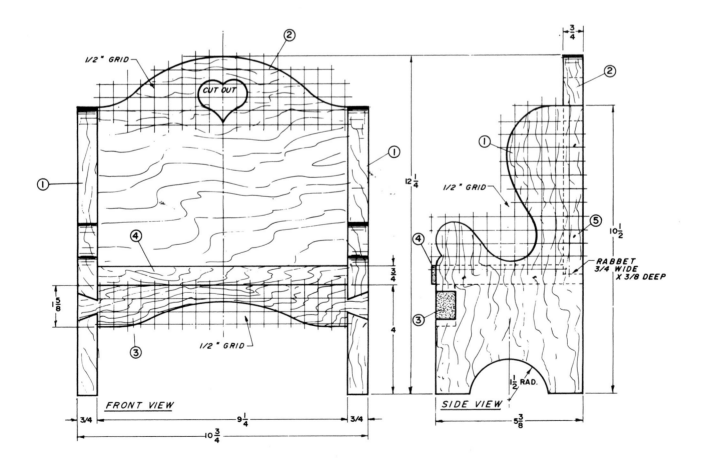

FRONT VIEW

SIDE VIEW

Child's Bench

This bench is a scaled-down version of a sleigh bench that was used for an extra seat in a horse-drawn open sleigh years ago. These slightly decorated sleigh benches were especially popular in Pennsylvania. Today this smaller version makes an excellent bench for a child's room. This project can be made of either soft or hard wood as its design produces a very sturdy construction.

MATERIALS LIST			
NO.	NAME	SIZE	REQ'D.
1	END	3/4 x 7½ – 12 LONG	2
2	SUPPORT	3/4 x 1½ – 5¾ LONG	2
3	SEAT	3/4 x 7½ – 12 LONG	1
4	SKIRT	3/4 x 1½ – 12 LONG	2
5	SCREW – FL. HD.	NO. 8 – 1¼ LONG	6
6	FINISH NAIL	6 d	14

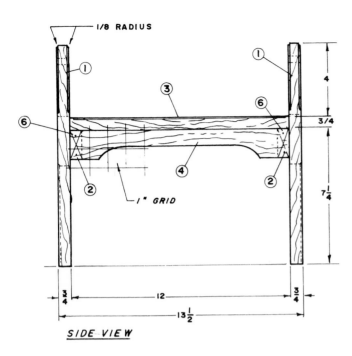

SIDE VIEW

END VIEW

1. Cut all the pieces to overall size, and sand all edges. Lay out the patterns for the ends and skirt. Transfer the patterns to the wood, and cut them out.

2. Using a router bit with a ⅛-inch-radius cove-cutter and ball-bearing follower, rout the top edge of the ends, the arched leg sections, and the seat, as shown in the drawings.

3. Locate and attach the seat supports to the ends. Glue and screw these in place. Note: the supports should be ¾ inch in from each side. Glue the skirt pieces and seat to the ends. Check that everything is square.

4. Finish to match the room in which you will put this bench, if possible.

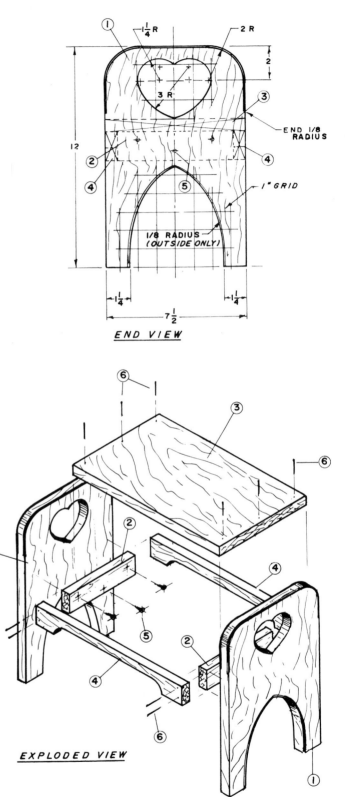

EXPLODED VIEW

Turtle Footstool

Here's my version of an interesting footstool I saw at an outdoor flea market a few years ago. It looked to be homemade. I didn't want to buy it, but the dealer didn't mind my taking a photo and a few overall measurements, so here's my take on it. I would guess the original was made in the 1940s. This footstool will brighten up any child's room.

1. Cut all pieces to overall size.

2. Transfer the shapes to the wood, and cut them out. Sand the edges as needed.

3. Using a ⅛-inch-radius cove cutter with a ball-bearing follower, make the cut around the seat (part 1).

4. Assemble according to the drawing of the exploded view.

5. Here's where you can really show off your creative abilities by painting your turtle in either a realistic or funky fashion.

		MATERIALS LIST	
NO.	**NAME**	**SIZE**	**REQ'D.**
1	SEAT	¾ x 9 – 9 LONG	1
2	LEG	¾ x 4¾ – 11½ LONG	2
3	HEAD	¾ x 2½ – 7 LONG	1
4	TAIL	¾ x 1½ – 6⅜ LONG	1
5	FINISH NAIL	6 d	12
6	EYE OVAL	⅝ SIZE	1 PR.

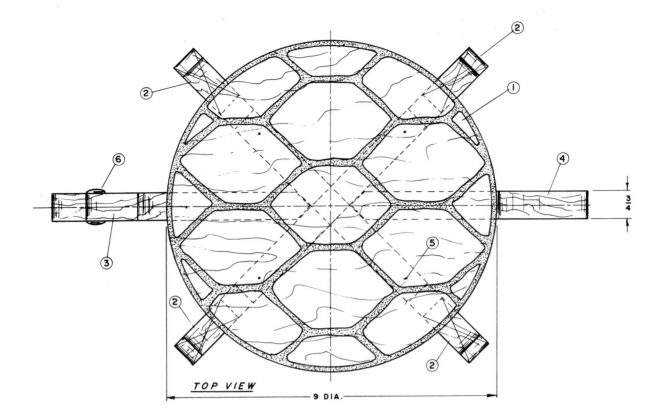

TOP VIEW

9 DIA.

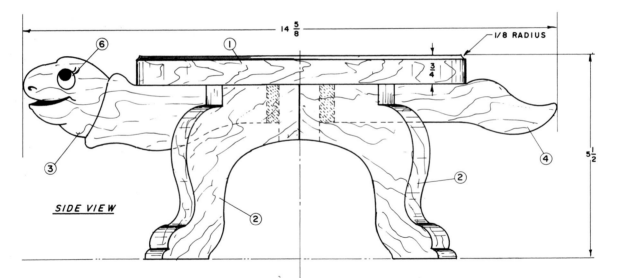

14 5/8

1/8 RADIUS

3/4

SIDE VIEW

5 1/2

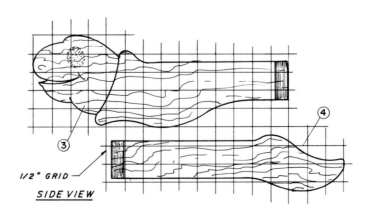

1/2" GRID

SIDE VIEW

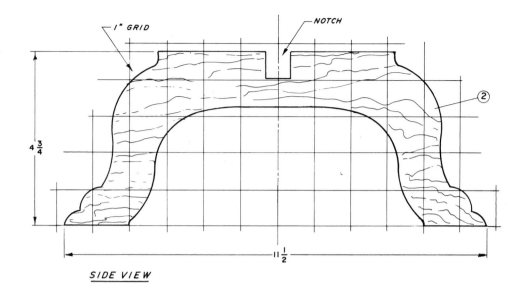

1" GRID

NOTCH

4 3/4

11 1/2

SIDE VIEW

②

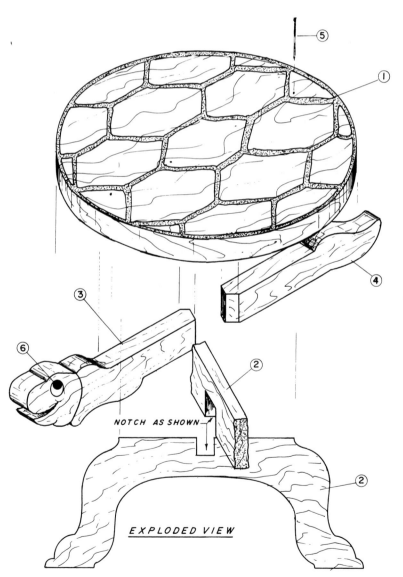

⑤

①

④

③

⑥

NOTCH AS SHOWN

②

②

EXPLODED VIEW

Dog Seat

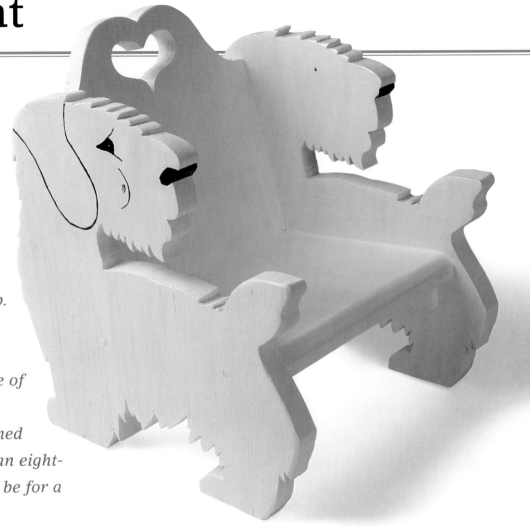

This is a neat project for any child's room. Most children like dogs, so here's one that will earn its keep. Its width can be changed slightly to accommodate the size of the child you want to make it for. The finished project pictured has an eight-inch seat. This would be for a very small toddler.

1. Lay out the side (part 1) using a 1-inch grid, and cut out two sides. Locate and drill the six holes for the screws (parts 4 and 5). Sand all over.

2. Cut the back (part 2), two supports (part 3), and seat (part 4) to size. Sand all over.

3. Glue and screw the two supports (part 3) to the sides (part 1).

4. Glue and screw the back (part 2) and seat (part 4) in place. Take care to keep everything square. Be sure all four feet sit flat on the floor.

5. Paint to suit, using non-toxic paint.

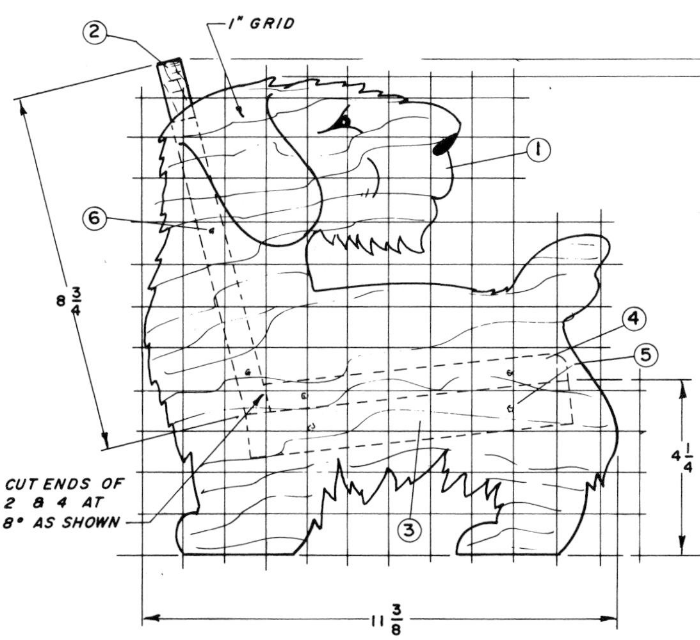
1" GRID
8 3/4
11 3/8
4 1/4
CUT ENDS OF 2 & 4 AT 8° AS SHOWN

SIDE VIEW

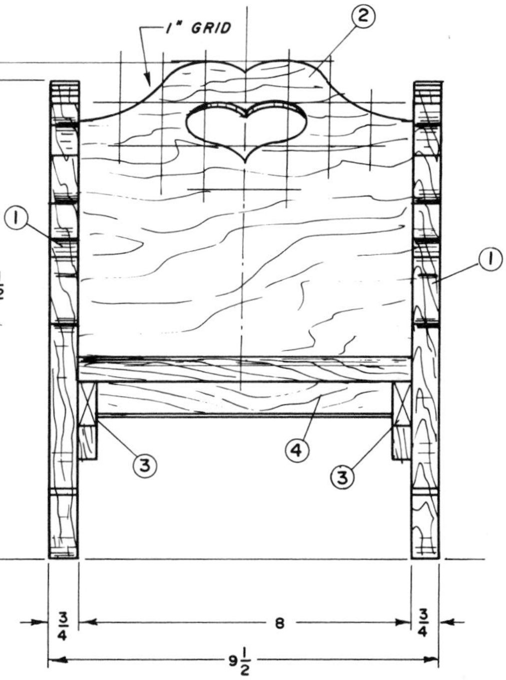
1" GRID
11 1/2
3/4
8
3/4
9 1/2

FRONT VIEW

MATERIALS LIST

NO.	NAME	SIZE	REQ'D.
1	SIDE	¾ x 11½ – 11⅜ LONG	2
2	BACK	¾ x 8¾ – 8 LONG	1
3	SUPPORT	½ x 1¼ – 8 LONG	2
4	SEAT	¾ x 7½ – 8 LONG	1
5	SCREW – FL. HD.	NO. 8 – 1 LONG	4
6	SCREW – FL. HD.	NO. 8 – 2 LONG	10

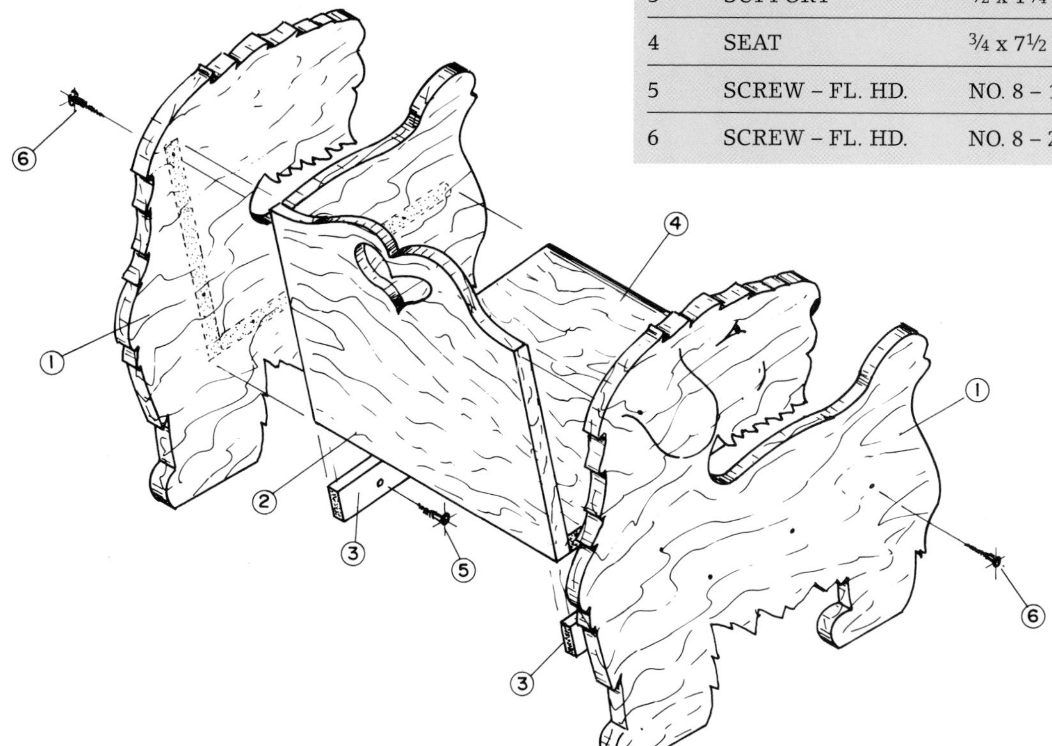

EXPLODED VIEW

Child's Small Chest of Drawers

The original chest of drawers from which this project is drawn was made expressly for Master Joseph Warren of Boston, Massachusetts, in 1745. He used the chest of drawers as his toy chest. Incidentally, Warren later became a doctor and eventually lost his life at the battle of Bunker Hill in 1775, at the age of 34. Today, this small chest of drawers can be used as a jewelry box or even as a child's toy chest—just as the original chest was.

MATERIALS LIST

NO.	NAME	SIZE	REQ'D.
1	SIDE	⅜ x 4⅛ – 5¾ LONG	2
2	DIVIDER	¼ x 3⅞ – 5¾ LONG	3
3	BACK	¼ x 5½ – 5¾ LONG	1
4	TOP	⅜ x 4½ – 7 LONG	1
5	SKIRT - FRONT	⅜ x 1¼ – 4½ LONG	1
6	SKIRT - SIDE	⅜ x 1¼ – 4½ LONG	2
7	FRONT	⅜ x 1¼ – 5½ LONG	1
8	SIDE	¼ x 1¼ – 3⅝ LONG	2
9	BACK	¼ x 1¼ – 5¼ LONG	1
10	BOTTOM	¼ x 3½ – 5½ LONG	3
11	FRONT	⅜ x 1½ – 5½ LONG	1
12	SIDE	¼ x 1½ – 3⅝ LONG	2
13	BACK	¼ x 1½ – 5¼ LONG	1
14	FRONT	⅜ x 2⅛ – 3⅝ LONG	1
15	SIDE	¼ x 2⅛ – 3⅝ LONG	2
16	BACK	¼ x 2⅛ – 5¼ LONG	1
17	PULL	⅜ DIA. – ¹³⁄₁₆ LONG	6
18	PIN	⅜ LONG	6

1. Cut all of the pieces to exact size and sand all edges. Important: be sure to make a right-hand and left-hand pair of sides. Carefully locate and cut the three ¼-inch-wide x ⅛-inch-deep dadoes in each side. Cut the ¼-inch-wide x ⅛-inch-deep rabbet on the back edge of the sides. Using a ¼-inch-radius cove cutter, cut the cove around the two ends and front of the top. Glue together the sides, dividers, and back. Sand all over.

2. Using a ¼-inch grid, lay out the leg detail, as shown in the side view. Using a router bit with an ogee cutter, cut the top edge of the front and side skirt. Temporarily fit the front and two side skirts to the case using a 45° miter cut at the corners, as shown. Remove the skirts and transfer the leg pattern to each skirt. Cut them out, and permanently reattach the skirts. Add the top.

3. Make up the drawers to fit the openings. The drawers are the flush type, but they should fit with a little room for any expansion.

The six pulls can be turned to the ⅜-inch diameter. I made mine up from ⅜-inch-diameter dowel. The original drawer pulls were pinned in place, as shown; I did not use the pins, but simply glued the pulls in place instead.

4. Distress very lightly; resand all over. A stain should be used, followed by a coat of satin-finish tung oil or Danish oil.

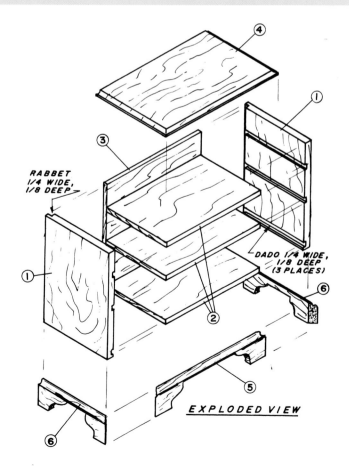

RABBET 1/4 WIDE, 1/8 DEEP

DADO 1/4 WIDE, 1/8 DEEP (3 PLACES)

EXPLODED VIEW

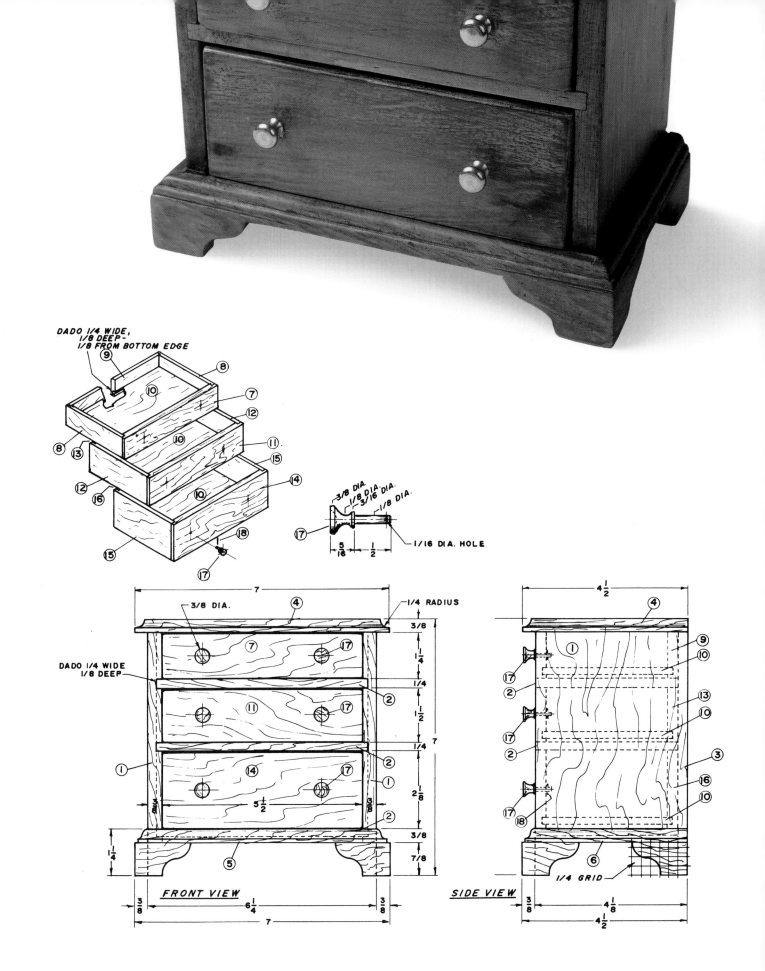

DADO 1/4 WIDE,
1/8 DEEP-
1/8 FROM BOTTOM EDGE

3/8 DIA.
1/8 DIA.
3/16 DIA.
1/8 DIA.

1/16 DIA. HOLE

5/16   1/2

3/8 DIA.

1/4 RADIUS

3/8

DADO 1/4 WIDE
1/8 DEEP

1 1/4

1/4

1 1/2

1/4

2 1/8

3/8

7/8

7

5 1/2

1 1/4

3/8   6 1/4   3/8

7

FRONT VIEW

4 1/2

9

10

13

10

3

16

10

6

1/4 GRID

3/8   4 1/8

4 1/2

SIDE VIEW

Child's Winged Rocking Chair

Historically, the rocking chair is attributed to Benjamin Franklin around 1770. Children's rocking chairs of this design were used from around 1790 to 1825 or so.

The high back and wings were added to ward off drafts. Usually located near and facing towards the fireplace, this chair kept the child warm, toasty, and protected on both sides from the cold. Children's rockers such as this one are very popular with just about everyone because they are still functional, will fit into any Early American decor, and add warmth to any room. The heart-shape cutout was a handhold so the rocker could be carried from place to place. Many antique children's chairs feature these cutout heart shapes.

If you collect dolls, this rocking chair, made half-size, would make an excellent way to display them. To make the rocker half-size, simply use ⅜-inch-thick material, halve all dimensions, and make the layout squares ½ inch instead of 1 inch.

| \multicolumn{4}{c}{MATERIALS LIST} |
NO.	NAME	SIZE	REQ'D.
1	BACK	⅝ x 8⅞ – 28 LONG	1
2	SIDE	⅝ x 8⅝ – 24½ LONG	2
3	SEAT	⅝ x 8¾ – 10⅞ LONG	1
4	NAIL – SQ. CUT	1¾ LONG	AS REQ'D.
5	ROCKER	¾ x 4 – 19 LONG	2

1. As with any woodworking project, carefully study all of the drawings to make sure that you fully see and understand how the chair is made and put together. On a piece of cardboard, draw 1-inch squares and carefully transfer the shapes of the parts exactly as illustrated. Carefully cut out the patterns and transfer the shapes to the wood. Cut the dadoes, $3/16$ inch deep x 5/8 inch wide, on the back (part 1) and sides (part 2) before cutting out the outer shape. After the dadoes have been made, cut out the shape of the parts, following the patterns. Note: The sides (part 2) must be a matching pair—one left-hand and one right-hand; be sure the dadoes are positioned correctly. Note also that the dadoes stop $3/8$ inch from the back edge as shown— see the plans.

2. Cut the seat (part 3) as shown, taking care that the grain is going the correct direction and that you hold the $10^7/8$-inch dimension as shown. Cut or plane the 6° angle into the back (part 1) as shown.

3. Cut and sand the rockers (part 5) as a pair, taking care that the $28^1/2$-inch-radius arc is continuous and does not have any flat spots in its entire length. Mark the front end of the rockers for identification, as the front end is slightly different from the back end. The pieces must be assembled with fronts facing the front of the rocker. You might want to cut out the top notch after you assemble the back, sides, and seat so that you will have a good, tight fit.

Dry-fit all of the parts to check that they all fit and go together correctly.

4. The back (part 1) and the sides (part 2) should fit exactly into the seat (part 3). Trim as necessary to ensure a tight fit. The sides (part 2) should fit into the 6° cut into the back (part 1), and the rabbets in these parts should fit nicely into the seat (part 3). Glue and nail together, once everything fits correctly.

5. Add the rockers (parts 5) along the sides of the seat (part 3). Glue and nail the assembly together taking care that the two fronts of the rockers are facing towards the front of the seat and parallel to the side edges of the seat.

After assembly, sand all over.

6. Distress lightly as you wish, and stain with a stain of your choice. Apply two or three coats of satin-finish tung oil. After this has thoroughly dried, steel wool the entire rocker with 0000 steel wool. Apply a coat of paste wax.

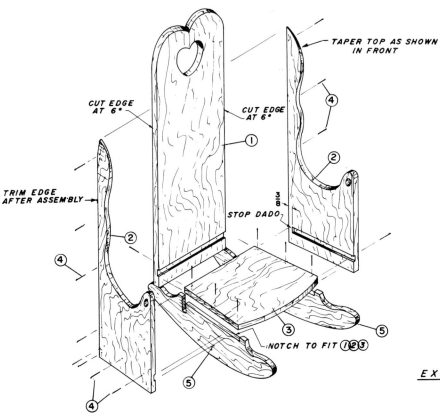

EXPLODED VIEW

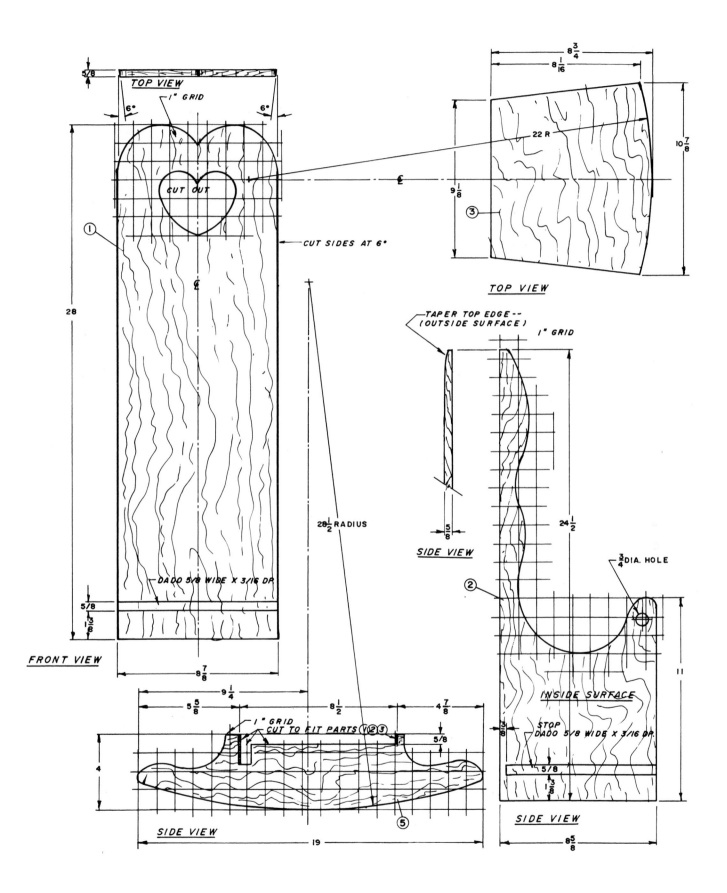

TOP VIEW

1" GRID

6°   6°

CUT OUT

CUT SIDES AT 6°

28

5/8

1 3/8

FRONT VIEW

8 7/8

①

℄

DADO 5/8 WIDE X 3/16 DP.

8 3/4

8 1/16

22 R

10 7/8

℄

9 1/8

③

TOP VIEW

TAPER TOP EDGE --
(OUTSIDE SURFACE)

1" GRID

SIDE VIEW

5/8

24 1/2

3/4 DIA. HOLE

②

INSIDE SURFACE

STOP
DADO 5/8 WIDE X 3/16 DP.

3/8

11

5/8

1 3/8

8 5/8

SIDE VIEW

28 1/2 RADIUS

9 1/4

5 5/8   8 1/2   4 7/8

1" GRID
CUT TO FIT PARTS ① ② ③

5/8

4

SIDE VIEW

⑤

19

Book House, c.1925

The original of this unusual book-case design was found in Surry, New Hampshire. It was sold by the Christian Scientists back in the 1920s. Books, I feel, are an important toy for children of all ages. This makes a neat place to store your child's reading materials. I would suggest you make it out of high-grade plywood.

MATERIALS LIST			
NO.	NAME	SIZE	REQ'D.
1	END	3/8 x 11 3/4 – 19 1/2 LONG	2
2	BASE	3/4 x 11 – 12 1/2 LONG	1
3	BACK	1/2 x 12 13/16 – 12 1/2 LONG	1
4	ROOF – FRONT	3/8 x 8 5/8 – 14 LONG	1
5	ROOF – BACK	3/8 x 13 3/8 – 14 LONG	1
6	CHIMNEY	3/4 x 3 5/8 – 4 LONG	2
7	FOOT	1/2 DIA.	4
8	BRAD	1 LONG	AS REQ'D.

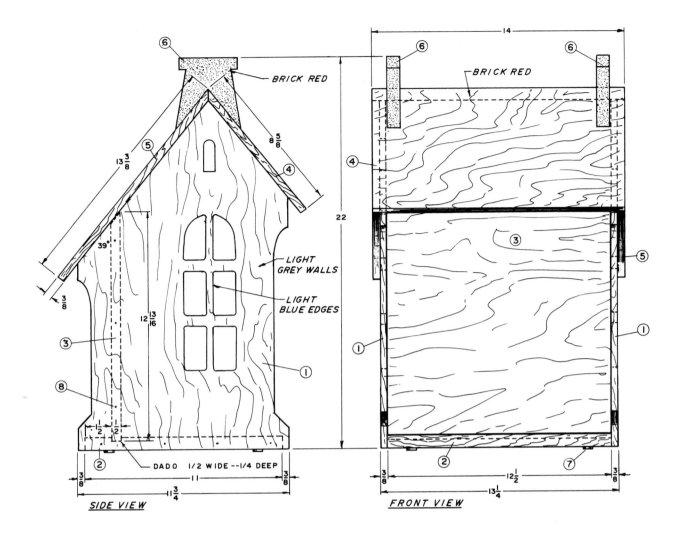

SIDE VIEW

BRICK RED

LIGHT GREY WALLS

LIGHT BLUE EDGES

DADO 1/2 WIDE --1/4 DEEP

FRONT VIEW

BRICK RED

1. Cut all pieces to overall size according to the Materials List. Use high-grade plywood for the ends (part 1), back (part 3), and roof (parts 4 and 5).

2. Using the detailed plan, lay out the ends (part 1) and cut out and sand all edges. (Temporarily tack the two sides together before cutting and sanding

3. Make the ½-inch-wide x ¼-inch-deep dado in the base (part 2) 1½ inches back from back edge, as shown.

4. Cut the top edge of the back (part 3) at an angle of 39°, as shown.

5. Cut the top edges of the roof pieces (parts 4 and 5) at an angle as close to 39° as you can manage.

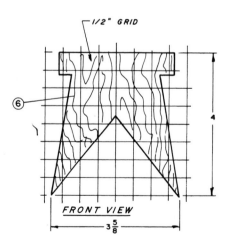

1/2" GRID

FRONT VIEW

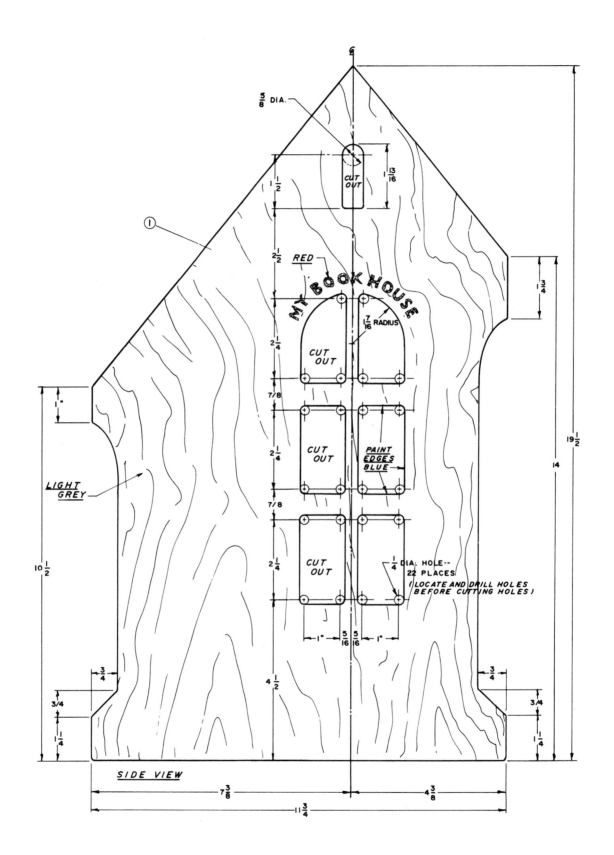

SIDE VIEW

6. Lay out and cut out the chimney (part 6).

7. Assemble all pieces with glue and nails. Set nails, and fill all nail holes.

8. Sand all over; round all sharp edges.

9. Paint to suit. The original was painted light gray with edges of light bone; the roof was brick red. It had My Book House lettered above the window, as shown. Once the paint has dried, add four rubber feet (part 7).

CUT AT 39°

DADO $\frac{1}{2}$ WIDE $\frac{1}{4}$ DEEP

EXPLODED VIEW

Hooded Doll Cradle

This hooded doll rocker is fun to make and will provide countless hours of play and a nook for a child to place a favorite doll to sleep at night.

Years ago, almost everyone believed that night air promoted lung disorders. Cradles such as this one, therefore, were made with solid sides, side wings, and hoods in order to ward off those dangerous drafts of the night. Full-size cradles were made as far back as 1660, but most of the ones we see today are from the 1800s. It is unusual to find a small doll cradle such as this one.

The cradle has simple flowing lines and follows the traditional lines of cradles made around the turn of the twentieth century. The original was made of pine in the New England area. Some were made of poplar, and many were painted. This model rocks from side to side, as was most common. However, some people of the time thought that rockers should be positioned lengthwise to deter colic. Although rockers had been used on cradles throughout the world, it was some time before anyone thought to add rockers to adults' chairs.

1. Carefully study all of the drawings to make sure that you fully see and understand how the cradle is made and put together.

I used regular No. 2 knotty pine for the cradle I made, but if I make another, I will be sure to use knot-free, No. 1 pine. I think it looks better. Note that the sides of the original cradle I copied were made in two pieces, so I made mine in two pieces. If you wish to eliminate a step, use one 9½-inch-wide piece of wood instead of gluing up two pieces as I did. If you have a biscuit joiner, use biscuits in place of the three dowels (part 4C), as shown.

Cut all of the pieces to size according to the Materials List. If you do not have a planer you will have to have the stock custom-planed to the required ⅜-inch thickness. Perhaps you can have this done at a local high school wood shop.

Lay out full-size patterns for the sides (parts 4A and 4B), the rocker (part 2), and the roof support (part 7). Transfer these patterns to the wood, and cut out the pieces.

2. Carefully lay out the foot and head (parts 5 and 6) according to the given dimensions. Be sure the bottom areas of both are exactly the same shape. The drawing shows the two pieces drawn on top of each other. Cut the bottom edges of both at 4°, as shown.

Note: the top and bottom edges of the assembled sides (parts 4A, 4B, and 4C) are cut at 10°. Important: be sure to make one right-hand and one left-hand side.

3. Assemble the two sides (part 4) to the foot (part 5) and head (part 6). Plane and/or sand the bottom for the assembly so that you have a flat surface along the bottom edges.

4. Assemble the cradle with glue and square-cut nails, keeping everything square and tight. Take care not to get glue on exposed surfaces, and wipe off any excess glue immediately. Attach the rockers (parts 2 and 3) to the bottom board (part 1), about 11⅜ inches apart, as shown on the plans. Add the bottom assembly to the side, foot, and head assembly.

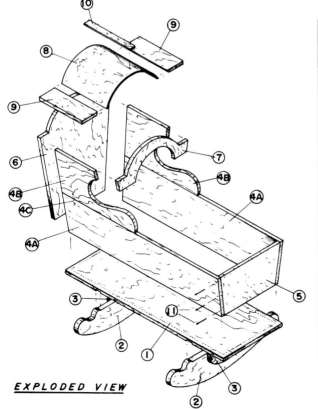

EXPLODED VIEW

NO.	NAME	SIZE	REQ'D.
	MATERIALS LIST		
1	BASE	⁷⁄₁₆ x 7¾ – 20⅝ LONG	1
2	ROCKER	⅝ x 2½ – 14¹⁵⁄₁₆ LONG	2
3	BRACE	¼ x 2⅛ – 5 LONG	2
4A	SIDE – BOTTOM	⅜ x 4½ – 20¾ LONG	2
4B	SIDE – TOP	⅜ x 5 – 9½ LONG	1
4C	PIN	³⁄₁₆ DIA. – 1 LONG	6
5	FOOT	⅜ x 7⅞ – 4½ LONG	1
6	HEAD	⅜ x 9⁹⁄₁₆ – 11⅞ LONG	1
7	ROOF SUPPORT	⅜ x 9⁹⁄₁₆ – 3¹³⁄₁₆ LONG	1
8	ROOF – CENTER	¼ x 9½ – 6¼ LONG	1
9	ROOF – SIDE	⅜ x 1⅞ – 6¼ LONG	2
10	ROOF – TRIM	³⁄₁₆ x ¾ – 6¼ LONG	1
11	NAIL – SQ. CUT	⅞ LONG	AS REQ'D.

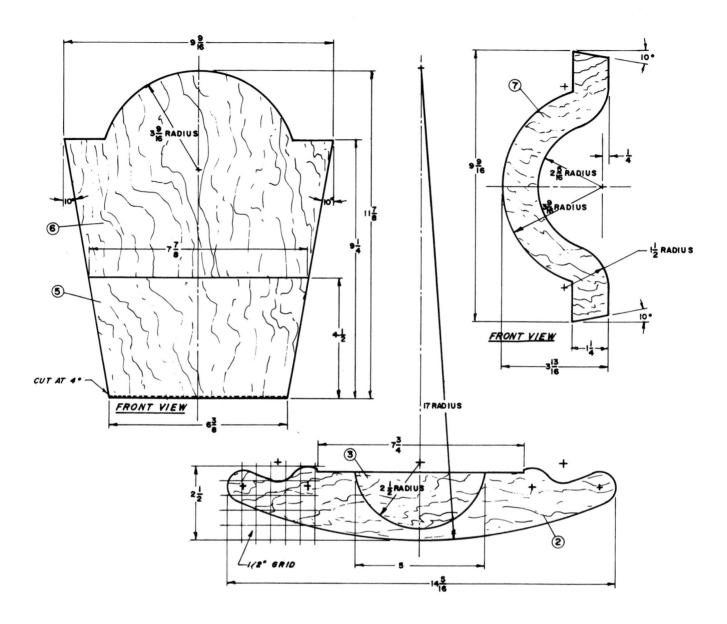

Attach the roof support (part 7) to the cradle assembly. Glue and clamp the center roof (part 8) in place. I made a series of parallel saw kerfs about 1/8 inch apart on the inside surface to make the bending easier. Note: The original cradle did not have these saw kerfs—the maker probably steam-bent its top. You can either steam-bend the top or make the saw kerfs.

After the glue sets, add the two roof sides (part 9). Last, add the roof trim (part 10).

5. After assembly, sand all over; distress lightly—remember, your reproduction should look 150 years old. The original cradle was painted a light powder blue inside and barn red outside.

After the paint dries, sand over with fine sandpaper; try to sand through the edges slightly where there would normally be wear. Rub the entire cradle, inside and out, with 0000 steel wool. Apply a top coat of light walnut stain over the paint—this will really add years to your cradle. Apply a coat of paste wax.

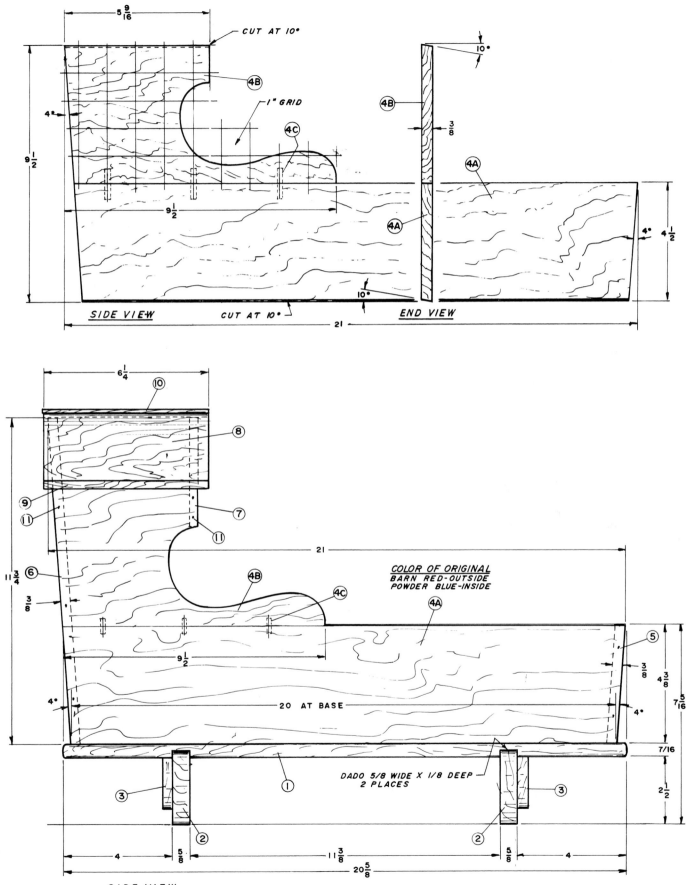

5 9/16

CUT AT 10°

4B

1" GRID

4C

4°

9 1/2

9 1/2

SIDE VIEW   CUT AT 10°

10°

4B

3/8

4A

4A

END VIEW

10°

4°   4 1/2

21

6 1/4

10

8

9
11

7

11

11 3/4

6

3/8

4B

4C

21

COLOR OF ORIGINAL
BARN RED-OUTSIDE
POWDER BLUE-INSIDE

4A

9 1/2

4A

5

3/8

4 3/8

4°   4°   7 5/16

20 AT BASE

7/16

DADO 5/8 WIDE X 1/8 DEEP
2 PLACES

3

1

3

2   2

2 1/2

4   5/8   11 3/8   5/8   4

20 5/8

SIDE VIEW

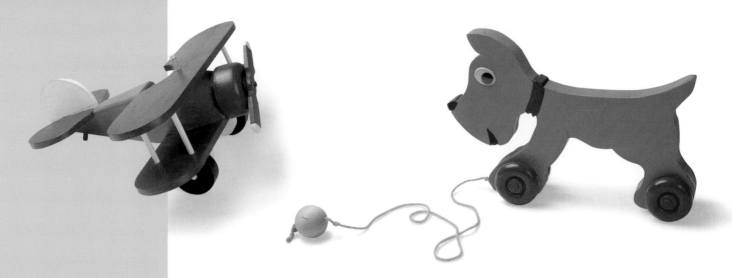

Toys, Games & Puzzles

With the creative patterns in this chapter, you can make a log cabin, a checkers game, cars and planes, and more. You can also help a little one experience the magic of time gone by when you fashion reproductions of antique favorites, including pull toys, rocking horses, a toy train, and a sled.

Walking Penguin Toy

Here's a toy that walks, yet it has no batteries or motors. It's a copy of a now-antique toy enjoyed by children in an earlier time. Years ago, walking toys came in all kinds of shapes and sizes—even four-legged animals. We found the penguin this one is based on in an antique shop in St. Johnsbury, Vermont. To make it walk, you need only a smooth, slightly inclined surface. Before you get started, note that you'll need a lathe to make this toy.

MATERIALS LIST

NO.	NAME	SIZE	REQ'D.
1	HEAD	1¼ DIA. x 1¼ LONG	1
2	BODY	1¾ DIA. x 2¾ LONG	1
3	BEAK	¼ DIA. x 1¼ LONG	1
4	LEG	¼ DIA. x 3¹⁄₁₆ LONG	2
5	FOOT	¼ x ⅝ – 1¼ LONG	2
6	FLIPPER (LEATHER)	¹⁄₁₆ x 1 – 2 LONG	2
7	TAIL (LEATHER)	¹⁄₁₆ x 1 – 1⅛ LONG	1
8	SPACER	³⁄₁₆ DIA. x ³⁄₁₆ LONG	1
9	PIN	¹⁄₁₆ DIA. x 1⅜ LONG	1

1. Turn the body in a lathe exactly as shown. Be sure to hollow out the interior. Locate and drill the ¹⁄₁₆-inch-diameter hole, ⁷⁄₁₆ of an inch down from the top as shown. Carefully make the ¹⁄₁₆-inch-wide saw kerf for the tail at a 45° angle as shown.

2. Turn the head on a lathe. Check that the ⅞ inch-diameter neck fits tightly into the body. Drill a ¼-inch-diameter hole ½ inch deep at 10° as shown for the beak. Make up a beak and glue it to the head.

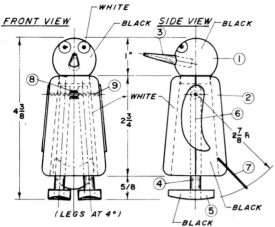

FRONT VIEW

WHITE

BLACK

SIDE VIEW

BLACK

WHITE

WHITE

BLACK

BLACK

(LEGS AT 4°)

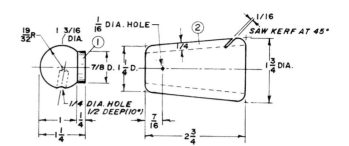

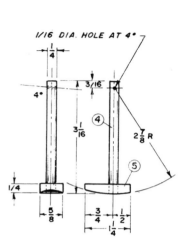

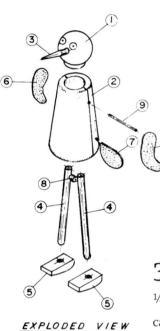

EXPLODED VIEW

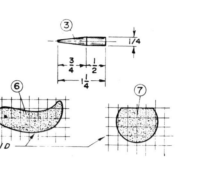

1/4 GRID

3. Cut the two legs from a ¼-inch-diameter dowel, and carefully locate and drill a ¹⁄₁₆-inch-diameter hole at 4°, as shown. Make up the feet and glue them to the legs. Important: be sure they are 90° to the ¹⁄₁₆-inch-diameter hole. Check the 2⁷⁄₈-inch radius from the hole to the bottom of the feet—this is crucial for the toy to walk.

4. Assemble the legs and feet to the body with ¹⁄₁₆-inch-diameter stiff wire and a small spacer piece between legs; a small piece of tubing or a large bead will do. There should be a tight fit between the wire and body, but a loose fit between the wire and legs; the legs must swing freely.

5. Paint the body, head, and legs white and black, to suit, using a nontoxic paint. Carefully cut the wings and tail from a piece of ¹⁄₁₆-inch-thick black leather or plastic (leather was used on the original). Attach the wings and tail, and your penguin is ready to walk. Place it at the top of a smooth, slightly inclined surface and watch him walk.

Monkey Business Balancing Trick

This is a take-off on the old pipe-shaped belt trick. I simply made the old trick into a monkey. To use the balancing monkey, center and balance a regular belt in the tail, as shown. Balance the monkey on your finger or the edge of a table at point A (see Front View, page 212).

1. Transfer the monkey pattern to a piece of high-grade ¼-inch to ⁵⁄₁₆ inch-thick plywood. (Marine or aircraft plywood is best.)

2. Carefully cut out, as shown. Sand all over.

3. Paint to suit, and apply three or four coats of varnish to help strengthen the wood.

$\frac{1}{4}''$ PLYWOOD

$5\frac{5}{8}$

BELT

FRONT VIEW

$4\frac{1}{8}$

Color/Shape Puzzle

This toy teaches counting, color, and shape. It's especially good for two- to three-year-old children, who will love this puzzle!

1. Cut pieces to overall sizes according to the Materials List.

   Sand the back (part 2).

   On the top board (part 1), carefully lay out the three overall cutouts using the given dimensions (top view).

2. Cut out the three holes and glue the top board (part 1) to the back (part 2).

   After the glue dries, sand all surfaces and edges.

   Using a rounding router bit with a ball-bearing follower, round the edges, as shown.

3. On ¾-inch or 1-inch-thick material, lay out the triangle, circle, and square.

   Cut out the three pieces, and round all edges. Sand all over.

   Cut the triangle in two pieces, the circle in three pieces, and the square in four pieces.

4. Sand all pieces.

   Prime and paint with bright colors, using non-toxic paint.

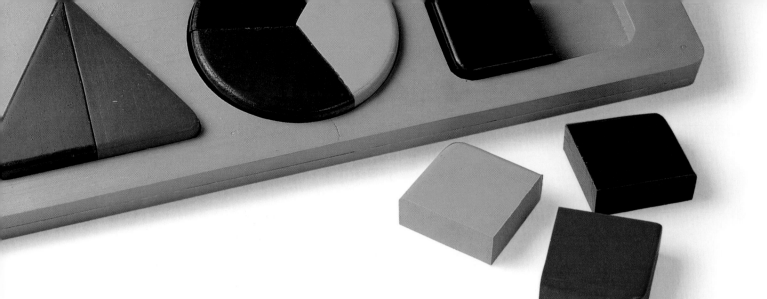

MATERIALS LIST

NO.	NAME	SIZE	REQ'D.
1	TOP BOARD	½ x 5½ – 14½ LONG	1
2	BACK	¼ x 5½ – 14½ LONG	1
3	FELT (OPTIONAL)	5¼ x 14¼ LONG	1
4	TRIANGLE	1 x 4 – 4½ LONG	1
5	CIRCLE	1 x 4 DIA.	1
6	SQUARE	1 x 4 SQUARE	1

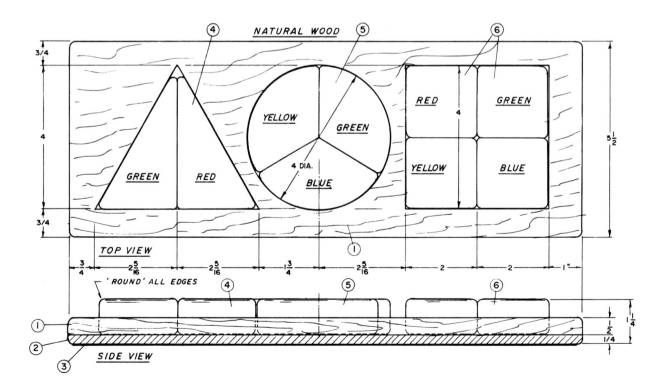

Stegosaurus Puzzle

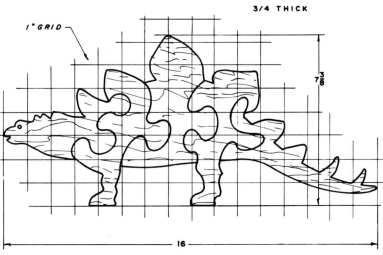

Dinosaurs are really big with kids. Our grandchildren have all kinds of dinosaur toys in all shapes, colors, and sizes. This is a simple puzzle that the very young will enjoy.

1. On a 1-inch grid, lay out the pattern. Transfer the pattern to the wood.

2. Cut the outside surfaces first, and slightly sand all edges. Sand along the bottom of the feet so that the assembled puzzle will stand up.

3. Paint to suit. Redraw the inner pieces.

4. Cut the inner pieces, as shown. If you stray slightly from the pattern, don't worry, no one will ever know.

5. Touch up all paint, as necessary.

3/4 THICK

1" GRID

7 3/8

16

SIDE VIEW

Pyramid Puzzle

Are you intrigued by three-dimensional puzzles? If so, you should like this one. It involves just two identical pieces, each made with four saw cuts. The trick is to assemble the pieces to form a three-sided pyramid. How difficult is this puzzle? You'll have to make it before you can find out. When assembled, the grain in one part is perpendicular to the grain in the other. This clue is the only one I give people, and it's great fun to watch them at work.

1. Select the stock. I suggest straight-grained hardwood. You'll need a block 2¼ x 2⅝ x 16 inches. You'll be able to get both puzzle pieces out of this block. If you can't come up with 2¼-inch stock, glue up three pieces of ¾-inch hardwood.

2. Cut the pieces. Cut the block into two 7½-inch lengths. The drawings give step-by-step illustrations for the remaining cuts. I made cuts on a band saw. Remember to make two identical puzzle pieces.

To make the first cut, set the saw blade to exactly 30° and cut, as shown. Turn the block 180° and make the second cut with the same blade setting. Be sure to keep the base a full 2⅝ inches wide.

For the third and fourth cuts, use the miter gauge to saw off the ends with the blade still set at 30°. These cuts must leave a base that is exactly 2⅝ inches square if the puzzle is to work

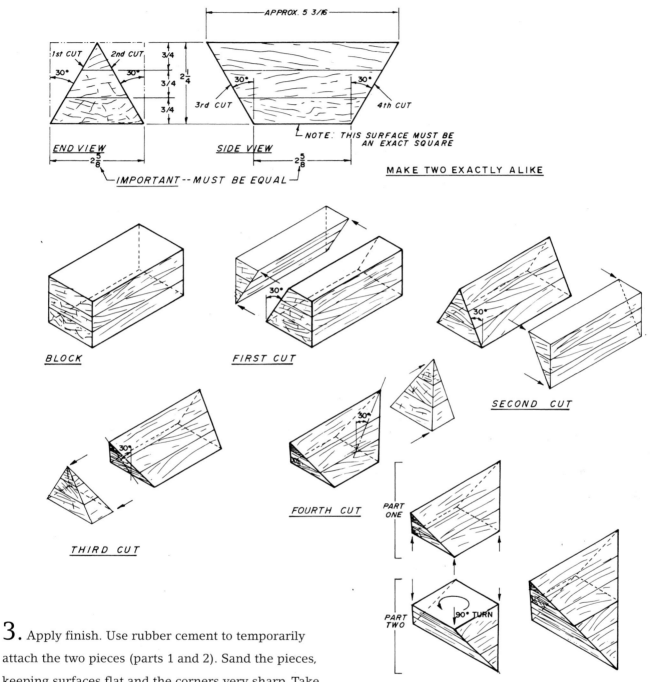

APPROX. 5 3/16

1st CUT   2nd CUT

30°   30°

3/4
3/4   2 1/4
3/4

END VIEW

2 5/8

IMPORTANT--MUST BE EQUAL

SIDE VIEW

30°   30°

3rd CUT   4th CUT

NOTE: THIS SURFACE MUST BE AN EXACT SQUARE

2 5/8

MAKE TWO EXACTLY ALIKE

BLOCK

FIRST CUT

30°

SECOND CUT

30°

THIRD CUT

30°

FOURTH CUT

PART ONE

PART TWO

90° TURN

COMPLETED PROJECT

3. Apply finish. Use rubber cement to temporarily attach the two pieces (parts 1 and 2). Sand the pieces, keeping surfaces flat and the corners very sharp. Take the pieces apart, and sand the square surfaces that were joined.

I've found that it's best to either leave the puzzle unfinished or to apply varnish so that the grain is visible.

Nail Puzzle

*Here's a great puzzle. At first, every-
one will say it is absolutely impossible
to do. The problem is to balance all
ten nails on top of the middle nail. The
balanced nails cannot touch anything
and must all be balanced above the
head of the center nail. Simple—any
genius can do it!*

1. Cut the three wood blocks (parts 1 and 2) to size and sand all over.

2. Carefully glue the three wood blocks together as shown.

3. Using a router and a 3/16-inch-radius cove cutter with a ball-bearing follower, make a cut along the top edge.

4. Carefully locate the 11 holes, using the given dimensions in the top view.

5. Drill the 10 outer holes so that an 8-penny common nail will fit loosely. Drill the center hole so that an 8-penny common nail will fit tightly.

6. Finish all over with a high-gloss finish. Sand all over and add a coat of paste wax.

7. Add the center nail (part 3), making it a tight fit. Add the 4 felt pads (part 4). Clean out the 10 outer holes so the 10 nails can be inserted and removed easily.

You're ready to test your puzzle. Try to balance the 10 nails on the head of the center nail. For the solution, see the four steps on page 442. Have fun!

MATERIALS LIST			
NO.	NAME	SIZE	REQ'D.
1	BLOCK (WALNUT)	¾ x 2½ – 3¼ LONG	2
2	BLOCK (MAPLE)	¾ x 2⅛ – 2⅞ LONG	1
3	NAIL – COMMON	8d	11
4	FELT PAD	½ DIA.	4

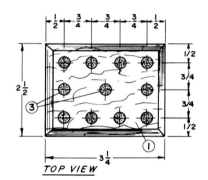

TOP VIEW

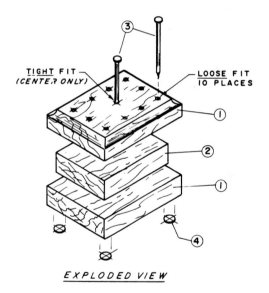

EXPLODED VIEW

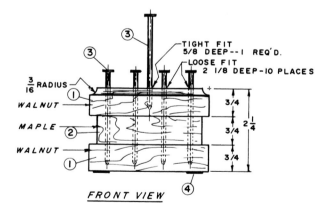

FRONT VIEW

Toy Blocks

If you tend to make an incorrect cut now and then and waste a little wood, as I do, you can recycle these leftovers by turning them into children's blocks. You don't have to reproduce the exact shapes shown here, of course. I offer these as examples.

To make it a little easier for kids to fit the blocks together, restrict yourself to a few overall widths and heights.

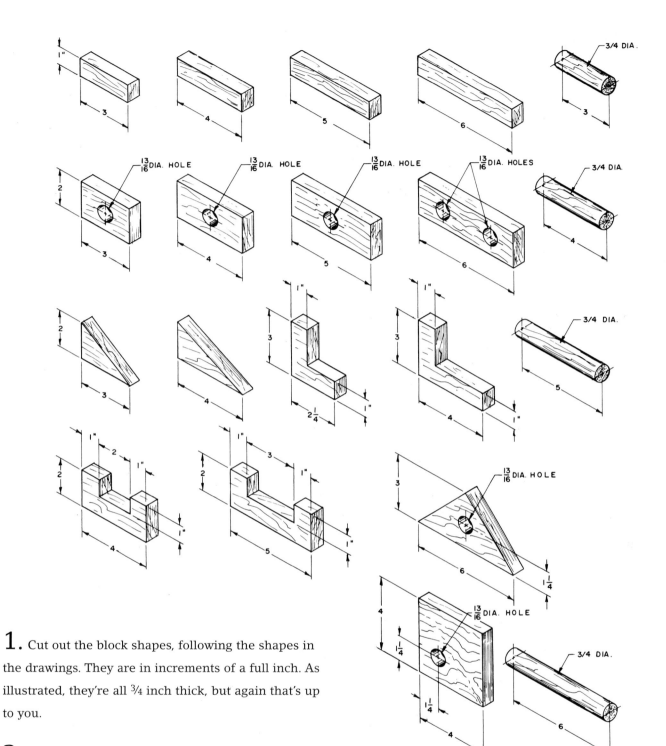

1. Cut out the block shapes, following the shapes in the drawings. They are in increments of a full inch. As illustrated, they're all ¾ inch thick, but again that's up to you.

2. Sand the blocks lightly, rounding the corners somewhat and removing splinters.

3. Finish the blocks with a coat of salad-bowl finish or a nontoxic paint For the safety of younger children who might gnaw on blocks, don't use leftover paints that may contain toxic chemicals.

Nutcracker Horse & Rider Toy

Our daughter Joy collects all kinds of toy rocking horses. This one is very different from all the others in her collection. It's a fun project to make. Let your imagination loose, and paint it as you wish—as you think a nutcracker should look. I would suggest that you make two or three of these at the same time, since everyone who sees it will want one.

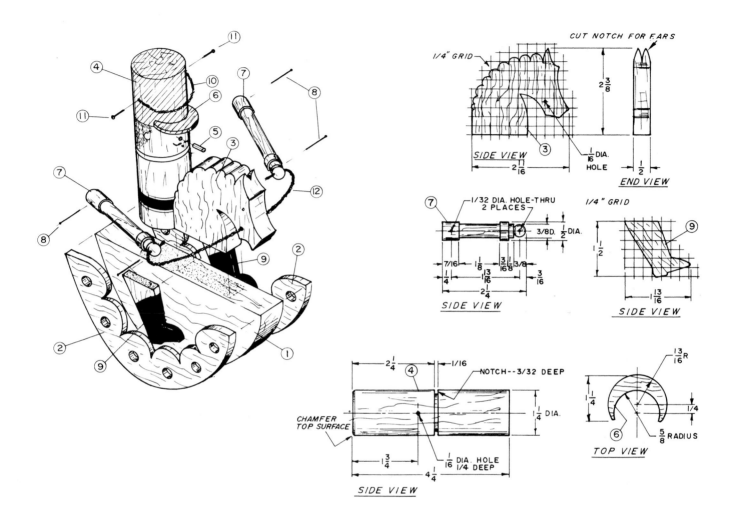

CUT NOTCH FOR EARS

1/4" GRID

SIDE VIEW
2 11/16

2 3/8

END VIEW
1/2

1/16 DIA.
HOLE

1/32 DIA. HOLE-THRU
2 PLACES

1/4" GRID

3/8D. 1/2 DIA.

7/16   1 1/8   3 1/6 3/8
1/4   1 13/16   3/16
2 1/4

SIDE VIEW

1 1/2

1 13/16

SIDE VIEW

2 1/4   1/16

NOTCH--3/32 DEEP

1 1/4 DIA.

CHAMFER
TOP SURFACE

1 3/4

1/16 DIA. HOLE
1/4 DEEP

4 1/4

SIDE VIEW

13/16 R

1 1/4

1/4

5/8 RADIUS

TOP VIEW

1. Cut all the flat parts to shape, and sand them all over. Drill all holes as shown.

2. Turn the body and arms on a lathe.

3. Assemble the rocker and two rocker trim pieces with glue. After the glue sets, sand along the bottom 2½-inch-radius curve. Glue the hat brim and nose to the body. Glue the body legs and horse's head to the rocker subassembly. Allow to set, and add temporarily the arms with small brads to check for fit.

4. Remove the arms after you are sure of the fit, and prime all parts. For speed, I recommend using fast-drying, easy-cleanup latex paint. Apply top coats, using either the suggested colors or colors you prefer. You can paint a smiling face if you wish, as my wife did.

After all the painting is done, reattach the arms with glue and brads. Attach the gold twine to the hat, and run string from one hand through the ¹/₁₆-inch-diameter hole in the horse's head to the other hand.

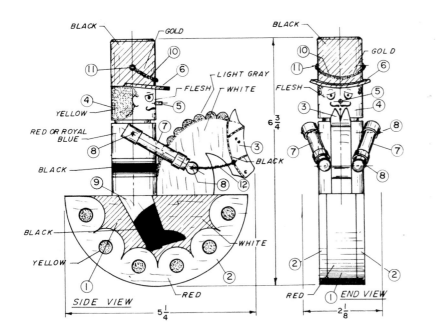

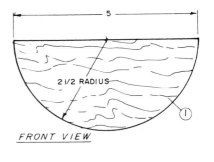

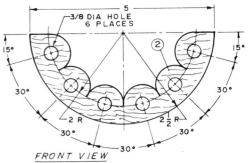

MATERIALS LIST

NO.	NAME	SIZE	REQ'D.
1	ROCKER	$3/4$ x $2\frac{1}{2}$ – 5 LONG	1
2	ROCKER TRIM	$1/4$ x $2\frac{1}{2}$ – 5 LONG	2
3	HEAD	$1/2$ x $2^{11}/_{16}$ – $2\frac{3}{8}$ LONG	1
4	BODY	$1\frac{1}{4}$ DIA. – $4\frac{1}{4}$ LONG	1
5	NOSE	$1/16$ DIA. – $7/16$ LONG	1
6	HAT BRIM	$1/16$ x $1\frac{1}{4}$ – $1\frac{5}{8}$ LONG	1
7	ARM	$1/2$ DIA. – $2\frac{1}{4}$ LONG	1
8	BRAD	$1\frac{1}{4}$ LONG	4
9	LEG	$1/4$ x $1^{13}/_{16}$ – $1\frac{1}{2}$ LONG	2
10	TWINE (GOLD)	$1\frac{1}{2}$ LONG	1
11	TACK (BRASS)	$1/2$ LONG	2
12	STRING (RED)	4 LONG	5

Rabbit Pull Toy

All children enjoy a pull toy at some time or another. When our granddaughter Hilary was two years old and even a little older, she loved them. See if your rabbit can catch your child, grandchild, or some other lucky youngster you have in mind.

	MATERIALS LIST		
NO.	**NAME**	**SIZE**	**REQ'D.**
1	BASE	¾ x 3 – 6 LONG	1
2	WHEEL	2¼ DIA.	4
3	AXLE PEG		4
4	BODY	¾ x 5 – 6 LONG	1
5	DOWEL PIN	¼ DIA. - 1½ LONG	2
6	PULL	¾ DIA. - 3 LONG	1
7	TWINE	TO SUIT	1

1. Make the base and drill four ⁵⁄₁₆-inch-diameter holes for the axle pegs. If you have a dowel-centering jig, use it to ensure that the holes are properly positioned. If the holes are not centered, the pull toy will rock. Drill a ¹⁄₁₆-inch-diameter hole at 45° in the front for the pull string or use a small eye screw as I did as shown in the photo. Locate and drill two ¼-inch-diameter holes for the dowel pins. Sand all over. Round all edges slightly to eliminate any sharp corners.

2. Lay out the rabbit design on a ½-inch grid. Transfer the pattern to the wood and cut it out. Drill a ⁵⁄₁₆-inch-diameter hole for the eyes. Sand all edges slightly as necessary.

3. Glue the rabbit in place. When the glue sets, drill up through the two ¼-inch-diameter holes in the base into the rabbit's legs and glue the two dowel pins in place. This will give the rabbit added strength.

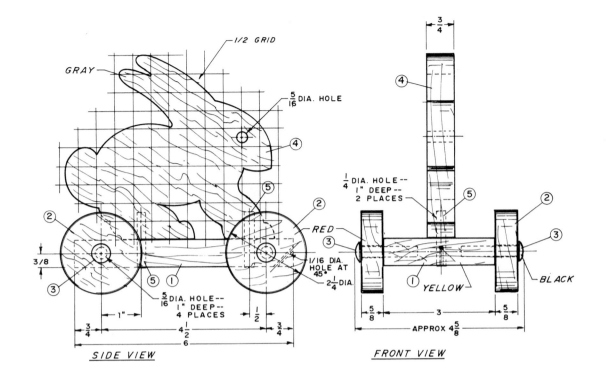

GRAY

1/2 GRID

5/16 DIA. HOLE

④

⑤

②

⑤

①

3/8

③

5/16 DIA. HOLE --
1" DEEP --
4 PLACES

3/4

1"

4 1/2

6

1/2

3/4

SIDE VIEW

②

RED

③

1/16 DIA.
HOLE AT
45°

2 1/4 DIA.

3/4

④

⑤

1/4 DIA. HOLE --
1" DEEP --
2 PLACES

②

③

①

YELLOW

BLACK

5/8

3

5/8

APPROX 4 5/8

FRONT VIEW

4. Use only nontoxic paint to paint the rabbit and base. Paint the wheels and hub of the axle pegs. When the paint dries, glue the axle pegs in place. Be sure not to get any glue on the wheels. Add the pull string and pull.

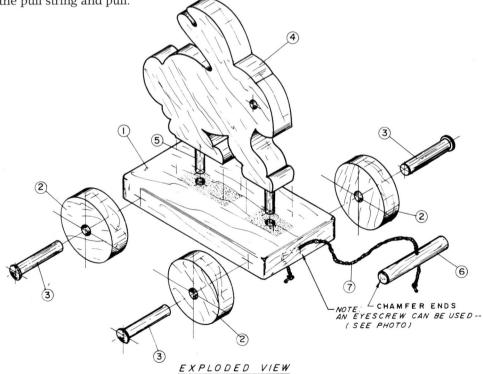

④

①

⑤

③

②

②

③

②

②

③

⑥

⑦

NOTE
CHAMFER ENDS
AN EYESCREW CAN BE USED --
(SEE PHOTO)

EXPLODED VIEW

Small Farm Tractor

Here is a heavy-duty farm tractor any child would love to have. It has a sense of freedom, fresh air, and power. Having spent many hours on a big green tractor on a farm in northern Vermont, I know the thrill of owning and operating a real tractor. Now you can give some special youngster the same thrill. The tractor will do some heavy farm work in the hands of an imaginative child. If you have a scroll saw, this project is very easy to make. I recommend that you use hardwood, especially for the fenders.

1. Lay out the body design on a ¼-inch grid, point by point. Transfer the pattern to the wood and cut it out. Locate and drill all of the holes. Sand all over.

2. Make a few saw kerfs along the front to simulate a grill. Trim the drawbar as shown in the exploded view. Don't forget to add the air filter to the left side. Cut the fenders from one piece of wood, ¾ inch by 1⅛ inches and 1¾ inches long, as shown.

| \multicolumn{4}{c}{**MATERIALS LIST**} | | | |
NO.	NAME	SIZE	REQ'D.
1	BODY	¾ x 2¼ – 4½ LONG	1
2	FENDER	¾ x 1⅛ – 1¾ LONG	2
3	STEP	⅛ x ⅝ – 1½ LONG	1
4	STACK	¼ DIA. – 2 LONG	1
5	COLUMN	⅛ DIA. – 2 LONG	1
6	WHEEL	¾ DIA. – ⅛ LONG	1
7	REAR AXLE	¼ DIA. – 2¾ LONG	1
8	REAR WHEEL	2 DIA. – ¾ LONG	2
9	FRONT AXLE	¼ DIA. – 2¼ LONG	1
10	SPACER	⅝ DIA. – ¼ LONG	2
11	FRONT WHEEL	1½ DIA. – ½ LONG	2
12	AIR CLEANER	⅜ DIA. - ⅜ LONG	1

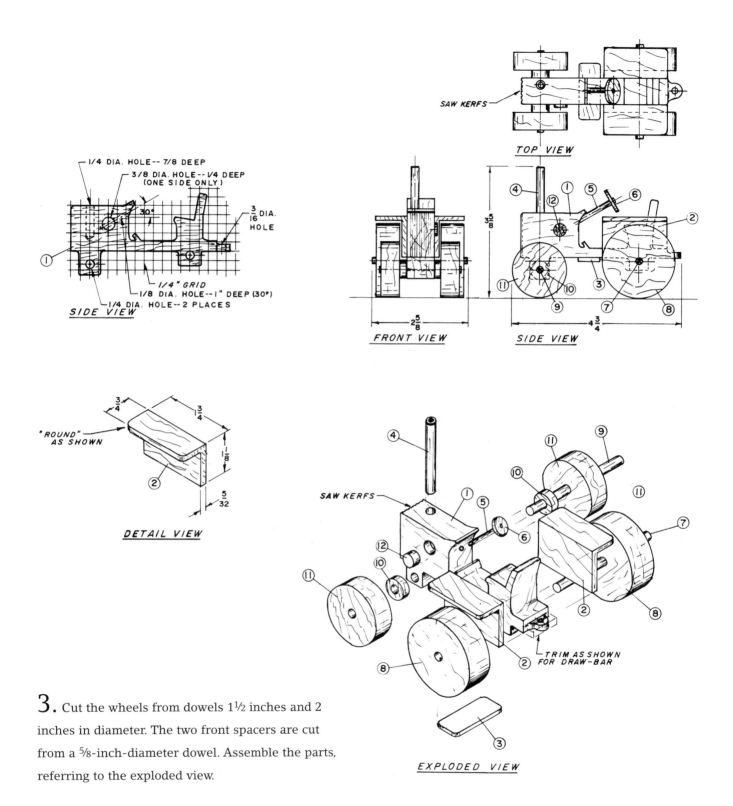

1/4 DIA. HOLE -- 7/8 DEEP
3/8 DIA. HOLE -- 1/4 DEEP (ONE SIDE ONLY)
30°
3/16 DIA. HOLE
1/4" GRID
1/8 DIA. HOLE -- 1" DEEP (30°)
1/4 DIA. HOLE -- 2 PLACES

SIDE VIEW

"ROUND" AS SHOWN

3/4
3/4
1 1/8
5/32

DETAIL VIEW

SAW KERFS

TOP VIEW

3 5/8
2 5/8
4 3/4

FRONT VIEW   SIDE VIEW

SAW KERFS

TRIM AS SHOWN FOR DRAW-BAR

EXPLODED VIEW

3. Cut the wheels from dowels 1½ inches and 2 inches in diameter. The two front spacers are cut from a ⅝-inch-diameter dowel. Assemble the parts, referring to the exploded view.

4. Paint with a nontoxic paint. Most tractors in North America are painted red, blue, or green. Paint the wheels black or to suit.

Toolbox with Tools

This project is both fun and educational, and it's a good one for girls as well as boys. When our three daughters were little, they would work along with me helping to make various woodworking projects. They still recall how much they enjoyed making them. I suggest you make the tool box first, then the tools.

1. Cut all pieces to size according to the cutting list.

2. Lay out the ends (part 1), and cut them out making two pieces exactly the same.

3. Locate and drill a ¾-inch hole for the handle.

4. Nail all pieces together with the finishing nails (part 5). Check that everything is square.

5. Sand all over, rounding the edges slightly.

6. The hammer and screwdriver can be made out of simple dowels and shaped, as shown.

7. The saw and the square should be laid out and made according to the given dimensions. Note: for very young children you may want to consider omitting the screwdriver, since a small child could get hurt with this tool.

8. The only tricky tool to make is the pliers. On a ½-inch grid lay out the jaws and cut, as shown. The left and right jaws are the same. Locate and drill the 3⁄16-inch-diameter hole. Locate and notch as shown. Check again that you have a left and right jaw, each the same as the other. Add the pin. (An axle pin used in holding wheels on toys makes a great pin for the pliers.) In gluing the pin in place, apply glue to the back jaw only so that the jaws operate freely.

9. Sand all over, rounding all corners.

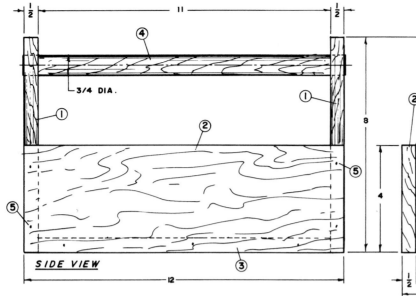

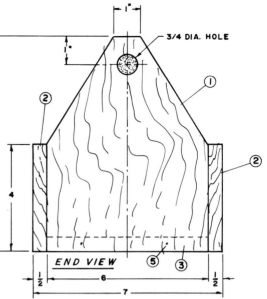

SIDE VIEW

END VIEW

10. Either paint or leave natural. I recommend that you paint the tool box with bright colors. The handle of the screwdriver and the square can be painted yellow. Everything else will look great left natural with a clear top coat.

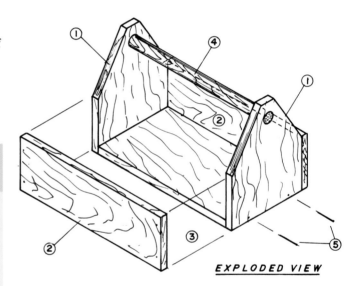

EXPLODED VIEW

NO.	NAME	SIZE	REQ'D.
1	END	½ x 6 – 8 LONG	2
2	SIDE	½ x 4 – 12 LONG	2
3	BOTTOM	½ x 6 – 11 LONG	1
4	HANDLE	¾ DIA. - 12 LONG	1
5	NAIL – FINISH	6d	18
6	HANDLE	½ x ¾ – 2¾ LONG	1
7	BLADE	⅛ x ⅝ – 5 LONG	1
8	HANDLE	¾ DIA. – 7 LONG	1
9	HEAD	1¼ DIA. – 2½ LONG	1
10	BLADE	⅜ DIA. – 6¼ LONG	1
11	HANDLE	¾ DIA. – 2½ LONG	1
12	HANDLE	½ x 1⅝ – 6⅝ LONG	2
13	PIN	3/16 DIA.	1
14	HANDLE	⅝ x 3½ – 3⅝ LONG	1
15	BLADE	¼ x 3⅛ – 8¾ LONG	1
16	PIN	3/16 DIA. – ⅝ LONG	2

MATERIALS LIST

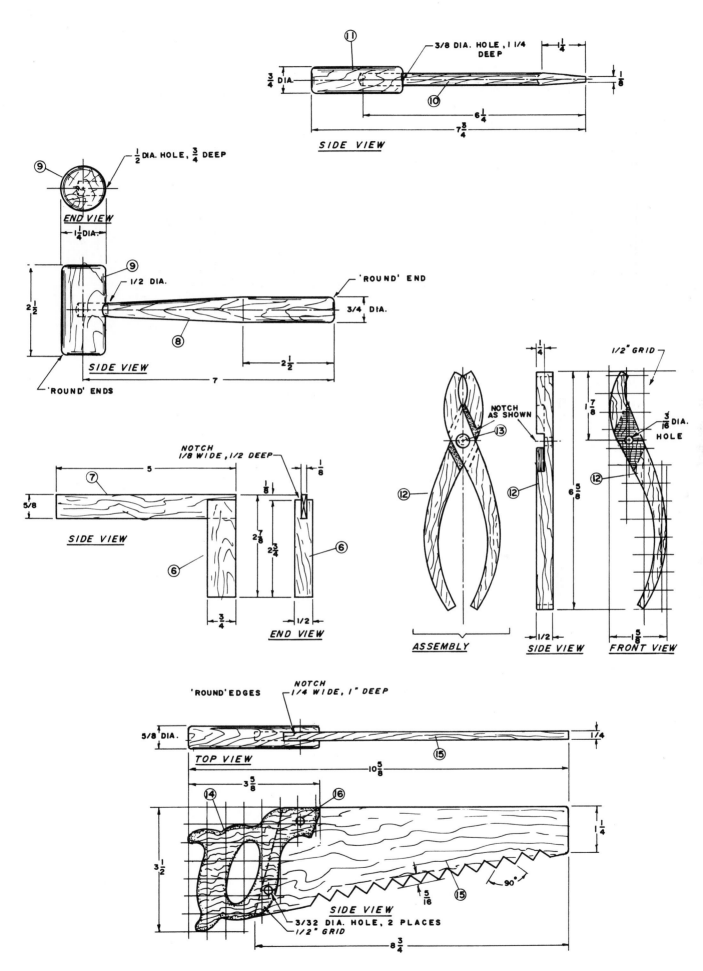

⑪

3/8 DIA. HOLE, 1 1/4 DEEP

1 1/4

3/4 DIA.

⑩

1/8

6 1/4

7 3/4

SIDE VIEW

⑨

1/2 DIA. HOLE, 3/4 DEEP

END VIEW

1 1/4 DIA.

⑨

1/2 DIA.

'ROUND' END

3/4 DIA.

2 1/2

⑧

'ROUND' ENDS

SIDE VIEW

2 1/2

7

NOTCH 1/8 WIDE, 1/2 DEEP

5

⑦

1/8

5/8

1/8

2 7/8

2 3/4

⑥

⑥

⑥

3/4

1/2

SIDE VIEW

END VIEW

NOTCH AS SHOWN

⑬

⑫

⑫

ASSEMBLY

1/2

SIDE VIEW

1/4

1/2" GRID

1 7/8

3/16 DIA. HOLE

6 5/8

⑫

5/8

FRONT VIEW

'ROUND' EDGES

NOTCH 1/4 WIDE, 1" DEEP

5/8 DIA.

⑮

1/4

TOP VIEW

10 5/8

3 5/8

⑭

⑯

1 1/4

3 1/2

5/16

90°

⑮

3/32 DIA. HOLE, 2 PLACES

1/2" GRID

SIDE VIEW

8 3/4

Toys, Games & Puzzles   231

Simple Toy Train, c.1920

*This is a classic toy train, and it's still as
popular today as it was in the 1920s. It's an old toy that is
easy to make and takes very little wood. In fact, a ³⁄₄-inch-thick
piece of wood 1½ inches wide and only 19 inches long is all you need
for a complete train, with hardly any waste. The wheels are made from
a ⁷⁄₈-inch-diameter dowel only 5 inches long. Watch the children's eyes
light up when they see their new train!*

1. Cut a board ³⁄₄ inch thick, 1½ inches wide, and 19
inches long. Sand all over. Apply a light primer coat.

2. Carefully lay out the cars, following the given
dimensions. Cut out all of the cars and sand. Note:
there are actually four cars; make two cars from the
middle car design.

3. Cut the wheels from the ⁷⁄₈-inch-diameter dowel
into ¼-inch-wide strips. Drill each wheel in the center
for the axle.

4. Paint the cars and all of the wheels with nontoxic
paint.

5. Add the wheels and eye screws. (Open every other
eye screw to make a hook).

6. Optional: sand all edges lightly, down to the bare
wood. Apply a coat of light wood stain to create an
original antique look.

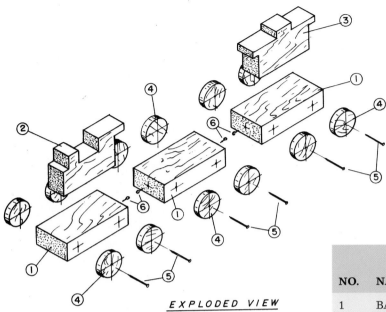

EXPLODED VIEW

NO.	NAME	SIZE	REQ'D.
1	BASE	¾ x 1½ – 3 LONG	4
2	ENGINE	¾ x 1½ – 3 LONG	1
3	CABOOSE	¾ x 1½ – 3 LONG	1
4	WHEEL	¼ x ⅞ DIA.	16
5	AXLE	1 LONG TACK	16
6	EYESCREW	SMALL	6

MATERIALS LIST

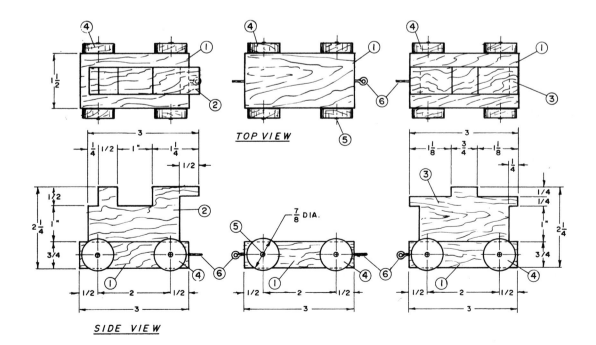

TOP VIEW

SIDE VIEW

Log Cabin

As a child, one of my favorite toys was a set of logs that kept me busy for hours. Naturally, this is one of my favorite projects. I also think this is a very educational toy, since it teaches children to think and use their imaginations. Many different structures can be built using these logs in various combinations. A special dado head and router bit will be needed for this project.

Important: In cutting the dadoes, extreme care must be taken, especially for the smaller parts. Use clamps, stops, or whatever else you have in cutting all dadoes. Be sure, as always, to wear safety glasses when making this project.

1. Cut overall sizes exactly to ¾ inch x ¾ inch and 5-foot or 6-foot lengths. Be sure to use knot-free, straight-grained wood. Cut about twice as much material as you think you will actually need.

2. Set up the router to make the curved cuts, and run all the stock through at the same time at the same setting, as shown in figure A.

Note: multiple parts must be exactly the same size and shape; therefore, use whatever stops or jigs you have at your disposal.

MATERIALS LIST			
NO.	NAME	SIZE	REQ'D.
1	LOCKING PIN	¾ x ¾ – 1½ LONG	96
2	WALL	¾ x ¾ – 3½ LONG	48
3	WALL	¾ x ¾ – 9 LONG	6
4	WALL	¾ x ¾ – 9 LONG	8
5	WALL	¾ x ¾ – 14½ LONG	4
6	WALL	¾ x ¾ – 14½ LONG	6
7	WALL	⅜ x ¾ – 14½ LONG	2
8	WALL	⅜ x ¾ – 14½ LONG	2
9	GABLE	¾ x ¾ – 10¼ LONG	2
10	GABLE	¾ x ¾ - 9 LONG	2
11	GABLE	¾ x ¾ – 7½ LONG	2
12	GABLE	¾ x ¾ – 6 LONG	2
13	GABLE	¾ x ¾ – 4½ LONG	2
14	GABLE	¾ x ¾ – 3 LONG	2
15	GABLE	¾ x ¾ – 1½ LONG	2
16	ROOF	¼ x 1⅜ – 15¼ LONG	20
17	ROOF TOP	⅝ x ⅝ – 15¼ LONG	2
18	CHIMNEY	¾ x 2¼ – 2¼ LONG	2

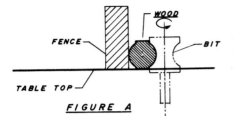

FENCE

WOOD

BIT

TABLE TOP

FIGURE A

3. Square one end.

4. Locate and cut ¾-inch-wide dadoes exactly ³⁄₁₆ inch deep, as shown.

5. Cut to specified length, again using stops to ensure uniformity.

   Note: all dadoes are made before each piece is cut to final length in order to give you something to hold on to while making the dado cuts. Again, take extreme care; these cuts could be dangerous.

6. Sand all over, removing any sharp edges

7. Roofing material (parts 16 and 17) and chimney (part 18) should be made as shown.

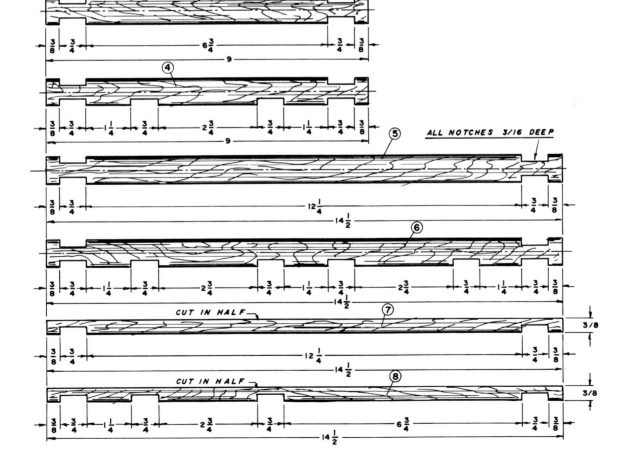

8. I recommend that you stain all the logs with a light walnut stain. Because there are so many pieces, you might want to consider just dipping them in a can of stain.

9. Paint roof material green or any color of your choice, and the chimney red.

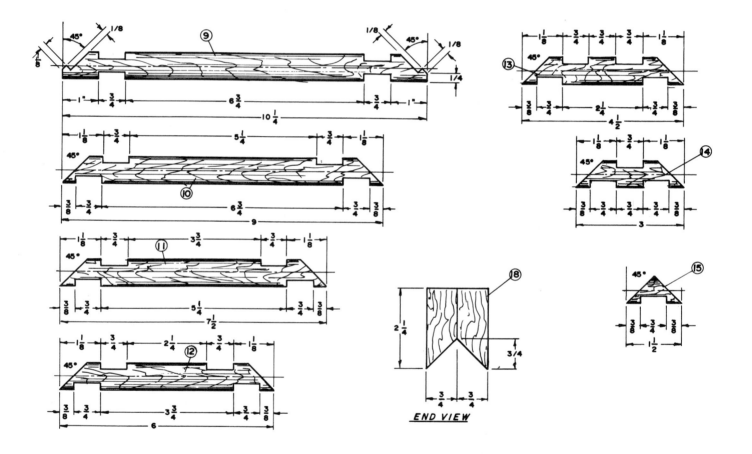

END VIEW

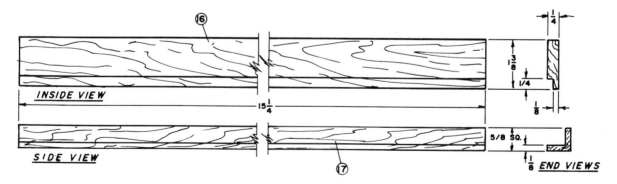

INSIDE VIEW

SIDE VIEW

END VIEWS

Rover Pull Toy, c.1935

This is a copy of an original pull toy that we found in an antique shop. It was a promotional toy for some company. The original one was painted lime green, thus the bright color on this one. You can paint yours any color you wish.

1. Cut the parts to overall size.

2. The 2-inch-diameter wheels can be purchased or cut from a 2-inch dowel, 1 inch thick, as the original toy was. If made from a dowel, use a $\frac{7}{8}$-inch-diameter Forstner bit to counterbore $\frac{3}{8}$ inch deep, as shown.

3. Using a 1-inch grid, lay out and cut out the body.

4. Locate and drill the $\frac{3}{8}$-inch-diameter holes in the body and wheels.

5. Sand all over, removing any sharp edges.

6. Paint to suit.

MATERIALS LIST			
NO.	NAME	SIZE	REQ'D.
1	BODY	$\frac{3}{4}$ x 6$\frac{5}{8}$ – 10 LONG	1
2	WHEEL	2 DIA. x 1 THICK	4
3	AXLE	$\frac{3}{8}$ DIA. – 2$\frac{1}{2}$ LONG	2

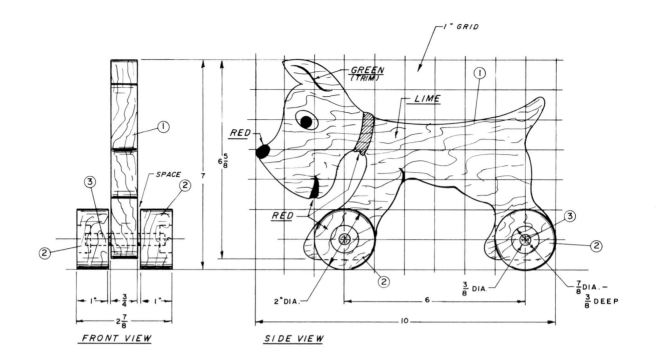

1" GRID

GREEN
(TRIM)

LIME

RED

RED

①

③

②

②

SPACE

③

②

②

7

6 5/8

1"   3/4   1"

2 7/8

FRONT VIEW

SIDE VIEW

2" DIA.

3/8 DIA.

7/8 DIA. –
3/8 DEEP

6

10

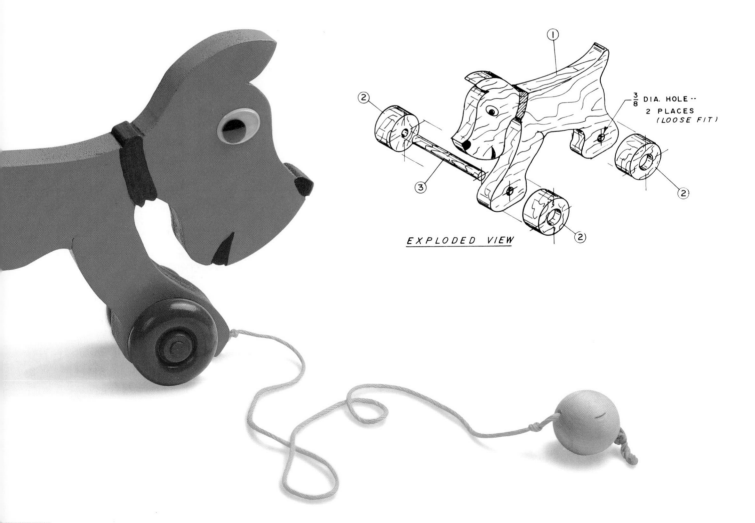

①

②

③

3/8 DIA. HOLE –
2 PLACES
(LOOSE FIT)

②

②

EXPLODED VIEW

Checkers Game

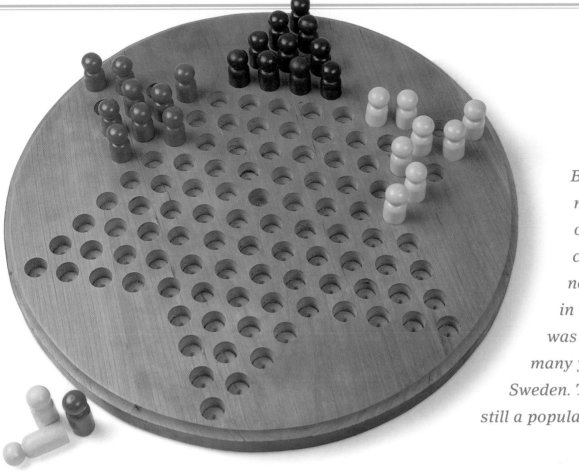

Believe it or not, the game of Chinese checkers was not invented in China; it was invented many years ago in Sweden. Today, it's still a popular game.

1. On heavy paper, lay out the grid for the location of the holes. The sheet should be about 16 inches square or so. It would be helpful if you have a drafting board, T-square, and a 30°/60° triangle.

2. Refer to the drawings for each step to locate the holes. Draw horizontal and vertical lines through the middle of the paper. At the center, draw a circle using a 6^{15}/$_{16}$-inch radius. Divide the circle into three equal parts. Make a triangle with 12-inch sides. Make another triangle (upside down) with 12-inch sides. Divide each leg of both triangles into 1-inch spaces. Draw

parallel lines from point to point as shown. Where the points cross is the exact center point for each hole.

3. Tape or glue your pattern to a piece of wood that is approximately 16-inches square. Be sure it cannot move. Using a prick punch, ice pick, or similar tool, prick punch the centers of all 121 holes.

4. Remove the pattern and locate the center hole. From this point, swing a 7^{3}/$_{4}$-inch radius for the outside edge. Cut and sand the outer edge.

5. Using a ¼-inch-radius cove cutter with a ball-bearing follower, make the cove cut around the upper, outer edge, as shown. Sand all over.

6. Using a drill press and a ½-inch-diameter drill with a ³⁄₁₆-inch-deep setting, drill the 121 holes.

7. Sand all over with fine-grit sandpaper. Apply a high-gloss coat of varnish. Optional: glue a piece of felt cloth to the bottom surface and trim along its edge. Use marbles or pegs for pieces.

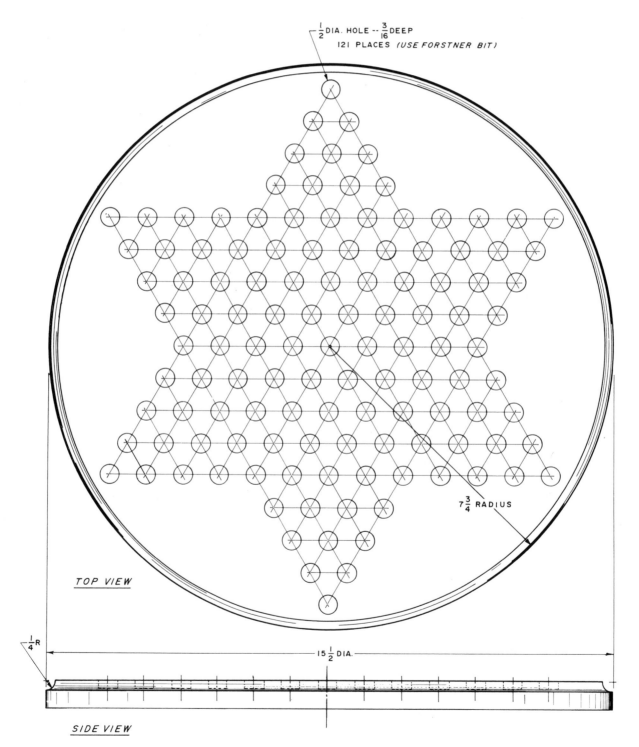

½ DIA. HOLE -- ³⁄₁₆ DEEP
121 PLACES *(USE FORSTNER BIT)*

7¾ RADIUS

TOP VIEW

¼ R

15½ DIA.

SIDE VIEW

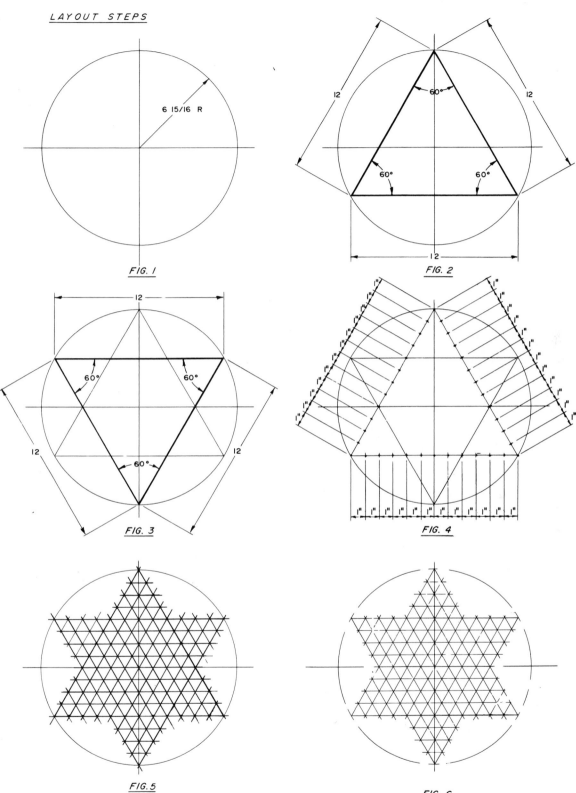

LAYOUT STEPS

6 15/16 R

FIG. 1

FIG. 2

FIG. 3

FIG. 4

FIG. 5

FIG. 6

Horse Pull Toy

For the most part, the child of yesterday did not have many toys. Childhood is a fairly modern idea; in years past, toys were thought to be frivolous. Life was hard, and kids did not have much time to play. But one prized toy may have been some sort of pull toy like this fine example of a horse on wheels.

MATERIALS LIST

NO.	NAME	SIZE	REQ'D.
1	BODY	¾ x 5 – 10 LONG	1
2	FRONT LEG	½ x 2 – 6 LONG	1
3	FRONT LEG	½ x 2½ – 6 LONG	1
4	BACK LEG	½ x 2½ – 5½ LONG	2
5	BASE	¾ x 4¾ – 9¼ LONG	1
6	SCREW – FLAT HEAD	NO. 6	4
7	WHEEL (CAST)	2 DIA.	4
8	TACK	1 LONG	4

1. Study the plans carefully. The body and legs are irregular in shape and will have to be laid out on a grid to make full-size patterns. The drawing notes a ½-inch and a 1-inch grid. Lay out the grids on heavy paper or cardboard, and transfer the shape of each piece to the appropriate grid, point by point.

The wheels (part 7) will have to be purchased early on so that you will have them handy when you need them. If you prefer, you can make the wheels of solid wood. This will also give an aged appearance.

2. Carefully cut the parts according to the materials fist. Take care to cut all of the parts to exact size and exactly square (90°). Stop and recheck all dimensions before going on.

Note: the handle used has been carefully selected because it is safe, even though a round ball may have been used originally for the pull. Do not use a round ball, because it could all too easily come loose and endanger a child. The recommended handle is a 2½-inch-long piece of ½-inch-diameter dowel.

3. Lightly sand all surfaces and edges with medium sandpaper to remove any burrs and all tool marks. Take care to keep all edges square and sharp at this time.

4. Make all parts according to the detailed dimensions. Transfer the full-size patterns to the wood, and cut out. Check all dimensions for accuracy. Resand all over with fine-grit sandpaper, still keeping all edges sharp.

5. Once all of the parts fit together correctly, assemble the project with glue, positioning everything as shown. Do not add the wheels at this time.

Note: the feet are attached to the base (part 5) with flathead wood screws.

6. Finish according to the drawings. Be sure to use a nontoxic paint if the toy is intended for a child.

Attach the wheels after the pull toy has been painted.

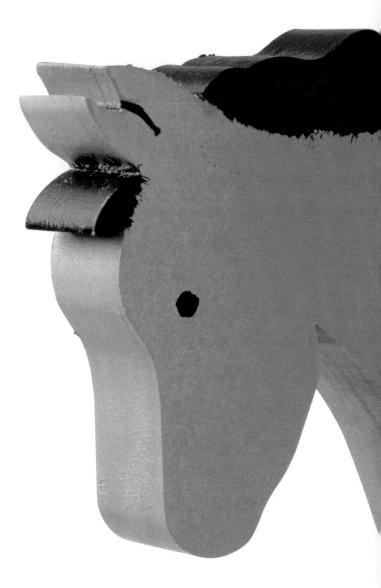

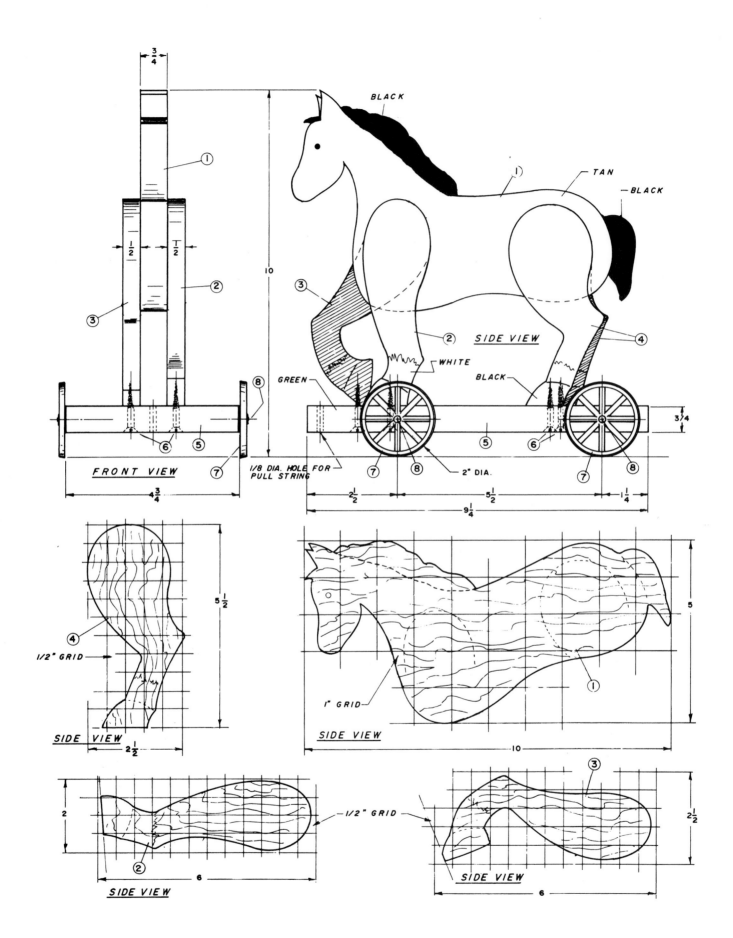

FRONT VIEW

SIDE VIEW

SIDE VIEW

BLACK

TAN

BLACK

GREEN

WHITE

BLACK

1/8 DIA. HOLE FOR PULL STRING

2" DIA.

1/2" GRID

1" GRID

Pushcart

Here's a toy cart that can be used for almost anything, from dolls to blocks or toy soldiers. Simple construction is used throughout for easy assembly. It even has a built-in stand. Mom might want to use it as a planter.

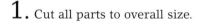

1. Cut all parts to overall size.

Assemble the body, using parts 1, 2, 3, and 4. Add the support and axle support (parts 5 and 6). Add the pull (part 7). I suggest that you glue and nail it in place.

2. Cut the wheels exactly to a 3-inch diameter, and drill a hole in the center of each for the screws. Temporarily add the wheels.

Glue and nail the handle (part 12) in place.

Sand all over, removing all sharp edges.

4. Remove the wheels, and paint to suit using bright colors. After the paint dries, reattach the wheels, checking that they turn freely.

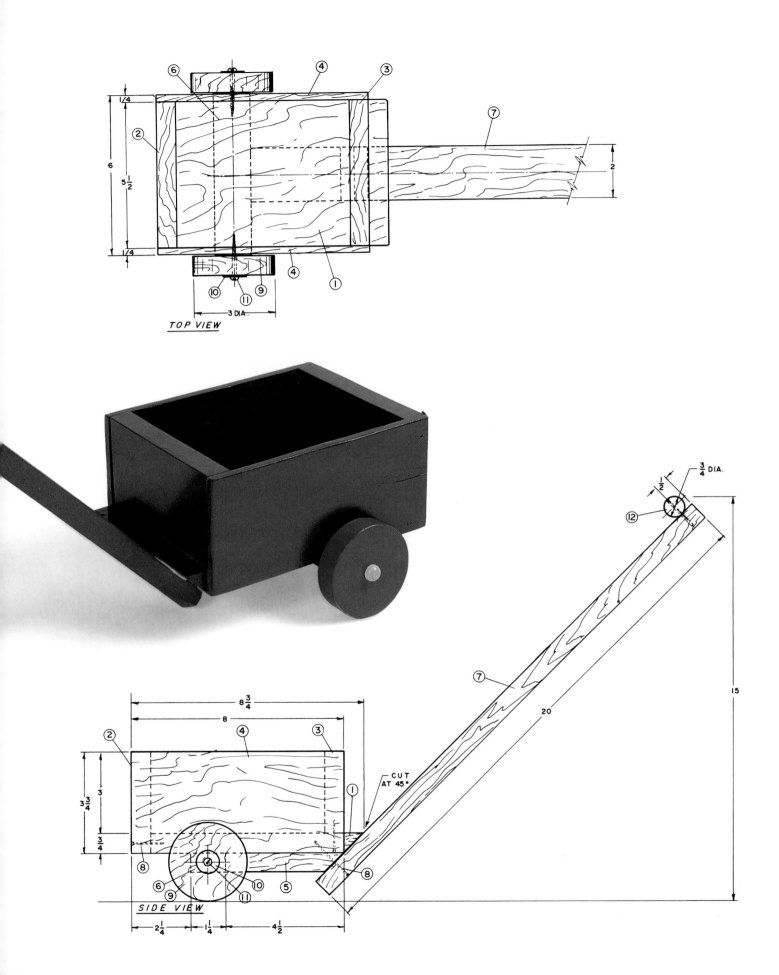

TOP VIEW

⁶⁄₄
6
5½
¹⁄₄
3 DIA.

8¾
8
3¾
3
¾
2¼
1¼
4½

SIDE VIEW

CUT AT 45°

¾ DIA.
½
20
15

MATERIALS LIST

NO.	NAME	SIZE	REQ'D.
1	BASE	¾ x 5½ - 8 LONG	1
2	BACK	¾ x 3¾ - 5½ LONG	1
3	FRONT	¾ x 3 - 5½ LONG	1
4	SIDE	¼ x 3¾ - 8 LONG	2
5	SUPPORT	¾ x 2 - 4½ LONG	1
6	AXLE SUPPORT	¾ x 1¼ - 6⅛ LONG	1
7	PULL	¾ x 2 - 20 LONG	1
8	FINISH NAIL	6d	14
9	WHEEL	3 DIA. – ¾ LONG	2
10	WASHER - FLAT	SMALL - ¾ DIA.	2
11	SCREW - RD. HD.	NO. 8 - 2 LONG	2
12	HANDLE	¾ DIA. – 6 LONG	1

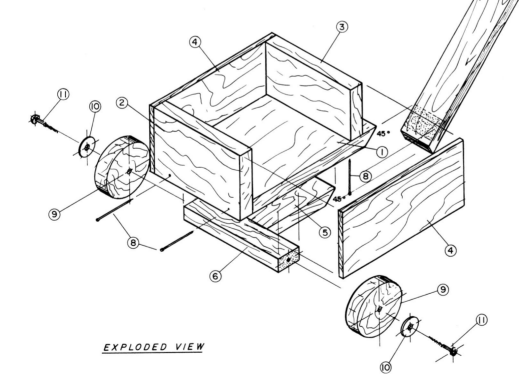

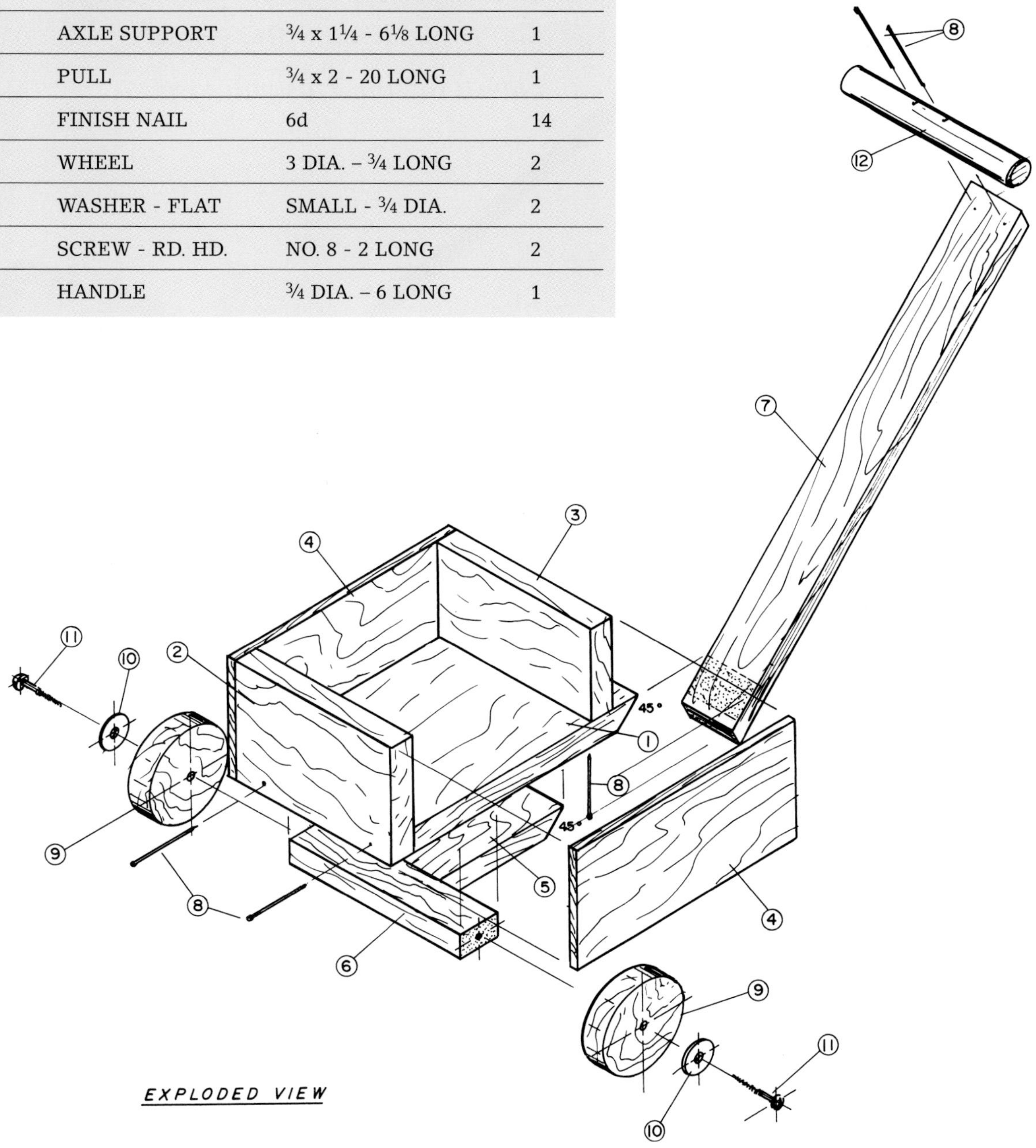

EXPLODED VIEW

Push Chicken

I found the neat old toy this project is based on in an antique shop. I would guess the original is more than fifty years old—a toy the kids will love.

1. Cut all parts to overall size.

2. On a 1/2-inch grid, lay out the pieces (parts 1, 2, and 3).

3. Carefully cut out, and sand all over.

4. Carefully locate and drill the ¼-inch-diameter holes in the sides (part 2).

5. Drill the ⅜-inch-diameter hole in the body center (part 1) at 45°, as shown, and 1½ inches deep.

6. Assemble all pieces according to the exploded view. Check that the wheel turns freely. Be sure to add the wheel before assembling the sides since the wheel will not fit in after assembly.

7. Paint with bright, nontoxic colors. Note: the oval eyes (part 5) should be painted on if the toy is for a very small child.

NO.	NAME	SIZE	REQ'D.
\multicolumn{4}{c}{**MATERIALS LIST**}			
1	BODY CENTER	⅞ x 5⅞ – 4¾ LONG	1
2	BODY SIDE	¼ x 5½ – 4¾ LONG	2
3	WING	⅛ x 2 – 3³⁄₁₆ LONG	2
4	WHEEL	¾ x 2½ DIA.	1
5	EYE	1 OVAL	1 PR.
6	HANDLE	⅜ DIA. – 18 LONG	1
7	TIP	1 SPHERE	1
8	AXLE	¼ DIA. – 1⁷⁄₁₆ LONG	1

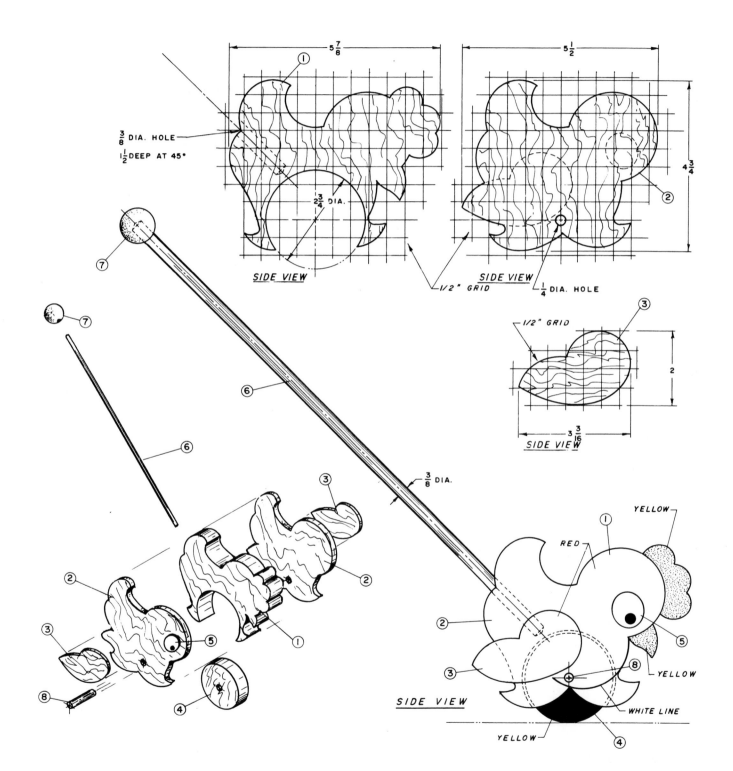

$\frac{5\,7}{8}$

$\frac{3}{8}$ DIA. HOLE

$1\frac{1}{2}$ DEEP AT 45°

$2\frac{3}{4}$ DIA.

SIDE VIEW

1/2" GRID

$5\frac{1}{2}$

$4\frac{3}{4}$

SIDE VIEW

$\frac{1}{4}$ DIA. HOLE

1/2" GRID

2

$3\frac{3}{16}$

SIDE VIEW

$\frac{3}{8}$ DIA.

YELLOW

RED

YELLOW

WHITE LINE

YELLOW

SIDE VIEW

Elephant Pull Toy

Here is another elephant project. The pattern is the same one used for the Elephant Bank on page 180.

MATERIALS LIST

NO.	NAME	SIZE	REQ'D.
1	BODY	1 x 7 ½ – 7½ LONG	1
2	EAR	½ x 4 – 5½ LONG	1
3	TAIL	3/16 DIA. – ¼ LONG	1
4	JIGGLE EYE		1 PR.
5	SADDLE	½ x 2 – 2 LONG	2
6	RIDER	1 DIA. – 2 LONG	1
7	BASE	¾ x 4 – 7¾ LONG	1
8	WHEEL	2 DIA. – ¾ LONG	4
9	AXLE PEG		4
10	SCREW – FL. HD.	NO. 8 – 1½ LONG	2
11	SCREW – EYE		1

1. Select the stock and cut the parts. The body (part 1) is made from 1 inch-thick stock. If you can't find wood that thick, glue up two ½-inch pieces. Cut the parts to the sizes given in the Materials List.

2. Make a paper pattern and cut the parts to shape. Draw a grid with ½-inch squares and enlarge the elephant and his ears onto it. Transfer the pattern to wood. Note that the ears (part 2) are a single piece of wood and that they slide into a notch cut in the bottom of the body. Cut the body and the ears to shape. Cut the notch with a band saw or jigsaw.

Cut the saddles (part 5) to shape and glue them to the body. Drill a 3/16-inch-diameter hole for the tail (part 3) and a 1 inch-diameter hole for the rider (part 6). The rider can be lathe-turned or carved from a 1 inch-diameter dowel.

You can either purchase the 2 inch-diameter wheels (part 8) or cut them yourself with a hole saw from ¾-inch-thick stock.

Drill ¼-inch holes in the base for the axle pegs (part 9).

3. Assemble the elephant. Glue the ears and tail to the body. Glue the body to the base (part 7). When the glue has set, drill and countersink for two flathead screws (part 10) and screw the elephant to the base. Slide the wheels over the axle pegs, and glue the pegs in place, making sure that the wheels have enough room to turn freely. Add the eye screw (part 11).

4. Apply finish. Paint with nontoxic colors of your choice and add the jiggle eyes (part 4), if you wish.

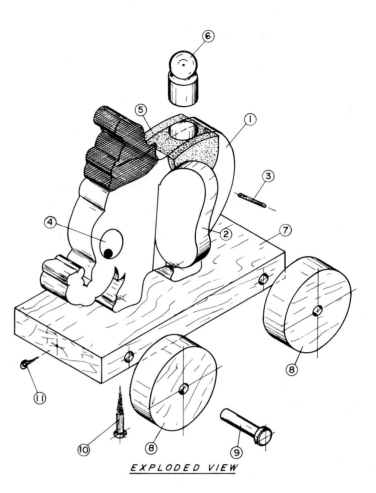

EXPLODED VIEW

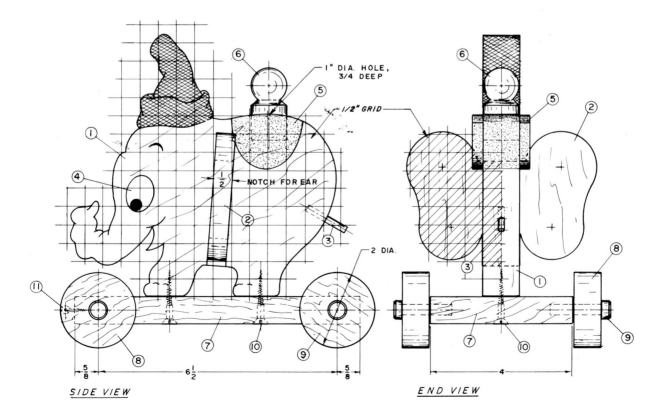

SIDE VIEW   *END VIEW*

Caterpillar Pull Toy

*Children are
fascinated with caterpillars;
now they can have one of their own. Just
hope it doesn't turn into a butterfly!*

1. Cut out all pieces to overall size. Sand all over.

Using the given dimensions, carefully lay out the body and head directly on the wood with a compass. Locate all holes. Cut out the body and head.

2. Drill all 5/16-inch-diameter holes. I drilled these holes with a 3/8-inch diameter so that the axles would be sloppy in the holes and not bind.

Cut the spacers (part 4) from a 1-inch-diameter dowel, 1/4-inch thick.

Since each wheel is a different diameter, each of the five pairs will have to be cut out individually.

3. Drill for the antennas (part 2).

Glue the spacers (part 4) onto the body (part 1). You might have to re-drill the 5 holes.

Drill a 1/8-inch-diameter hole for the nose.

4. Temporarily assemble all of the pieces. Check that everything fits correctly.

5. Disassemble and paint. Use your imagination; a caterpillar is typically green and yellow, but this one is painted green and orange. Assemble after painting, and add the eye screw (part 5) and string.

MATERIALS LIST

NO.	NAME	SIZE	REQ'D.
1	BODY	¾ x 3¾ – 10⅞ LONG	1
2	ANTENNA	³⁄₁₆ DIA. – 1¼ LONG	2
3	AXLE	⁵⁄₁₆ DIA. – 3 LONG	5
4	SPACER	1 DIA. – ¼ LONG	10
5	SCREW – EYE	SMALL	1
6	WHEEL 1	2 DIA. – ¾ LONG	2
7	WHEEL 2	1⅞ DIA. – ¾ LONG	2
8	WHEEL 3	1¾ DIA. – ¾ LONG	2
9	WHEEL 4	1⅝ DIA. – ¾ LONG	2
10	WHEEL 5	1½ DIA. – ¾ LONG	2

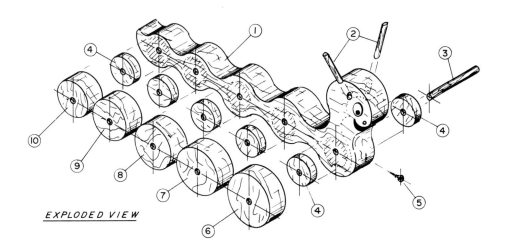

EXPLODED VIEW

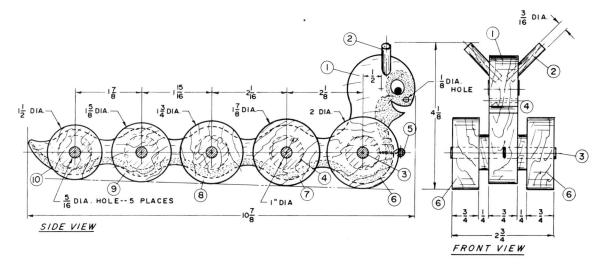

SIDE VIEW

FRONT VIEW

Crayon Tractor-Trailer

This toy truck is great for your budding artist. It provides a handy place to hold crayons when they're not in use. It can be made from a piece of 2 x 4-inch wood.

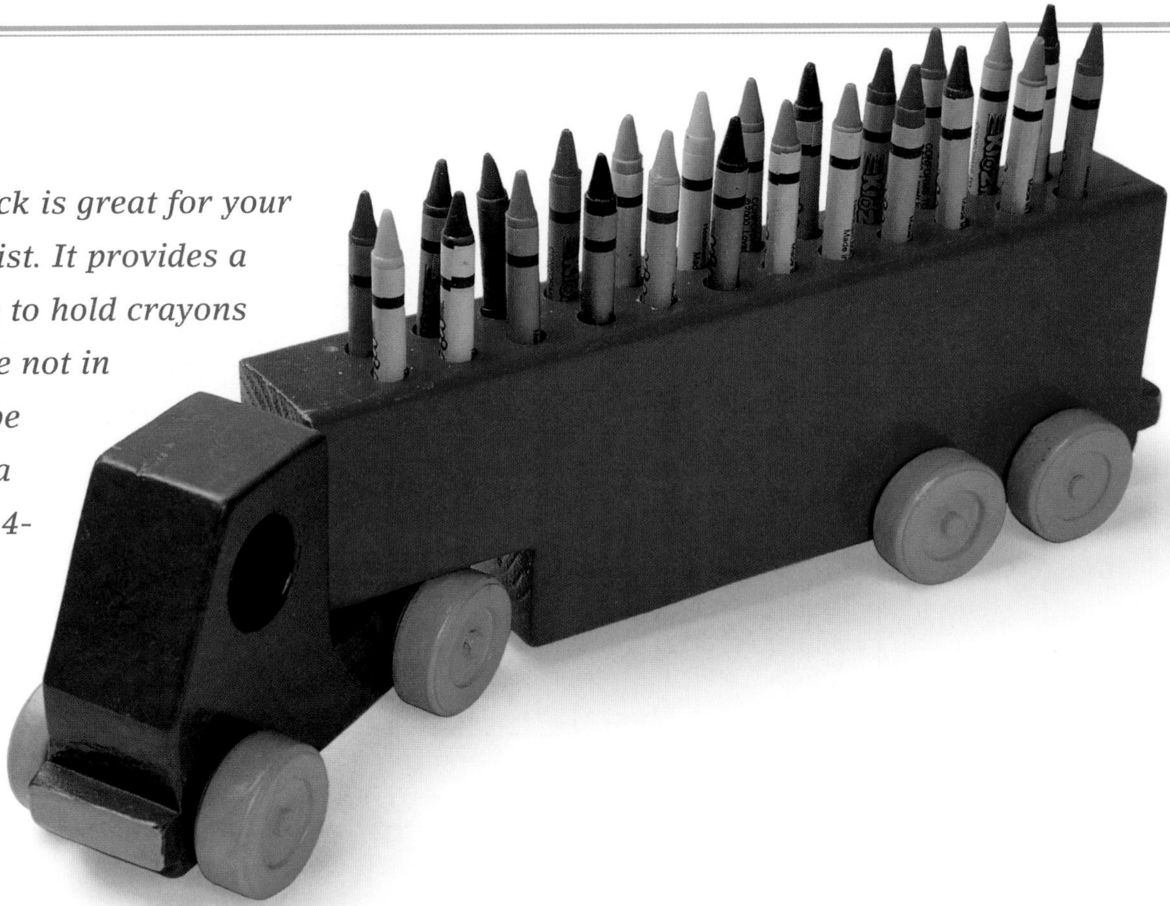

1. Cut pieces to overall size.

2. Carefully lay out the cab (part 1) and box (part 2).

3. Drill all required holes, as shown.

4. The wheels (part 4) can be cut from a 1½-inch-diameter dowel (½ inch wide) or you can purchase 1½-inch-diameter wheels.

5. Dry-fit all pieces.

6. Paint to suit, and assemble.

7. Glue the wheels to the axles. Let them turn freely inside the cab or box. Add a set of crayons, and the tractor-trailer is ready for the artist.

MATERIALS LIST

NO.	NAME	SIZE	REQ'D.
1	CAB	1½ x 3⅛ – 5¼ LONG	1
2	BOX	1½ x 3½ – 10¾ LONG	1
3	AXLE	¼ DIA. – 2¾ LONG	4
4	WHEEL	1½ DIA. – ½ LONG	8
5	PEG	⅜ DIA. – 2¼ LONG	1
6	CRAYON SET	ALL COLORS	24

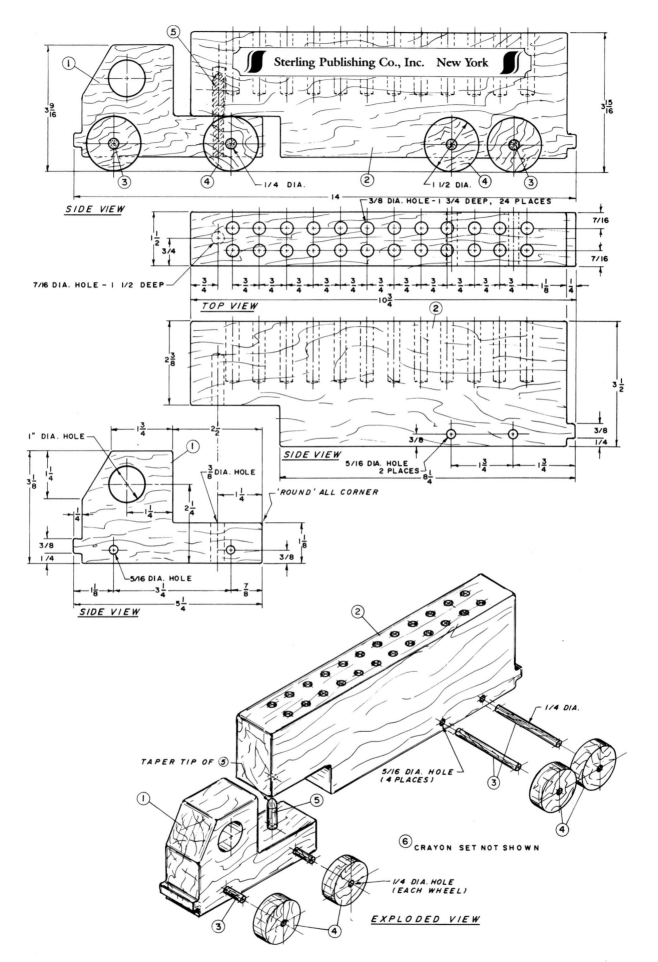

SIDE VIEW

Sterling Publishing Co., Inc.   New York

3/8 DIA. HOLE - 1 3/4 DEEP, 24 PLACES

TOP VIEW

7/16 DIA. HOLE - 1 1/2 DEEP

SIDE VIEW

1" DIA. HOLE

3/8 DIA. HOLE

'ROUND' ALL CORNER

5/16 DIA. HOLE

SIDE VIEW

5/16 DIA. HOLE
2 PLACES

1/4 DIA.

TAPER TIP OF ⑤

5/16 DIA. HOLE
(4 PLACES)

⑥ CRAYON SET NOT SHOWN

1/4 DIA. HOLE
(EACH WHEEL)

EXPLODED VIEW

1/4 DIA.

Dog Pull Toy

A good friend of ours bought a miniature dachshund and spent hours teaching the dog to do tricks. I was impressed with the dog and based this toy on it.

MATERIALS LIST

NO.	NAME	SIZE	REQ'D.
1	BODY	½ x 6½ – 14 LONG	1
2	EAR	⅛ x 2 – 2¾ LONG	2
3	HINGE PIN	⅛ DIA. – 2½ LONG	2
4	AXLE	¾ x ¾ – 4 LONG	2
5	WHEEL	⅝ - 2 DIA.	4
6	AXLE PEG	7/32 DIA. – 1½ LONG	4
7	SCREW – EYE		1
8	STRING	CUT TO FIT	

1. Select the stock and cut the body segments. I suggest using straight-grained maple or birch. First, make paper patterns of both the dog and his ears (parts 1 and 2). Draw a grid with ½-inch squares and enlarge the parts onto it. Transfer the enlargements to the stock, leaving at least ½ inch between the segments. Cut the parts to shape.

2. Drill the hinge pinholes. Temporarily assemble the three body segments and tape them together. Make sure that they are in proper alignment and that the hinge joints are snug. Locate and drill the holes for the two hinge pins (part 3), as shown in the top view, taking care to drill straight down.

Temporarily put the hinge pins—made from ⅛-inch-diameter hardwood dowels—in place and remove the tape. Sand the profile of the dog so that one segment seems to flow into the other along the length of the body. This work goes quickly on a drum sander mounted on a drill press.

Remove the hinge pins and round the hinge joints with a rasp so that the segments can each swivel approximately 90° in either direction. Refer to the exploded view to see the finished shape of the hinges. As you work, check your progress by reassembling the dog. The fit should be loose but not sloppy.

3. Make the wheels and axles. You can either cut the wheels (part 5) out of ⅝-inch-thick stock with a circle cutter in a drill press or buy them.

Cut out the axles (part 4). Notch them to take the feet of the dog. Drill ⁷⁄₃₂-inch-diameter holes, roughly 1¼ inch deep, in the center of the axle ends to take the axle pegs (part 6).

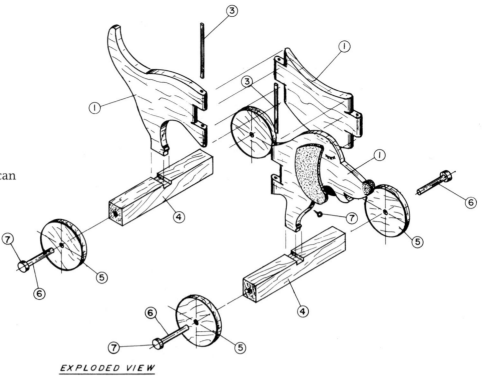

EXPLODED VIEW

4. Assemble the dog. You can glue up axle pegs or turn them if you have a lathe, but I've found it's easier to purchase them. Slip the pegs through the wheel holes and glue them in the axles, making sure the cap on the end of the axle doesn't bind against the wheel. Glue the dog's feet to the axles and glue on the ears.

5. Apply finish. You can leave the dog unfinished or apply a varnish or fanciful paint job. When the finish has dried, glue the hinge pins in place. Place the glue in the top and bottom holes only, or the joints won't turn.

Install the eye screw (part 7), tie on a length of string (part 8), and take your dog for a walk.

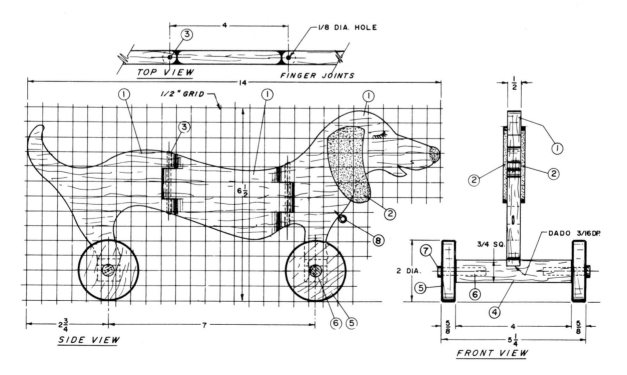

Walking Dog Pull Toy

Now this is my kind of dog. You don't have to feed, walk, or brush him. He doesn't bark or smell, and you don't have to apply flea powder to him. This dog's legs move as you pull him, making him look like a real dog walking. This kind of dog used to be a common addition to many kids' toy chests.

1. Carefully lay out all of the parts on a ½-inch grid, point by point. Don't forget to locate all of the drilling points for the holes. I suggest that you simply glue two ¾-inch-thick pieces together to get the 1½-inch thickness for the body.

2. Transfer the patterns to the wood. Locate and drill all of the holes first, before you cut out all of the pieces. After cutting them out, sand all over. Multiple parts that are the same should be drilled, cut out, and

NO.	NAME	SIZE	REQ'D.
\multicolumn{4}{c}{**MATERIALS LIST**}			
1	BODY	1½ x 4½ – 17½ LONG	1
2	WHEEL	¾ x 2½ DIA.	1
3	AXLE	⅜ DIA. - 3¹⁄₁₆ LONG	2
4	BACK LEG – TOP	¾ x 1¾ – 4 LONG	2
5	BACK LEG – BOTTOM	⅝ x 2 – 4 LONG	2
6	FRONT LEG – TOP	¾ x 1⅝ – 3¾ LONG	2
7	FRONT LEG – BOTTOM	⅝ x 1⁹⁄₁₆ – 4 LONG	2
8	AXLE PEG	1⅜ LONG	12
9	EAR	⁵⁄₁₆ x 2¼ – 4½ LONG	2
10	TEETH	³⁄₁₆ DIA. - 1⅛ LONG	3
11	EYE – JIGGLE		2
12	SCREW - EYE		1

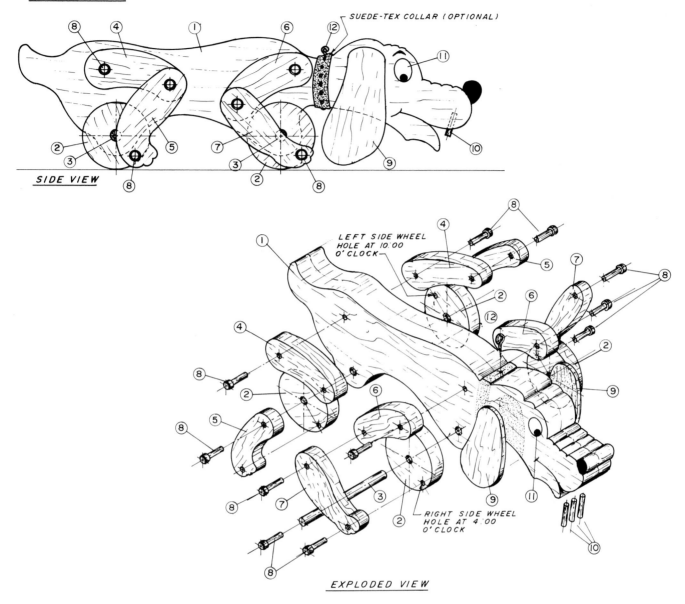

ASSEMBLY VIEW

SUEDE-TEX COLLAR (OPTIONAL)

SIDE VIEW

LEFT SIDE WHEEL
HOLE AT 10:00
O'CLOCK

RIGHT SIDE WHEEL
HOLE AT 4:00
O'CLOCK

EXPLODED VIEW

sanded along the edges while they are taped or tacked together to ensure that each matches exactly.

3. Dry-fit all of the parts to ensure that everything works correctly. Adjust as necessary. Make sure that all of the parts are a little on the loose side so that the dog will pull easily and the four legs will move smoothly without any binding.

4. Disassemble and paint your walking dog as you wish. If you have always wanted a spotted dog, here is your chance to have one. Don't forget the collar. Apply a coat of paste wax to all of the parts before final assembly, but do not get any wax inside any hole where you will be gluing an axle peg.

5. Carefully glue the axle pegs in place with the wheels on the peg. Be sure the glue does not get on the wheels. Check that all parts move freely. Add an eyescrew to the collar.

Toys, Games & Puzzles   259

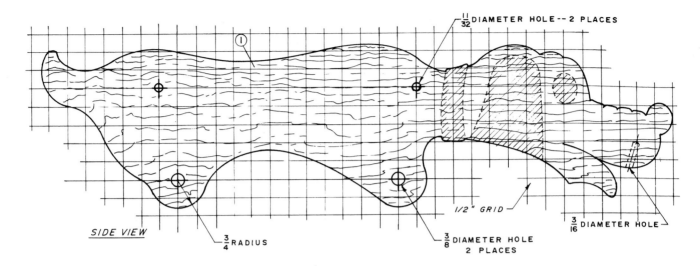

$\frac{11}{32}$ DIAMETER HOLE -- 2 PLACES

①

$\frac{3}{16}$ DIAMETER HOLE

1/2" GRID

SIDE VIEW

$\frac{3}{4}$ RADIUS

$\frac{3}{8}$ DIAMETER HOLE 2 PLACES

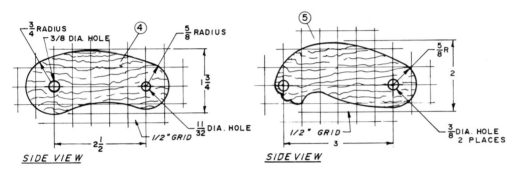

$\frac{3}{4}$ RADIUS
3/8 DIA. HOLE
④
$\frac{5}{8}$ RADIUS

$1\frac{3}{4}$

$\frac{11}{32}$ DIA. HOLE

1/2" GRID

$2\frac{1}{2}$

SIDE VIEW

⑤
$\frac{5}{8}$ R

2

1/2" GRID

3

$\frac{3}{8}$ DIA. HOLE 2 PLACES

SIDE VIEW

$\frac{3}{4}$ DEEP -- 3 PLACES
$\frac{3}{8}$ DIA. HOLE

$2\frac{1}{2}$ DIA.

1"

②

$\frac{11}{32}$ DIA. HOLE

SIDE VIEW

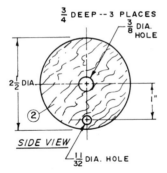

$\frac{9}{16}$ RADIUS
⑥
$\frac{5}{8}$ RADIUS

$1\frac{5}{8}$

3/8 DIA. HOLE

$\frac{11}{32}$ DIA. HOLE

1/2" GRID

$2\frac{1}{2}$

SIDE VIEW

$\frac{9}{16}$ RADIUS
1/2" GRID

$1\frac{9}{16}$

⑦

3

3/8 DIA. HOLE -- 2 PLACES

SIDE VIEW

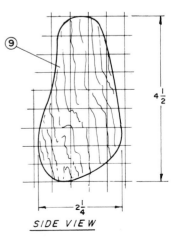

⑨

$4\frac{1}{2}$

$2\frac{1}{4}$

SIDE VIEW

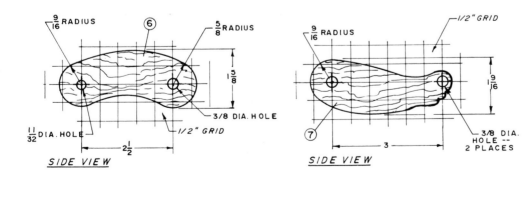

Train with Passengers

MATERIALS LIST

NO.	NAME	SIZE	REQ'D.
1	BASE	½ x 1¾ – 3⅞ LONG	1
2	BASE	½ x 1¾ – 2¾ LONG	1
3	BASE	½ x 1¾ – 3¼ LONG	2
4	BASE	½ x 1¾ – 4½ LONG	1
5	WHEEL	1 DIA. - 3/16 LONG	20
6	TACK		28
7	MAGNET	½ DIA.	8
8	CAB	¾ x 1½ – 1⅞ LONG	2
9	BOILER	1¼ DIA. – 1½ LONG	1
10	CHIMNEY	⅜ DIA. – 1⅛ LONG	1
11	LIGHT	¾ DIA. – ½ LONG	1
12	ROOF	¼ x 1¾ – 2 LONG	1
13	PLUG	¾ DIA. – 7/16 LONG	6
14	GUIDE	CUT FROM 6d NAIL	1
15	SIDE	¼ x 1½ – 2¼ LONG	2
16	FRONT	¼ x 1½ – 1 LONG	1
17	SUPPORT	5/16 DIA. – 2⅛ LONG	2
18	CARGO	1¼ DIA. – ½ LONG	6
19	CAB	¾ x 1⅞ – 4 LONG	2
20	ROOF	¼ x 1¾ – 4½ LONG	1
21	CAB	¾ x 1⅞ – 2¾ LONG	2
22	ROOF	¼ x 1¾ – 3¼ LONG	1
23	LOOKOUT	½ x ¾ – 1¼ LONG	1
24	ROOF	¼ x 1 – 1¾ LONG	1
25	CHIMNEY	3/16 DIA. – ¾ LONG	1
26	PASSENGER	11/16 DIA. – 1¾ LONG	6

One of the most popular toys ever is the toy train. I tried to come up with a simple train that could be made up of all those scrap pieces of wood you usually burn or throw away. I chose modern round magnets and tacks to hook the train cars together. This project can be left natural or painted.

1. Cut all pieces to overall size. Glue up required pieces as necessary. Drill all holes according to the sizes given. Dry-fit all pieces.

2. Glue up each car (refer to the exploded view). Don't forget to add the passengers.

3. The wheels can be cut from a 1-inch-diameter dowel (3/16 inch thick) or you can purchase 1-inch wheels. Add wheels to cars last.

4. Paint cars to suit or leave them natural. Add the magnets. Don't forget to orient the magnets north to south so that the cars will attach correctly.

Paint and add wheels; check that they turn freely.

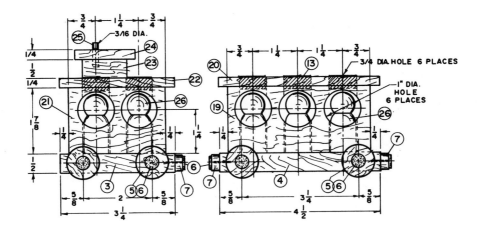

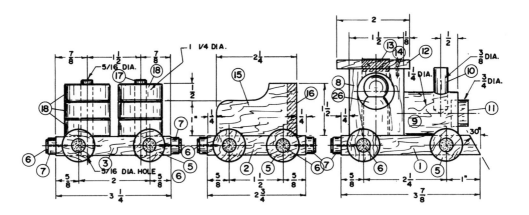

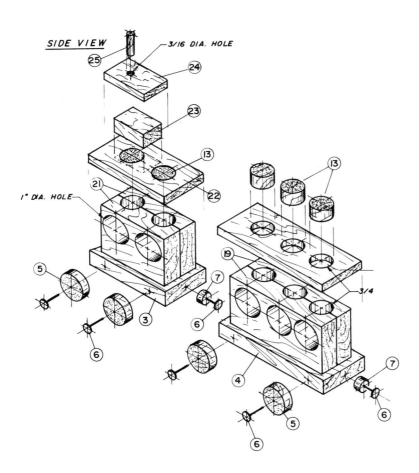

SIDE VIEW

3/16 DIA. HOLE

25

24

23

13

21

22

1" DIA. HOLE

5

3

7

6

6

19

13

13

3/4

4

7

6

5

6

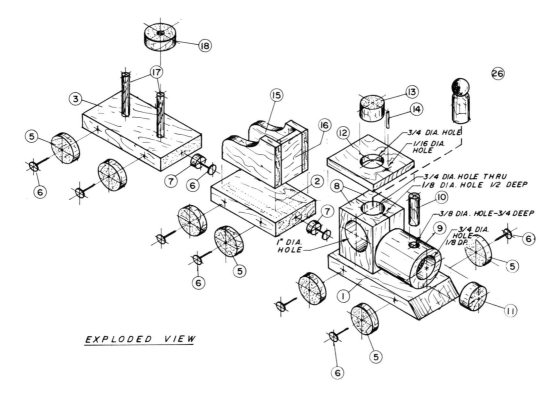

18

17

3

15

16

13

12

26

14

3/4 DIA. HOLE

1/16 DIA. HOLE

3/4 DIA. HOLE THRU

1/8 DIA. HOLE 1/2 DEEP

3/8 DIA. HOLE-3/4 DEEP

3/4 DIA. HOLE 1/8 DP.

5

6

7

6

1" DIA. HOLE

7

2

8

10

9

6

5

5

EXPLODED VIEW

1

5

6

11

Doll Tricycle

Even dolls and teddy bears need a toy, so here's one for them. I suggest that you make this out of hardwood, especially the handlebars.

1. Cut all parts to overall size, according to the cutting list.

2. On a half-inch grid lay out the seat, and transfer the pattern to the wood.

3. Using a compass, lay out the axle support (part 2) and handlebar (part 6) according to the given dimensions.

4. Cut out the four 3 inch-diameter wheels, and drill holes in the center of each for the axles.

MATERIALS LIST			
NO.	NAME	SIZE	REQ'D.
1	BASE	¾ x 1 – 5⅝ LONG	1
2	WHEEL SUPPORT	¾ x 4 ¾ – 3 LONG	1
3	NAIL – FINISH	6 d	5
4	SEAT	¾ x 5½ – 5 LONG	1
5	VERTICAL BAR	¾ x ¾ – 2¼ LONG	1
6	HANDLE BAR	¾ x 3 – 6 LONG	1
7	PIN	5/16 DIA. – 1½ LONG	1
8	VERTICAL BAR	¾ x ¾ – 2¼ LONG	1
9	PIN	5/16 DIA. – 2¼ LONG	1
10	AXLE – FRONT	5/16 DIA. – 2¼ LONG	1
11	FOOT REST	5/16 DIA. – 1¾ LONG	2
12	AXLE – REAR	5/16 DIA. – 6 LONG	1
13	WHEEL	¾ x 3 DIA.	4

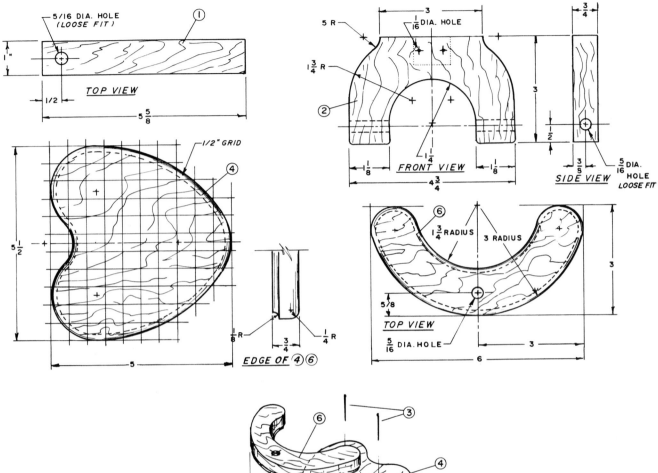

5/16 DIA. HOLE
(LOOSE FIT)

①

1"

1/2

5 5/8

TOP VIEW

5 R

1/16 DIA. HOLE

3

3/4

1 3/4 R

②

3

1 1/8

1 1/4

1 1/8

1/2

3/8

5/16 DIA. HOLE
LOOSE FIT

FRONT VIEW

SIDE VIEW

4 3/4

1/2" GRID

④

5 1/2

5

⑥

1 3/4 RADIUS

3 RADIUS

3

5/8

5/16 DIA. HOLE

TOP VIEW

6

1/8 R

3/4

1/4 R

EDGE OF ④ ⑥

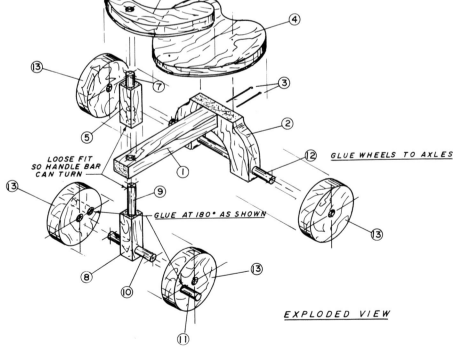

⑥

③

④

⑬

⑦

⑤

LOOSE FIT
SO HANDLE BAR
CAN TURN

①

②

③

⑫

GLUE WHEELS TO AXLES

⑬

⑬

⑨

GLUE AT 180° AS SHOWN

⑬

⑧

⑩

⑬

⑪

EXPLODED VIEW

5. Complete all other pieces, according to the dimensions given.

6. Using a ⅛-inch cove-cutter bit with a ball-bearing follower, rout the bottom of the seat and handlebars.

7. Using a ¼-inch-radius router bit, round the edges of the seat and handlebars.

8. Assemble the tricycle, using the exploded view. Check that the front wheels move and steer freely.

9. Sand all over, removing all sharp edges.

10. Paint to suit, using bright colors.

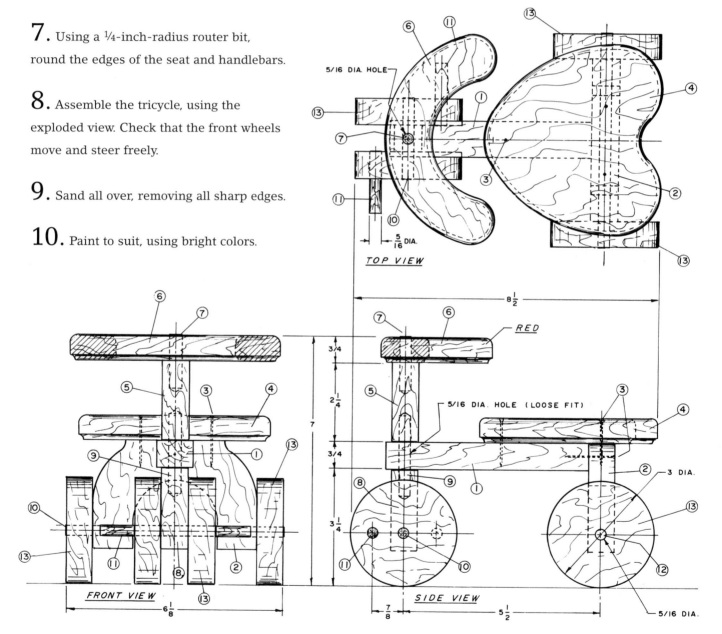

Model T Truck

This is a toy that teaches both history and thrift. It's a 1925 Model T Ford truck. The Model T Ford was made from 1909 through 1927, and it single-handedly put America on wheels. In addition to being fun to play with, this toy is also a bank.

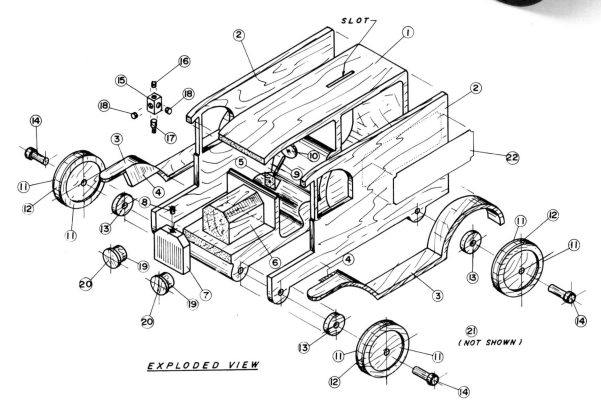

SLOT

EXPLODED VIEW

(NOT SHOWN)

1. Cut all pieces to overall size according to the Materials List.

2. On a ½-inch grid, lay out all pieces. Take care that the outer shape of the body (parts 1 and 2) is exactly the same.

3. Cut the interior of the center (part 1). Locate and cut the slot, as shown. Cut out the window on the two sides (part 2). Glue the two sides (parts 2) over the center section, and cut out the outer edges of the car.

4. Locate and drill the two ¼-inch-diameter holes for the axles.

5. Sand all over.

6. Add the hood (part 6) and radiator (part 7) in place.

7. Cut out the fenders (part 3). Be sure to make a right and left matched pair of fenders.

8. Fit the filler (part 4) to the fenders (part 3) as shown. Fit the fenders to the body, and glue in place.

9. Assemble all other miscellaneous pieces according to the exploded view.

10. Make up wheels by gluing the tires (part 11) to the wheels (part 10). (See the exploded view.)

11. Temporarily add the wheels to the body. Check that everything fits correctly.

12. Paint all over to suit. Add wheels and axles.

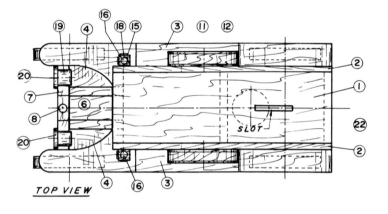

TOP VIEW

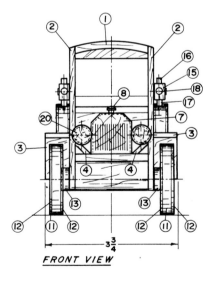

FRONT VIEW

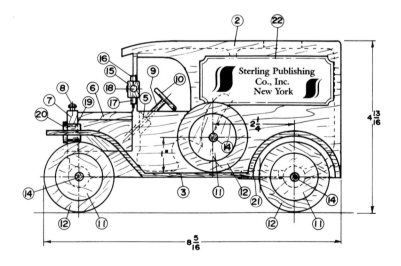

MATERIALS LIST			
NO.	NAME	SIZE	REQ'D.
1	CENTER	2 x 4¼ - 7¾ LONG	1
2	SIDE	3⁄16 x 4¼ – 7¾ LONG	2
3	FENDER	1 ¼ x 15⁄16 – 8¼ LONG	2
4	FILLER	⅛ x 1 – 1⅜ LONG	2
5	SUPPORT – COLUMN	½ x ½ – ½ LONG	1
6	HOOD	11⁄16 x 1⅛ – 1½ LONG	1
7	RADIATOR	5⁄16 x 1⅛ – 1¼ LONG	1
8	CAP	3⁄16 DIA. – 7⁄16 LONG	1
9	COLUMN	⅛ DIA. – 1¼ LONG	1
10	WHEEL	⅞ DIA. – ⅛ LONG	1
11	TIRE	1⁄16 x 2 SQUARE	12
12	RIM	¼ x 2 SQUARE	6
13	SPACER	⅝ DIA. - 3⁄16 LONG	4
14	AXLE PEG		6
15	PARKING LAMP	5⁄16 x 5⁄16 – ½ LONG	2
16	TOP	3⁄16 DIA. - 5⁄16 LONG	2
17	BOTTOM	3⁄16 DIA. - ⅜ LONG	2
18	LENS	3⁄16 DIA. - ⅛ LONG	4
19	BODY	½ DIA. - ⅜ LONG	2
20	LENS	⅝ DIA. - ⅛ LONG	2
21	STOPPER		1
22	SIGN (TO SUIT)	1 ⅜ - 3¾ LONG	2

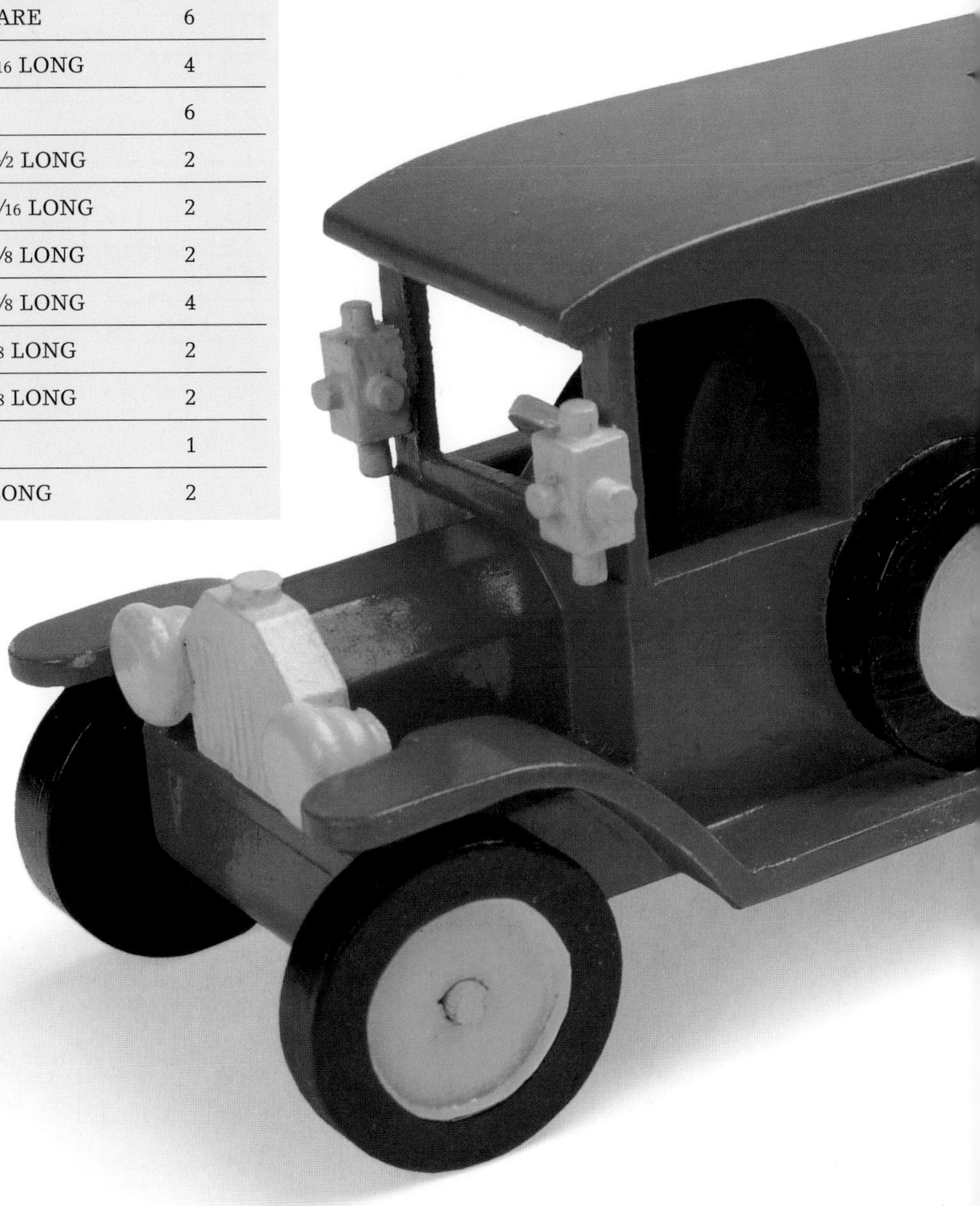

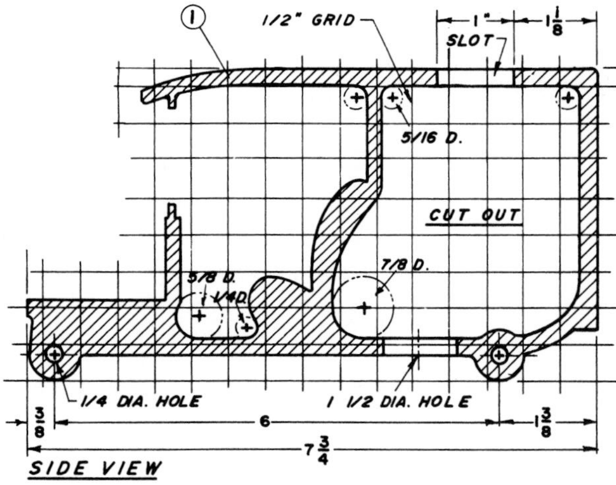
1
1/2" GRID
1"
1 1/8
SLOT
5/16 D.
CUT OUT
4 1/4
5/8 D.
1/4 D.
7/8 D.
1/4 DIA. HOLE
1 1/2 DIA. HOLE
3/8
6
1 3/8
7 3/4
SIDE VIEW

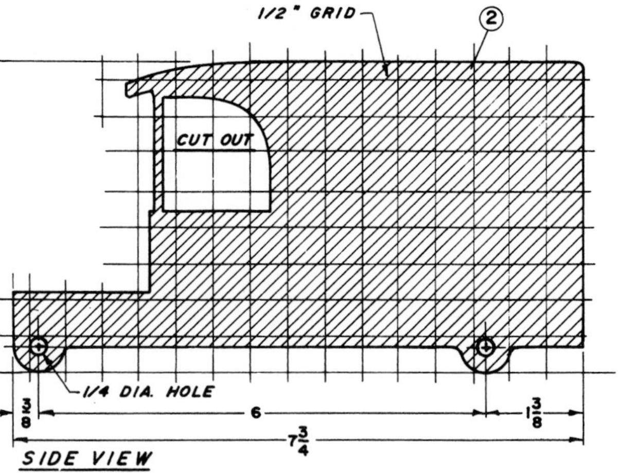
1/2" GRID
2
CUT OUT
1/4 DIA. HOLE
3/8
6
1 3/8
7 3/4
SIDE VIEW

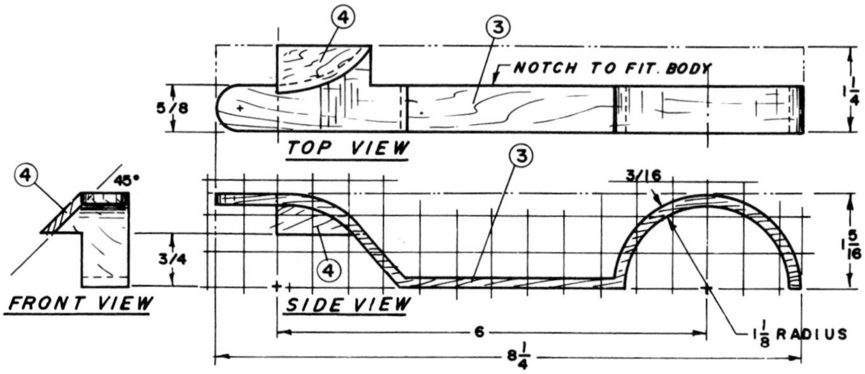
4
3
NOTCH TO FIT BODY
5/8
1 1/4
TOP VIEW
4
45°
3/4
FRONT VIEW
3
3/16
4
1 5/16
SIDE VIEW
6
1 1/8 RADIUS
8 1/4

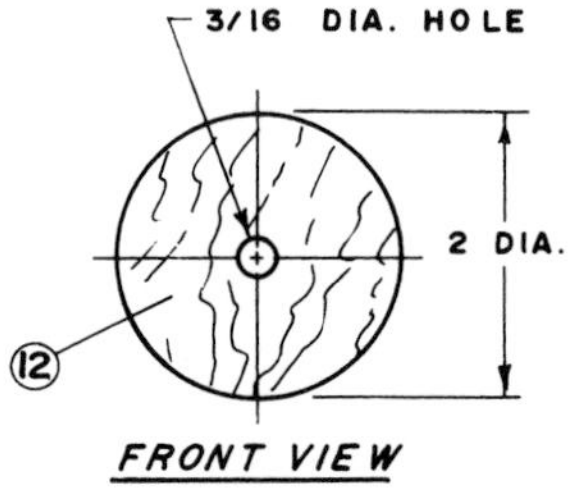
3/16 DIA. HOLE
2 DIA.
12
FRONT VIEW

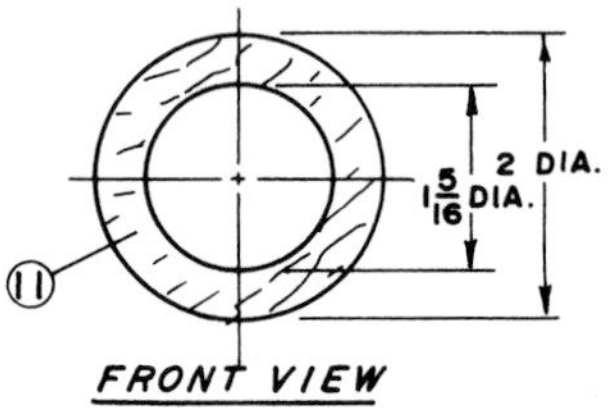
2 DIA.
1 5/16 DIA.
11
FRONT VIEW

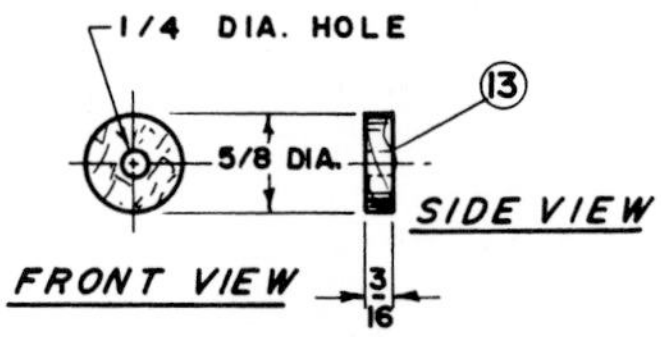
1/4 DIA. HOLE
5/8 DIA.
13
SIDE VIEW
FRONT VIEW
3/16

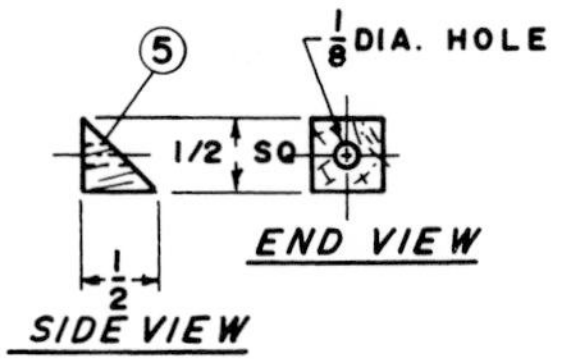
5
1/8 DIA. HOLE
1/2 SQ.
END VIEW
1/2
SIDE VIEW

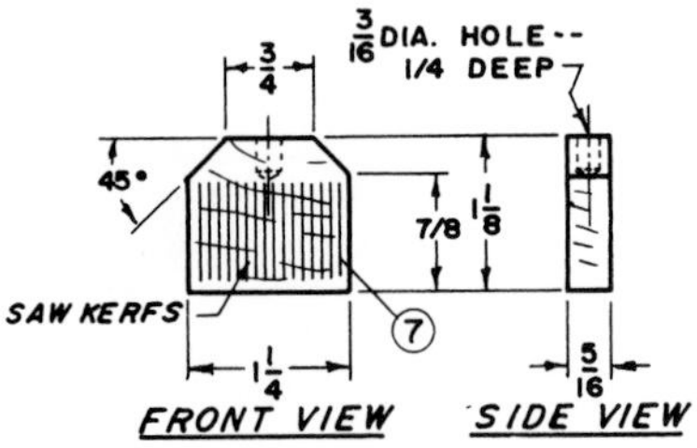
3/4
3/16 DIA. HOLE
1/4 DEEP
45°
7/8
1 1/8
SAW KERFS
7
1 1/4
5/16
FRONT VIEW
SIDE VIEW

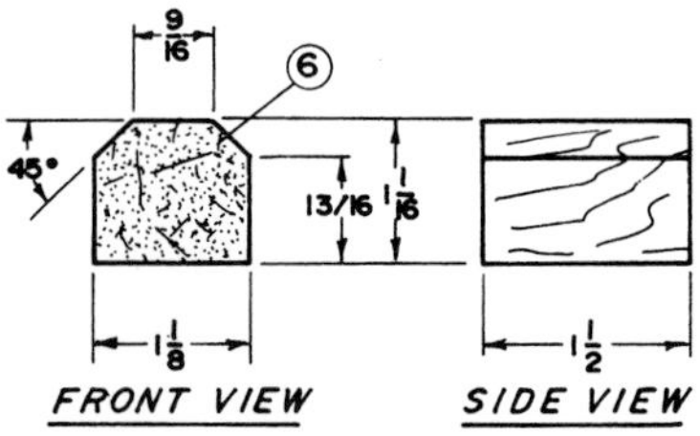
9/16
6
45°
13/16
1 1/16
1 1/8
1 1/2
FRONT VIEW
SIDE VIEW

Noah's Ark with Animals

Noah's Ark seems very popular today. I find replicas at all the big craft fairs we go to, so here's my version. I tried to make it with a folk-art flair. You'll be all set for the next flood.

1. Study the exploded view before starting. Note that the boat sides (part 4) are simply nailed or glued to a frame made up of parts 1, 2, and 3. Cut all pieces to overall size, according to the cutting list.

2. Make up the frame subassembly as shown, using parts 1, 2, and 3.

3. Lay out the two side pieces (part 4), using the given dimensions. Drill the three 1 inch-diameter holes. On one side panel, locate the door and make the two notches. Drill the 1/16-inch-diameter holes for the nails (part 7).

Note: drill the two 1/16-inch-diameter holes 2¼ inches deep before cutting out the door.

MATERIALS LIST			
NO.	**NAME**	**SIZE**	**REQ'D.**
1	DECK	¾ x 4 – 11¾ LONG	1
2	END	¾ x 4 – 5 LONG	2
3	BOTTOM	¾ x 4 – 7¾ LONG	1
4	SIDE	¾ x 6⅛ – 12 LONG	2
5	CABIN	1½ x 3 – 6 LONG	1
6	ROOF	¼ x 1 ¾ – 6¾ LONG	2
7	PIN	1/16 DIA. – 2¼ LONG	2
8	WHEEL	1¾ DIA. – ⅝ LONG	4
9	AXLE	¼ DIA. – 7 LONG	2
10	NAIL – FINISH	6d	18
11	ANIMALS	½ x 6 –16½ LONG	2

4. Cut out the door.

5. Locate and drill the ¼-inch-diameter holes for the axles (part 9).

6. Attach the sides (part 4) to the frame assembly.

7. Sand all over.

8. Re-drill the ¼-inch-diameter holes for the axles through the bottom (part 3). (You might want to drill a ⁵⁄₁₆-inch-diameter hole so the axle will turn more easily.)

9. Make up the remaining pieces (parts 5 and 6).

10. Install the door using the 2 pins (part 7).

11. Add the axles and wheels (glue the wheels to the axle). Check that they turn freely.

12. Paint to suit.

13. On a ½-inch grid, lay out the animals (part 11) onto ½-inch-thick wood. Make two of each animal. You might wish to make one set slightly smaller to represent the female of each. (But remember that for some animals, lions for instance, the male and female look quite different.)

Paint the animals to suit. If you use a nice hardwood, they could be left natural.

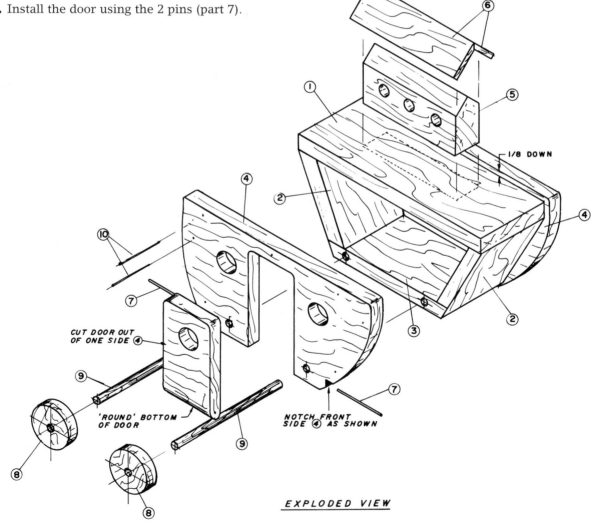

1/8 DOWN

CUT DOOR OUT
OF ONE SIDE ④

'ROUND' BOTTOM
OF DOOR

NOTCH FRONT
SIDE ④ AS SHOWN

EXPLODED VIEW

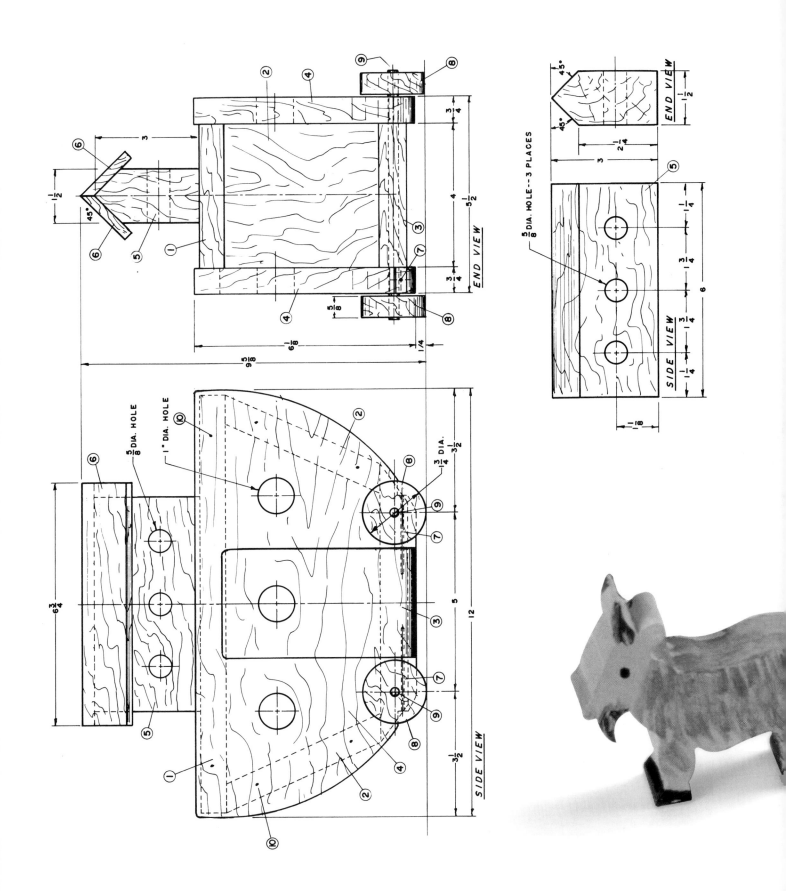

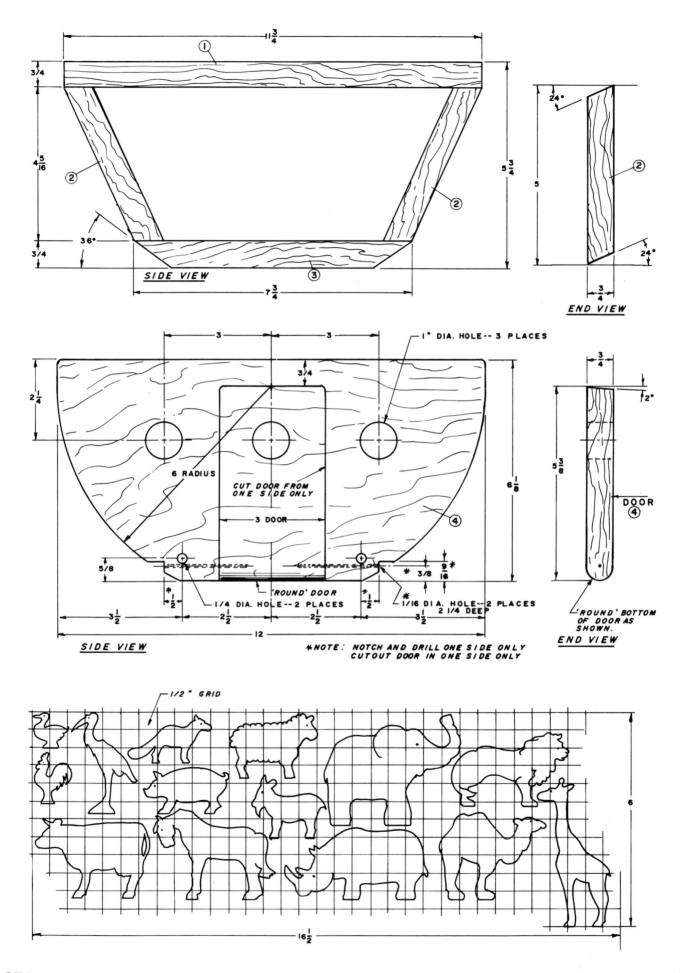

SIDE VIEW

END VIEW

1" DIA. HOLE—3 PLACES

6 RADIUS

CUT DOOR FROM
ONE SIDE ONLY

3 DOOR

'ROUND' DOOR

1/4 DIA. HOLE—2 PLACES

1/16 DIA. HOLE—2 PLACES
2 1/4 DEEP

DOOR
④

'ROUND' BOTTOM
OF DOOR AS
SHOWN.

END VIEW

SIDE VIEW

*NOTE: NOTCH AND DRILL ONE SIDE ONLY
CUTOUT DOOR IN ONE SIDE ONLY

1/2" GRID

Model T Runabout

This toy is patterned after a 1914 Model T, a car with a crank starter, carbide headlights, kerosene cowl lights, and a rubber bulb horn. As the by-now famous saying goes, it came in any color you wanted, as long as you wanted black. I owned one of them a few years ago, and it was a lot of fun to drive. Since even a slight deviation may affect the assembly of this toy, dry-fit each part before gluing it. You'll find that cutting the parts is far easier if you have a parallel-arm scroll saw, but you can make do with a coping saw.

1. Select the stock. Because of the intricate cutting that you'll have to do, use a wood with tight, straight grain. Maple and birch are good choices. I used ash because I have a plentiful supply, but it was hard work.

Cut the parts to the sizes given in the Materials List. Make the engine compartment (part 4) 12 inches long for now so that it will be easier to chamfer when the time comes. Cut the base (part 1) to the profile shown.

2. Make paper patterns. Draw grids with the appropriately sized squares and enlarge the outer body and fenders onto it. Transfer the patterns to the stock.

3. Make the body. The body is a sandwich made of two outer bodies and one inner body. The two outer bodies (part 2) are particularly complex. Cut them at the same time, temporarily gluing two 3/16-inch-thick

pieces of stock to each other with rubber cement. Cut out the parts with a jigsaw or coping saw. Begin the two cutouts, as marked in the side view, by drilling a small hole. Slip the saw blade into the hole before attaching the blade to the saw.

Use one of the outer bodies as a pattern to draw the inner body (part 3) on a piece of stock. Leave out the roof supports but add a seat, as shown in the detail of the inner body Cut out the inner body.

Lay out and drill a ⅛-inch-diameter steering wheel hole through the front of the inner body; it is ⅜ inch from the left side, roughly ⅝ inch up from the bottom and at a 45° angle to the floor.

Make a saw kerf, ¹⁄₁₆ inch wide and ¼ inch deep, to accept the windshield in the inner body. Locate and cut out the rear window, as shown.

Glue the outer bodies to either side of the inner body. After the glue has dried, sand the edges between the parts. This completes the body subassembly.

4. Make the engine compartment. Cut the 45° chamfers, as shown in the front view of the engine compartment (part 4). You can rip these on the table saw if you begin with a piece at least 12 inches long. Chamfer it and then cut it to the proper length.

Lay out and drill the two holes for the headlights, as shown in the front view of the engine compartment Position the holes exactly as shown. The drill bit overhangs the edge of the compartment when drilling, leaving a hole with one flat side.

Cut a slot around the engine compartment with a thin-bladed saw, as shown in the side view of the engine compartment. Lay out and drill the hole for the radiator cap.

5. Assemble the body, base, engine compartment, and trunk. Glue the base and engine compartment to the body subassembly. When the glue has dried, fill any gaps with a matching wood putty and sand thoroughly, smoothing the edges between the parts. Glue the trunk (part 5) in place.

6. Make the fenders. Use the pattern you made earlier to lay out the fenders (part 7). Sand or file as necessary to fit the fender to the car body. Only the top of the left-hand fender is shown. You'll need to make a set of right-hand and left-hand fenders. Glue the fenders to the body and fill and sand as necessary to eliminate any gaps.

7. Complete the assembly. Drill ³⁄₁₆-inch-diameter holes through the length of the axle supports (part 6). To position

MATERIALS LIST

NO.	NAME	SIZE	REQ'D.
1	BASE	⅜ x 2 – 5 LONG	1
2	OUTER BODY	³⁄₁₆ x 3⅛ – 3⅝ LONG	2
3	INNER BODY	1⅝ x 3⅛ – 3⅝ LONG	1
4	ENGINE COMPARTMENT	1⅛ x 1½ – 1⅜ LONG	1
5	TRUNK	⁹⁄₁₆ x 1⅜ – 1³⁄₁₆ LONG	1
6	AXLE SUPPORT	¼ x ¼ – 2 LONG	2
7	FENDER	⅝ x 1⅛ – 6 LONG	2
8	CAP	³⁄₁₆ DIA. – ⅜ LONG	1
9	HEADLIGHT BODY	½ DIA. – ¼ LONG	2
10	HEADLIGHT LENS	⅝ DIA. – ¹⁄₁₆ LONG	2
11	STEERING POST	⅛ DIA. - 1¼ LONG	1
12	STEERING WHEEL	⅝ DIA. – ⅛ LONG	1
13	LAMP	³⁄₁₆ x ³⁄₁₆ – ⁵⁄₁₆ LONG	2
14	LAMP DETAIL	⅛ DIA. – ⅛ LONG	8
15	WHEEL	1½ DIA. – ¼ LONG	4
16	AXLE PINS	³⁄₁₆ DIA. – 2¾ LONG	2
17	WINDSHIELD	1½ x 2 (THICKNESS VARIABLE)	1

the axle supports, temporarily mount the wheels in them. Put the supports underneath the car so that the wheels are centered inside the fender wells. Glue the supports in place.

After the glue dries, check the fit of the axle pins (part 16) in the axle supports. Slide the axle pins into the supports, and make sure the wheels can turn freely. You might have to sand the pins slightly. Adjust as necessary; slip an axle pin through the supports, and glue the wheels in place.

Glue the steering post (part 11) and steering wheel (part 12) in place.

Glue the lamp details (part 14) onto the lamps (part 13). Note that on each lamp, one detail is aimed away from the car—the right-hand and left-hand lamps will not be identical. Mount the lamps on the body, as illustrated.

Slice the headlight bodies and lenses (parts 9 and 10) from sections of ½-inch and ⅝-inch-diameter dowels. Glue them together, and then glue the assembly to the body.

Glue the cap (part 8) on top of the radiator.

Cut out the windshield (part 17) from a piece of clear plastic measuring up to $\frac{1}{16}$ inch thick. I used plastic from an overhead projector transparency. Outline the border in black as shown, with a pen that will write on plastic. Attach the plastic in the kerf with all-purpose household cement designed for plastics.

8. Apply finish. You can leave the car as it is, or add a couple coats of clear varnish. Of course, you also can paint it black like the original Model T.

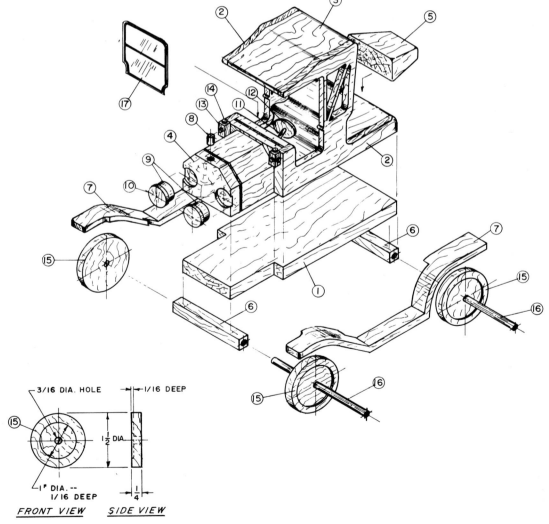

3/16 DIA. HOLE · 1/16 DEEP · 1½ DIA. · 1" DIA. 1/16 DEEP · ¼

FRONT VIEW   SIDE VIEW

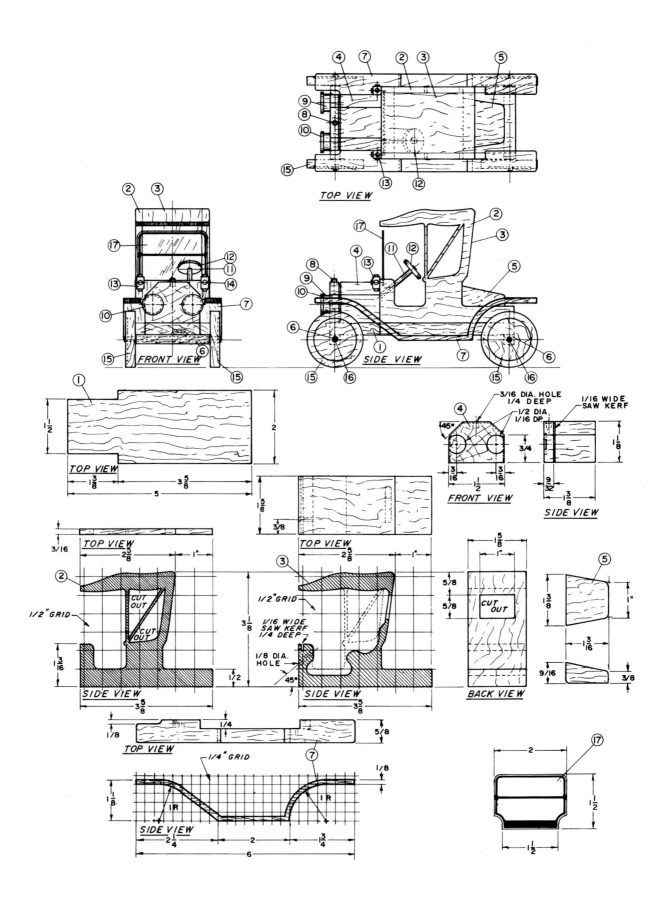

TOP VIEW

FRONT VIEW

SIDE VIEW

3/16 DIA. HOLE
1/4 DEEP

1/2 DIA.
1/16 DP.

1/16 WIDE
SAW KERF

45°

FRONT VIEW

SIDE VIEW

TOP VIEW

TOP VIEW

TOP VIEW

1/2" GRID

CUT OUT

CUT OUT

SIDE VIEW

1/2" GRID

1/16 WIDE
SAW KERF
1/4 DEEP

1/8 DIA.
HOLE

45°

SIDE VIEW

CUT OUT

BACK VIEW

TOP VIEW

1/4" GRID

SIDE VIEW

1R

1R

Jeep

*The Jeep was literally the
workhorse of the Army in World War II,
replacing the horses used in World War I. This toy
borrows the more graceful lines of today's Jeep. When making
small-scale projects such as this vehicle, even a slight deviation from
the given sizes may affect the assembly. So, as you proceed, dry-fit
each part before gluing it, and make adjustments as necessary.*

1. Select the wood and cut the parts. Use a hardwood for the Jeep, and cut the parts to the dimensions given in the Materials List. You may have to glue up the hood (part 3) and seat (part 16) because they require thicker pieces.

2. Transfer the patterns, and cut the parts to shape. Draw full-size patterns on the individual pieces of wood. Cut the shapes. Note the two fenders (part 5) are not identical: they are mirror images of each other. Drill holes, as indicated on the drawing, except for the holes on the grill that you will drill later.

3. Make the wheels (part 18), or buy them. You can cut them with a circle cutter or turn them on a lathe. I made my wheels with a circle cutter that had a $5/16$ inch-

diameter drill in the center, so I had to adjust the diameter of the axles (part 17) to fit. You might also have to adjust the axle size if you order the wheels by mail.

4. Assemble the body. Glue the hood (part 3) and the rear panel (part 4) between the sides (part 2). When the glue dries, sand thoroughly.

Cut a $1/8$-inch-thick slice from the front of the assembled body to make the grill (part 7), as shown in the exploded view. Lay out and drill the holes for the headlights and parking lamps. You can leave the larger holes, as shown in the plans, or make headlights with $3/16$-inch lengths of $3/4$-inch-diameter dowel, as in the photograph.

Create the grill effect by cutting grooves about $1/16$ inch deep in the grill with a hand saw. Space the slots evenly, as shown. Cut seven fillers from a piece of scrap that is the width and depth of the kerfs and about 7 inches long. Each filler is about ⁵⁄₁₆ inch long. Glue them into the lower ends of the kerfs.

Glue the grill back onto the front of the body. When the glue has dried, sand the joint smooth.

5. Assemble the Jeep. Glue the body subassembly to the base (part 1), and when the glue dries, sand the joint between the two to make it inconspicuous.

Taper the top of the hood about 2°, as shown in the side view of part 3. Start the taper just ahead of the door openings and sand or plane the hood to create the slope. Round the edges of the hood, as shown in the side view of the completed vehicle, with a rasp and sandpaper. This shaping gives the Jeep an up-to-date look.

The fenders, which you cut to shape in step 1, may need some final shaping to fit the body. Shape as needed and glue the fenders in place.

Add the post and steering wheel (parts 14 and 15). Make the windshield (part 13) from four ⅛ inch-thick scraps, as shown in the detail for it. Sand and glue it in place. Attach the wheel wells (part 6), seat (part 16), bumper supports (part 9), bumper (part 10), and parking lights (part 11).

6. Add the wheels. Glue the spare tire (part 18) to the tire support (part 12) and glue the support in the hole provided for it in the body. Glue the wheels to the axles. The wheels and axles are held in place by the axle supports (part 8). Make the supports by cutting a groove ¼ inch wide and ⅛ inch deep, down the center of a piece ¾ inch wide, as shown. Chamfer the edges to approximate the illustrated shape. To simplify adding a finish, you might want to add the wheels after completing Step 7.

7. Apply finish. Either paint the Jeep with brilliant nontoxic colors, or apply a clear varnish.

NO.	NAME	SIZE	REQ'D.
\multicolumn{4}{c}{**MATERIALS LIST**}			
1	BASE	⅜ x 4 – 9⅜ LONG	1
2	SIDE	⅜ x 1⅞ – 8⅞ LONG	2
3	HOOD	1⅞ x 3¼ – 3 LONG	1
4	REAR PANEL	⅜ x 1⅝ – 3¼ LONG	1
5	FENDER	1 x 1¾ – 9⅛ LONG	2
6	WHEEL WELL	⅛ x 1⅛ – 3 LONG	2
7	GRILL	CUT FROM PARTS 2 AND 3	1
8	AXLE SUPPORT	⅜ x ¾ – 3¼ LONG	2
9	BUMPER SUPPORT	¼ DIA. – ⅝ LONG	2
10	BUMPER	³⁄₁₆ x ¾ – 5 LONG	1
11	PARKING LIGHT	³⁄₁₆ DIA. – ³⁄₁₆ LONG	4
12	TIRE SUPPORT	¼ DIA. – 1 LONG	1
13	WINDSHIELD	⅛ x ½ – 12 LONG	1
14	POST	³⁄₁₆ DIA. – 1¼ LONG	1
15	STEERING WHEEL	⅞ DIA. – ³⁄₁₆ LONG	1
16	SEAT	1¾ x 2⅛ – 3⅛ LONG	1
17	AXLE	¼ DIA. – 4¾ LONG	2
18	WHEEL	2¼ DIA. – ¾ LONG	5

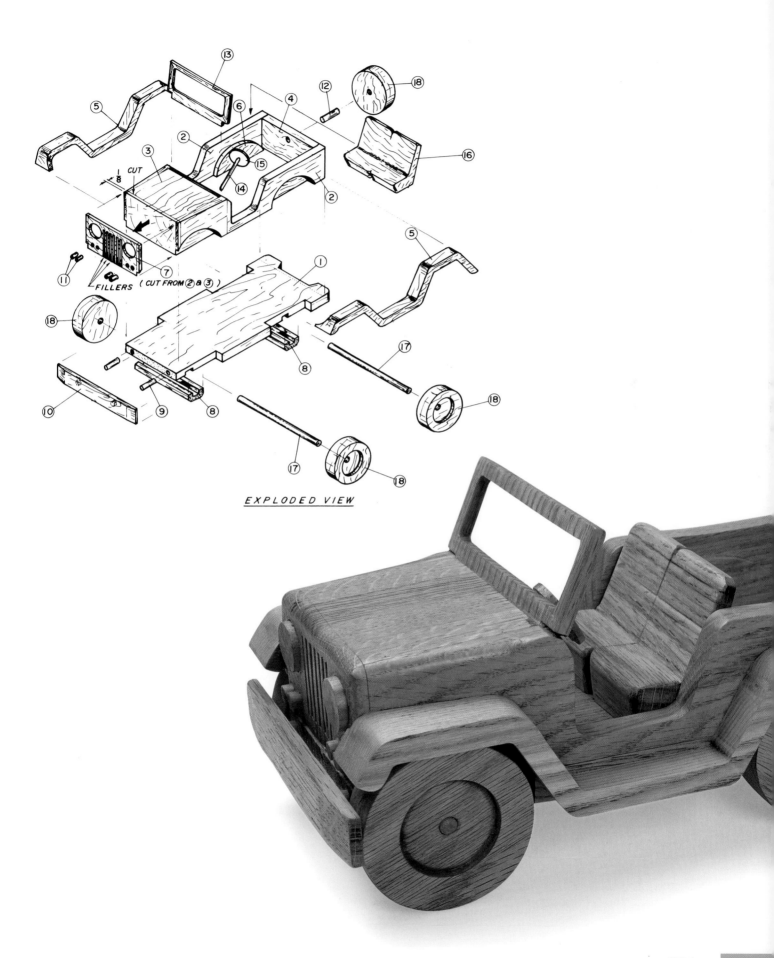

EXPLODED VIEW

CUT

8

CUT FROM ② & ③

FILLERS

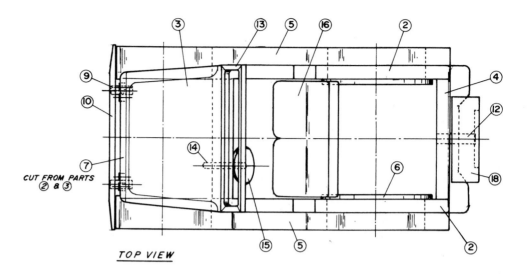

TOP VIEW

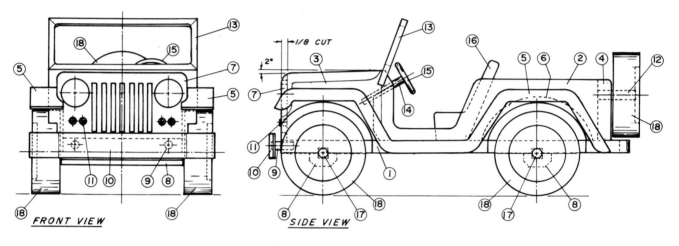

CUT FROM PARTS
② & ③

FRONT VIEW

SIDE VIEW

‑1/8 CUT

2°

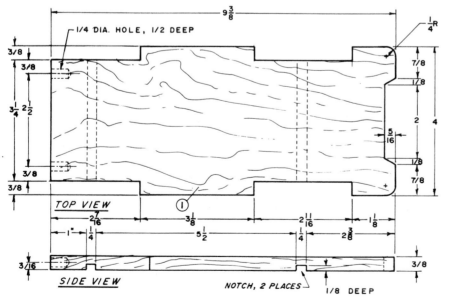

9 3/8

1/4 DIA. HOLE, 1/2 DEEP

1/4 R

3/8

3/8

3 1/4   2 1/2

3/8

3/8

7/8

1/8

2

5/16

1/8

7/8

4

TOP VIEW

2 7/16

3 8

2 11/16

1 1/8

1"

1/4

5 1/2

1/4

2 3/8

3/16

3/8

SIDE VIEW

NOTCH, 2 PLACES

1/8 DEEP

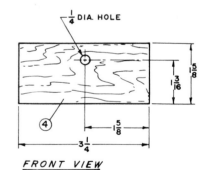

1/4 DIA. HOLE

5/8

1 3/16

1 5/8

3 1/4

FRONT VIEW

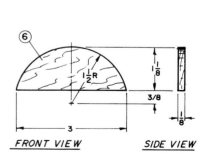

1 1/2 R

1 1/8

3/8

1/8

3

FRONT VIEW

SIDE VIEW

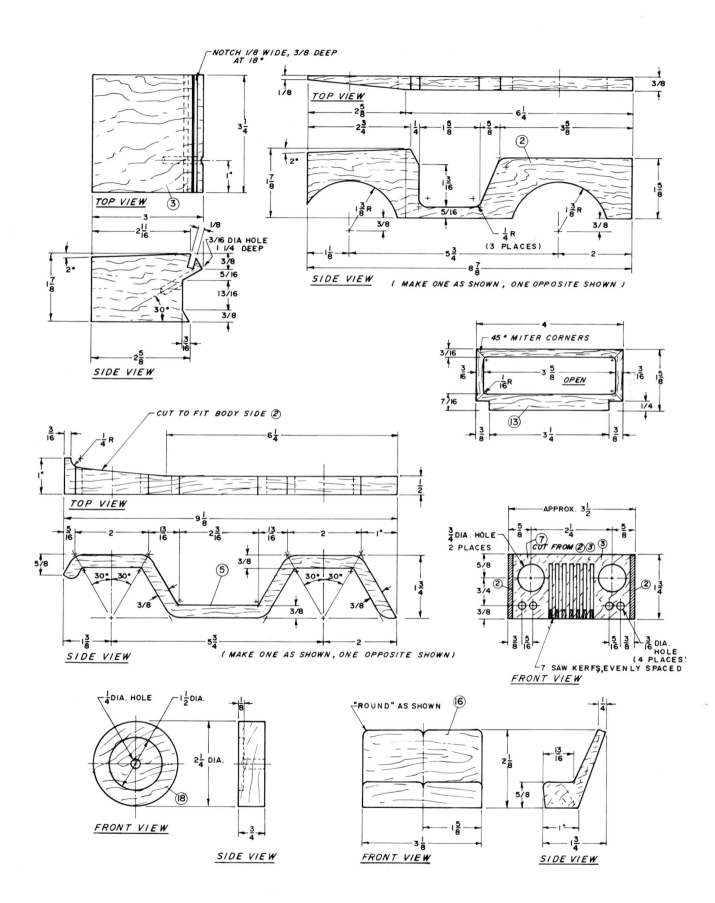

NOTCH 1/8 WIDE, 3/8 DEEP AT 18°

TOP VIEW ③

3

2 11/16

1/8

3/16 DIA HOLE 1 1/4 DEEP

3/8

5/16

13/16

3/8

30°

3/16

2 5/8

SIDE VIEW

3 1/4

1"

3 1/2°

2°

1 7/8

1 7/8

TOP VIEW

1/8

2 5/8

2 3/4

6 1/4

1/4

1 5/8

5/8

3 5/8

②

2°

1 7/8

1 3/16

3/8

1 3/8 R

3/8

5/16

1/4 R
(3 PLACES)

1 3/8 R

3/8

1 5/8

1 1/8

5 3/4

8 7/8

2

SIDE VIEW   (MAKE ONE AS SHOWN , ONE OPPOSITE SHOWN)

45° MITER CORNERS

4

3/16

3/8
3/16

1/8 R

3 5/8   OPEN

3/8
3/16

1 5/8

7/16

1/4

3/8

3 1/4

3/8

⑬

CUT TO FIT BODY SIDE ②

3/16

1/4 R

6 1/4

1"

1/2

TOP VIEW

9 1/8

5/16

2

13/16

2 3/16

13/16

2

1"

5/8

30° 30°

3/8

⑤

3/8

30° 30°

3/8

3/8

1 3/4

1 3/8

5 3/4

2

SIDE VIEW   (MAKE ONE AS SHOWN, ONE OPPOSITE SHOWN)

APPROX. 3 1/2

3/4 DIA. HOLE
2 PLACES

5/8

2 1/4

5/8

⑦

CUT FROM ② ③

②

5/8

3/4

3/8

③

②

1 3/4

3/8
5/16

5/16
3/8

3/16 DIA.
HOLE
(4 PLACES)

7 SAW KERFS, EVENLY SPACED

FRONT VIEW

1/4 DIA. HOLE

1 1/2 DIA.

1/8

2 1/4 DIA.

3/4

FRONT VIEW

⑱

SIDE VIEW

"ROUND" AS SHOWN   ⑯

2 1/8

5/8

1 5/8

3 1/8

FRONT VIEW

1/4

13/16

1"

1 3/4

SIDE VIEW

Toys, Games & Puzzles   283

Dump Truck

This toy truck is built for rugged play. I based the design on a couple of actual dump trucks, but if you want, you can omit the dump subassembly to make a simpler utility truck. You can buy treaded wheels, and I think their realism adds a lot to the project. This project looks difficult at first glance, but it fits together as nicely as a puzzle. Note that four parts are turned on a lathe.

1. Select the stock and cut the parts. Order the axle pegs and wheels (parts 16 and 23). Use any hardwood for this one. I made the truck shown here out of ash.

Cut the parts to the sizes given in the Materials List. To save yourself the trouble of cutting tight radii in the corners of the cab front (part 4) and sides (part 5), lay out and drill the ¼-inch-diameter holes before cutting out the parts.

2. Lay out the parts and cut them to shape. Use the measurements in the drawing to lay out the various parts. Drill all holes before cutting the parts to their final shapes so that the parts will be easier to hold.

If you're building the dump subassembly, drill the ¼-inch-diameter hole in the dump support (part 32), and use this hole as a guide for drilling the ¼-inch-

diameter holes in the wheel housing (part 18).

As you cut out the parts, dry-fit them so that you can catch any errors at the earliest possible stage.

3. Turn the gas tanks and mufflers. Turn the gas tanks (part 17) and mufflers (part 25) on a lathe. If you don't have a lathe, substitute dowels: make the gas tanks from two 1⅝-inch lengths of 1 inch-diameter dowel; make the mufflers from three dowels with diameters of ⅞, 11/16, and ¼ inches.

4. Make subassemblies. Assemble the truck in a series of smaller subassemblies.

First, make two rear wheel wells from parts 18, 19, and 20. Make front fender assemblies from parts 21 and 22. Make the grill subassembly from parts 7, 8, 9,

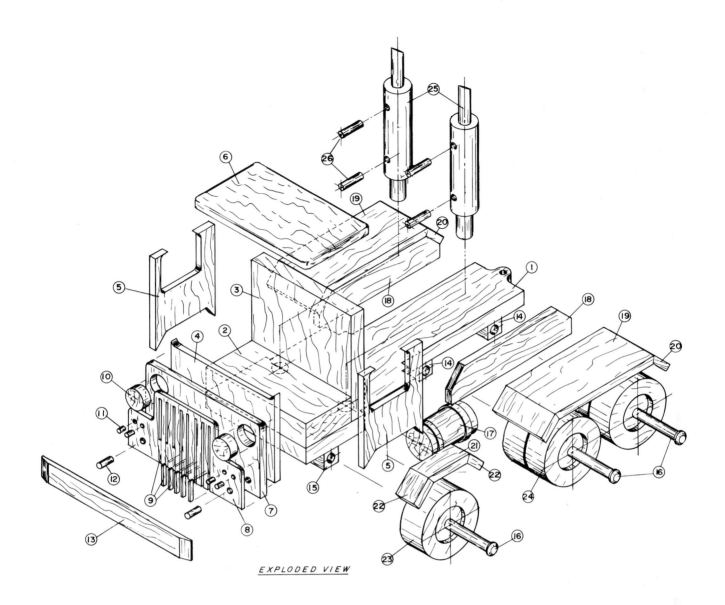

EXPLODED VIEW

10, and 11. Make the cab from parts 2, 3, 4, 5, and 6 and dry-fit the cab to the base (part 1). Trim the base if necessary. Glue the cab to the base and then glue the grill subassembly to it.

Cut the bumper (part 13). Drill holes in it for the bumper support (part 12). Glue one end of the bumper support in the bumper and the other end in the grill. Glue it in place.

Glue the rear wheel wells to the base. Fit the front fenders to the cab. You may have to notch the front fender slightly to fit over the hood. Glue the fenders in place.

Glue the muffler to the base and cab. Glue the gas tank in place.

Make the dump subassembly from parts 27, 28, 29, and 31, but don't attach the dump support (part 32) to

it yet. Attach the dump board (part 30) with 4d finishing nails or ³/₄-inch lengths of ¹/₁₆-inch-diameter dowel. Be sure to drill before nailing to avoid splitting the wood. Check that the dump board moves freely.

5. Dry-fit the wheels. Drill holes in the supports to suit the peg length and diameter. Make sure the wheels turn freely, but do not glue them in place.

Glue the six axle supports (parts 14 and 15) in place, as shown in the side view of the assembled truck. The given distances between the axle centers are only an approximate guide. Center the wheels within the wheel wells, as shown in this view.

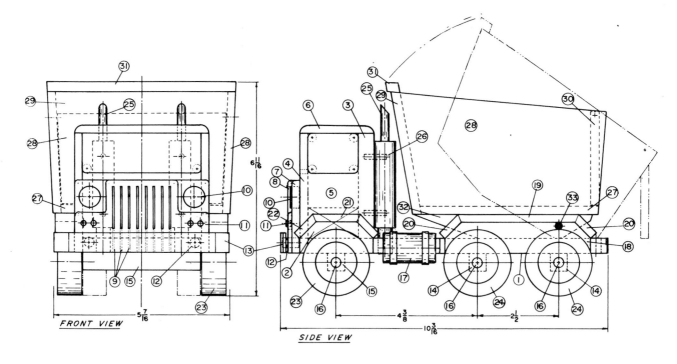

FRONT VIEW

SIDE VIEW

6. Add the dump subassembly. If you don't care to have an operable dumping bed, simply glue the bed to the base. Otherwise, proceed as follows:

Enlarge the ¼-inch-diameter hole in the dump support with a 9/32-inch drill bit. Attach the dump support to the truck by putting the pin (part 33) through the hole in one of the wheel wells, into the hole in the dump support, and out through the second wheel well.

Glue the dump to the dump support, positioning it so it will not hit any parts as it moves. Make sure that the dump subassembly looks centered when seen from the top, both sides, and the rear. Use large rubber bands to hold everything together until the glue sets.

7. Apply finish. The truck can be left unfinished, protected with clear varnish, or painted. Glue the axle pegs in place.

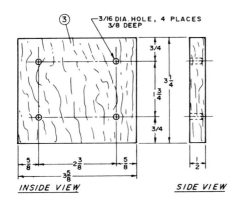

INSIDE VIEW   SIDE VIEW

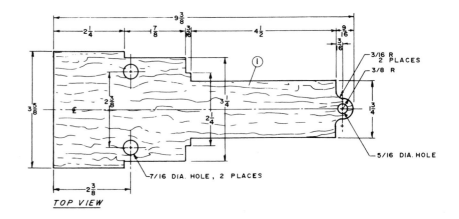

TOP VIEW

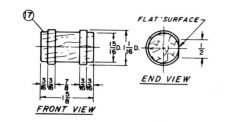

FRONT VIEW

END VIEW

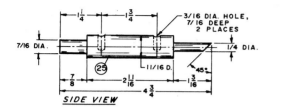

SIDE VIEW

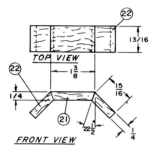

TOP VIEW

FRONT VIEW

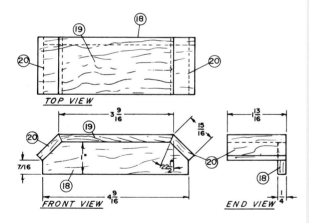

TOP VIEW

FRONT VIEW

END VIEW

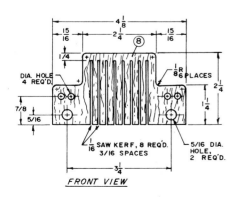

FRONT VIEW

MATERIALS LIST

NO.	NAME	SIZE	REQ'D.
1	BASE	$\frac{1}{2}$ x $3\frac{5}{8}$ – $9\frac{3}{8}$ LONG	1
2	SEAT	1 x $1\frac{1}{2}$ – $3\frac{5}{8}$ LONG	1
3	BACK	$\frac{1}{2}$ x $3\frac{5}{8}$ – $3\frac{1}{4}$ LONG	1
4	FRONT	$\frac{1}{4}$ x $3\frac{5}{8}$ – $2\frac{5}{8}$ LONG	1
5	SIDE	$\frac{1}{4}$ x $2\frac{1}{4}$ – 3 LONG	2
6	TOP	$\frac{1}{4}$ x $2\frac{1}{4}$ – $4\frac{1}{8}$ LONG	1
7	HOOD	$\frac{1}{4}$ x $4\frac{1}{8}$ – $2\frac{1}{4}$ LONG	1
8	GRILL	$\frac{1}{8}$ x $4\frac{1}{8}$ – $2\frac{1}{4}$ LONG	1
9	LOWER GRILL	$\frac{1}{16}$ x $\frac{1}{8}$ – $\frac{3}{4}$ LONG	8
10	HEADLIGHT	$\frac{5}{8}$ DIA. – $\frac{5}{16}$ LONG	2
11	PARKING LIGHT	$\frac{3}{16}$ DIA. – $\frac{3}{16}$ LONG	4
12	BUMPER SUPPORT	$\frac{5}{16}$ DIA. – $\frac{9}{16}$ LONG	2
13	BUMPER	$\frac{3}{16}$ x $\frac{5}{8}$ – $5\frac{5}{8}$ LONG	1
14	AXLE SUPPORT	$\frac{1}{2}$ x $\frac{1}{2}$ – $2\frac{1}{4}$ LONG	2
15	AXLE SUPPORT	$\frac{1}{2}$ x $\frac{1}{2}$ – $3\frac{5}{8}$ LONG	1
16	AXLE PEG	$\frac{5}{16}$ DIA. (LENGTH TO SUIT)	6
17	GAS TANK	$\frac{1}{16}$ DIA. – $1\frac{5}{8}$ LONG	2
18	HOUSING	$\frac{1}{4}$ x 1 – $4\frac{9}{16}$ LONG	2
19	WHEEL TOP	$\frac{1}{4}$ x $1\frac{13}{16}$ – $3\frac{9}{16}$ LONG	2
20	WHEEL END	$\frac{1}{4}$ x $1\frac{13}{16}$ – $\frac{15}{16}$ LONG	4
21	WHEEL TOP	$\frac{1}{4}$ x $\frac{13}{16}$ – $1\frac{3}{8}$ LONG	2
22	WHEEL END	$\frac{1}{4}$ x $\frac{13}{16}$ – $\frac{15}{16}$ LONG	4
23	FRONT WHEEL	$\frac{3}{4}$ x 2 DIA.	2
24	REAR WHEEL	$\frac{3}{4}$ x 2 DIA.	8
25	MUFFLER	$\frac{11}{16}$ DIA. – $4\frac{3}{4}$ LONG	2
26	MUFFLER SUPPORT	$\frac{3}{16}$ DIA. – $\frac{3}{4}$ LONG	4
27	DUMP BASE	$\frac{1}{4}$ x 5 – $5\frac{9}{16}$ LONG	1
28	DUMP SIDE	$\frac{1}{4}$ x $3\frac{3}{4}$ – $6\frac{3}{4}$ LONG	2
29	DUMP FRONT	$\frac{1}{4}$ x $3\frac{7}{8}$ – $5\frac{7}{8}$ LONG	1
30	DUMP BOARD	$\frac{1}{4}$ x 3 – $5\frac{1}{4}$ LONG	1
31	TOP BOARD	$\frac{5}{16}$ x $\frac{1}{2}$ – $5\frac{7}{8}$ LONG	1
32	DUMP SUPPORT	$\frac{3}{4}$ x $1\frac{3}{4}$ – $5\frac{9}{16}$ LONG	1
33	PIN	$\frac{1}{4}$ DIA. – $2\frac{1}{4}$ LONG	1

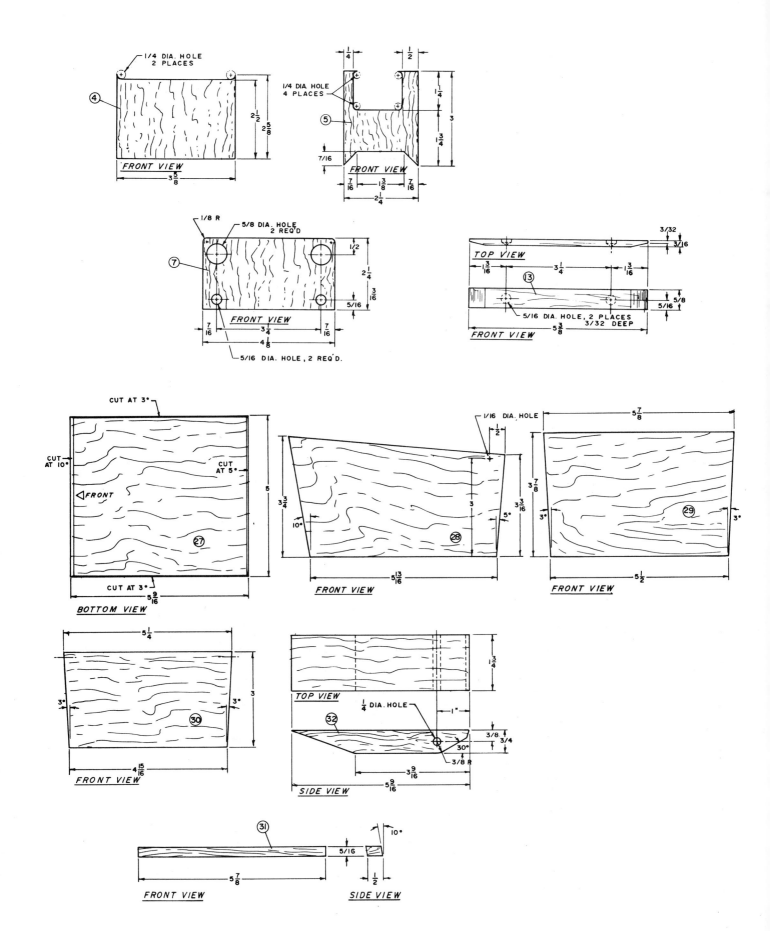

World War I Aeroplane, c.1916

Here comes the Red Baron in his red triplane. Children are usually fascinated with planes, so here is a very old aeroplane for them with a lot of history, too. In World War I, it was a notorious German airplane, and it has been a favorite among history buffs and children alike ever since. Planes such as this toy are also fun to make.

MATERIALS LIST

NO.	NAME	SIZE	REQ'D.
1	BODY	¾ x 1⅝ – 7⅛ LONG	2
2	ELEVATOR	¼ x 2½ – 4½ LONG	1
3	RUDDER	¼ x 1⅞ – 1⅞ LONG	1
4	WING	¼ x 2⅛ – 10¾ LONG	3
5	STRUTT	⅜ DIA. – 3⅛ LONG	2
6	BRACE	⅜ DIA. – 2 LONG	1
7	COWL	1¾ DIA. – ½ LONG	1
8	GUN BARREL	¼ DIA. – 1¼ LONG	2
9	GUN BARREL	⅛ DIA. – ½ LONG	2
10	PIN	⅛ DIA. – ¾ LONG	1
11	LANDING GEAR	¾ x 1½ – 2½ LONG	1
12	AXLE	3/16 DIA. – 3⅛ LONG	1
13	WHEEL	1 DIA. – ¼ LONG	4
14	PROP	⅛ x ⅞ – 4 LONG	1
15	WASHER	⅛ SIZE	1
16	SCREW – RD. HD.	NO. 6 – 1 LONG	1

1. Cut all pieces to overall size according to the Materials List. Sand all over.

2. Glue up two ¾-inch-thick pieces to make up the body (part 1).

3. Stack all three wings; cut and drill them at the same time. Note that the top wing has four extra scallop cutouts in the center and that the middle wing will have to be cut to fit the body.

4. Cut out the body profile (part 1). Round the front section, as shown.

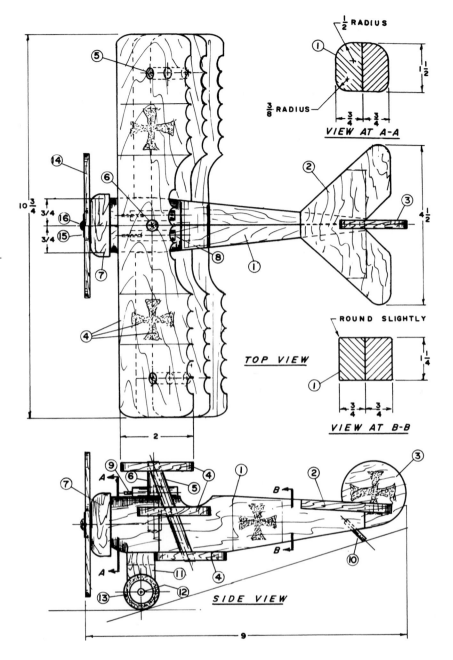

5. Locate and drill all holes in the body. Sand all over.

6. Lay out and cut out the elevator, rudder, cowl, propeller, and landing gear (parts 2, 3, 7, 14, and 11).

7. Make up material for the gun barrel (parts 8 and 9).

8. Round the front edge of the cowl (part 7).

9. Dry-fit all pieces; trim as necessary.

10. Glue all pieces together.

11. Paint to suit. Red is a good choice for this particular plane.

VIEW AT A-A

½ RADIUS

⅜ RADIUS

1½

¾   ¾

TOP VIEW

ROUND SLIGHTLY

VIEW AT B-B

1¼

¾   ¾

SIDE VIEW

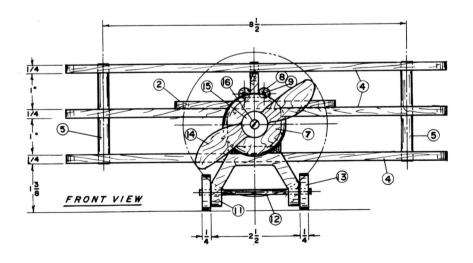

FRONT VIEW

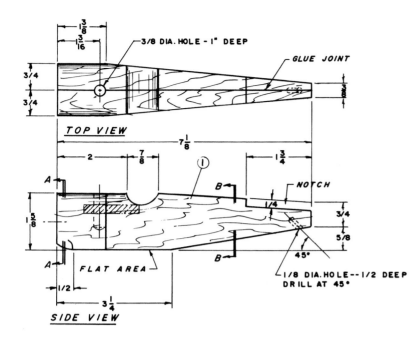

TOP VIEW

3 1/8
3 3/16
3/8 DIA. HOLE - 1" DEEP
GLUE JOINT
3/4
3/4

SIDE VIEW

7 1/8
2
7/8
①
1 3/4
NOTCH
1/4
B
A
1 3/8
B
FLAT AREA
3/4
5/8
45°
1/8 DIA. HOLE--1/2 DEEP
DRILL AT 45°
A
1/2
3 1/4

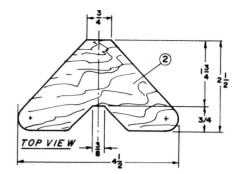

TOP VIEW

3/4
②
1 3/4
2 1/2
3/4
3/8
4 1/2

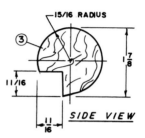

15/16 RADIUS
③
1 7/8
11/16
11/16
SIDE VIEW

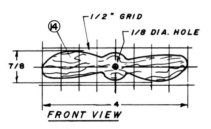

FRONT VIEW

1/2" GRID
1/8 DIA. HOLE
⑭
7/8
4

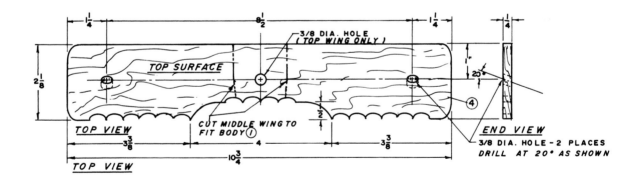

TOP VIEW

1/4
8 1/2
1 1/4
1/4
3/8 DIA. HOLE
(TOP WING ONLY)
TOP SURFACE
2 1/8
20°
④
CUT MIDDLE WING TO
FIT BODY ①
2
END VIEW
3/8 DIA. HOLE - 2 PLACES
DRILL AT 20° AS SHOWN
TOP VIEW
3 3/8
4
3 3/8
10 3/4

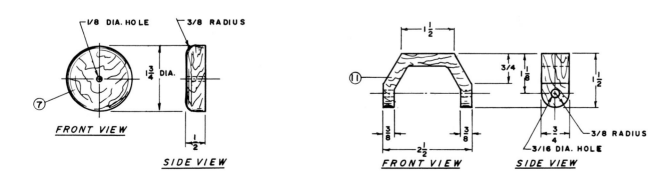

1/8 DIA. HOLE
3/8 RADIUS
1 3/4 DIA.
1/2
⑦
FRONT VIEW
SIDE VIEW

1 1/2
3/4
1 1/8
1 1/2
⑪
3/8
3/8
2 1/2
3/4
3/8 RADIUS
3/16 DIA. HOLE
FRONT VIEW
SIDE VIEW

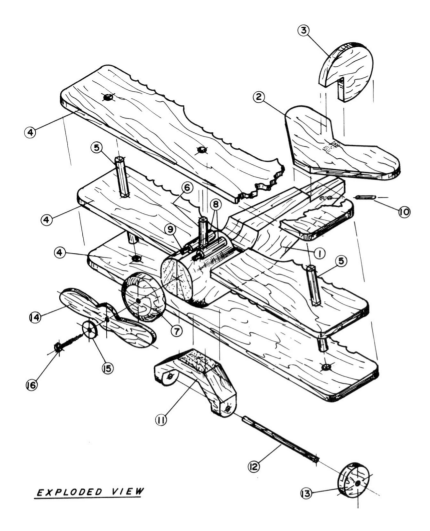

EXPLODED VIEW

Toy Airplane

As a child growing up in the early 1940s in Rhode Island next to the state airport, I can remember small biplanes, such as this one, taking off and landing. Even today, I can still remember the sound of their long-stroke engines putting along overhead. It's a sound you just don't hear anymore. There is an aerodrome in Rhinebeck, New York, that still flies wonderful old airplanes, where you can hear that sound.

MATERIALS LIST			
NO.	NAME	SIZE	REQ'D.
1	BODY SIDE	$1\frac{1}{4}$ x $2\frac{1}{2}$ – $8\frac{5}{16}$ LONG	2
2	WING	$\frac{1}{4}$ x 3 – 13 LONG	2
3	STRUT	$\frac{1}{4}$ DIA. - $2\frac{3}{4}$ LONG	4
4	PIN FOR WING	$\frac{1}{4}$ DIA. - 1 LONG	1
5	TAIL PIN	$\frac{3}{16}$ DIA. - $\frac{3}{4}$ LONG	1
6	COWEL	$2\frac{1}{2}$ DIA. - $1\frac{1}{2}$ LONG	1
7	ELEVATOR	$\frac{1}{4}$ x $3\frac{1}{4}$ – $6\frac{1}{8}$ LONG	1
8	PIN FOR RUDDER	$\frac{3}{16}$ DIA. - $1\frac{1}{2}$ LONG	2
9	RUDDER	$\frac{1}{4}$ x 3 – $3\frac{1}{2}$ LONG	1
10	SUPPORT	$\frac{3}{4}$ x $1\frac{5}{8}$ – $1\frac{5}{8}$ LONG	2
11	WHEEL	$\frac{3}{4}$ x $1\frac{3}{4}$ SQUARE	2
12	AXLE	$\frac{1}{4}$ DIA. - $6\frac{7}{8}$ LONG	1
13	PROP	$\frac{3}{16}$ X $\frac{3}{4}$ – $4\frac{1}{2}$ LONG	1
14	PEG	$\frac{1}{2}$ DIA. - $1\frac{1}{4}$ LONG	1

1. Glue up material to cut the body from. You should have a block of wood $2\frac{1}{2}$ x $2\frac{1}{2}$ x $8\frac{5}{16}$ inches long.

2. Using a band saw, cut out the airplane body (part 1). Locate and drill all holes as noted. Round the edges as shown in the front view, section A-A, section B-B, and section C-C.

3. Cut the two wings (part 2) to size, as shown. Note that the top wing has a $1\frac{3}{4}$-inch radius cut out of it. Locate and drill the five $\frac{1}{4}$-inch-diameter holes.

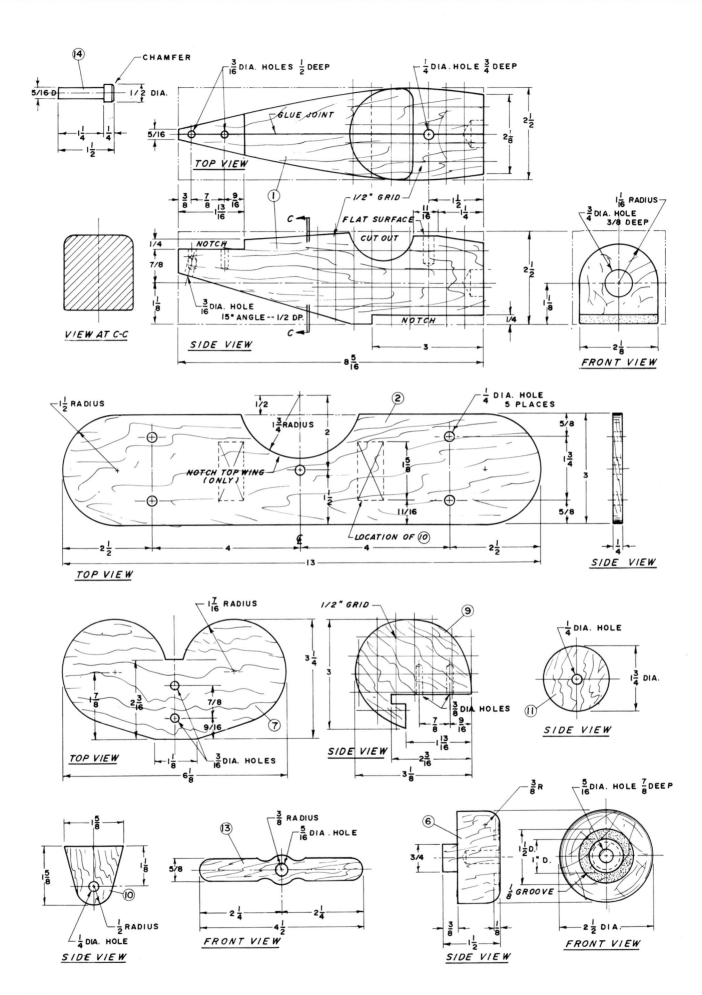

4. Make the remaining pieces, according to the detail drawings.

Note: a lathe is needed to make the cowl (part 6). Sand all over.

5. Assemble all of the pieces, following the drawing of the exploded view.

6. Lightly sand, and paint to suit.

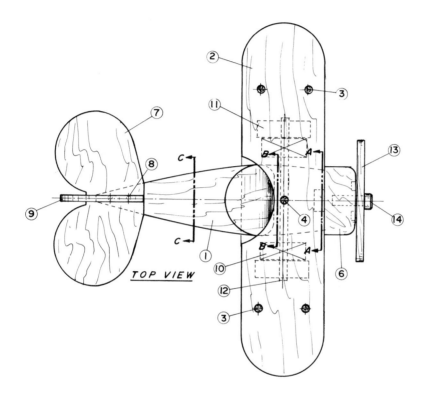

TOP VIEW

VIEW AT A-A

VIEW AT B-B

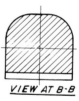

VIEW AT C-C

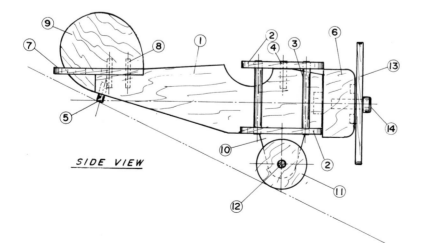

SIDE VIEW

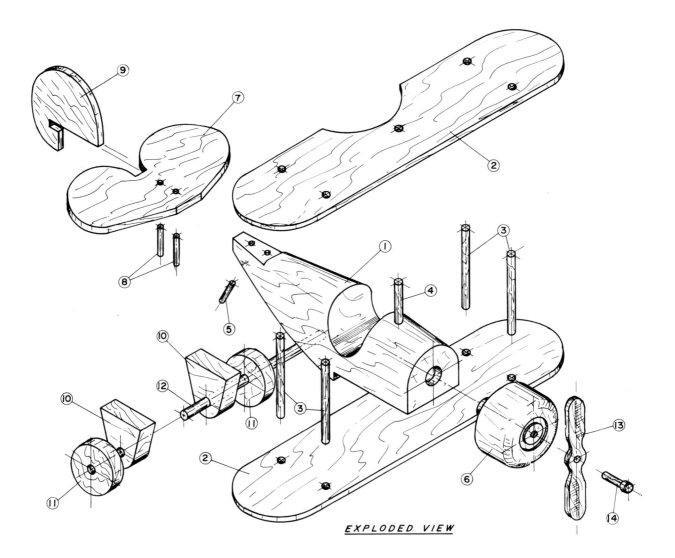

EXPLODED VIEW

Child's Swedish Sled

For those woodworkers who live in a snow-belt area and have young children or grandchildren, this sled is just perfect. For those in warmer climes, it will make a great decorative piece, or you could use it to put your plants on. Any kind of wood can be used, but oak or ash would be best. Your sled can be painted green like the one pictured, or it could be left plain. A project such as this one makes a great tole painting or rosemaling project. Once you're finished, all you need is a snowstorm.

1. Cut all the wood to overall size. Be sure to order and have on hand the spindle, or other purchased turning for the pull, before starting. As these turnings vary in length slightly from vendor to vendor, you may have to trim the length to hold the 10¼ inch dimension shown in the top view.

2. Tape or tack the two pieces of stock together, and transfer the pattern for the runners to the top board. Locate and drill a ¹⁄₁₆-inch-diameter hole where the larger hole for the pull (spindle) will be drilled. Locate and cut out the two ¾ x ¾-inch notches for the two braces. Cut out the remaining shape. While the two run-

ners are still taped or tacked together, sand all edges. You should have an exact pair of runners. Separate the two runners and on the inside surface of both runners, drill a blind hole for the pull, ⅝ inch deep. Use the small ¹⁄₁₆ inch-diameter hole to locate each larger hole and to ensure that both holes line up exactly.

Be careful to start on the inside, and do not drill all the way through.

3. Lay out the seat. If your spindle or pull is too long, you will either have to trim it or widen the seat. Be sure to check this before you cut the seat to the 10¼-inch width.

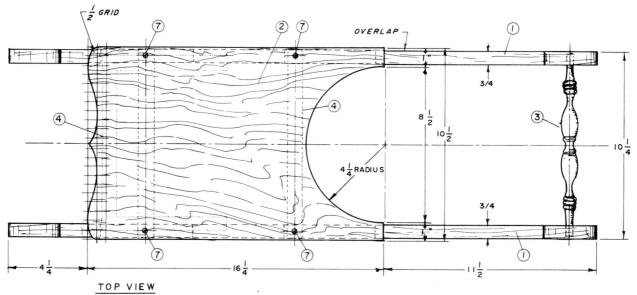

TOP VIEW
(SHOWN WITHOUT PARTS ⑤⑥ & ⑧ IN PLACE)

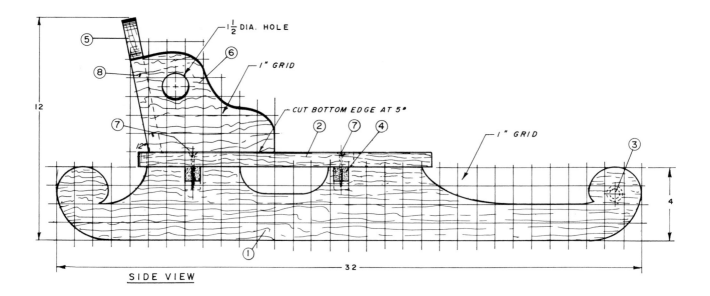

SIDE VIEW

Cut the seat to size, and drill and countersink holes for the four flathead screws. Cut out two matching braces as indicated in the drawing. Sand all pieces, taking care not to round any edges.

4. Dry-fit all the parts, and adjust if necessary. If okay, glue the two braces and the pull to the two runners, keeping everything square. Glue and screw the

seat in place. If hardwood is used, pre-drill for the four screws so that the wood does not split.

5. Carefully cut the bottom edge of the two sides at about 6°. Lay out the pattern, and cut the two sides while the two pieces are taped or tacked together so that both sides will be an exact pair, exactly the same. Locate and drill the 1½-inch-diameter holes. Separate the parts and sand all over.

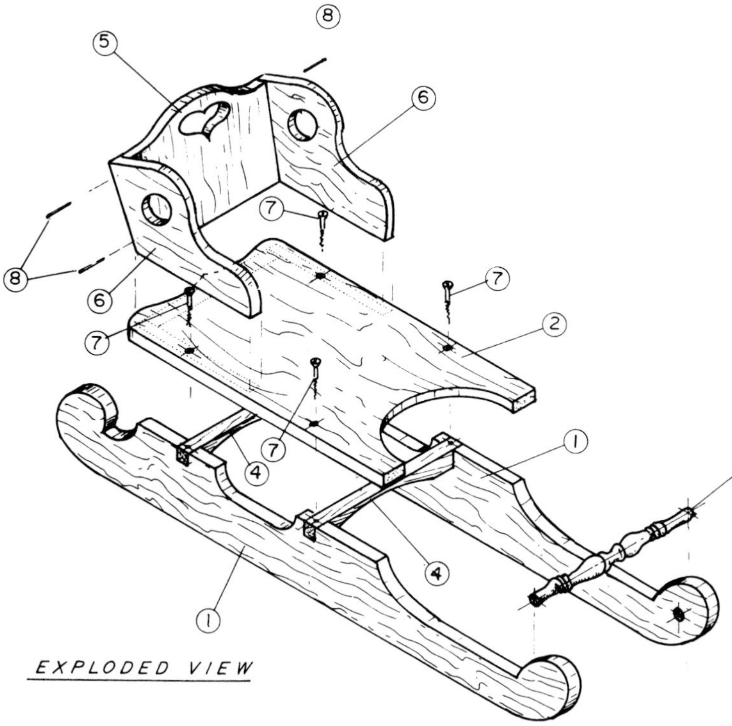

8
5
6
7
8
6
7
2
7
4
1
3
4
1
EXPLODED VIEW

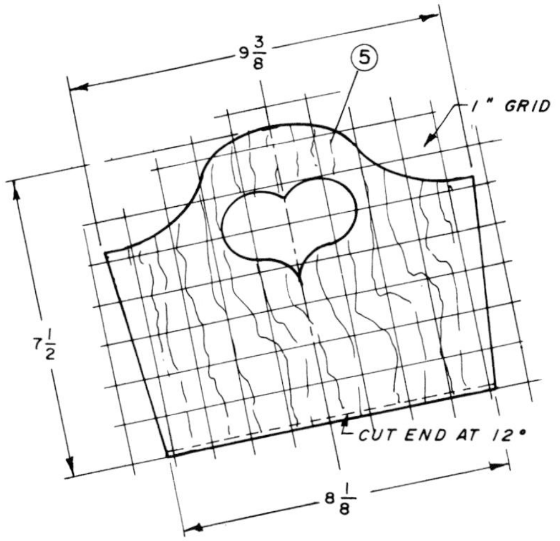

9 3/8
5
1" GRID
7 1/2
CUT END AT 12°
8 1/8

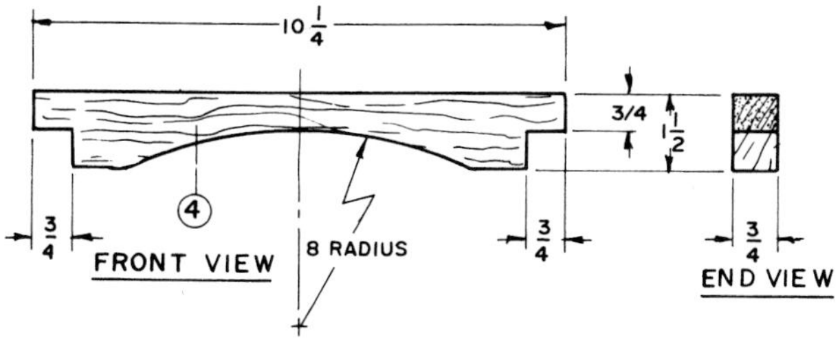

10 1/4
3/4
1 1/2
4
3/4
FRONT VIEW
8 RADIUS
3/4
3/4
END VIEW

MATERIALS LIST			
NO.	**NAME**	**SIZE**	**REQ'D.**
1	RUNNER	¾ x 4 – 32 LONG	2
2	SEAT	¾ x 10½ – 16¼ LONG	1
3	PULL	⅞ DIA. x 10 LONG	1
4	BRACE	¾ x 1¼ – 10¼ LONG	2
5	BACK	¾ x 9⅜ – 7½ LONG	1
6	SIDE	¾ x 5¼ – 8 LONG	2
7	SCREW – FL. HD.	NO. 8 – 2 LONG	4
8	NAIL – FINISH	6 d	4

6. Lay out the shape of the back. Make the 12° cut across the bottom edge first. Then cut out the shape of the back, and sand all over. Glue the two sides and back together. Drill and fasten with finishing nails for added strength after the glue sets. Note: if you are going to use the sled in the snow, be sure to use waterproof glue.

Check that the bottom surface of the two sides and back are perfectly flat after assembly. If not, sand so that the three parts will sit flush on a smooth, flat surface. Locate and glue the sides and back in place.

7. Sand all over, and round all exposed edges slightly. Finish to your liking.

Country Rocking Horse, c.1935

I made a rocking horse for each of our grandchildren, and I think it was by far the most popular toy I ever made them, at least until they outgrew it. It always fascinated me that they knew instinctively exactly how to ride the horse. This one is a copy of one I bought at a flea market in southern New Hampshire. It was painted yellow with red and black edges.

Note: This is a very simple project except for fitting the legs to the seat. Refer to View at A-A, page 302. This is a cross section of the final assembly. Note that the ½-inch-diameter holes must be drilled at an angle of 70°, as shown. Fit the top section of the legs (part 2) to the seat (part 1).

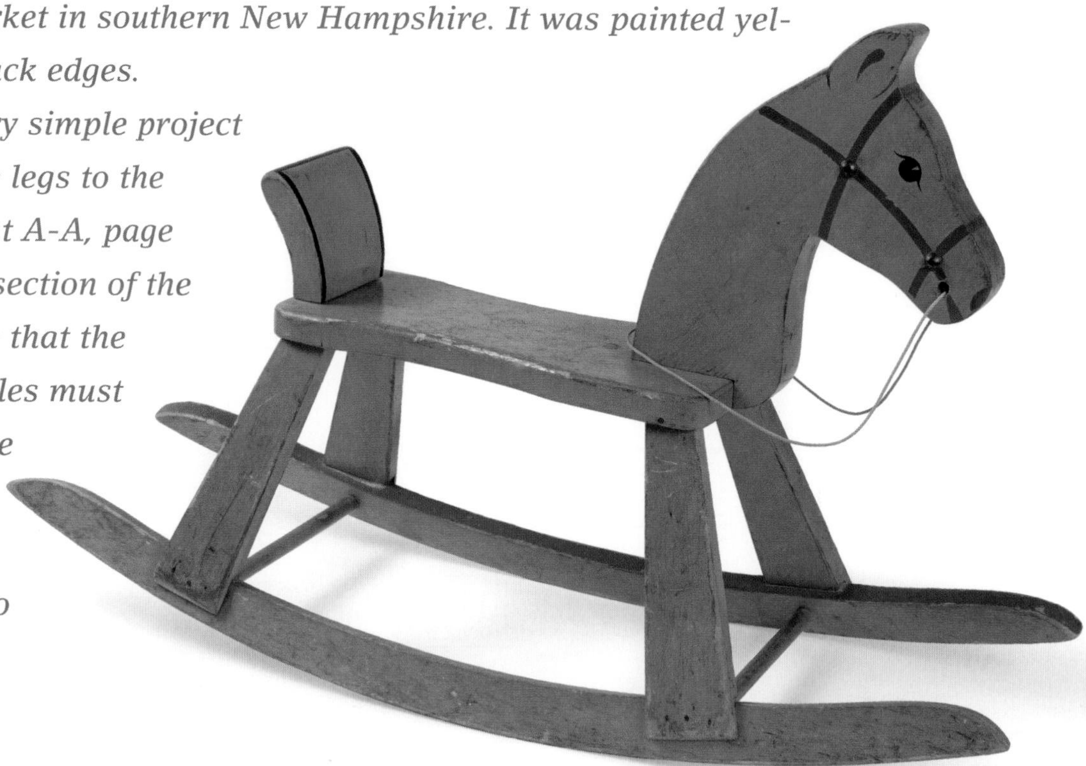

MATERIALS LIST

NO.	NAME	SIZE	REQ'D.
1	SEAT	¾ x 5¼ – 12¾ LONG	1
2	LEG	¾ x 2⅜ – 8⅝ LONG	4
3	PIN	¼ DIA. – 1 LONG	2
4	ROCKER	¾ x 4 – 30 LONG	2
5	SPACER	½ DIA. – 8½ LONG	2
6	BRAD	1 LONG	12
7	HEAD	1¼ x 7½ – 10⅞ LONG	1
8	TACK	⅜ DIA. HEAD	4
9	TAIL	2⅛ x 3½ – 3¾ LONG	1
10	SCREW – FL. HD.	NO. 8 – 2 LONG	4
11	TWINE	TO SUIT	1

1. Cut all pieces to overall size according to the cutting list.

Lay out the seat (part 1), following the given dimensions.

Cut out the seat, and drill all holes. Important: note that the four ¼-inch-diameter holes are drilled from the bottom, ⅝ inch deep. Sand all over.

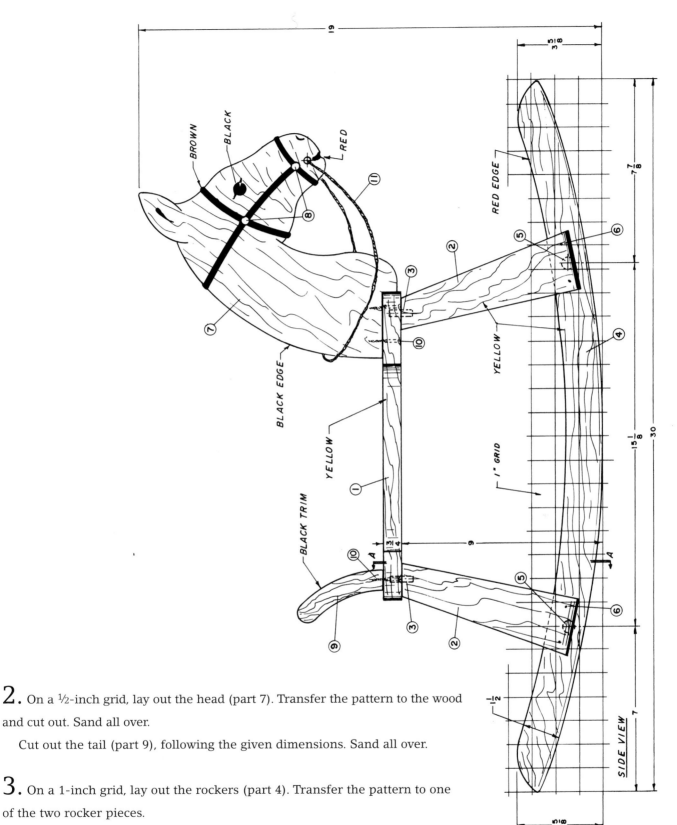

2. On a ½-inch grid, lay out the head (part 7). Transfer the pattern to the wood and cut out. Sand all over.

Cut out the tail (part 9), following the given dimensions. Sand all over.

3. On a 1-inch grid, lay out the rockers (part 4). Transfer the pattern to one of the two rocker pieces.

Tack the two pieces together, and cut out. Sand all over. Be sure to round the bottom edge.

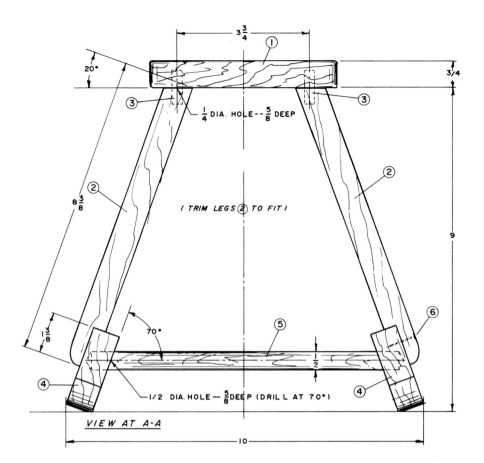

$3\frac{3}{4}$

①

20°

$\frac{3}{4}$

③   ③

$\frac{1}{4}$ DIA. HOLE -- $\frac{5}{8}$ DEEP

② ②

$8\frac{3}{8}$

(TRIM LEGS ② TO FIT)

9

$1\frac{3}{8}$

70°

⑤ ⑥

$\frac{1}{2}$

④ ④

1/2 DIA. HOLE — $\frac{5}{8}$ DEEP (DRILL AT 70°)

VIEW AT A-A

10

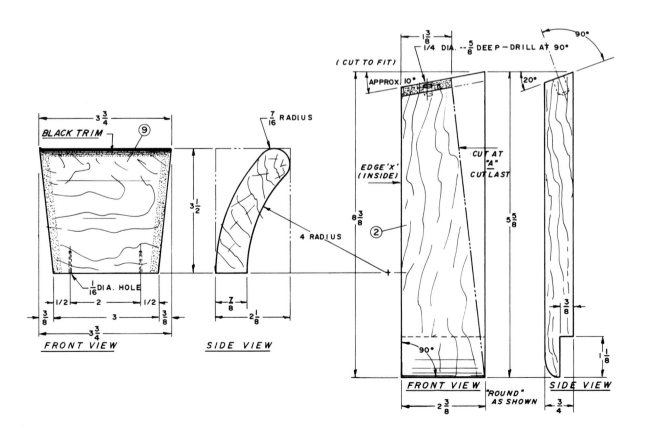

$3\frac{3}{4}$

BLACK TRIM ⑨

$\frac{7}{16}$ RADIUS

$3\frac{1}{2}$

4 RADIUS

$\frac{1}{16}$ DIA. HOLE

1/2   2   1/2

$\frac{7}{8}$

$\frac{3}{8}$ 3 $\frac{3}{8}$

$2\frac{1}{8}$

$3\frac{3}{4}$

FRONT VIEW   *SIDE VIEW*

$\frac{3}{8}$

1/4 DIA. -- $\frac{5}{8}$ DEEP - DRILL AT 90°

(CUT TO FIT)

90°

APPROX. 10°

20°

EDGE 'X' (INSIDE)

CUT AT "A" CUT LAST

$8\frac{3}{8}$

②

$5\frac{5}{8}$

$\frac{3}{8}$

90°

$1\frac{1}{8}$

FRONT VIEW   "ROUND" AS SHOWN   *SIDE VIEW*

$2\frac{3}{8}$ $\frac{3}{4}$

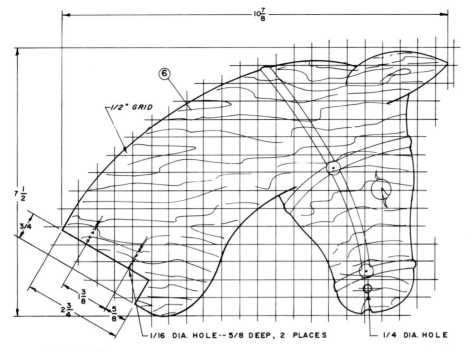

SIDE VIEW

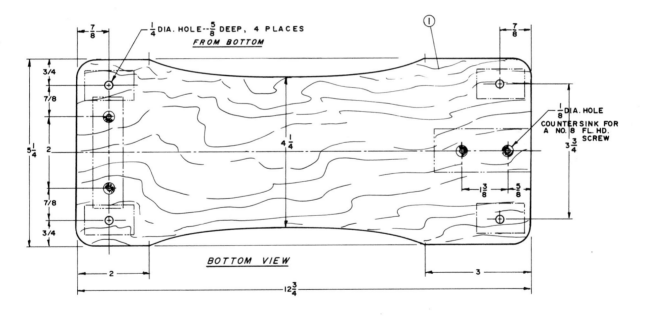

BOTTOM VIEW

4. Carefully cut out the four legs (part 2) as shown. (See the front and side views for details.)

Locate and drill all holes, as shown. In the legs (part 2), add dowel pins (part 3).

Dry-fit the legs (part 2) and spacers (part 5) to the rockers (part 4). Use the ¼-inch-diameter holes in the bottom of the seat and the pins (part 3) as a guide in dry-fitting the pieces. If necessary, trim to suit.

5. Glue and screw the head and tail to the seat.

Glue and nail the legs to the rockers and seat. Add the spacers (part 5) at the same time.

6. Sand all over, rounding all sharp edges.

7. Paint to suit. Note the colors that were used on the original horse.

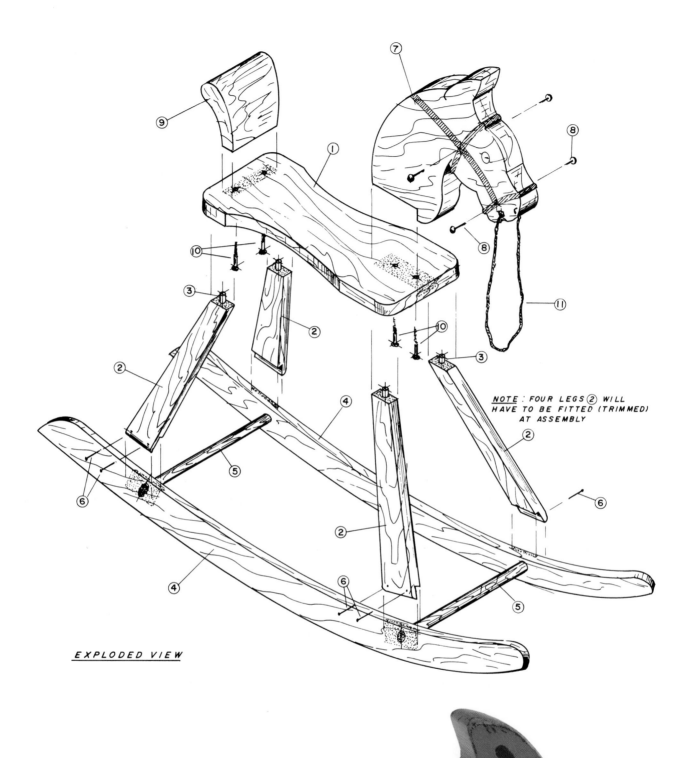

NOTE : FOUR LEGS ② WILL
HAVE TO BE FITTED (TRIMMED)
AT ASSEMBLY

EXPLODED VIEW

Circus Toy

There are a lot of details in this project, but none of the steps is particularly difficult. Because the toy will appeal to small children, take great care to glue the parts securely. Annular (or ring) nails are used to help keep the wheels and magnets in place.

1. Select the stock and cut the parts. Use any wood for the wagon; the animals should be hardwood for durability. In selecting wood for the animals, arrange the shapes so that thin areas will run with the grain, such as along the neck of the giraffe. Note that the clown is cut from two stock thicknesses. Purchase any hardware items before beginning the project.

Leave parts that require shaping slightly longer and wider than listed in the Materials List and cut them to size as you shape. Cut the rest of the parts to the sizes given in the Materials List.

2. Cut the wagon parts to shape. Cut a notch in the base (part 1) to take the ramp, as shown in the section View at A-A.

Cut the ends of the long and short top rails (parts 2 and 3) to make tight-fitting lap joints, as shown in the side and end views. Glue the four rails together to make a frame, checking to see that it is square; the overall dimensions of this frame should be exactly the same as those of the base.

Drill the holes for the bars (part 4) next. Lay out the holes on the bottom of the base. Clamp the top support on top of the base, lining up the sides exactly. Using a stop on a drill bit or drill press, drill each of the holes for the bars through the base and $5/8$ inch into the supports. This ensures that the holes will be aligned for the bars.

Rout coves in the base and top rails with a $1/8$ inch-radius cove bit and a ball-bearing guide. The profile of the cove is shown in the View at C-C. The section View at A-A shows the location of the coves.

Cut the bars, and chamfer the edges slightly so that they will fit into place more easily. Glue the bars into the base, and allow the glue to dry before adding the top support frame to the bars. Make sure the support and base are parallel and 7¼ inches apart, as shown in the side view.

Next, cut the four axle supports (part 5) to the shape shown in the side view. It's easiest if you chamfer a long block and cut it to form the four axle supports. Drill a ⅜-inch-diameter axle hole through the center of each support.

Cut the two axles (part 6) and chamfer the ends slightly. Temporarily slide the axles through the axle supports to align the supports. Position the supports, as shown in the side and end views. After the glue sets, reinforce the joint with finishing nails (part 32).

3. Make the ramp. Cut the ramp (part 8) to shape and saw the 1/16-inch-deep kerfs, as shown in the side view, with a handsaw. Drill the 3/16-inch-diameter holes in the base for the ramp hinge pins (part 9).

To hang the ramp, drill through the holes you just made from the base into the ramp. Drill about 1 inch from each side into the ramp. Put the ramp temporarily in place. Before gluing the hinge pins in place, make sure that the ramp works as it should. Make necessary adjustments so that the ramp closes just below the short, top support. Then glue the ramp hinges in place, taking care to glue them to the base only. Add the ramp stop (part 15) to the short top support.

Glue the ramp handle (part 10) to the ramp, as shown.

The ramp lock (part 11) is simply a ¼-inch-thick slice of a ¾-inch-diameter dowel mounted through an off-center hole. Drill a

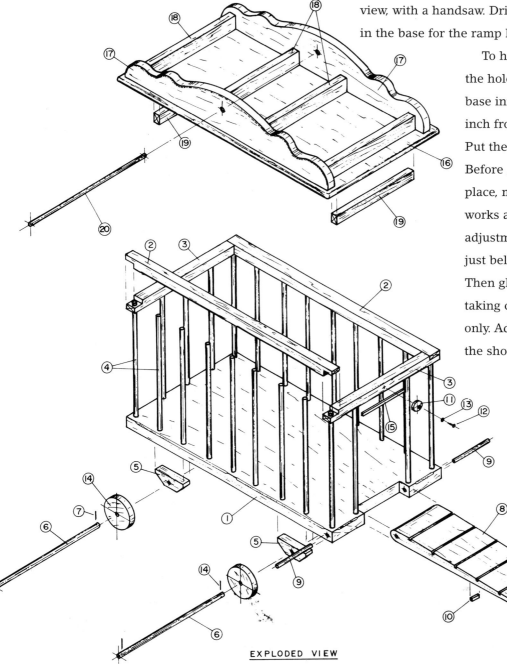

EXPLODED VIEW

clearance hole for the screw $\frac{3}{16}$ inch from the center of the dowel. Counter bore it to take a #4 x 1-inch round-head screw and #4 washer (parts 12 and 13). Screw the ramp lock to the top support.

4. Make the wagon wheels (part 20). They can be made with an adjustable circle cutter in a drill press.

Cut the wheels (part 14) from $\frac{5}{8}$-inch-thick stock with an adjustable circle cutter First, set the cutter to score a shallow $2\frac{1}{4}$-inch-diameter groove that defines the edge between the tire and wheel, as shown in the detail of the wagon wheel. Then set the cutter to a diameter of $2\frac{7}{8}$ inches, and cut out the wheel. If necessary, re-drill the center hole to fit the axle.

Put the axles temporarily in the axle supports; slide on the wheels, and mark the proper location of the wheel pins on the axles. Allow about $\frac{1}{32}$-inch clearance between the wheels and the base; then drill the $\frac{1}{8}$-inch-diameter holes for the pins. Cut the four wheel pins (part 7), but do not drill holes for them yet.

5. Make the top board and trim. Rout the edges of the top board (part 16) with a $\frac{1}{8}$-inch-radius router bit, and sand to the profile shown.

On paper, draw a grid with $\frac{1}{2}$-inch squares and enlarge the top trim (part 17) onto it. Transfer the pattern to the stock and cut the trim to shape. To make

certain the two trim pieces will match, attach them to one another with rubber cement or double-sided tape and then cut them out. Drill the $\frac{5}{16}$-inch-diameter hole and sand the edges before taking them apart.

NO.	NAME	SIZE	REQ'D.
	MATERIALS LIST		
1	BASE	$\frac{3}{4}$ x $7\frac{1}{4}$ – $13\frac{3}{4}$ LONG	1
2	LONG TOP SUPPORT	$\frac{3}{4}$ x $\frac{3}{4}$ – $13\frac{3}{4}$ LONG	2
3	SHORT TOP SUPPORT	$\frac{3}{4}$ x $\frac{3}{4}$ – $7\frac{1}{4}$ LONG	2
4	BAR	$\frac{5}{16}$ DIA. x $7\frac{1}{8}$ LONG	23
5	AXLE SUPPORT	$\frac{3}{4}$ x $\frac{3}{4}$ – $2\frac{1}{4}$ LONG	4
6	AXLE	$\frac{3}{8}$ DIA. x 9 LONG	2
7	WHEEL PIN	$\frac{1}{8}$ DIA. x $\frac{3}{4}$ LONG	4
8	RAMP	$\frac{3}{4}$ x $3\frac{1}{16}$ – $5\frac{3}{4}$ LONG	1
9	RAMP HINGE	$\frac{3}{16}$ DIA. x 3 LONG	2
10	RAMP HANDLE	$\frac{1}{4}$ x $\frac{1}{4}$ – 1 LONG	1
11	RAMP LOCK	$\frac{3}{4}$ DIA. x $\frac{1}{4}$ LONG	1
12	ROUNDHEAD SCREW	NO. 4 x 1 LONG	1
13	FLAT WASHER	NO. 4	1
14	WAGON WHEEL	$2\frac{7}{8}$ DIA. x $\frac{5}{8}$ LONG	4
15	RAMP STOP	$\frac{1}{4}$ x $\frac{1}{4}$ – $3\frac{1}{4}$ LONG	1
16	TOP BOARD	$\frac{5}{16}$ x $7\frac{1}{2}$ – 14 LONG	1
17	TOP TRIM	$\frac{9}{16}$ x $2\frac{1}{8}$ – $13\frac{3}{4}$ LONG	2
18	BRACE	$\frac{5}{8}$ x $\frac{3}{4}$ – 6 LONG	4
19	CLEAT	$\frac{5}{8}$ x $\frac{3}{4}$ – $5\frac{3}{4}$ LONG	2
20	LADDER SUPPORT	$\frac{5}{16}$ DIA. x 8 LONG	1
21	LADDER RAIL	$\frac{3}{8}$ x $\frac{3}{4}$ – $14\frac{1}{2}$ LONG	4
22	LADDER RUNG	$\frac{1}{4}$ DIA. x $2\frac{1}{2}$ LONG	18
23	ANIMALS	$\frac{3}{4}$ x 8 – 54 LONG (MAKES 7)	1
24	ANIMAL WHEEL	$1\frac{1}{4}$ DIA. x $\frac{5}{16}$ LONG	32
25	BALL	$1\frac{5}{8}$ DIA. x $\frac{3}{4}$ LONG	1
26	MAGNET	$\frac{1}{2}$ DIA.	17
27	NAIL – RD. HD. ANNULAR	$\frac{3}{4}$	18
28	NAIL – FL. HD. ANNULAR	$\frac{3}{4}$	32
29	CLOWN BODY	$\frac{1}{2}$ x 2 – 5 LONG	1
30	CLOWN ARM/LEG	$\frac{1}{4}$ x 2 – 6 LONG	2 EA.
31	POST AND SCREW	2 x $1\frac{1}{8}$ LONG	1 EA.
32	NAIL – FINISH	4 d	AS REQ'D

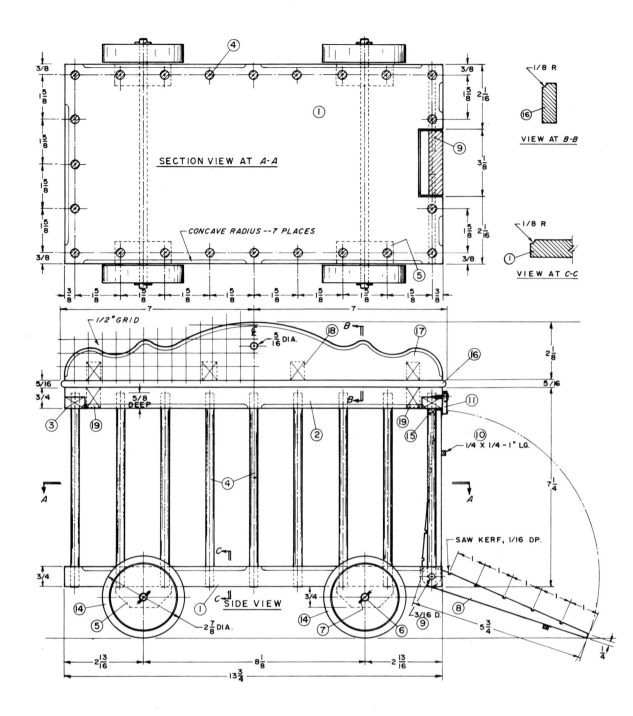

SECTION VIEW AT *A-A*

CONCAVE RADIUS --7 PLACES

VIEW AT *B-B*

VIEW AT *C-C*

1/2" GRID

5/16 DIA.

5/8 DEEP

1/4 X 1/4 - 1" LG.

SAW KERF, 1/16 DP.

SIDE VIEW

2 7/8 DIA.

3/16 D.

Rout a ⅛-inch-radius cove in the edge, as shown in the view at B-B. Don't cut all the way to the edges, as indicated by the side view.

Glue the top trim to the top board. For now, glue only the front and back braces (part 18) to the trim and top board, placing them about 1 inch from the front and back of the top. You will add the two inner braces later.

Glue the two cleats (part 19) to the underside of the top, allowing approximately ¹⁄₁₆-inch clearance with

the top support frame. The cleats serve to keep the top, which is removable, centered on the wagon.

6. Make the ladders. There are two of them. One is attached to the roof by the ladder support (part 20). The other ladder simply leans against the wagon.

Drill rung holes in the ladder rails and drill the hole for the ladder support, as shown in the detail of the ladder. Make sure that the holes on the pairs of rails are aligned. Glue up the rails and rungs (parts 21 and

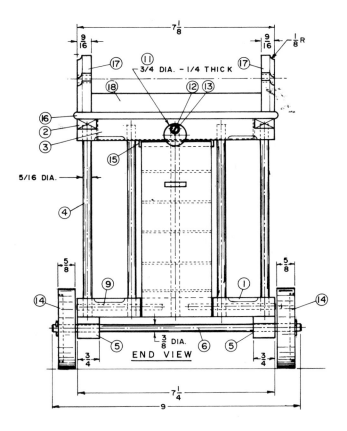

7⅛

9/16   9/16   ⅛R

⑰   ⑪ ¾ DIA. – 1/4 THICK   ⑰

⑱   ⑫ ⑬

⑯
②
③
⑮

5/16 DIA.

④

⑤   ⑤
⑨   ①
⑭   ⑭

⑤   ⅜ DIA. ⑥ ⑤
¾   END VIEW   ¾

7¼
9

22), keeping everything square.

Round the ends of the ladder support. Attach the ladder to the wagon by running the ladder support through the holes, both in the top trim and in the ladder rails; glue the support in the holes in the trim. Position the two remaining braces so that they keep the ladder at roughly a 60° angle. Glue the braces in place, and tack them in place when the glue has dried.

7. Cut the animal and clown parts to shape. The wagon is done; now it's time to build a clown and some animals for it. Sand the face of the boards from which you'll cut the animals before making any cuts. It will make the job of sanding easier later. Draw the patterns on a ½-inch grid; transfer the patterns to the wood and cut out the parts.

The animal wheels (part 24) are 5/16-inch-thick slices of 1¼-inch dowel. Counterbore the wheels so the heads of the nails that attach them will be recessed. If you have a drill press, a simple jig makes this easy.

To make the jig, clamp a piece of scrap to the drill press. Drill a 1¼-inch-diameter hole ¼ inch deep in the scrap. Without moving the scrap, put a ⅜-inch-diameter bit in the chuck. Set the depth stops for a hole ⅛ inch deep. Put each wheel in turn into the jig and drill the counter bore. Then put a drill bit, slightly wider than the annual nails that will hold the wheels in place, into the drill press. Drill holes through all the wheels.

Glue the ears on the elephant, the mane on the lion, and the assorted tails on the animals.

8. Apply finish. Paint the circus wagon and animals with bright, nontoxic colors. For inspiration, you might go to the library for a book with color photos of circuses.

9. Add the magnets and wheels and assemble the clown. After the paint has dried, attach the ceramic magnets (part 26) with roundhead annular nails (part 27). The polarity of the magnets is marked with plus and minus symbols; make sure that all of the pluses are at the front and the minuses at the back, or the animals won't parade around obediently. The seal gets a roundhead nail in its nose (part 23) to attract the magnet in the ball (part 25).

When attaching the animal wheels, put a bit of candle wax into the counterbored holes for lubrication. Attach the wheels to the bodies with flathead annular nails (part 28).

Attach the wagon wheels to the wagon. Glue the wheel pins in place.

Assemble the clown (parts 29 and 30) with a self-locking post and screw (part 31). If necessary for a snug fit, place thin flat washers between the body and the arms and legs. Make sure that the posts and screws are very tight so that they won't come apart in a child's hands. Check them for tightness from time to time. You might ask at a hardware store for a special adhesive that locks threaded parts, and use it on the screw.

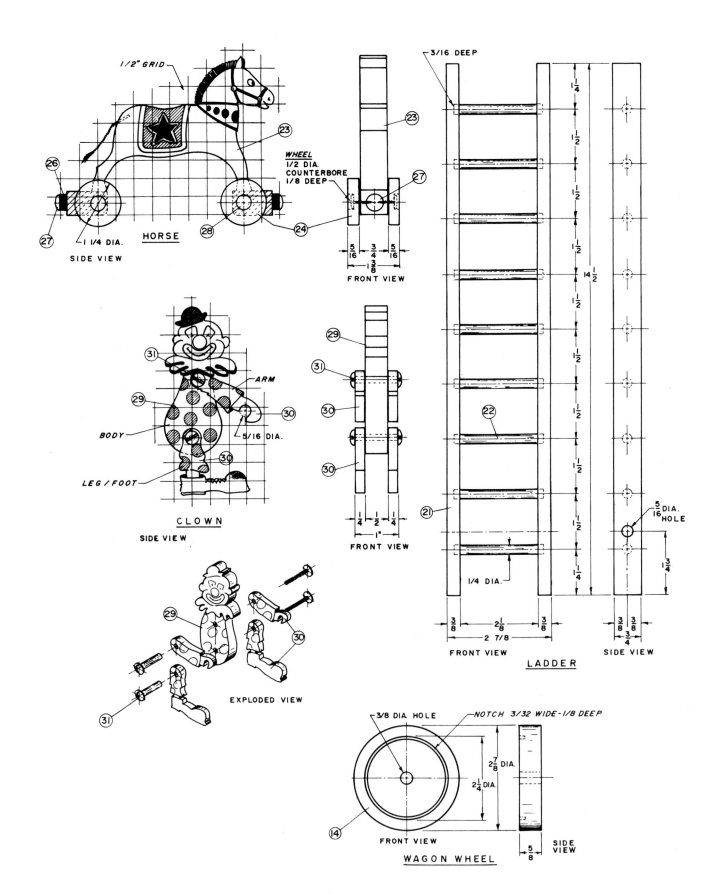

1/2" GRID

WHEEL
1/2 DIA.
COUNTERBORE
1/8 DEEP

HORSE
SIDE VIEW

FRONT VIEW

1 1/4 DIA.

3/16 DEEP

LADDER

FRONT VIEW

SIDE VIEW

14 1/2

1 1/4
1 1/2
1 1/2
1 1/2
1 1/2
1 1/2
1 1/2
1 1/2
1 1/4

3/8   2 1/8   3/8
2 7/8

3/8 3/8
3/4

5/16 DIA. HOLE

1 3/4

1/4 DIA.

CLOWN
SIDE VIEW

ARM

BODY

5/16 DIA.

LEG/FOOT

FRONT VIEW

1/4   1/2   1/4
1"

EXPLODED VIEW

3/8 DIA HOLE

NOTCH 3/32 WIDE-1/8 DEEP

2 7/8 DIA.

2 1/4 DIA.

5/8

FRONT VIEW

SIDE VIEW

WAGON WHEEL

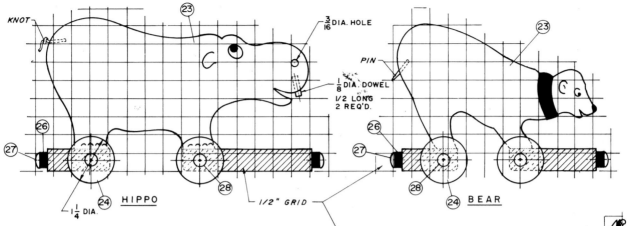

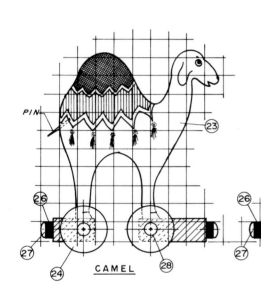

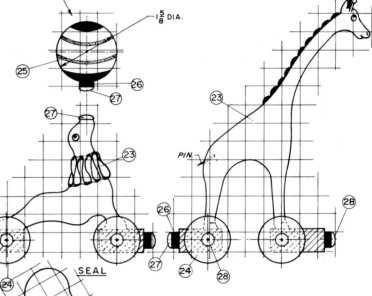

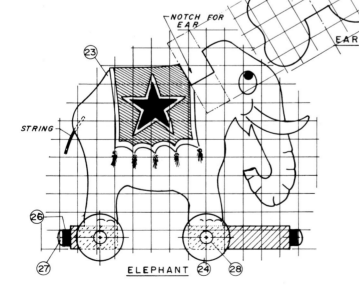

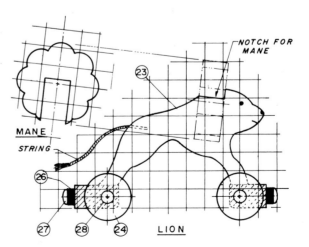

Riding Rocking Horse

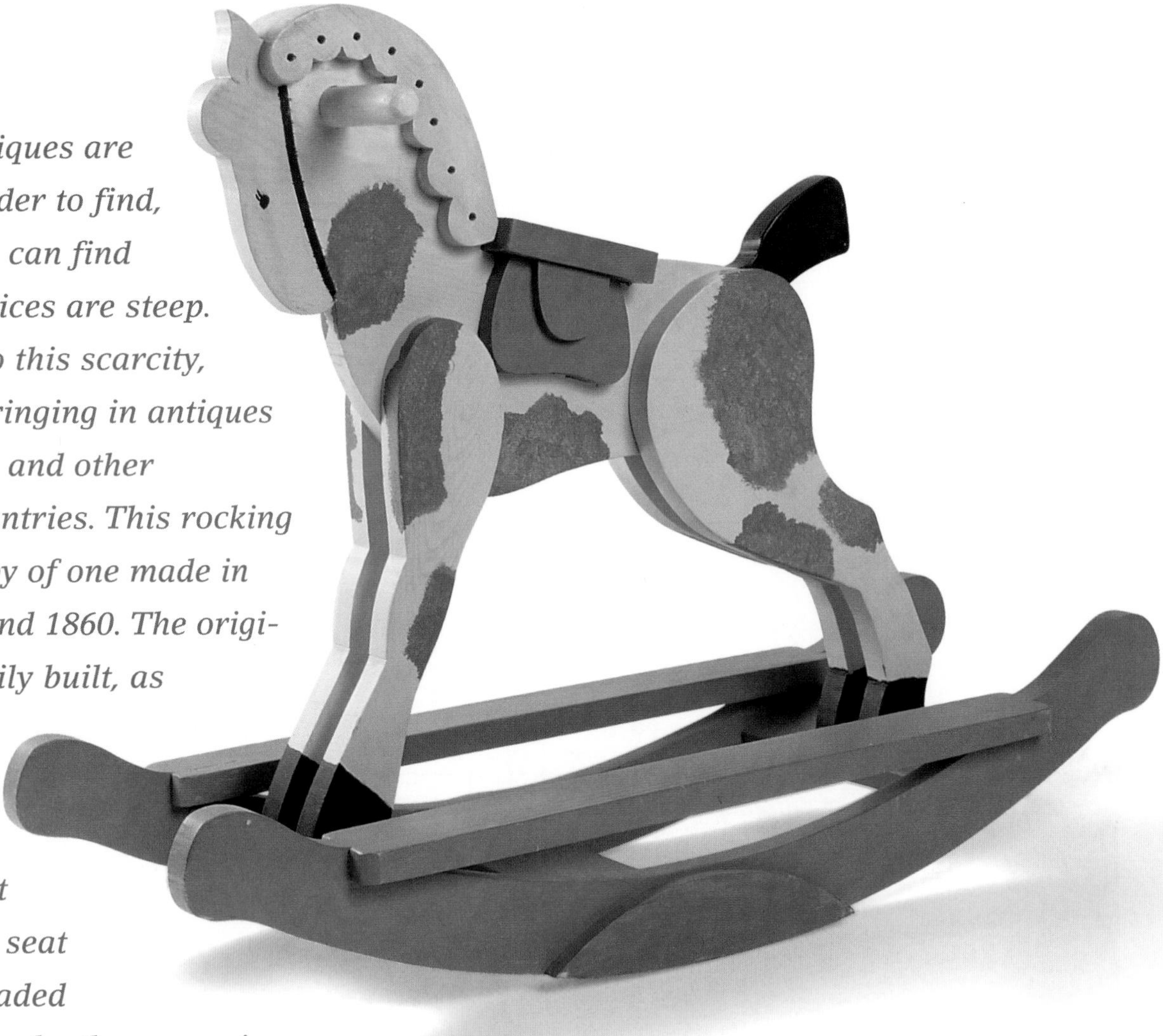

American antiques are becoming harder to find, and when you can find them, their prices are steep. In response to this scarcity, dealers are bringing in antiques from England and other European countries. This rocking horse is a copy of one made in England around 1860. The original was sturdily built, as testified to by at least five generations of use. It had a padded seat with large-headed tacks holding a leather cover in place. Note that this design is different from most rocking horses made in the United States because it has footrests on each side but doesn't have the hand-hold dowels found on most of our horses. You may find it a good idea to add them, as I've done on the one pictured here. This copy has relatively simple joinery and is easy to cut out and assemble.

MATERIALS LIST

NO.	NAME	SIZE	REQ'D.
1	BODY	¾ x 11 – 21 LONG	1
2	FRONT LEG	¾ x 3 – 14 LONG	3
3	REAR LEG	¾ x 6 – 16 LONG	2
4	MANE	½ x 4 – 9 LONG	2
5	ROCKER	¾ x 6½ – 31 LONG	2
6	FOOTREST	¾ x 2¼ – 22 LONG	2
7	RUNNER	½ x 2¼ – 8½ LONG	2
8	SPACER	¾ x 3 – 8 LONG	3
9	SEAT	¾ x 2¾ – 4¾ LONG	1
10	SEAT SUPPORT	½ x 2½ – 4¾ LONG	2
11	SEAT SUPPORT	½ x 2¼ X 2 LONG	2
12	SCREW – FL. HD.	NO. 8 – 2 LONG	12
13	SCREW – FL. HD.	NO. 8 – 1½ LONG	4
14	NAIL – FINISH	4 d	AS REQ'D.
15	NAIL – FINISH	6 d	AS REQ'D.
16	DOWEL	⅜ DIA. – 1⅛ LONG	12

1. Select the stock and cut the parts. I recommend using a hardwood such as maple, oak, or ash for this project. Softwood may not hold up over the decades as well as the ash used to make the original.

Cut the parts to the sizes given in the Materials List.

2. Make paper patterns of all parts. Draw the separate grids with the size squares noted on the drawings and enlarge each individual piece onto the grids. Take special care to draw a smooth 28½-inch radius for the rocker (part 5). Note that the top of the rocker has a step that accepts the notched footrest. Measure accurately so that these pieces will come together properly. Transfer the patterns to the wood.

3. Cut the parts to shape. To save time, double up when cutting identical parts. Tape the pairs together with double-sided tape, or temporarily tack them together with small finishing nails. The holes can be filled in later. After cutting all the parts to shape, sand their edges while the pairs are still together. This saves time and ensures that the matching parts really match. Take particular care when cutting the bottom edge of the rockers so that the horse will rock evenly.

Two cross pieces run between the rockers and are attached with screws. Before taking the two rockers apart, drill and countersink six screw holes slightly larger than the screw shank, as shown in the front view. Then separate the rockers.

You'll need to drill holes in the spacers (part 8), too, to keep the screws from splitting them. The easiest way to locate these holes is to temporarily clamp the spacers in place and drill through the rocker holes into the spacers. Drill holes slightly smaller than the screw shank.

4. Assemble the horse. Dry-fit all parts, making any necessary adjustments. Glue the footrests (part 6) to

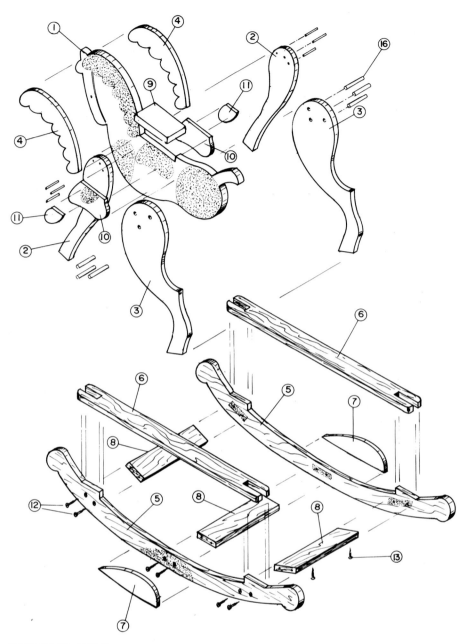

EXPLODED VIEW

the rockers. Screw the spacers between the rockers with #8 2-inch flathead screws. Make sure everything is square. Glue the runners (part 7) in place. Sand the entire rocker, rounding the edges slightly.

Glue the mane (part 4) and the seat supports (parts 10 and 11) to the body, as shown. Attach the seat (part 9) with glue. To ensure that these parts don't move, drive 4d finishing nails (part 14) through the mane and supports, and 6d finishing nails (part 15) through the seat.

Clamp the legs (parts 2 and 3) onto the body (part 1) and adjust them until all four rest squarely on the spacers. Trace the outline of the legs on the body. Remove the clamps and add glue. Guided by the outlines, clamp the legs to the body again. After the glue has set, reinforce this joint by running a ⅜-inch-diameter dowel (part 16) through each pair of legs and halfway into the body. Glue the dowels in place and sand the ends flush with the legs.

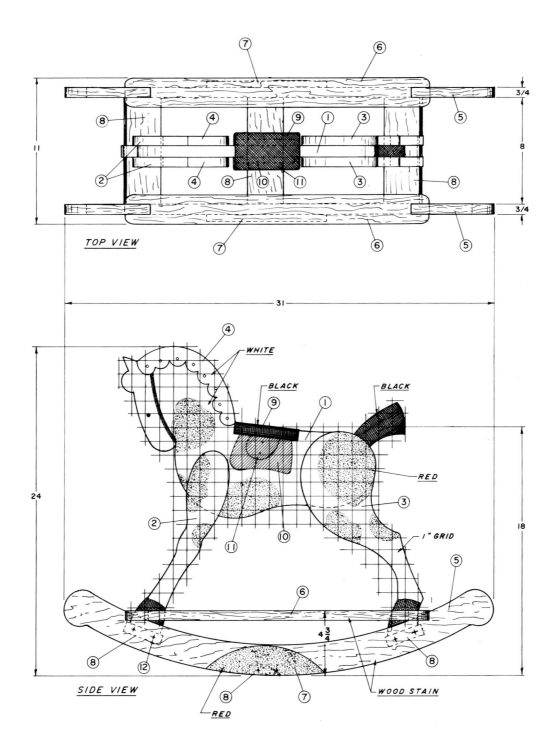

TOP VIEW

SIDE VIEW

Finally, glue the legs to the spacers and screw them in place with #8 ½-inch-flathead wood screws (part 13).

5. Apply finish. The original horse was painted and had a stained rocker assembly, as shown in the side view. My wife wanted to make the horse brighter, so she painted the rockers solid blue. The brown spots were actually an orangey-brick red on the original. Be sure to use nontoxic paint.

To make the horse look older, paint it as noted in the plans and, when thoroughly dry, sand all the edges slightly to give them a worn look. Then apply a light coat of cherry stain over all the painted surfaces.

A simpler alternative is to stain the entire horse rather than paint it.

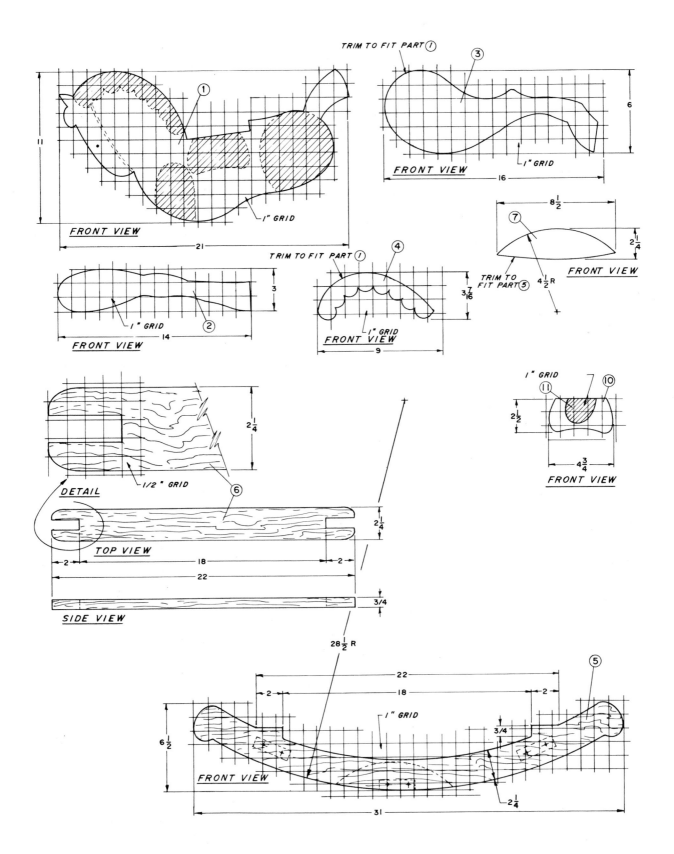

TRIM TO FIT PART ①

③

FRONT VIEW

6

1" GRID

16

①

FRONT VIEW

11

1" GRID

21

8½

⑦

2¼

TRIM TO
FIT PART ⑤

4½ R

FRONT VIEW

③

1" GRID

②

14

FRONT VIEW

TRIM TO FIT PART ①

④

3 7/16

1" GRID

FRONT VIEW

9

1" GRID

⑪   ⑩

2½

4¾

FRONT VIEW

DETAIL

2¼

1/2" GRID

⑥

TOP VIEW

2   18   2

22

2¼

SIDE VIEW

3/4

28½ R

22

18

2   2

1" GRID

3/4

⑤

6½

FRONT VIEW

2¼

31

Folk Art Projects

Whether you start with the weather vane, the cranberry scoop, or the whimsical lawn bird, when you construct some of the useful and decorative items in this chapter, a bit of America's past can be yours to enjoy today.

Folk Weather Vanes

Weather vanes are as popular today as they were a hundred years ago. Both of these patterns are taken directly from antique weather vanes. You can distress these if you want yours to look old. Weather vanes have been used for centuries, perhaps even millennia. The rooster is an old symbol used to identify places of worship. The arrow points into the wind and stays aligned as the wind changes. The cock weather vane on church steeples signified how easily faith could be swayed.

These weather vanes also make great wall hangings.

1. Lay out either or both patterns on a ½-inch grid.

2. Transfer the pattern(s) to the wood and cut out.

3. Paint to suit. I prefer sanding the edges slightly and staining over the paint to get an old look.

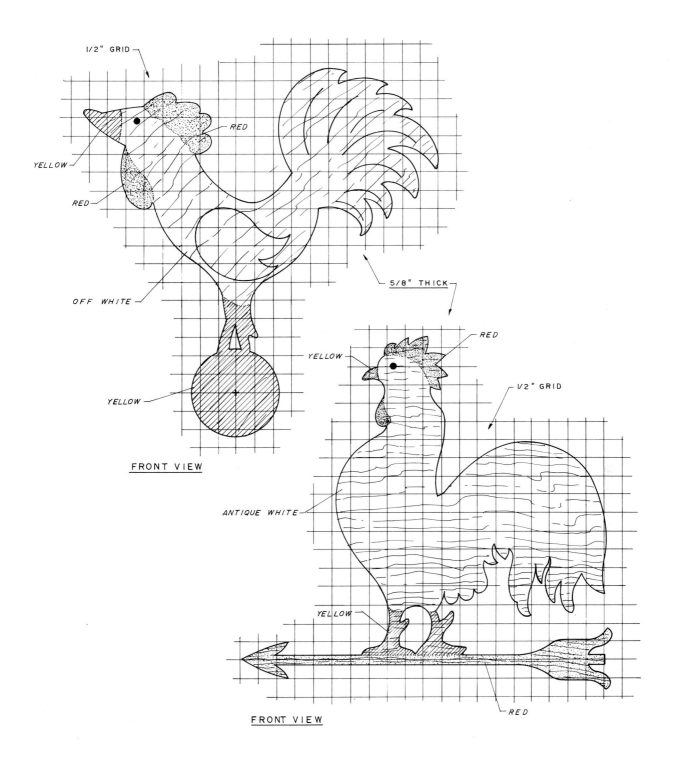

1/2" GRID

YELLOW

RED

RED

OFF WHITE

YELLOW

FRONT VIEW

RED

5/8" THICK

RED

YELLOW

1/2" GRID

ANTIQUE WHITE

YELLOW

RED

FRONT VIEW

Swan Cutting Board

I've found that the most popular animal shape for cutting boards is that of the pig, but this board takes the shape of a resting swan. We saw one like it at a flea market, and the dealer claimed to know that it was old and came from South Carolina. The original was about one-third larger than this pattern, a size that might be too large for today's kitchens.

1. Select the stock. Use knot-free, straight-grained hardwood, ¼ or 1 inch thick. If possible, find a 12 inch-wide board and make the project out of one piece of wood. Otherwise, you'll have to glue up the blank from two or more pieces. You can make good use of scrap pieces in this way.

2. Transfer the pattern. Draw the swan's body directly on the wood with a large compass, following the dimensions shown on the drawing.

   Make a paper pattern for the swan's head. Draw a grid with ½-inch squares and enlarge the swan's head and neck onto it. Line up the enlarged drawing so that the dots marked End of Arcs run into the 5¾-inch-radius curves on the swan's body. The centerline of the

head pattern, indicated by long and short dashes, should align with the centerline of the body. Transfer the drawing to the wood.

3. Cut out the cutting board. Cut just outside the layout line with a band saw, saber saw, or jigsaw. Drill a hole in the cutout within the bend of the neck, slip a coping or jigsaw blade through it, and saw out the teardrop shape. Sand the entire piece, and round the ends slightly to remove any rough edges.

   Use a sharp carving knife or wood-burning tool to define the beak and neck as shown in the photograph.

4. Apply finish. Sand the piece and buff it with 0000 steel wool. Protect it with a non toxic salad-bowl finish.

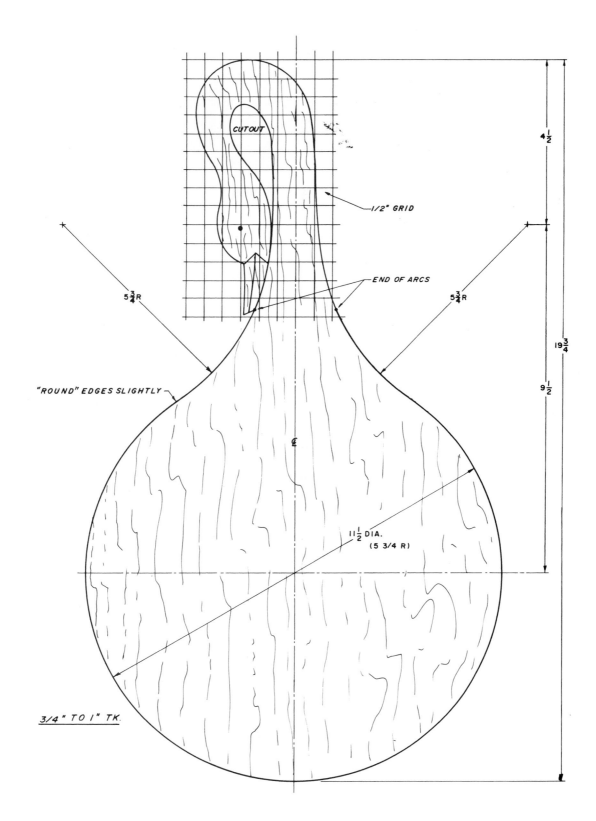

CUTOUT

1/2" GRID

4½

5¾R

END OF ARCS

5¾R

19¾

9½

"ROUND" EDGES SLIGHTLY

11½ DIA.
(5 3/4 R)

3/4" TO 1" TK.

Early Toy Roadster

On a summer's day we were browsing at a local antique shop when I found the peculiar small toy car on which I based this project. While the original is probably not an actual antique, it is rather old—I estimate about sixty years old—since it depicts an early 1930s roadster, perhaps a Cadillac. What fascinated me the most about this unique find was that the body was made of only two simple pieces. They were interlocked in such a way that they created a full-bodied car. I purchased it and drew up the plans just as the original toy was. The roadster is easy to make, does not take much time, and would make an excellent gift for any child. The child will have fun and get a sense of what another child may have played with in the early part of the 1900s.

Note: This project is more properly termed folk art rather than the reproduction of an antique. Therefore, the painted finish does not have to be perfect. It should look handmade, so if you are not an expert painter, as I surely am not, don't be afraid to do this project. You can always buy a perfect plastic toy at any toy store.

1. Cut two pieces of knot-free softwood such as pine; one, $\frac{3}{4}$ x $2\frac{1}{8}$ x $6\frac{1}{4}$ long, and another $\frac{3}{4}$ x $1\frac{3}{4}$ x 7 inches. Sand the top and bottom surfaces.

2. Transfer the shapes of the body and base to the wood, and cut the $\frac{3}{4}$-inch-wide, $\frac{1}{2}$-inch-deep notch in the base piece. Check that the body fits snugly into the notch in the base.

3. Cut the body and base to shape, according to the drawing, and sand all edges. Take care to line up the wheel wells for the two pieces.

4. Glue these two pieces together, and the major part of the roadster is complete. Fill, if necessary, with wood filler, and resand all over.

5. Cut the wheels and spare tires from a 1 inch-diameter dowel— two pieces $1\frac{1}{2}$ inches long, and two pieces $\frac{1}{4}$ inch long.

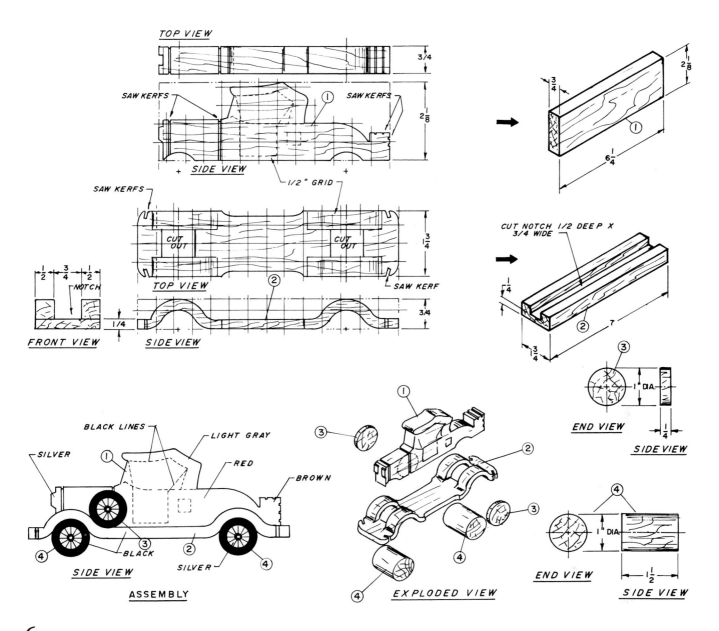

6. Glue them in place as shown.

7. Prime all over, and lightly sand when dry.

8. Paint the roadster as you desire. The original colors are noted if you wish to follow them.

9. (Optional) If you want your car to look 60 years old, you might want to carefully sand some of the edges down to the bare wood where you think it might have been worn naturally in normal use. Apply a glaze coat of dark-walnut stain over the entire painted car, even over the white paint. This will give it an authentic old look and feel.

Your car is now ready to be enjoyed for another 60 years. As this might become a family heirloom, you might want to cut your name and date into the bottom of the car. Perhaps in the middle of the twenty-first century some woodworker will find your car in an antiques shop and be as fascinated with it as I was with the original I found.

MATERIALS LIST			
NO.	NAME	SIZE	REQ'D.
1	BODY	¾ x 2⅛ – 6¼ LONG	1
2	BASE	¾ x 1¾ – 7 LONG	1
3	TIRE – SPARE	1 DIA. – ¼ LONG	2
4	WHEEL (DOWEL)	1 DIA. – 1½ LONG	2

Maiden Plant Holder

A friend wanted a wall plant holder. She wanted something different. Well, here it is. It is bright and different.

MATERIALS LIST

NO.	NAME	SIZE	REQ'D.
1	SUPPORT	¾ x 2 - 14 LONG	1
2	BODY	¾ x 9½ – 7½ LONG	1
3	SCREW – FL. HD.	NO. 6 – 1¾ LONG	2

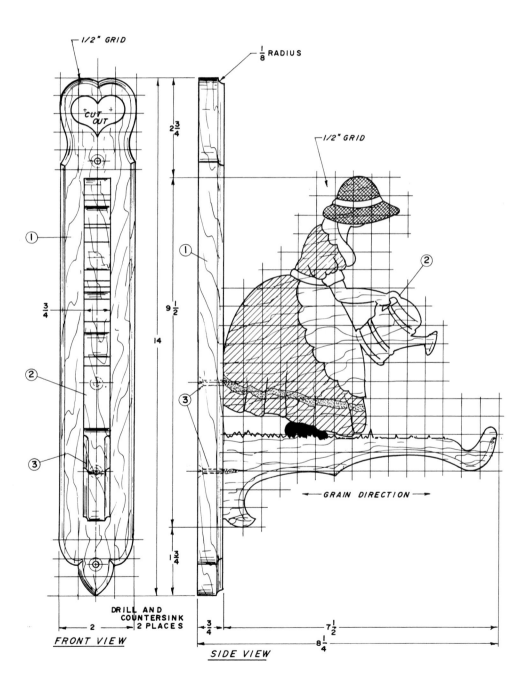

FRONT VIEW

SIDE VIEW

1. Lay out the patterns for parts 1 and 2 on heavy paper.

2. Transfer the pattern to the wood, and cut out parts 1 and 2. Sand all over.

3. Using a ⅛-inch-radius cove cutter with a ball-bearing follower, cut out the outer edge of the support (part 2).

4. Drill the holes in the support (part 1).

5. Glue and screw the body (part 2) to the support (part 1) using screws (part 3).

6. Prime and paint with bright colors to suit. Hang on the wall, and add your favorite plant

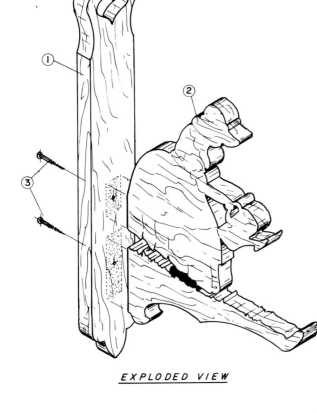

EXPLODED VIEW

Christmas Tree Decoration

Here's a simple decoration that's easy to make and that will add a festive flair to any setting. This also makes a great craft-fair project.

1. Using a ¾-inch-thick board 7½ inches wide x 16 inches long, lay out all pieces. If you plan to make a few of these, make a pattern of each part out of heavy cardboard or hardboard.

2. Locate and drill all ¼-inch-diameter holes. Do not drill through the base (part 1).

3. Cut out all of the pieces, and sand all over. Round all edges slightly.

4. Glue the base (part 1) to the center stem (part 9).

5. Drill a ¼-inch-diameter hole into the star (part 10) as shown. You might want to use a clamp to hold the star while drilling the hole. Do not drill through.

6. Assemble all parts and paint to suit.

TOP VIEW

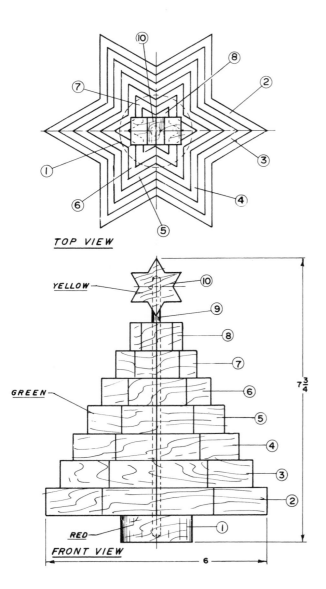

FRONT VIEW

YELLOW

GREEN

RED

$7\frac{3}{4}$

6

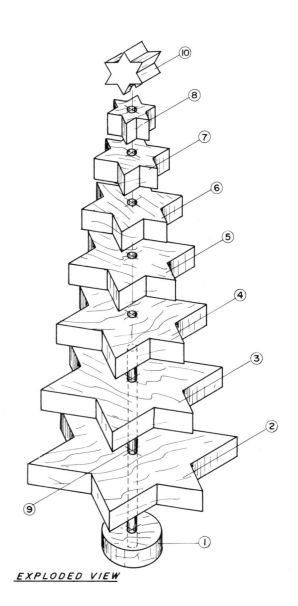

EXPLODED VIEW

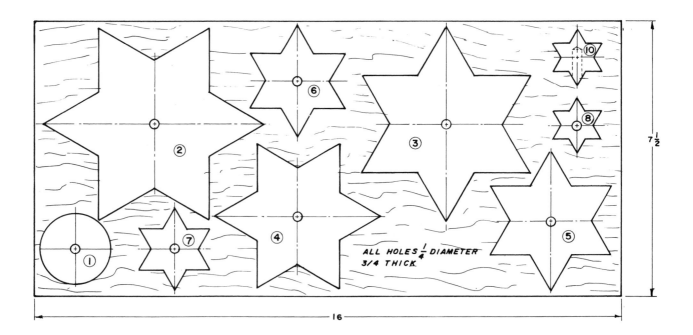

ALL HOLES $\frac{1}{4}$ DIAMETER
3/4 THICK

$7\frac{1}{2}$

16

Cat Plant Stand

Now this is a folk art project right out of the 1930s. The original was actually used for a smoking stand to support an ashtray. As a kid, I can remember them. I have seen more and more of these smoking stands in local antique shops. They are becoming collectibles. Today, of course, they're better for holding plants instead of ash trays.

MATERIALS LIST			
NO.	NAME	SIZE	REQ'D.
1	BODY	¾ x 13½ – 24¾ LONG	1
2	BASE	¾ x 8 - 10 LONG	1
3	LOWER SUPPORT	¾ - 5 DIA.	1
4	SUPPORT	¾ - 6 DIA.	1
5	SCREW – FL. HD.	NO. 8 – 3 LONG	1
6	SCREW – FL. HD.	NO. 8 – 2 LONG	2

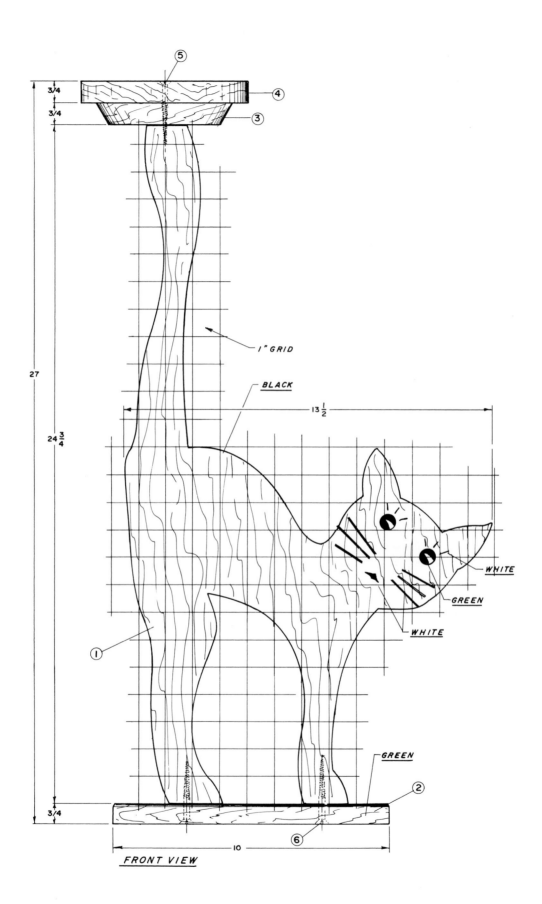

1" GRID

BLACK

13 ½

3/4 ⑤ ④

3/4 ③

27

24 ¾

WHITE

GREEN

WHITE

①

GREEN

②

3/4

⑥

10

FRONT VIEW

1. Make a full-size pattern of the body (part 1). Cut all pieces to overall size, and sand.

Transfer the pattern of the body (part 1) to the wood, and cut out. Sand all edges slightly.

2. Cut the base (part 2) and two supports (parts 3 and 4) to shape, and sand all over.

Drill for the screws (parts 5 and 6).

3. Assemble the pieces according to the drawing of the exploded view.

Prime and paint to suit. If desired, paint on eyes, whiskers, and a mouth, per the illustration. Now your stand is all ready to use.

EXPLODED VIEW

Small Decorative Rocking Horse

All children should have a rocking horse. This small one is meant to hold rather than ride, but nevertheless it's a rocking horse. It is fun to make and paint, as well as to play with.

MATERIALS LIST			
NO.	NAME	SIZE	REQ'D.
1	BODY	½ x 3⅝ – 8 LONG	1
2	FRONT LEG	¼ x 1½ – 4 LONG	2
3	BACK	¼ x 2 – 4¼ LONG	2
4	EAR	⅛ x ⅜ – ¾ LONG	2
5	SADDLE	⅛ x 1¼ – 2 LONG	1
6	SUPPORT	¼ x 1 – 1⅜ LONG	3
7	ROCKER	¼ x 2½ – 10½ LONG	2

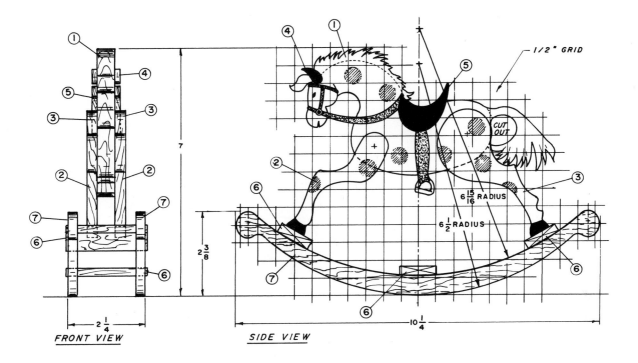

FRONT VIEW   SIDE VIEW

1. Lay out the horse and rocker on a ½-inch grid.

   Note: it could be made twice the size if you lay it out on a 1-inch grid.

2. Cut all pieces to overall size according to the cutting list. Sand all over.

3. Transfer the shapes of the horse, legs, and rocker to the wood and cut out. Sand all pieces, rounding all edges slightly.

4. Assemble the rocker section first (parts 6 and 7). Keep the rockers parallel to each other.

   Note: if you expect hard use, you might want to consider gluing and nailing the pieces together.

5. Glue the legs to both the horse's body and the rocker assembly at the same time. This will ensure correct alignment of the leg (parts 2 and 3) with the supports (part 6). (It also takes three hands to do it!)

6. Prime the toy. You might consider staining the rockers (part 7).

7. Now comes the fun part. Paint and decorate your horse as you wish. Use your imagination and have fun.

Small Wheelbarrow Planters With Boy & Girl Figures

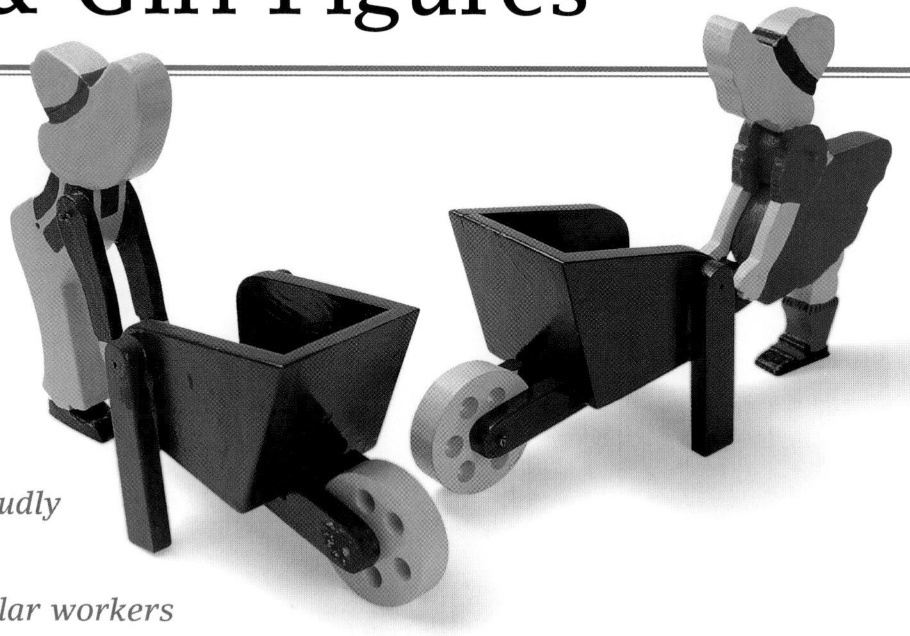

This is the kind of project that was very popular in the early 1940s. Today they are collectibles. As a kid, I can remember most everyone made small projects such as these and displayed them proudly around the house. I found the originals of these two particular workers at a flea market and would guess that they are from this period. My newly purchased collectibles were in bad shape, but enough was left to create a pattern and redraw the plans. They are brightly colored and will add a lot to your plants. You can make one or the other, or both, if you choose.

1. Lay out all the parts full size on a sheet of heavy paper or cardboard. Be sure to note the location of all holes. Transfer the pattern and hole locations to the wood. Cut out all the pieces according to the plans. Don't forget to make a saw kerf to divide the legs of the figures.

2. To make the wheelbarrow, glue the bottom and front together; then attach the two sides. Sand all over when the glue sets. Make up the left and right-hand handles. Make up the wheel and attach the two handles with the wheel temporarily attached. Add the two legs, and the wheelbarrow is done, ready for painting.

3. To make the figures, simply attach the arms to the body. To get the exact position of the arms, temporarily attach the hands to the wheelbarrow. Check that the

MATERIALS LIST			
NO.	NAME	SIZE	REQ'D.
1	BODY (EITHER)	⅝ x 4 – 8 LONG	1
2	ARM	¼ x 2⅛ X 3½ LONG	2
3	BOTTOM	¾ X 2 – 2¹¹⁄₁₆ LONG	1
4	FRONT	¼ x 2 – 3¹⁄₁₆ LONG	1
5	SIDE	¼ x 3 – 3¾ LONG	2
6	HANDLE	¼ x ⅝ – 6⅜ LONG	2
7	LEG	¼ x ⅝ – 3⅛ LONG	2
8	WHEEL	½ - 2 SQUARE	1
9	BRAD	½ LONG	8
10	PIN (WHEEL)	⅛ DIA. - 1⅛ LONG	1

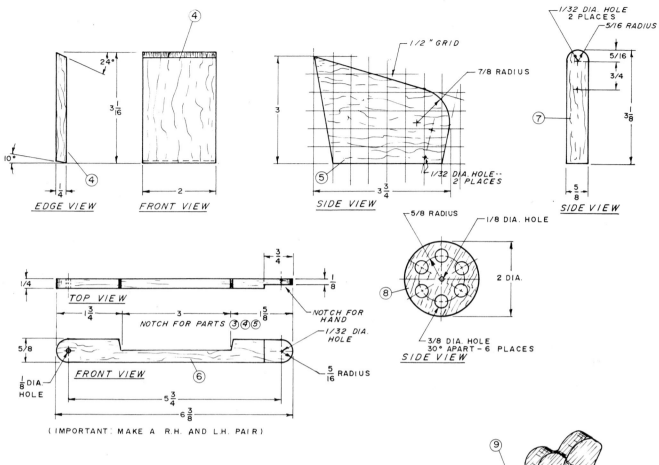

4

24°

3 1/16

10°

1/4

EDGE VIEW

2

FRONT VIEW

1/2" GRID

7/8 RADIUS

3

5

3 3/4

1/32 DIA. HOLE-- 2 PLACES

SIDE VIEW

1/32 DIA. HOLE 2 PLACES

5/16 RADIUS

5/16

3/4

3 1/8

7

5/8

SIDE VIEW

3/4

1/4

TOP VIEW

1 3/4

3

5/8

NOTCH FOR PARTS ③④⑤

NOTCH FOR HAND

1/32 DIA. HOLE

1/8

5/8

FRONT VIEW

6

1/8 DIA. HOLE

5/16 RADIUS

5 3/4

6 3/8

(IMPORTANT: MAKE A R.H. AND L.H. PAIR)

5/8 RADIUS

1/8 DIA. HOLE

8

2 DIA.

3/8 DIA. HOLE 30° APART – 6 PLACES

SIDE VIEW

wheelbarrow and feet are resting flush on the surface. Note: You will have to trim the handles of the wheelbarrow and the hands slightly to get the proper fit. The originals had the arms set at a slight angle.

4. Separate the wheel and hands from the wheelbarrow, and prime all of the parts. Using fast-drying latex paint, paint the features similar to what is shown in the plans. Use your imagination as you wish.

The colors called off in the plans are the colors used on the originals I purchased, but any color combination can be used. Permanently reattach the wheel and hands to the wheelbarrow. Make sure the feet rest squarely on the surface before the glue sets.

5. Add a small plant, and you're back in the forties.

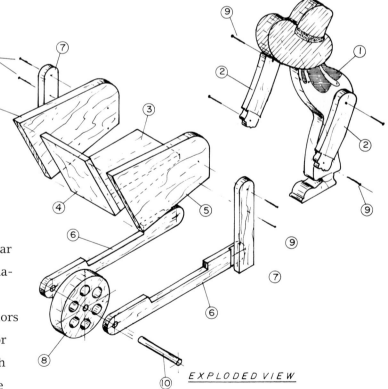

EXPLODED VIEW

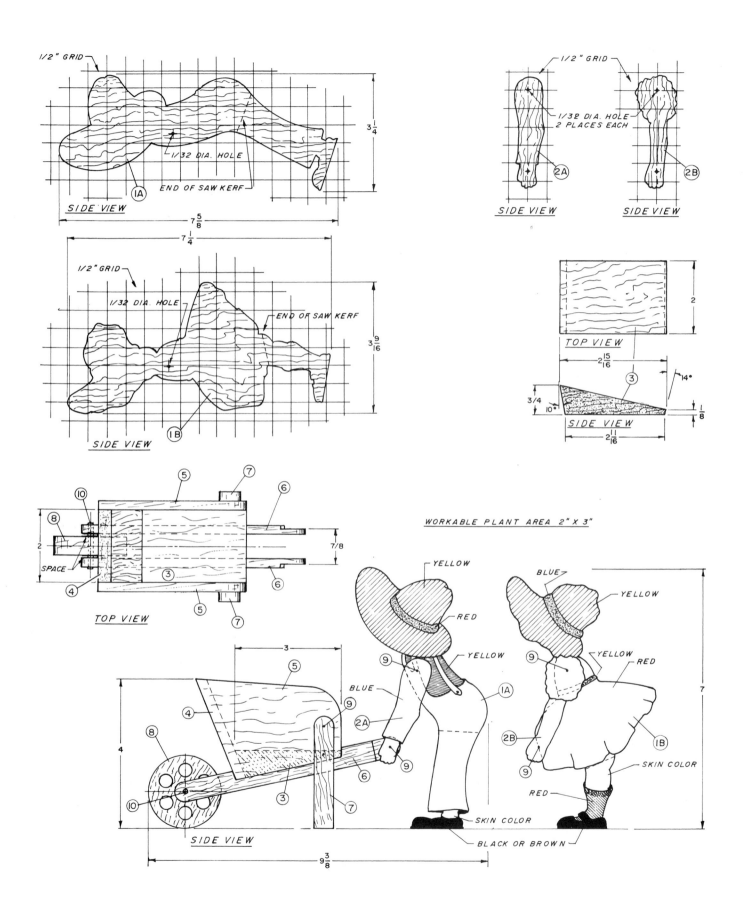

1/2" GRID

1/32 DIA. HOLE

END OF SAW KERF

1A

SIDE VIEW

7 5/8

7 1/4

1/2" GRID

1/32 DIA. HOLE

END OF SAW KERF

3 9/16

1B

SIDE VIEW

1/2" GRID

1/32 DIA. HOLE
2 PLACES EACH

2A

SIDE VIEW

2B

SIDE VIEW

TOP VIEW

2

2 15/16

3

14°

3/4

10°

1/8

SIDE VIEW

2 11/16

10

8

5

7

6

2

SPACE

4

3

5

6

7

7/8

TOP VIEW

WORKABLE PLANT AREA 2" X 3"

YELLOW

RED

YELLOW

BLUE

YELLOW

RED

3

5

8

4

9

2A

9

6

3

10

7

9

BLUE

9

9

1A

SKIN COLOR

BLACK OR BROWN

9

2B

9

SKIN COLOR

RED

1B

4

SIDE VIEW

9 3/8

7

336   Folk Art Projects

Alligator, c.1930

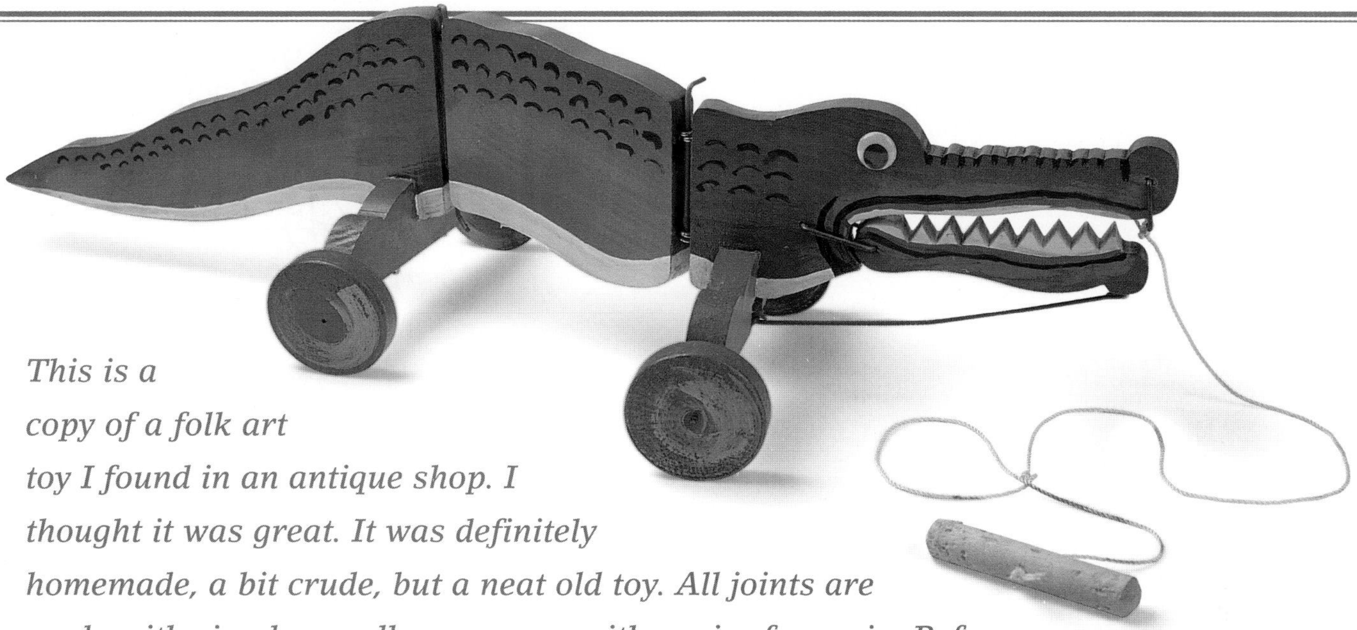

This is a
copy of a folk art
toy I found in an antique shop. I
thought it was great. It was definitely
homemade, a bit crude, but a neat old toy. All joints are
made with simple, small eye screws with a wire for a pin. Refer
to the exploded view. The jaw moves up and down as it rolls along. It
has an interesting hinge that I found especially unusual.

1. Cut all pieces to overall size. (If you don't have a plane, substitute ¾-inch-thick wood in place of the ⅝-inch thick.)

On a ½-inch grid, lay out the body pieces (parts 1, 2, 3, 4, and 9). Note the ⅝ inch-wide by ⁵⁄₁₆ inch-deep notches in parts 1, 4, and 9.

Transfer the patterns to the wood and cut out. (The front axle support has an extra notch.)

2. Sand all over. Round all edges slightly.

Glue the axle supports to the body. Check that they are square (90°).

Add all eye screws as shown, except the four holding the front axle in place.

Assemble the jaw (part 2) to the head (part 1) with a wire (part 10). Bend over after assembly.

Form the front axle (part 7) as shown. A coat hanger wire works great for this.

MATERIALS LIST			
NO.	NAME	SIZE	REQ'D.
1	HEAD	⅝ x 4 – 8½ LONG	1
2	JAW	⅝ x 1¼ – 5 LONG	1
3	CENTER BODY	⅝ x 5 – 5½ LONG	1
4	TAIL	⅝ x 5 – 10½ LONG	1
5	SCREW – EYE	SMALL SIZE	15
6	AXLE – REAR	⅛ DIA. – 7⅛ LONG	1
7	AXLE – FRONT	⅛ DIA. – 8¼ LONG	1
8	DRIVE ROD	⅛ DIA. – 7½ LONG	1
9	AXLE SUPPORT	⅝ x 1½ – 6 LONG	2
10	JAW HINGE	⅛ DIA. – 4 LONG	1
11	PIN	⅛ DIA. – 4½ LONG	2
12	PULL LOOP	⅛ DIA. – 3⅛ LONG	1
13	WHEEL	2¼ DIA. - ½ LONG	4

3. Locate and drill four small holes in the front axle support for the four eye screws (part 5).

4. Assemble the drive rod (part 8) to the front axle, and hammer the eye screws into the four small holes drilled. Secure the drive rod to the jaw with a small eye screw. Experiment to find the best location for the eye screw.

5. Paint to suit. I have noted the colors and detailing that were on the original if you want yours the same.

  Assemble all parts using two pins (part 11). Bend them over at the top and bottom to hold them in place.

6. Epoxy the wheels (part 13) to the axles (parts 6 and 7).

7. Add the pull loop (part 12), and your alligator is set to go.

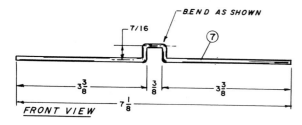

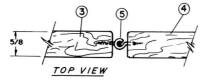

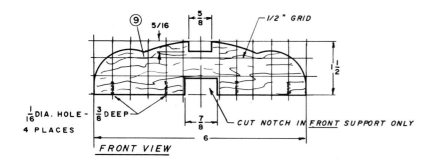

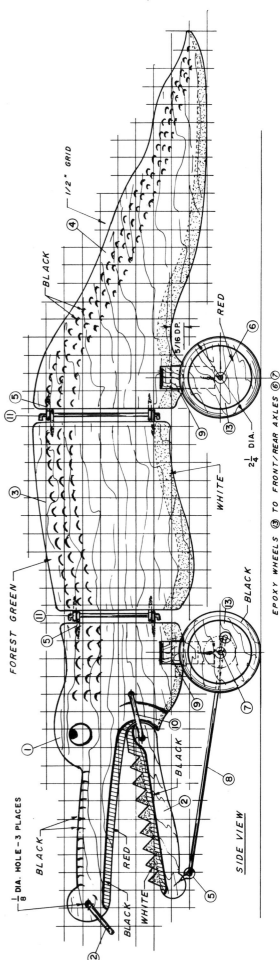

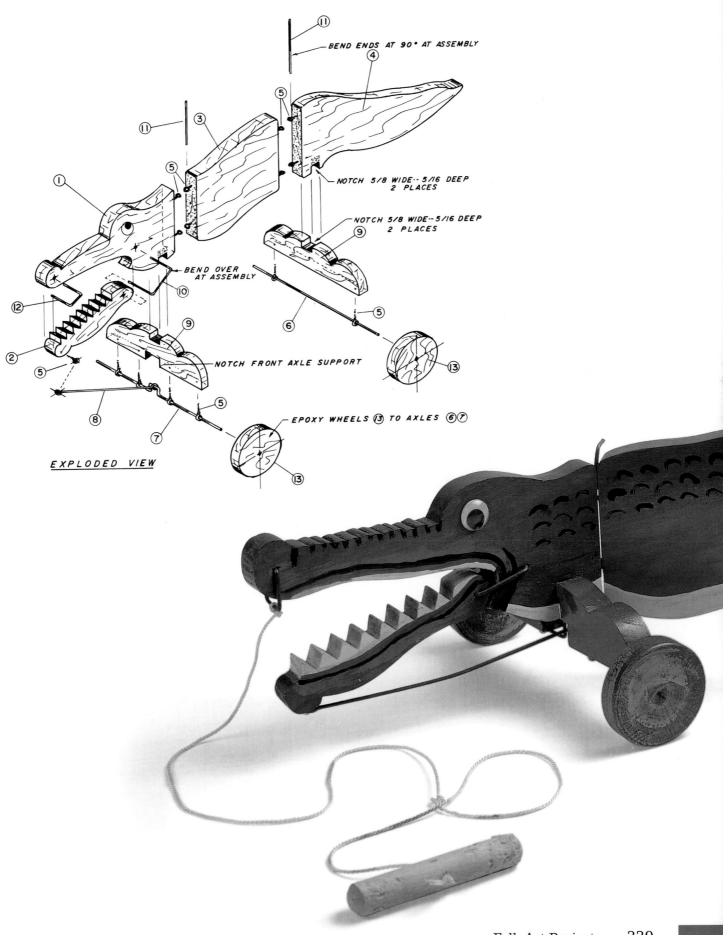

BEND ENDS AT 90° AT ASSEMBLY

NOTCH 5/8 WIDE – 5/16 DEEP
2 PLACES

NOTCH 5/8 WIDE – 5/16 DEEP
2 PLACES

BEND OVER
AT ASSEMBLY

NOTCH FRONT AXLE SUPPORT

EPOXY WHEELS ⑬ TO AXLES ⑥⑦

EXPLODED VIEW

Cranberry Scoop

This is a copy of a real cranberry scoop that was used in the cranberry bogs of Massachusetts. Today this scoop makes a functional wall decoration for plants or, perhaps, out-going mail. Or you could use it for a small magazine rack. If you use old wood, or if you distress new wood, yours will look like the original.

1. Cut all of the pieces to overall size. Note: one each of parts 2, 3, and 4 will be cut one inch shorter, to a 7-inch length.

   The shape of the handle (part 7) will have to be laid out on a 1-inch grid and cut out.

2. Cut an inch off one of the two (parts 2, 3, and 4). The 8 inch-long piece is for the front; the 7 inch-long one is for the back.

3. Locate and drill nine ⅜-inch-diameter holes along the top edge of the 7-inch-long board (part 2). Use the given dimensions at the top of the front view.

   Shape the two sides (part 1) as shown. Make an exact pair.

   Cut the ends of the nine teeth at 50°, as shown.

4. Assemble the scoop, using old-style, square-cut nails (part 8) if you can get them. Be sure everything is square. Don't forget to add the handle before adding the back boards.

5. Glue the nine teeth in place.

   Sand all over. Since this was a tool, use a rasp to create wear wherever you think it would have occurred in normal use.

6. You can either paint or stain this project. If you want it to look old, distress it and apply a glaze top coat.

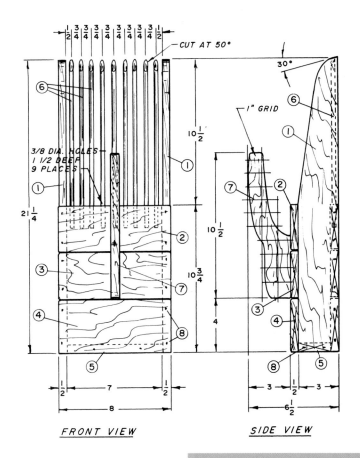

FRONT VIEW SIDE VIEW

MATERIALS LIST

NO.	NAME	SIZE	REQ'D.
1	SIDE	½ x 3 – 21¼ LONG	2
2	FRONT/BACK	½ x 3¼ – 8 (7) LONG	2
3	FRONT/BACK	½ x 3½ – 8 (7) LONG	2
4	FRONT/BACK	½ x 4 – 8 (7) LONG	2
5	BOTTOM	½ x 2½ – 7 LONG	2
6	TEETH	⅜ DIA. - 12 LONG	9
7	HANDLE	½ x 3 – 10½ LONG	1
8	NAIL – SQ. CUT	6 d	34

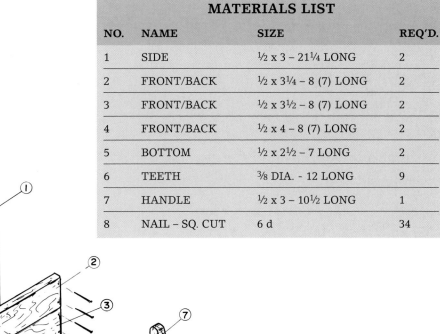

EXPLODED VIEW

Lawn Bird, c.1935

As a young boy growing up in Rhode Island in the early 1940s, I can remember seeing these crazy birds all over. It seems every street had at least one of these birds, with its head bobbing in the wind. By the time I was a teenager, I noticed they had all disappeared. For years I had been looking for one so I could make my own. I finally found one in an antique shop in southern Connecticut, but it was just too expensive, and the shop owner wouldn't let me photograph or measure it. A couple of years later I found another, in northern Vermont. I was able to make a pattern from it, and I made a couple of them and have one on my front lawn right now. My bird disappears for three or four days at a time, but then it all of a sudden returns as mysteriously as it left. It makes for a lot of neighborhood fun and is a great conversation piece. If anyone knows where these birds originally came from and why, I would love to know more about them.

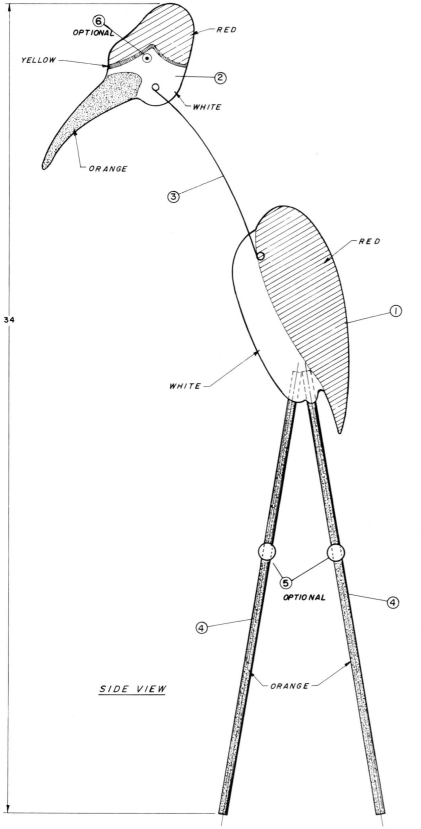

6
OPTIONAL

YELLOW

RED

2

WHITE

ORANGE

3

34

RED

1

WHITE

5
OPTIONAL

4

4

4

SIDE VIEW

ORANGE

1. Make up a full-size pattern, and cut out the head and body. Sand all edges. Don't forget to make a saw kerf for the spring.

2. Locate and drill the two ³⁄₈ inch-diameter holes for the legs and the ⁵⁄₁₆ inch-diameter holes for the spring.

3. The spring can be purchased from a supplier or from a clock repair shop. It is part of a 30-day spring-driven clock. Keep the neck as long as possible so it just supports the head. The head should bob in a gentle wind. Add purchased jiggle eyes and knees if desired.

4. Prime and paint your bird, coloring it as you wish. I used red and white, but any color combination should upset your neighbors. Be sure to use exterior paint.

MATERIALS LIST			
NO.	NAME	SIZE	REQ'D.
1	HEAD	¾ x 5½ – 14 LONG	1
2	BODY	¾ x 7½ – 15 LONG	1
3	NECK	.03 x ¾ – 9 LONG (SPRING STEEL)	1
4	LEG	⅜ DIA. - 36 LONG	2
5	KNEE (OPTIONAL)		2
6	EYE (OPTIONAL)		2

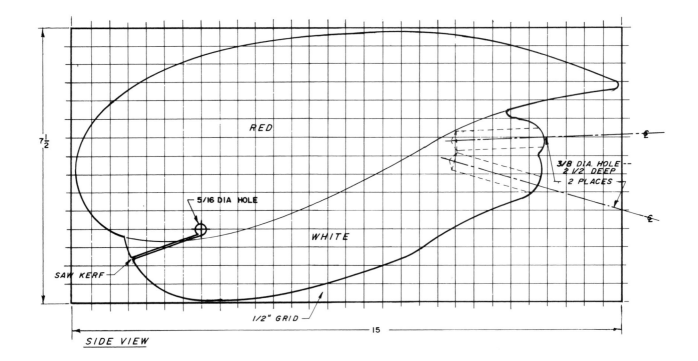

SIDE VIEW

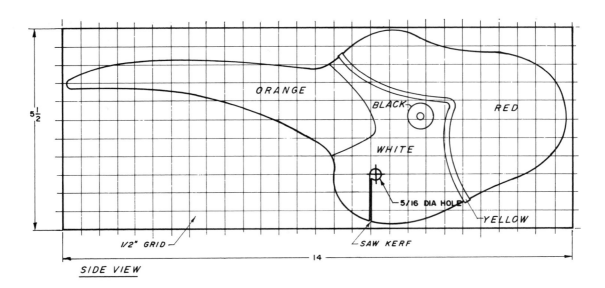

SIDE VIEW

Fretsaw Projects

Here's a selection of projects featuring ornamental openwork. The narrow blade and fine teeth of the saw create the interesting architectural details characteristic of these items.

Bootjack

Here is an item that isn't quite as useful today as it was in the days when tall boots were standard footwear. Still, a bootjack is an interesting novelty, and I don't believe I've ever seen a more ornate one.

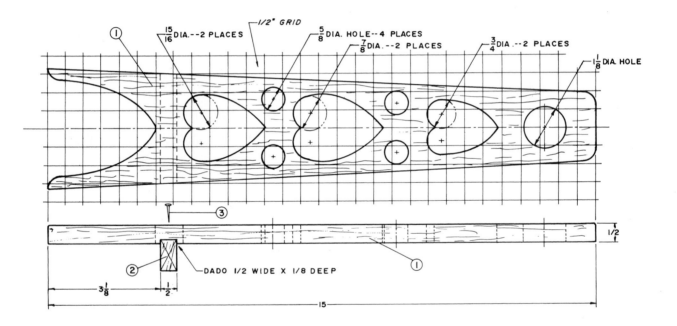

1. Select the stock and cut the parts. Both the bootjack and the leg it sits on are cut out of ¼-inch-thick stock. For a functional bootjack, pine will serve well, but consider a more attractive hardwood if the piece will be largely ornamental.

2. Make a paper pattern. Draw a grid with 1/2-inch squares and enlarge the bootjack (part 1) onto it. The pattern should include the location of all the holes and of the dado for the leg. Transfer the pattern to the wood; cut the dado, and drill the holes. Cut out the remaining area of the hearts with a coping saw or jigsaw.

Nail the leg (part 2) in the dado with 6d finishing nails (part 3). Cut out the outline of the bootjack, and sand all surfaces and edges.

3. Apply finish. Apply varnish. The bootjack can be hung on the wall when not in use to show off its unusual shape.

MATERIALS LIST			
NO.	NAME	SIZE	REQ'D.
1	BOOTJACK	¾ x 4 – 15 LONG	1
2	LEG	½ x 1 x 4 LONG	1
3	NAIL – FINISH	6 d	AS REQ'D.

Fretsaw Knickknack Shelf

The intricate decorative cuts shown here were especially popular with woodworkers back in the 1930s and 1940s. The designs are cut out of ¼-inch-thick stock with a jigsaw.

1. Select the stock. Use a knot-free wood such as mahogany. If you can't plane your own wood, you can buy ¼-inch-thick wood.

2. Make a paper pattern. Draw a grid with ½-inch squares and enlarge the parts onto it. Transfer the enlargement to the wood.

3. Cut the parts to size. To make the cutouts, first drill ¼ inch-diameter holes in each so that you can start cutting with the jigsaw. After making the cutouts, saw along the outside of the design. Sand thoroughly but don't round the comers.

4. Assemble the shelf. This project is put together with glue and finishing nails (part 4). If you think the wood might split, then drill pilot holes before nailing. Attach the shelf (part 3) to the brace (part 2), then add the backboard (part 1).

5. Apply finish. If you wish, apply stain and varnish. Hang the shelf through the teardrop-shaped hole at the top of the backboard.

MATERIALS LIST

NO.	NAME	SIZE	REQ'D.
1	BACKBOARD	¼ x 7½ – 12 LONG	1
2	BRACE	¼ x 3⅞ – 4⅝ LONG	1
3	SHELF	¼ x 4⅛ – 6¾ LONG	1
4	NAIL – FINISH	4 d	AS REQ'D.

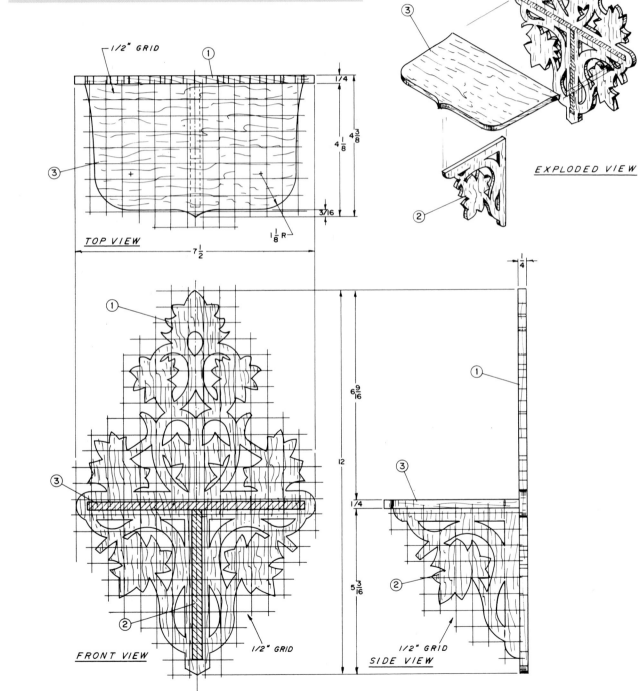

EXPLODED VIEW

TOP VIEW

FRONT VIEW

SIDE VIEW

Fretwork Wall Shelf 1

Fretwork projects such as this one and the one following were very popular around 1880 or so. They became popular again in the 1930s. Very early patterns were cut with a foot-powered scroll saw. Later, in the thirties and forties, the electric jigsaw was used to cut them out. This is an example of a simple fretwork wall shelf.

MATERIALS LIST

NO.	NAME	SIZE	REQ'D.
1	BODY	½ x 12⅜ – 17 LONG	1
2	BRACE	½ x 4¾ – 5 LONG	1
3	SHELF	½ x 5 - 10 LONG	1

1. Study the plans carefully. Note how each part is to be shaped. The back piece (part 1) is irregular in shape and should be laid out on a 1-inch grid to make a full-size pattern. Lay out the grid on heavy paper or cardboard, and transfer the shape of the piece to the grid, point by point.

2. Carefully cut all parts to overall size according to the materials list. Lightly sand all surfaces and edges with medium sandpaper to remove all tool marks.

3. I have had good luck by finishing the surfaces at this time, before cutting the pieces out. I add a coat of wood filler, sand all over, and apply a top coat or two of satin finish. I then resand, and apply the pattern. It is easier to get a pleasing finish on the outer surface at this time rather than after cutting out the pattern. A final light sanding and top coat will have to be added after cutting out.

4. Transfer the full-size patterns to the wood, and cut out the pieces. For fretwork projects such as these, I usually make a full-size copy of the design on paper, glue it directly on the wood, and cut it out. I then remove the paper and sand all over.

Lay out and cut out the shelf, following the detailed drawings and given dimensions.

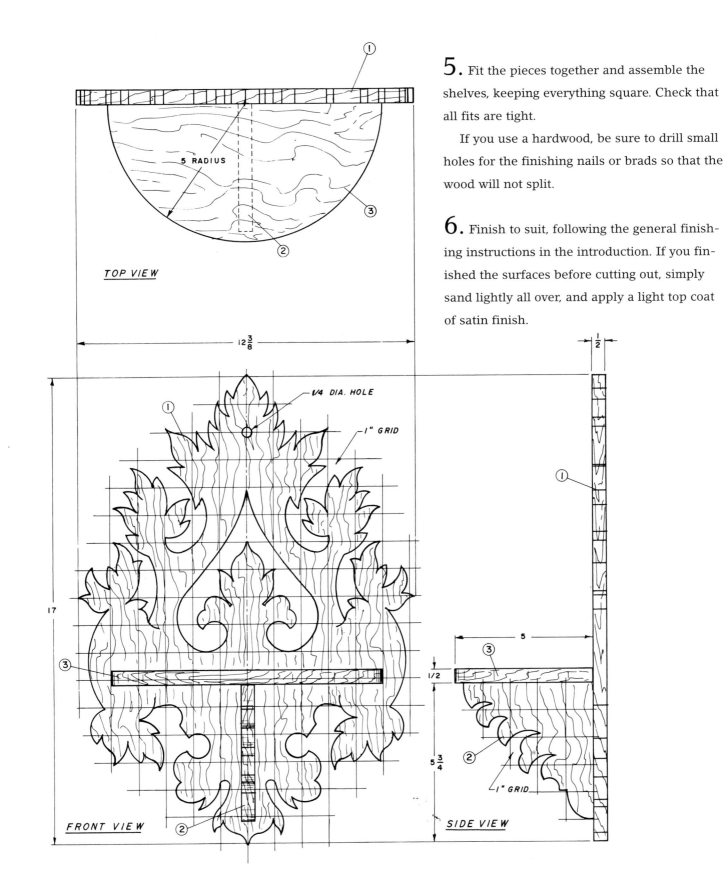

5. Fit the pieces together and assemble the shelves, keeping everything square. Check that all fits are tight.

If you use a hardwood, be sure to drill small holes for the finishing nails or brads so that the wood will not split.

6. Finish to suit, following the general finishing instructions in the introduction. If you finished the surfaces before cutting out, simply sand lightly all over, and apply a light top coat of satin finish.

TOP VIEW

5 RADIUS

12 3/8

1/4 DIA. HOLE

1" GRID

17

FRONT VIEW

1/2

5

1/2

5 3/4

1" GRID

SIDE VIEW

Fretwork Wall Shelf 2

This wall shelf is especially for any woodworker with a new parallel-arm scroll saw. I found the original of this one in an antique shop on Martha's Vineyard a few summers ago. The antique dealer dated it in the late 1920s. The project is a little time consuming, but it's a lot of fun to make. You should use a straight-grain hardwood for projects such as these. Walnut is a very good choice and cuts nicely. Most of the wall shelves of this vintage were made of walnut.

1. Draw a midline down the middle of a sheet of paper that is about 10 x 16 inches. On the left side of the midline, draw a ½-inch grid. Carefully transfer the design to the left side, point by point. Be sure to locate the hole labeled A and the holes labeled B. Note the location of the shelf, brace, and the ¼ inch-diameter hole. Fold the paper along the midline, and cut out the pattern. This will ensure that you have a pattern that is exactly the same size and shape but reversed on either side of the midline.

2. Cut and sand the surfaces of all the pieces. Glue the paper pattern to the wood using rubber cement or removable spray mount. Locate and drill the two ¾-inch-diameter holes as noted by A. Locate and drill the nine ½-inch-diameter holes as noted by B. Drill the ¼-inch-diameter hole, and countersink it slightly to give it a finished look.

3. Carefully cut out the back, following as close as possible to the pattern. If you do get off a little, try to do the same thing on the opposite side. Remember, this does not have to be exact; if you do stray here and there, no one will ever know once you remove the pattern. The original piece I purchased must have been cut out by hand as it was very crude.

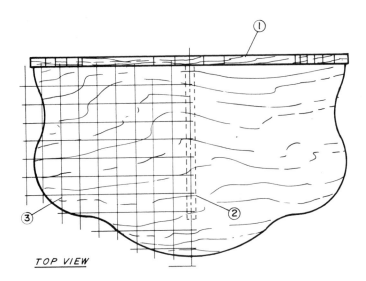

TOP VIEW

MATERIALS LIST

NO.	NAME	SIZE	REQ'D.
1	BACK	$\frac{1}{4}$ x $8\frac{3}{4}$ – $14\frac{1}{2}$ LONG	1
2	BRACE	$\frac{1}{4}$ x $8\frac{3}{4}$ – $4\frac{5}{8}$ LONG	1
3	SHELF	$\frac{1}{4}$ x $5\frac{1}{4}$ – $8\frac{5}{8}$ LONG	1
4	BRAD	$\frac{3}{4}$ LONG	8

EXPLODED VIEW

4. The brace pattern is nothing more than one half of the bottom, left side of the backboard. To get the shape, simply trace the cutout backboard onto a piece of wood, and then cut it out. Make a simple pattern of the shelf, and cut it out. The paper pattern can be easily sanded off, if you used the rubber cement. Resand all parts before assembly. Drill small holes for all brads before nailing so that the wood will not split.

5. Glue and tack all the parts together as shown in the exploded view. Check that everything is square. Apply two coats of a clear, satin finish, such as varnish, shellac, or lacquer. Your shelf is ready to be put up, and it will be enjoyed for years and years to come.

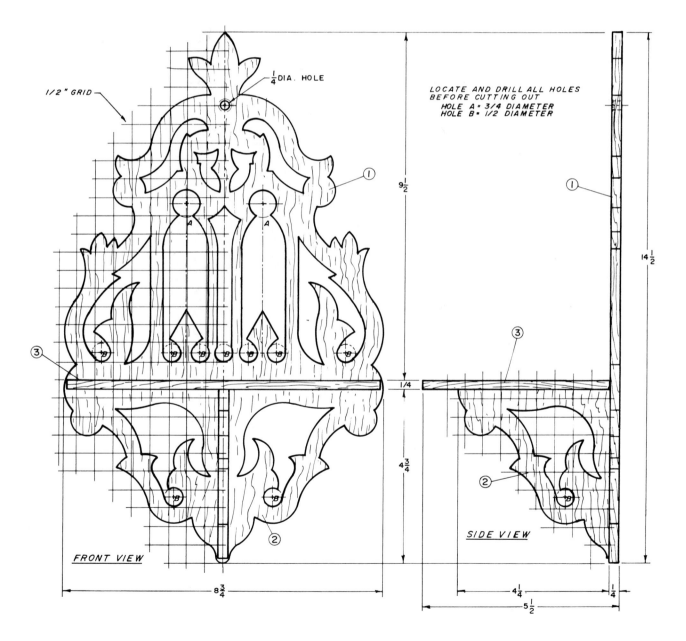

Fretsaw Wall Mirror

This is another interesting project, especially for those with scroll saws or for very ambitious individuals with a hand coping saw. It's a takeoff of a popular mirror design from the 1930s. With a parallel-arm scroll saw, it takes about two hours to make all the intricate interior cuts. There are over forty interior cuts, so it helps if your scroll saw blade can be removed and reattached in about thirty seconds. I recommend a straight-grained hardwood such as walnut for this.

1. Cut all of the wood to size, per the cutting list. Sand the face board, using fine grit sandpaper.

2. On a piece of tracing paper (or vellum) that is about 10 x 16 inches, draw a vertical midline. To the left of the midline draw a ½-inch grid. Carefully transfer the design to the grid, point by point. Locate the two ½-inch-diameter holes. Fold the paper along the midline, and retrace the pattern on the right-hand side. This will ensure an exact pattern for both sides.

3. Glue the paper pattern to the wood, using rubber cement or a spray-mount adhesive. Carefully locate and drill the four ½-inch-diameter holes. Also drill, with care a, ⅛-inch-diameter hole in the middle of each of the forty or so inner openings for inserting the blade to make the interior cuts. Take care not to rip through the back while drilling the holes. Resand the bottom surface to remove all burrs made by drilling the holes. You want to have a smooth back surface while sawing so the blade will not hang up any place.

4. Carefully make all interior cuts. If you go off the lines a little, try to do the same thing on the opposite side so that both sides will be the same. Lightly resand the back surface again to remove any burrs. Cut the outer edge with care. Remove the paper pattern, and resand the top and bottom surfaces.

Using a router with a ball-bearing follower, make a ⅛-inch-radius cove cut around the inside 4½-inch by 7½-inch opening. On the back surface, glue the stiles and rails in place. Note the direction of grain in the rails; it is important that the grain run in this direction so the mirror will not warp.

Purchase a mirror slightly smaller than the opening within the stile and rail assembly, and cut a backboard about the same size. Note: the back edge of the backboard is cut at a 10° angle leaving about a 3/32-inch edge on all four sides. See detail of backboard.

NO.	NAME	SIZE	REQ'D.
	MATERIALS LIST		
1	FACE	¼ x 8¾ – 14¼ LONG	1
2	STILE	¼ x 9/16 – 8⅝ LONG	2
3	RAIL	¼ x 4⅞ – 9/16 LONG	2
4	MIRROR	3/32 x 4¹³/16 – 7⁷/16 LONG	1
5	BACK BOARD	¼ x 4¹³/16 – 7⁷/16 LONG	1
6	NAIL – SQ. CUT/FINISH	¾ LONG	8

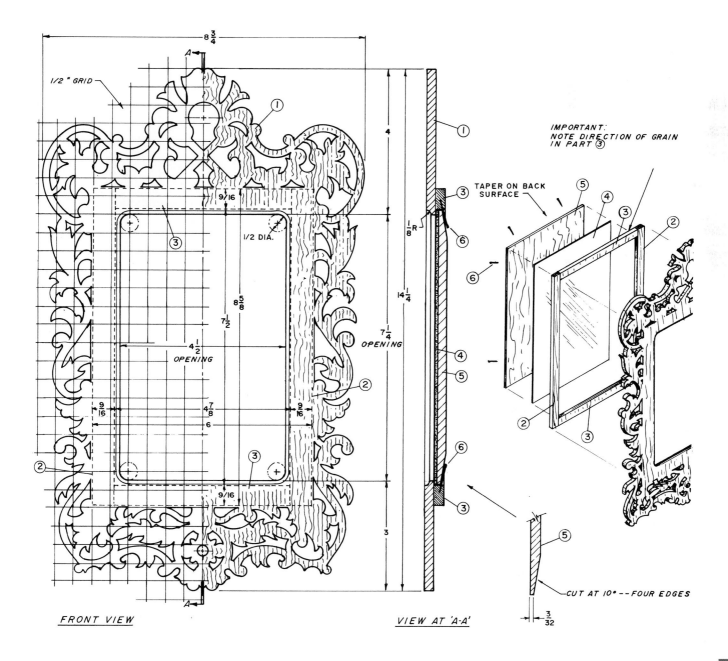

FRONT VIEW

VIEW AT 'A-A'

Gothic Wall Mirror

In my search for unusual and different projects to make, I was delighted to find this Gothic wall mirror. In the right setting, it can be great. It's simple to make since it's cut out of one piece of wood.

MATERIALS LIST

NO.	NAME	SIZE	REQ'D.
1	BODY	$11/16$ x $7^5/16$ – $19^1/4$ LONG	1
2	MIRROR	$3/32$ x $4^9/16$ x $7^9/16$ LONG	1
3	BACKING	$1/4$ x $4^9/16$ x $7^9/16$ LONG	1

1. Study the plans carefully. Note how the body is irregularly shaped. It will have to be laid out on a $1/2$-inch grid to make a full-size pattern. Lay out the grid on heavy paper or cardboard, and transfer the shape of the piece to the grid, point by point.

2. Transfer the full-size pattern to the wood, and carefully cut out the body. Check all dimensions for accuracy. Sand all over with fine-grit sandpaper, keeping all edges sharp.

3. Carefully cut the interior for the mirror. Sand all edges smooth.

4. Using a router and a 45° cutter with a ball-bearing follower, cut the 45° bevel all around the body, inside and outside.

5. Using the router and a $5/16$-inch-rabbet cutter with a ball-bearing follower, cut a rabbet $5/16$ inch wide and $5/16$ inch deep as shown. You will have to chisel out square corners to get a clean rectangular notch and flat surface in the back for the mirror and backing (parts 2 and 3).

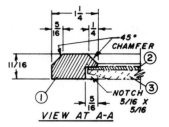

$\frac{1}{4}$

$\frac{5}{16}$ $\frac{1}{4}$

45° CHAMFER

11/16

② ① NOTCH 5/16 X 5/16

③

$\frac{5}{16}$

VIEW AT A-A

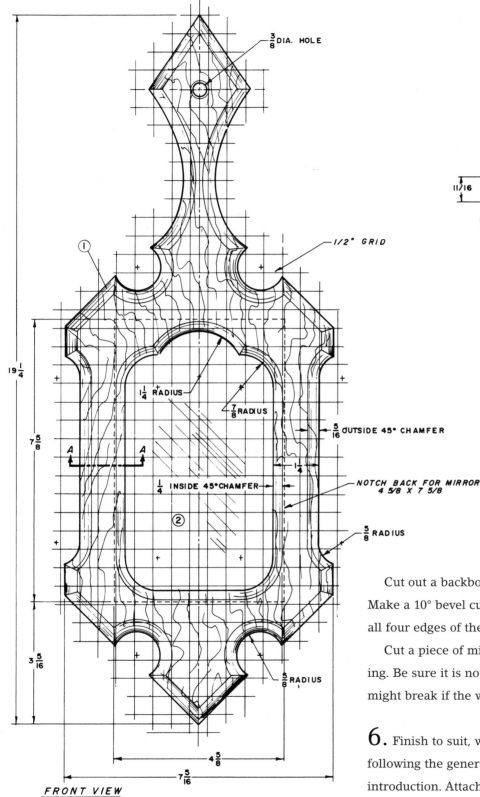

$\frac{3}{8}$ DIA. HOLE

①

1/2" GRID

$1\frac{1}{4}$ RADIUS

$\frac{7}{8}$ RADIUS

$\frac{5}{16}$ OUTSIDE 45° CHAMFER

$\frac{1}{4}$

A   A

$\frac{1}{4}$ INSIDE 45° CHAMFER

NOTCH BACK FOR MIRROR
4 5/8 X 7 5/8

②

$\frac{5}{8}$ RADIUS

$19\frac{1}{4}$

$7\frac{5}{8}$

$3\frac{5}{16}$

$\frac{5}{8}$ RADIUS

$4\frac{5}{8}$

$7\frac{5}{16}$

FRONT VIEW

Cut out a backboard (part 3) to fit the opening. Make a 10° bevel cut on the outside surface along all four edges of the backboard, as the original had.

Cut a piece of mirror to loosely fit into the opening. Be sure it is not a tight fit since the mirror might break if the wood expands or contracts.

6. Finish to suit, with the mirror out of the frame, following the general finishing instructions in the introduction. Attach the mirror and backboard, using small brads or small, square-cut finish nails. I added two picture-frame eyebolts with wire to hang the mirror on the wall.

Fretwork Corner Wall Shelf

This is another of the old fretwork projects that became popular again in the 1930s.

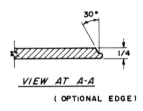

VIEW AT A-A

(OPTIONAL EDGE)

MATERIALS LIST			
NO.	NAME	SIZE	REQ'D.
1	SIDE	$^5/_{16}$ x $8^3/_{16}$ – 21 LONG	2
2	BOTTOM SHELF	$^1/_4$ x $8^1/_4$ – $11^1/_4$ LONG	1
3	TOP SHELF	$^1/_4$ x 6 – 8 LONG	1
4	NAIL - FINISH	$^3/_4$ LONG	12

1. The back piece (part 1) is irregular in shape and should be laid out on a ½-inch grid to make a full-size pattern. Lay out the grid on heavy paper or cardboard, and transfer the shape of the piece to the grid, point by point.

2. Carefully cut all parts to overall size according to the Materials List. Lightly sand all surfaces and edges with medium sandpaper to remove all tool marks.

3. I have had good luck by finishing the surfaces at this time, before cutting out the pieces. I add a coat of wood filler, sand all over, and apply a topcoat or two of satin finish. I then resand, and apply the pattern. It is easier to get a pleasing finish on the outer surface at this time rather than after cutting out the pattern. A final light sanding and topcoat will have to be added after cutting out.

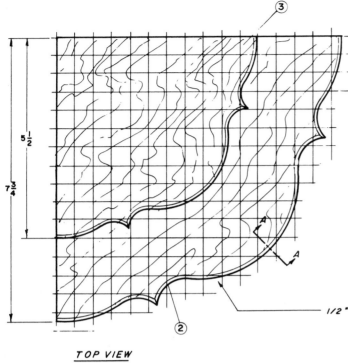

$5\frac{1}{2}$

$7\frac{3}{4}$

TOP VIEW

1/2" GRID

21

$\frac{5}{16}$

SIDE VIEW

$8\frac{3}{16}$

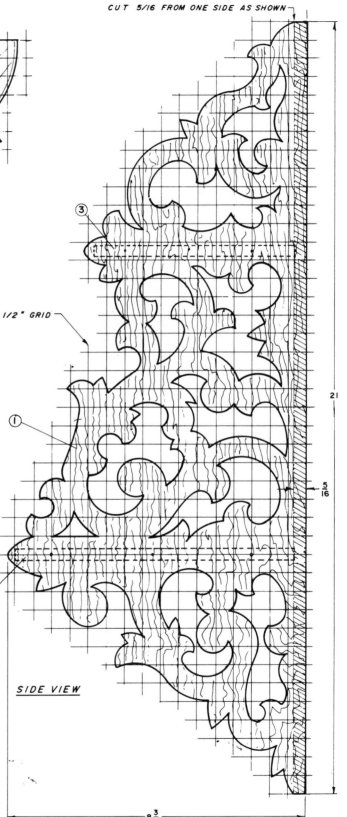

4. Transfer the full-size patterns to the wood, and cut out the pieces. For fretwork projects such as these, I usually make a full-size copy of the design on paper, glue it directly on the wood, and cut it out. I then remove the paper and sand all over.

Tack the two sides together with small brads before cutting out, so you will get two sides exactly the same size and shape.

5. Lay out and cut out the shelves, following the detailed drawings and given dimensions.

Fit the pieces together, and assemble the shelves, keeping everything square. Check that all fits are tight.

6. Finish to suit, following the general finishing instructions in the introduction. If you finished the surfaces before cutting out, simply sand lightly all over, and apply a light topcoat of satin finish.

Wall Boxes

The charming boxes in this chapter are reproductions of those made by craftsmen centuries ago. The originals were used to store items such as knives, candles, salt, and seeds. Today, you can fill yours with everything from dried flowers to the day's mail. Bonus: boxes are one of the easiest forms to build.

Heart Wall Box

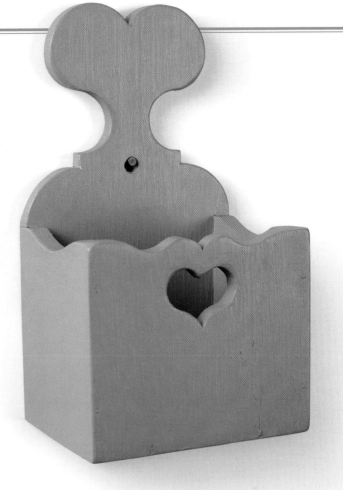

Wall boxes are always popular. They come in all shapes and sizes. This is a fancy wall box. It is not an exact copy of an antique; it is simply a composite of two or three antique wall boxes that I have liked.

1. Cut material to overall size. Sand all over.

2. Lay out the patterns for the pieces. Transfer the shapes to the wood, and cut them out.

3. Dry-fit all of the pieces. If everything fits correctly, nail the pieces together. Keep everything sharp and square as you go.

4. Prime; then paint or stain to suit.

MATERIALS LIST			
NO.	NAME	SIZE	REQ'D.
1	BACK	$3/8$ x $5^{1}/2$ – 10 LONG	1
2	FRONT	$3/8$ x $5^{1}/2$ – $4^{11}/16$ LONG	1
3	SIDE	$3/8$ x $3^{5}/8$ – $4^{11}/16$ LONG	2
4	BOTTOM	$3/8$ x $3^{1}/4$ – $4^{3}/4$ LONG	1
5	SQ. CUT – FINISH NAIL	1 LONG	15

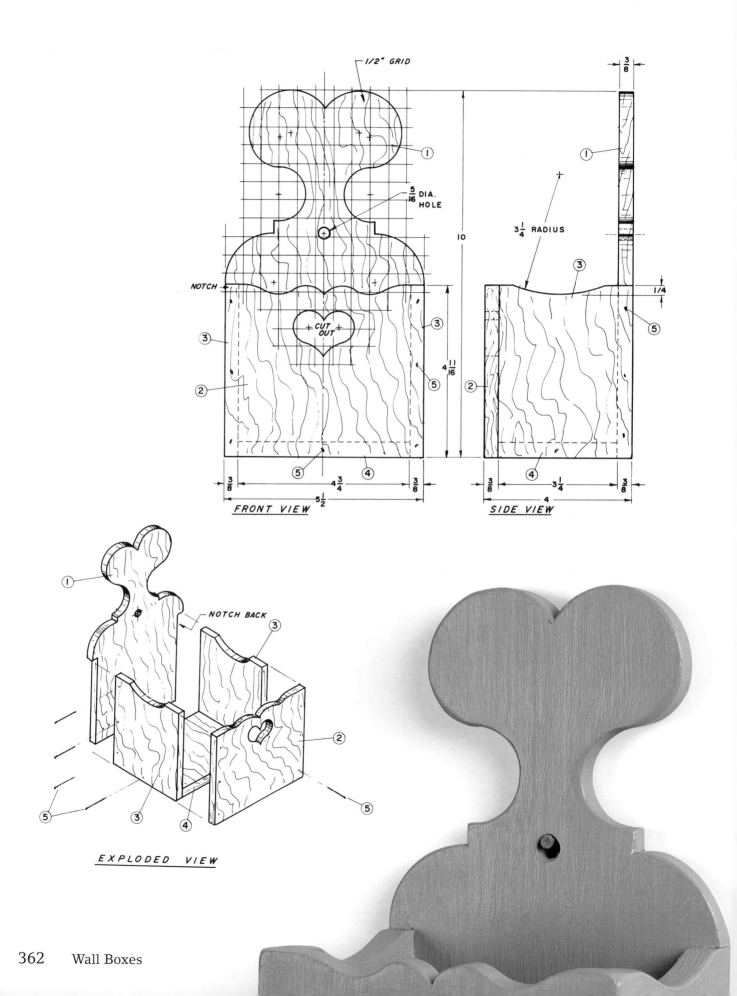

— 1/2" GRID

1/2" GRID

$\frac{3}{8}$

①

10

$\frac{5}{16}$ DIA. HOLE

$3\frac{1}{4}$ RADIUS

③

1/4

⑤

③

②

CUT OUT

③

⑤

$4\frac{11}{16}$

②

$\frac{3}{8}$

$4\frac{3}{4}$

$\frac{3}{8}$

⑤

④

$\frac{3}{8}$

④

$3\frac{1}{4}$

$\frac{3}{8}$

$5\frac{1}{2}$

4

NOTCH

FRONT VIEW

SIDE VIEW

①

NOTCH BACK

③

②

⑤

③

④

⑤

EXPLODED VIEW

Small Wall Box

Here's a small wall box with a design I find interesting and unusual. I found the original I based it on in northern Vermont, near Burlington. This project can be painted or stained, as desired.

1. Study the plans carefully. Note how each part is to be shaped. As you study the plans, try to visualize how you will make each part.

2. The back (part 1) has an irregular shape, so it should be laid out on a ½-inch grid, as shown, to make the full-size pattern. Lay out the grid, and transfer the shape of the piece to the grid, point by point.

3. Carefully cut all of the parts according to the Materials List. Take care to cut all parts to exact size and exactly square (90°).

Lightly sand all surfaces and edges with medium sandpaper to remove any burrs and all tool marks. Take care to keep all edges square and sharp at this time.

4. Cut all of the parts following the detailed illustrations as well as the given dimensions. Check all dimensions for accuracy. Resand all over with fine grit sandpaper, still keeping all edges sharp. Take care to cut the ⁷/₁₆-inch by 5¾-inch notches in the two sides of the backboard (part 1).

5. After all of the pieces have been carefully made, dry-fit all parts—that is, put the complete project together without glue or nails to check for accuracy and good-fitting joints. If anything needs refitting, now is the time to correct it.

6. Once all of the parts fit together correctly, assemble the project, keeping everything square as you go. Check that all fits are tight. As usual, leave the square-cut nails showing, and don't try to hide them; the original had them showing. Round all edges slightly.

7. Finish to suit.

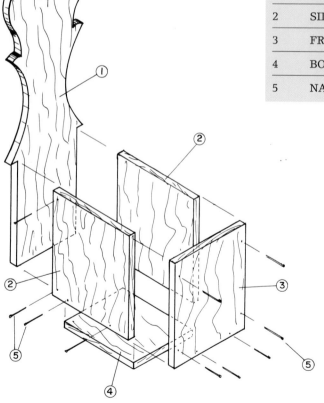

EXPLODED VIEW

MATERIALS LIST			
NO.	NAME	SIZE	REQ'D.
1	BACK	$7/16$ x $4\frac{3}{4}$ – $16\frac{1}{2}$ LONG	1
2	SIDE	$7/16$ x $4\frac{13}{16}$ – $5\frac{3}{4}$ LONG	2
3	FRONT	$7/16$ x $4\frac{5}{8}$ – $5\frac{3}{4}$ LONG	1
4	BOTTOM	$7/16$ x $4\frac{3}{8}$ – $3\frac{3}{4}$ LONG	1
5	NAIL – SQ. CUT	1 LONG	14

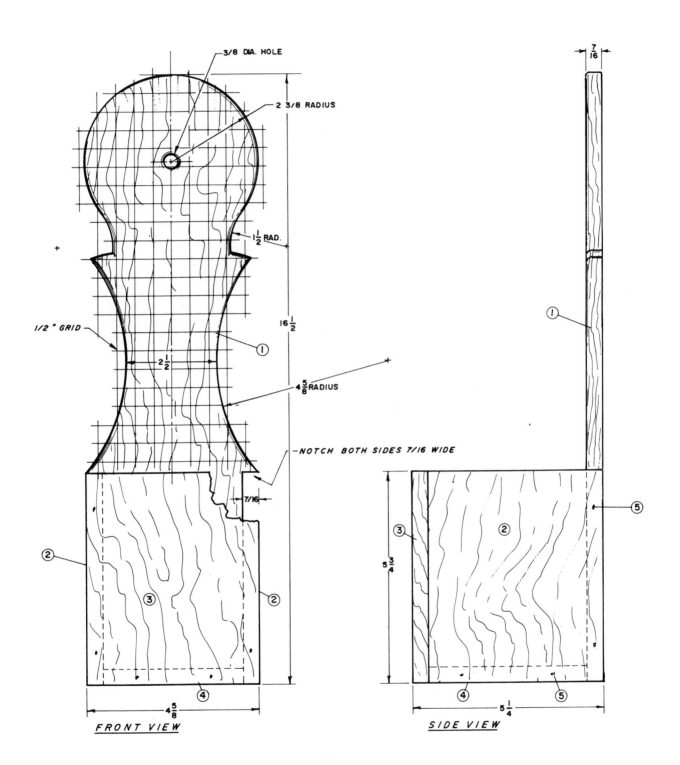

3/8 DIA. HOLE

2 3/8 RADIUS

1½ RAD.

16½

1/2 " GRID

2½

4⅝ RADIUS

NOTCH BOTH SIDES 7/16 WIDE

7/16

2

3

2

4

4⅝

FRONT VIEW

7/16

1

5

3

2

5¾

4

5

5¼

SIDE VIEW

Fish-Tail Wall Box

This interesting wall box has the old, familiar fishtail design. The original probably was made at or near an early American fishing community. I took the liberty of using an already-split piece of wood for the front to give it that old look. This also helped get rid of some otherwise unusable wood.

EXPLODED VIEW

1. On a 1-inch grid, carefully lay out the fish tail on the back piece. Notch for the two side pieces. Cut the top and bottom edges of the front at 5°, as shown. Cut the front edge of the bottom also at 5° while the saw is still set at 5°. Lay out the two matching sides, 4⅛ inches at the top and 3¾ inches at the bottom, to make an approximate 5° cut, as shown in the side view.

2. Sand all of the pieces. Dry fit the box. If the fit is all right, glue and nail the box together, keeping everything square. Sand all of the edges slightly.

3. Distress and paint as you desire. I painted my copy with two coats of paint, and then I sanded through the topcoat here and there where I thought it would have worn under normal use through the years.

MATERIALS LIST

NO.	NAME	SIZE	REQ'D.
1	BACK	$3/8$ x $8^1/2$ –14 LONG	1
2	FRONT	$3/8$ x $8^1/2$ – $5^1/8$ LONG	1
3	SIDE	$3/8$ x $4^1/8$ – 5 LONG	2
4	BOTTOM	$3/8$ x $3^3/4$ - $7^3/4$ LONG	1
5	NAIL – SQ. CUT/FINISH	1 LONG	16

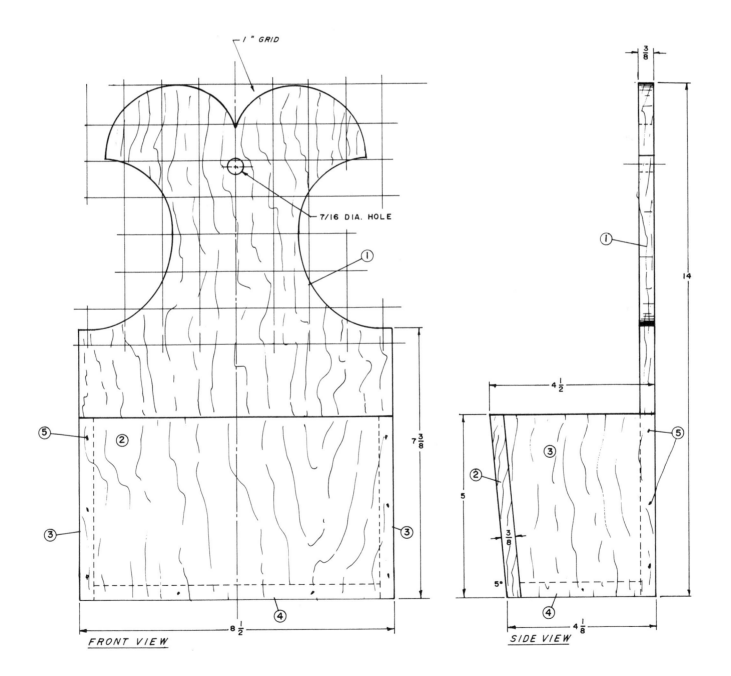

FRONT VIEW

SIDE VIEW

Salt Box

This is a scaled-down version of a somewhat larger salt box. The original was painted a dark, blackish-green color.

1. Cut material to overall size. Sand all over.

2. Lay out the patterns for the pieces. Transfer the shapes to the wood, and cut them out.

3. Dry-fit all of the pieces. If everything fits correctly, nail the pieces together. Keep everything sharp and square as you go.

4. Prime; then paint or stain to suit.

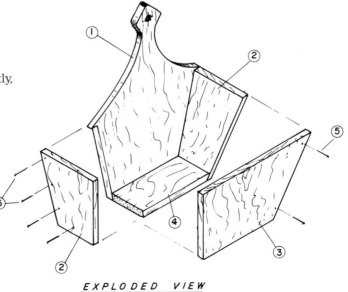

EXPLODED VIEW

MATERIALS LIST

NO.	NAME	SIZE	REQ'D.
1	BACK	½ x 9 – 13 LONG	1
2	SIDE	½ x 4 – 6⁵⁄₁₆ LONG	2
3	FRONT	½ x 9 – 6¾ LONG	1
4	BOTTOM	½ x 2 – 5⅜ LONG	1
5	NAIL – SQ. CUT/FINISH	1¼ LONG (SQUARE CUT)	15

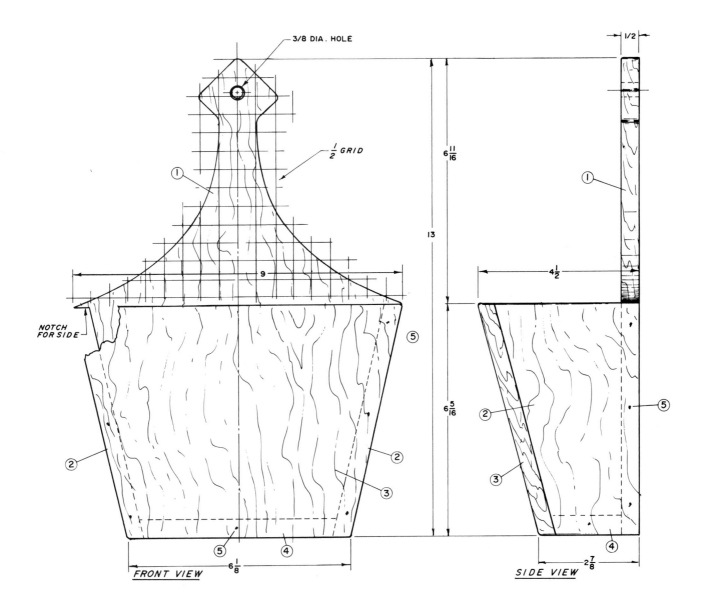

Canted Wall Box

As noted before, I am always looking for projects that are different. I really like this box, even though I'm not sure where to use it. I found the original years ago, and I can- not even remember where. According to my notes, the original was very large, so I had to scale it down. It was made around 1840 and was painted. This one is a two-thirds version of the original.

1. Cut to overall size the sides (part 2), and lay out the two inside dadoes and one rabbet on each. Note that the dadoes and rabbets are blind; that is they are not cut to the back edge. See the exploded view.

2. Make the two dado and one rabbet cuts on the inside surfaces of the two sides. Be sure to make one right-hand and one left-hand side. Make these cuts before cutting the outside shape of the sides so that you will have a straight edge to line up against your fence.

3. The back and sides (parts 1 and 2) are irregular in shape and will have to be laid out on a ½-inch grid to make full-size patterns. Lay out the grids on heavy paper or cardboard, and transfer the shape of each piece to the grid, point by point.

MATERIALS LIST

NO.	NAME	SIZE	REQ'D.
1	BACK	⅜ x 4¾ – 23 LONG	1
2	SIDE	⅜ x 3½ – 17 LONG	2
3	SHELF	⅜ x 3⅛ – 4⅛ LONG	2
4	SHELF – TOP	⅜ x 2⅛ – 4⅛ LONG	1
5	NAIL - SQ. CUT/FINISH	3/4 LONG	16

Transfer the full-size patterns to the wood, and carefully cut out the pieces. Sand all over with fine-grit sandpaper, keeping all edges sharp.

Don't forget to cut the two notches along the sides of the back (part 1) for the sides (part 2) to fit into.

4. Carefully line up the dado and rabbet cuts, and tape the two sides together with the cuts on the inside. Draw the pattern on the outside surface, and cut out both sides at the same time. Sand the edges while they are still taped together.

5. Cut the three shelves to size according to the Materials List. Take care to cut all parts to exact size and exactly square (90°). Stop and recheck all dimensions before going on. Note that the top shelf is cut at an angle along its front edge to match the sides.

Lightly sand all surfaces and edges with medium sandpaper to remove all tool marks. Take care to keep all edges square and sharp.

After all of the pieces have been carefully made, dry-fit the parts—that is, put the complete project together without glue or nails to check for accuracy and good-fitting joints. If anything needs refitting, now is the time to correct it.

Once all of the parts fit together correctly, assemble the project, keeping everything square as you go. Check that all fits are tight.

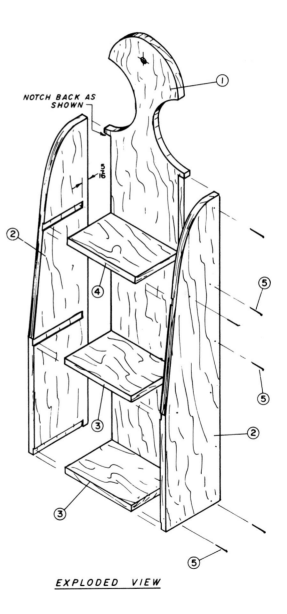

NOTCH BACK AS SHOWN

EXPLODED VIEW

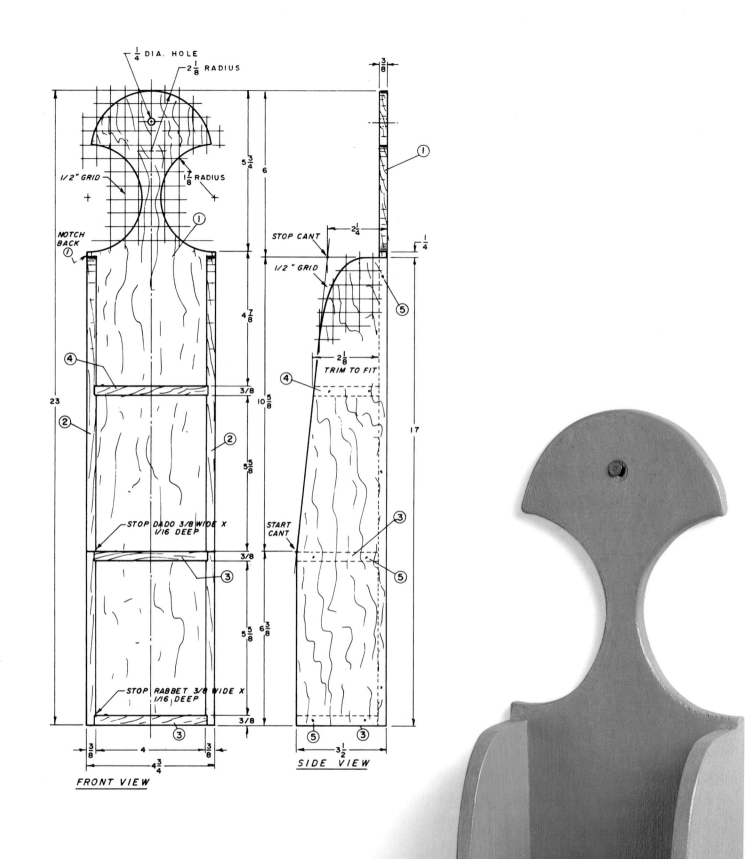

¼ DIA. HOLE

2⅛ RADIUS

1/2" GRID

1⅛ RADIUS

NOTCH
BACK
①

①

6

5¾

4⅞

3/8

10⅝

5⅝

STOP DADO 3/8 WIDE X
1/16 DEEP

3/8

6⅜

5⅝

STOP RABBET 3/8 WIDE X
1/16 DEEP

3/8

④

②

②

②

③

③

3/8   4   3/8

4¾

FRONT VIEW

3/8

①

STOP CANT

2¼

¼

1/2" GRID

2⅛

TRIM TO FIT

START
CANT

④

⑤

17

③

⑤

⑤   ③

3½

SIDE VIEW

Wall Candle Box

This is a great wall box. It is unusual, easy to make, and very functional. I found the one I based this on years ago, took several photographs, and, as usual, noted carefully the overall dimensions and patterns. This project is particularly suited to practicing your crackle-painting finish.

MATERIALS LIST

NO.	NAME	SIZE	REQ'D.
1	BACK	$\frac{3}{8}$ x $8\frac{11}{16}$ – $10\frac{1}{4}$ LONG	1
2	FRONT	$\frac{3}{8}$ x 3 – 11 LONG	1
3	SIDE	$\frac{3}{8}$ x 3 – $4\frac{5}{8}$ LONG	2
4	BOTTOM	$\frac{5}{16}$ x $5\frac{3}{8}$ – $11\frac{3}{4}$ LONG	1
5	NAIL - SQ. CUT/FINISH	$\frac{3}{4}$ LONG	14

1. Study the plans carefully. Notice how each part is to be made. The back (part 1) is the only irregularly shaped part and should be laid out on a 1-inch grid to make a full-size pattern. Lay out a grid on heavy paper or cardboard, and transfer the shape of the piece to the grid, point by point. Don't forget to locate the $\frac{5}{8}$-inch-diameter hole.

2. Carefully cut all of the parts according to the Materials List. Take care to cut all parts to exact size and exactly square (90°). Stop and recheck all dimensions before going on.

Lightly sand all surfaces and edges with medium sandpaper to remove any burrs and all tool marks. Take care to keep all edges square and sharp at this time.

3. Cut out all parts, following the detailed dimensions. Transfer the full-size patterns to the wood and cut out the pieces. Check all dimensions for accuracy. Resand all over with fine-grit sandpaper, still keeping all edges sharp.

4. After all of the pieces have been carefully made, dry-fit the parts; that is, put the complete project together without glue or nails to check for accuracy and good-fitting joints. If anything needs refitting, now is the time to correct it.

5. Once all of the parts fit together correctly, assemble the project keeping everything square as you go. Check that all fits are tight.

6. Finish to suit, following the general finishing instructions in the introduction.

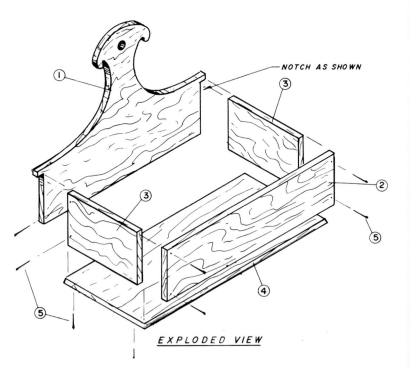

NOTCH AS SHOWN

EXPLODED VIEW

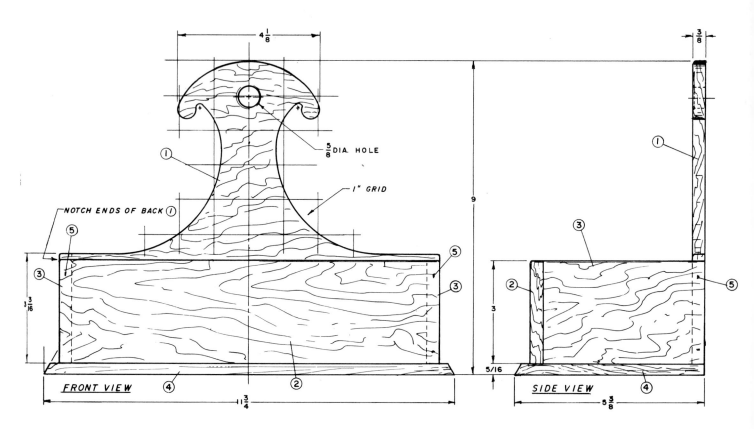

5/8 DIA. HOLE

1" GRID

NOTCH ENDS OF BACK ①

FRONT VIEW

SIDE VIEW

Early Wall Box

This is a copy of a simple wall box I found in northern Massachusetts. It probably was used for candles. The original was made of pine and painted a dark brick-red color. This project is very easy to make, as it has simple butt joints throughout.

1. Cut all of the pieces to size, and sand all surfaces. Make a full-size pattern of the back, and transfer the pattern to the wood. Locate and drill the ¾-inch-diameter hole. Cut the back out and sand all the edges. Assemble with glue and nails. The nails on the original wall box were showing, so don't attempt to hide them unless they bother you. Round all of the edges slightly.

2. Paint or stain as you desire. This project is perfectly suited to distressing slightly and sanding the edges to give that old worn look. Hang it on the wall, add candles, and you will be ready for that next power failure.

MATERIALS LIST			
NO.	NAME	SIZE	REQ'D.
1	BACK	⁵⁄₈ x 10 – 15 LONG	1
2	FRONT	¹⁄₂ x 4¹⁄₂ – 11¹⁄₄ LONG	1
3	END	⁵⁄₈ x 4¹⁄₂ – 5¹⁄₄ LONG	2
4	BOTTOM	⁵⁄₈ x 4⁷⁄₁₆ – 10 LONG	1
5	FINISH NAIL	4 d	18

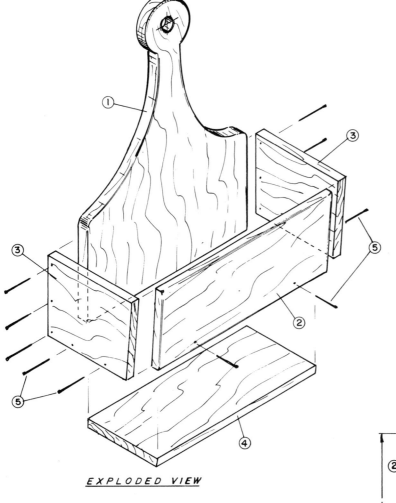

EXPLODED VIEW

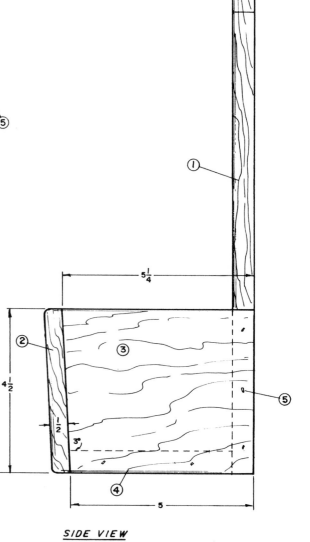

SIDE VIEW

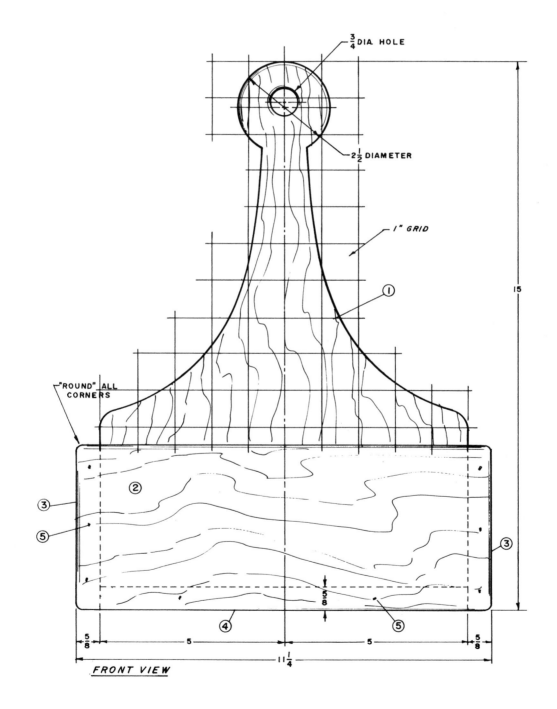

FRONT VIEW

Antique Projects

Antiques never go out of style, and their prices just keep rising. Think of all the money you'll save by making your own reproduction heirlooms. Best of all, imagine how handsome these pieces, including mirrors, a lantern, a miniature blanket chest, and a wall cupboard, will look in your home.

Early American Candlestick

This project is an exact copy of an antique candlestick I found in Maine. The original was maple, but you might also try turning one from cherry or walnut.

1. Select the stock. This candlestick is a two-piece construction. The base is turned from a blank, 9/16 inch thick and 4¼ inches square. The stem is turned from a blank, 1¼ inches square and 10 inches long.

2. Turn the base. Scribe a 4½-inch circle on the base with a compass, and cut out this circle with a band saw or saber saw.

The 1/16-inch recess, shown in the dashed lines at the bottom of the base, is designed to keep the candlestick from rocking on an uneven surface.

3. Turn the recess first. Mount the base between centers on the lathe. Center the drive spur on the center of the circle you drew, and center the tailstock against the other side of the wood. Scrape the recess, using standard turning techniques. There will be a small plug you cannot reach because of the tailstock. Remove the base from the lathe, and pare off the plug with a chisel. Center a faceplate in the recess, and screw the faceplate to the base. Make sure the screws are as long as possible, but not long enough to come through the top of the base.

Turn the base to the profile shown. Looking at the drawing, note the hidden line on the top surface of the base: it indicates a shallow groove turned into the top of the base.

4. After you've turned the groove, drill a hole in the top of the base to hold the stem. You can do this while the piece is still on the lathe. First, put a chuck in the tailstock and then put a drill bit in the chuck. Lock the tailstock in place and, with the lathe running slowly, advance the bit to drill the hole. Sand the piece while it is turning on the lathe. Remove it from the lathe but not from the faceplate.

5. Turn the stem. Mount the stem blank on the lathe and turn it to the profile shown. The stub tenon that fits into the base should be the closest to the headstock. Turn it carefully; it must fit snugly into the ½ inch-diameter hole in the base. Turn the section immediately above the cup that holds the candle to a diameter of ¾ inch. Sand the entire profile. Drill a hole for the candle. Remove the stem from the lathe.

6. The lathe makes a perfect clamp for holding the pieces together during the glue-up. Put the faceplate and base back on the lathe. Put glue both on the stub tenon and in the hole for it. Insert the tenon in the hole, center the tailstock against the stem, and tighten it gently. Allow the glue to set for at least 24 hours, and remove the candle stand from the lathe and from the faceplate.

7. To finish, apply two coats of a satin-luster finish of your choice.

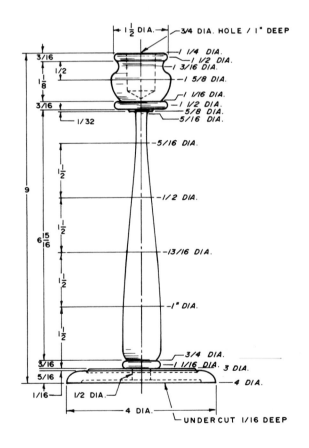

Country Mirror

This is a takeoff of a larger country mirror we saw in a museum years ago. The original was about one-third larger. Scaled down, it makes a suitable mirror for use in a child's room or in a small room. It will add a country look wherever it is hung. The original was painted a mustard color, but it looks good either painted or stained.

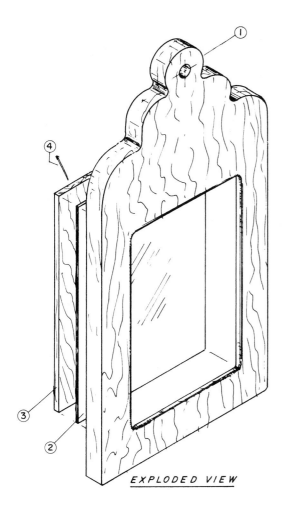

EXPLODED VIEW

1. Cut the body to overall size.

2. Carefully lay out the outer and interior details of the body (part 1). Transfer the shape to the wood and cut out. Drill a ½-inch hole at the top, as shown in the drawings.

3. Using a straight router bit with a ball-bearing follower, make a rabbet cut on the inside cutout, back surface for the mirror (part 2).

4. Using a ⅛-inch-radius router bit with a ball-bearing follower, round the front edges inside and out, as shown.

MATERIALS LIST

NO.	NAME	SIZE	REQ'D.
1	BODY	¾ x 7¼ – 13½ LONG	1
2	MIRROR	³⁄₃₂ x 5⅜ – 8 LONG	1
3	BACKBOARD	⅜ x 5⅜ – 8 LONG	1
4	FINISH NAIL	SQUARE-CUT – 1 LONG	4

5. Cut the backboard (part 3) to size, to fit the opening. Cut the back edge on a sharp bevel, 10° or so, as shown in the View at A-A.

6. Sand all over.

7. Paint or stain to suit. If you paint the mirror, distress it slightly to look somewhat old.

8. Add the mirror (part 1) and backboard (part 3) with the nails (parts 4).

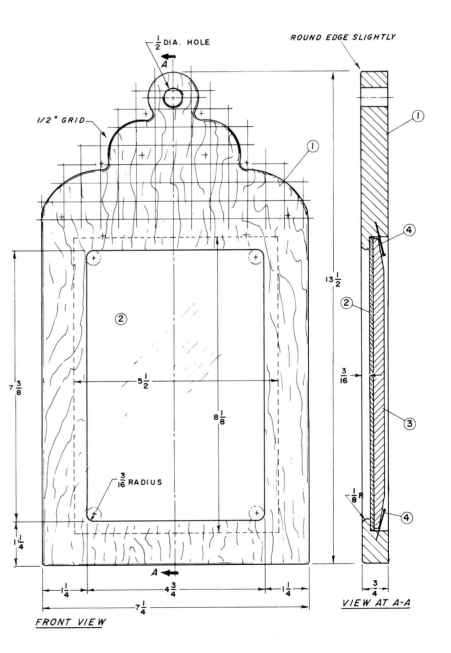

FRONT VIEW

VIEW AT A-A

Courting Mirror

In Colonial America, glass was so expensive that some very early mirrors were made with broken pieces of other mirrors, held in a crude makeshift frame. The design shown here is more refined. It is a courting mirror, presented by a man when proposing to a prospective bride. It was said that if the woman smiled into the mirror, she surely would accept. This early mirror is decorated with dentils and three hearts, one of them right side up and the others upside down. It is made of walnut, but you can use almost any hardwood. You might hang a courting mirror on a wall where a larger mirror or picture can't be squeezed in.

NO.	NAME	SIZE	REQ'D.
1	BOTTOM SECTION	¼ x 9¾ – 11⁵⁄₁₆ LONG	1
2	TOP SECTION	¼ x 8¾ – 7½ LONG	1
3	SIDE BATTEN	¼ x 7⁷⁄₈ – 1¹⁄₁₆ LONG	2
4	BOTTOM BATTEN*	¼ x 5¼ – ¾ LONG	1
5	MIRROR GLAZING	³⁄₃₂ x 5³⁄₁₆ – 7¹⁄₁₆ LONG	1
6	BACKBOARD	¼ x 5³⁄₁₆ – 7⅛ LONG	1
7	BRAD – HEADLESS, SQ. CUT	⅞ LONG	8
8	SCREW - EYE	⅞ LONG	2

MATERIALS LIST

* NOTE THAT GRAIN DIRECTION RUNS THE WIDTH OF THE PART.

1. Select the stock and cut the parts. The entire mirror is made of ¼-inch hardwood. Cut the parts to the sizes given in the Materials List. Study the exploded drawing. To prevent warping, the grain runs across the bottom batten (part 4) in the same direction as that in the bottom section (part 1).

2. Make a paper pattern. Draw a grid with ½-inch squares, and enlarge the entire mirror onto it. The three hearts in the top section are laid out with a compass. Transfer the patterns to the stock.

3. Cut the parts to shape. Lay out and drill the holes for each heart in the top section. Cut out the remaining area of the hearts with a jigsaw or coping saw. Cut the outline of the top section.

In the bottom section, carefully locate the centers of the holes that form the corners of the cutout for the mirror. Drill the holes; then saw the rest of the cutout. With a router and a ¼-inch-roundover bit, round the edges of the cutout to the profile shown in the cross section.

Locate and drill the two ⅜-inch-diameter holes that help to define the top corners of the bottom section. Then cut out the remainder of the section's outline.

Lay out the dentils along the top edge. You can cut them on a table saw with a dado blade. Hold the bottom section with its top edge down, and guide it through repeated passes with the miter gauge.

The pinwheel can be scratched into the stock at any time in the construction process. Scratch the outline into the wood. You can either follow the pattern, or scratch a series of arcs with a drafting compass that has a steel point instead of pencil lead.

Taper the backboard (part 6) on all four sides, as shown in the cross section with a hand plane.

4. Assemble the mirror frame. Dry-assemble the wood parts of the frame. As shown in the cross section, the top, the sides, and the bottom battens combine to form a rabbet that holds the mirror glazing and backboard in place. For the mirror to fit properly, the rabbet should be ¼ inch wide all around the mirror cutout, as shown. Trim the battens, if necessary. Glue up the frame. Glue the two side battens (part 3) flush with the sides of the bottom section. Glue the top (part 2) in place so that the overall height of the mirror frame is 17½ inches. Glue the bottom batten ¼ inch below the lower edge of the cutout. Attach two small eye screws to the back, and string a length of picture wire between them.

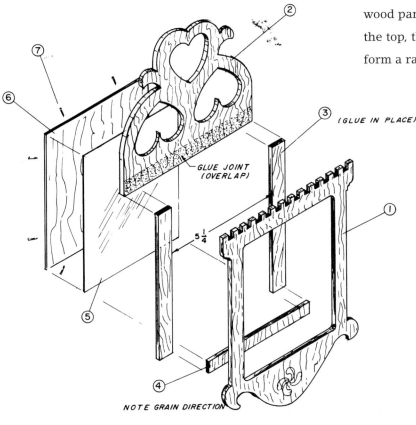

GLUE JOINT
(OVERLAP)

(GLUE IN PLACE)

5¼

NOTE GRAIN DIRECTION

EXPLODED VIEW

5. Apply finish. Before installing the mirror glazing (part 5) and backboard, varnish the frame.

6. Cut the mirror glazing to size, and check the fit. It should not be snug, or the expansion of the surrounding wood might crack the glass. Add the backboard, and hold it in place securely by driving eight square-cut headless brads (part 7) into the lip.

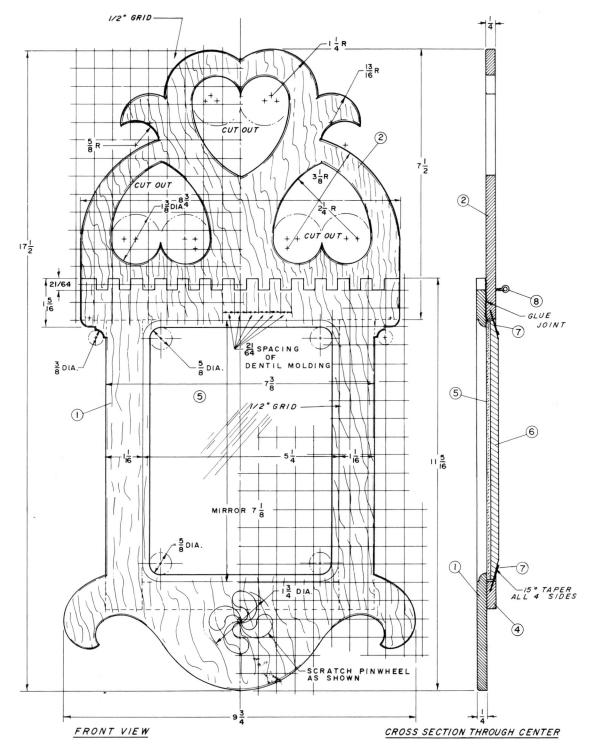

FRONT VIEW

CROSS SECTION THROUGH CENTER

Cricket Footstool

Footstools were very popular in years gone by. They were found in just about every early Colonial American home. Originally they were called crickets, although I don't know why. Footstools came in all shapes and sizes. Formal footstools, such as this one, were made of a fine hardwood and usually stained. More country footstools were very plain, made of a soft wood, and usually painted. However, I found an interesting combined treatment in many footstools from Vermont that had stained tops with painted legs and rails.

MATERIALS LIST

NO.	NAME	SIZE	REQ'D.
1	TOP	½ x 6½ – 15 LONG	1
2	RAIL	½ x 2¼ – 13⅞ LONG	2
3	LEG	⅝ x 4⅞ – 6⅛ LONG	2
4	NAIL -SQ. CUT/FINISH	1 LONG	18

1. Study the plans carefully. Note how each part is to be shaped. As you study the plans, try to visualize how you will make each part and how the project will be assembled. Note which parts you will put together first, second, and so on, exactly how you will put it together.

2. The matching rails (part 2) are irregular in shape and will have to be laid out on a 1-inch grid to make a full-size pattern. Lay out the grid on heavy paper or cardboard, and transfer the shape of the piece to the grid, point by point. A compass would come in handy to lay out this pattern.

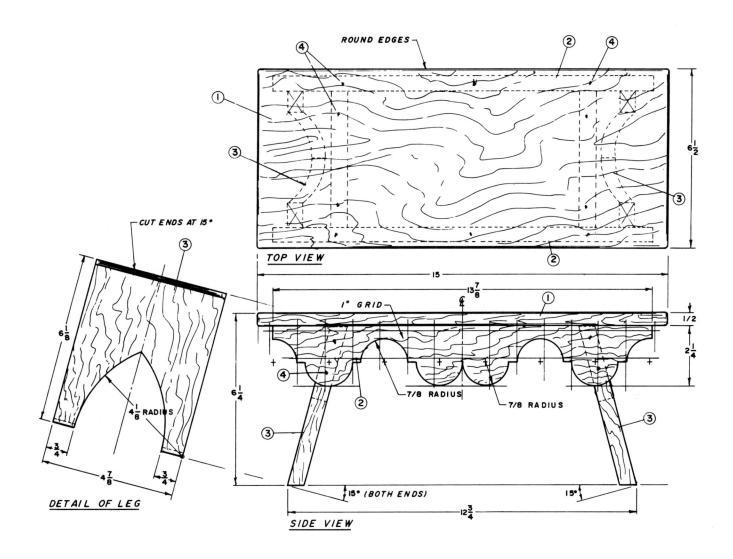

ROUND EDGES

TOP VIEW

CUT ENDS AT 15°

6⅛

¾

4⅞

¾

4⅛ RADIUS

DETAIL OF LEG

15

13⅞

1" GRID

¢

½

2¼

6¼

7/8 RADIUS

7/8 RADIUS

15° (BOTH ENDS)

15°

12¾

SIDE VIEW

3. Transfer the full-size pattern to the wood, and carefully cut out the pieces. Check all dimensions for accuracy. Sand all over with fine-grit paper, keeping all edges sharp. I recommend that you tack or tape the two rails together when cutting out and sanding so that your rails will be a perfectly matching pair.

4. Carefully cut the remaining parts to size according to the Materials List. Take care to cut all parts to exact size and exactly square (90°). Stop and recheck all dimensions before going on. The top and bottom ends of the legs (part 3) are cut at 15°, as shown. Be sure to make one right-hand and one left-hand leg.

Lightly sand all surfaces and edges with medium sandpaper to remove all tool marks. Take care to keep all edges square and sharp.

5. After all of the pieces have been carefully made, dry-fit the parts, that is, put the complete project together without glue or nails to check for accuracy and good-fitting joints. If anything needs refitting, now is the time to correct it.

6. Once all of the parts fit together correctly, assemble the project, keeping everything square as you go. Check that all fits are tight. If you used a hardwood, be sure to drill pilot holes for the nails so that the wood will not split.

7. Finish to suit, following the general finishing instructions in the introduction. This project can be stained or painted.

Early American Lantern

I had always wanted an original antique wooden lantern, but could never afford one. The few I had seen for sale seemed prohibitively expensive and were not in all that great condition. I came upon the original of this lantern at last, and discovered that it is not very difficult to make, and it really adds a lot to any room it is hung in.

MATERIALS LIST

NO.	NAME	SIZE	REQ'D.
1	STILE	$^{11}/_{16}$ SQ. - $10^{3}/_{4}$ LONG	4
2	RAIL	$^{11}/_{16}$ x $^{7}/_{8}$ – $4^{1}/_{16}$ LONG	8
3	GLASS	$^{3}/_{32}$ x 4 – $9^{5}/_{8}$ LONG	3
4	NAIL - SQ. CUT	$^{1}/_{2}$ LONG	20
5	TOP/BOTTOM	$^{1}/_{2}$ x 6 – 6 LONG	2
6	PIN	$^{1}/_{8}$ DIA. – $^{3}/_{4}$ LONG	8
7	HOOD (TIN)	$^{1}/_{32}$ x 3 – $4^{7}/_{8}$ LONG	1
8	TACK	$^{3}/_{8}$ LONG	4
9	HANDLE	$^{1}/_{4}$ x $^{1}/_{2}$ – 18 LONG	1
10	PIN	$^{1}/_{8}$ DIA. - $^{5}/_{8}$ LONG	4
11	CANDLE HOLDER	TO SUIT	1
12	SCREW – FL. HD.	NO. 6 - $1^{1}/_{4}$ LONG	1
13	STILE (DOOR)	$^{1}/_{2}$ x $^{5}/_{8}$ – $9^{1}/_{4}$ LONG	2
14	RAIL (DOOR)	$^{1}/_{2}$ x $^{11}/_{16}$ – $4^{5}/_{16}$ LONG	2
15	GLASS	$^{3}/_{32}$ x $3^{1}/_{2}$ – $8^{1}/_{4}$ LONG	1
16	DOOR PULL	TO SUIT	1
17	LOCKING ARM	TO SUIT	1
18	COTTER PIN	$1^{1}/_{8}$ LONG	4
19	DOOR STOP	$^{1}/_{4}$ SQ. - $9^{1}/_{4}$ LONG	1

1. Study the plans carefully. Note how each part is to be shaped. As you study the plans, try to visualize how you will make each part.

The handle (part 9) should be steam-bent. I have seen this done and am pretty sure I could do it, but for this project, I used an alternative approach. I simply cut $^{1}/_{16}$-inch-thick strips about $^{9}/_{16}$ inch wide. Then I glued them together over a $^{3}/_{4}$-inch-thick by $3^{3}/_{4}$-inch-wide board. I cut this board into the shape

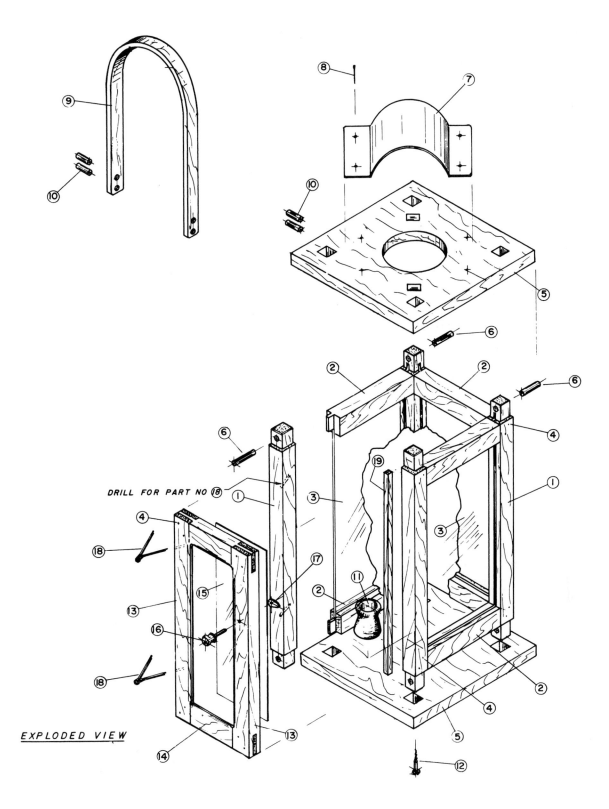

DRILL FOR PART NO ⑱

EXPLODED VIEW

of the interior of the bend. I then sanded the sides smooth to get the same ½-inch-wide handle as the original had. If you are set up to steam-bend the handle, then do. If not, simply glue up the ¹⁄₁₆-inch strips as I did. It is easy and really doesn't look like strips after the handle is sanded and finished.

As you study the plans, also try to visualize how the project will be assembled. Note which parts you will put together first, second, and so on, and exactly how you will put it together.

Note: this project is mostly pinned together using the eight pins (part 6).

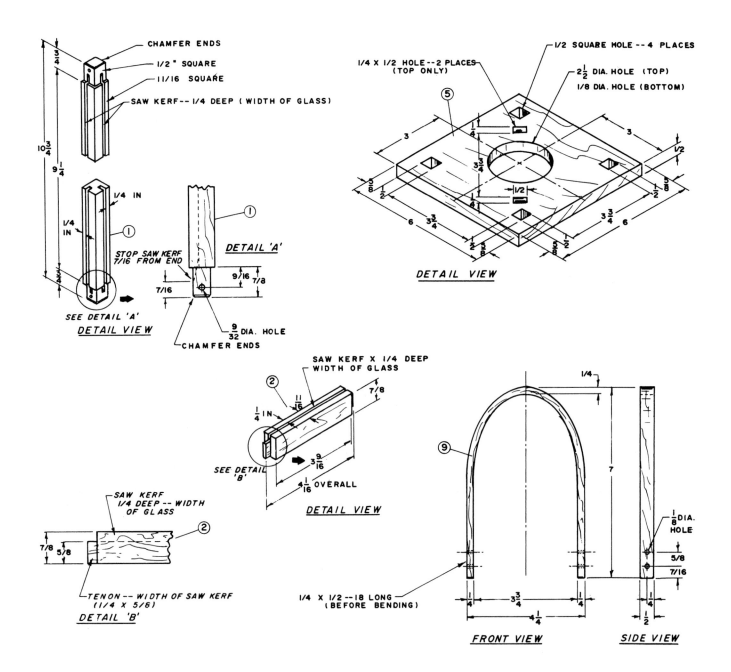

2. Carefully cut all of the parts to size according to the Materials List. Take care to cut all of the parts to exact size, keeping them precisely square (90°). Stop and recheck all dimensions before going on. Lightly sand all surfaces and edges with medium sandpaper to remove all tool marks. Take care to keep all edges square and sharp.

3. Make each piece according to the given detail drawings. I made the pieces and fit each to the other as I went. I suggest that you cut the four ½-inch-square holes in the top and bottom piece (part 5) after you make the other pieces. Fit the four ½-inch-holes to the lantern body. I'm not exactly sure in what order the original was assembled, but I installed the glass at the same time that I assembled the pieces. It made finishing a little more difficult, but the construction was easy.

Don't forget that the top and bottom are only pinned in place.

4. The tin hood (part 7) is cut out of a large tin juice can. After cutting it to size, bend it around some cylindrical object about 3½ inches in diameter. Blue it by heating it with a torch until it turns blue, and it will

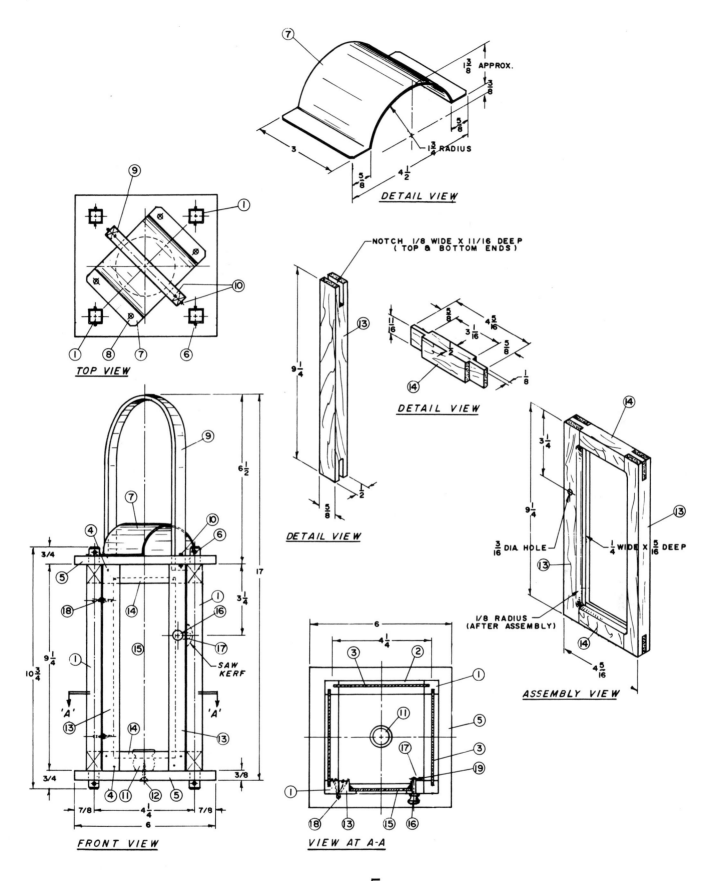

⑦

$1\frac{3}{8}$ APPROX.

$\frac{3}{8}$

$\frac{5}{8}$

3

$1\frac{3}{4}$ RADIUS

$\frac{5}{8}$ $4\frac{1}{2}$

DETAIL VIEW

⑨

①

⑩

① ⑧ ⑦ ⑥

TOP VIEW

NOTCH 1/8 WIDE X 11/16 DEEP
(TOP & BOTTOM ENDS)

⑬

$9\frac{1}{4}$

$\frac{1}{2}$

$\frac{5}{8}$

DETAIL VIEW

$\frac{5}{8}$ $4\frac{5}{16}$

$\frac{11}{16}$ $3\frac{1}{16}$ $\frac{5}{8}$

⑭ $\frac{1}{2}$ $\frac{1}{8}$

DETAIL VIEW

⑭

$\frac{3}{4}$

$9\frac{1}{4}$

$\frac{3}{16}$ DIA HOLE

⑬

⑬

$\frac{1}{4}$ WIDE X $\frac{5}{16}$ DEEP

1/8 RADIUS
(AFTER ASSEMBLY)

⑭

$4\frac{5}{16}$

ASSEMBLY VIEW

$6\frac{1}{2}$

⑨

⑦

④

$\frac{3}{4}$

⑤

⑱

①

⑩

⑥

①

⑯

17

$3\frac{1}{4}$

⑮

⑰

SAW KERF

$9\frac{1}{4}$

$10\frac{3}{4}$

①

'A'

⑬

⑭

⑬

$\frac{3}{4}$

$\frac{3}{8}$

④ ⑪ ⑫ ⑤

$\frac{7}{8}$ $4\frac{1}{4}$ $\frac{7}{8}$

6

FRONT VIEW

6

$4\frac{1}{4}$

③ ②

①

⑪

⑤

⑰

③

⑲

①

⑱ ⑬ ⑮ ⑯

VIEW AT A-A

look very old. I used old carpet tacks to hold it in place.

If all parts fit together correctly, assemble the project, keeping everything square as you go. Check that all fits are tight.

5. Finish to suit, following the general finishing instructions given in the introduction.

Coasting Sled

*Until the
first half of the 1800s,
most sleds were built by the
father or a grandfather of the family, a
local woodworker or cabinetmaker, or the local
blacksmith. These early sleds were not used as toys but for the
practical purpose of hauling supplies over the snow. As attitudes toward children's
play changed over the years, the sled evolved into something on which to slide
down hills. By the mid 1800s, at least twelve companies were manufacturing sleds
in the United States. These early sleds were gaily decorated with bright colors and
gold stripes to catch the consumer's eye. It took a lot of body English to steer these
sleds because the one-piece runners didn't flex like those on today's sleds. This
project is an exact copy of an early coasting sled I found in Rhode Island.*

MATERIALS LIST			
NO.	NAME	SIZE	REQ'D.
1	TOP	1 x 11 – 24 LONG	1
2	RAIL	1 x 4 – 30 LONG	2
3	BRACE	1 x 2 – 10 LONG	3
4	HANDLE	¾ DIA. – 12 LONG	1
5	RUNNER	⅛ x ⅝ – 38 LONG	2
6	SCREW – FL. HD.	NO. 8 – ¾ LONG	18
7	NAIL – SQ. CUT		AS REQ'D.

1. Select the stock and cut the parts. The old sleds were extremely sturdy and usually made from a hardwood such as oak or rock maple. But the choice of wood is up to you. You may find it necessary to glue up boards to make the top. The iron for the runners can be bought at metal supply firms.

Cut the parts to their overall sizes given in the Materials List.

2. Make a paper pattern and cut the parts to size. Draw a grid with 1-inch squares and enlarge the top (part 1) and rails (part 2) onto it. Transfer the pattern to the stock. Include the outline of the heart in the top. To save time, trace the pattern onto just one rail and join the two rails temporarily by tacking them with two finishing nails where they won't interfere with the cut. Cut out the rails and the top with a saber saw, jigsaw, or coping saw.

To cut the heart-shaped hole in the top, drill a hole within the traced outline, and start to saw from there. Locate and drill a $\frac{1}{4}$-inch-diameter hole in the rails for the handle (part 4).

Cut the braces (part 3) and the handle to size. Sand all cut edges. To ensure strong glue joints, avoid rounding off edges where the pieces will meet.

3. Make the runners. It's a simple matter to bend the runners (part 5) to shape as you attach them. Before you attach them, however, flatten the ends to the profile shown in the runner detail.

Each runner is attached to its rail with nine #8 flat-head screws (part 6). Mark the location of the holes on each runner by dimpling the metal with an awl or center punch. The dimple keeps the bit from wandering as you drill the hole. Select a bit that will just allow the full width of the screw shank to pass through, and then drill the holes. Counter bore the holes so that the mounting screws will be slightly recessed.

4. Attach the runners. Put one end of the still-unbent rail in position on the runner. Mark the location of the end hole on the rail, and drill a pilot hole to make it easier to drive the screw.

After driving the first screw, press the runner to conform to the rail. Then mark, drill, and drive the screw into the second hole. Continue until all nine screws are in place. You'll find that the runners can be bent easily by hand. Repeat the process on the second rail.

5. Assemble the sled. Test-fit all parts, and make any adjustments necessary. Nail the sled together with square-cut nails (part 7). First, nail the braces to the top. Before you nail the top to the rails, align them by temporarily slipping the handle through the holes in the rails. Then nail the top to the rails and remove the handle.

Put glue into the hole for the handle; slip the handle in place, and wipe off any excess glue with a damp rag. Further secure the handle with $\frac{1}{8}$-inch dowels driven through holes in the handle shown in the top view.

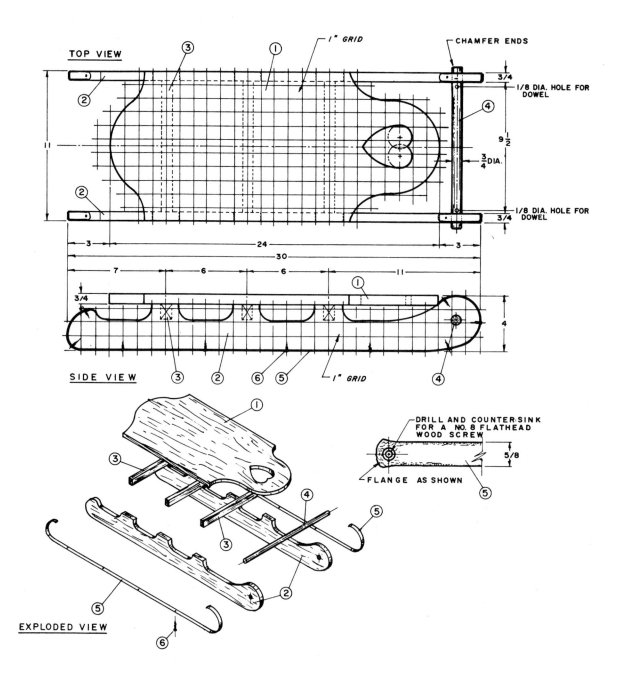

TOP VIEW

SIDE VIEW

EXPLODED VIEW

6. Finish the sled. If you've used an attractive wood, consider applying a clear weather-resistant finish. I chose to paint my sled blue with white pinstriping. I used oil-base exterior enamel for the base coat. When it dried, I added pinstripes with thinned enamel.

Don't be afraid to try your hand at pinstriping. The job on the antique sled itself was not perfect by any means. The trick is to use a long pinstriping brush, available at art supply stores. Practice on a piece of scrap wood until you get the hang of it. You can make a straighter line if you clamp a strip of wood to the top of the sled and run your hand along it. Clean up any mistakes with a rag or cotton swab dampened with paint thinner.

Candle Box with Sliding Lid

The candle box with sliding lid is as popular today as it was in the days when it actually was used to store candles. I have made many of these in all sizes for all kinds of uses. They are very handy boxes to have around the house, and they're a popular item at craft shows. These boxes do not use much material, and there is almost no waste. I suggest distressing the box, and I often add a painted, crackle finish to mine. The dimensions given are for the box pictured, but your box can be made any size, using whatever hardwood you have around. Be sure to use a straight-grained hardwood, as softwood is not strong enough for the notch cutouts.

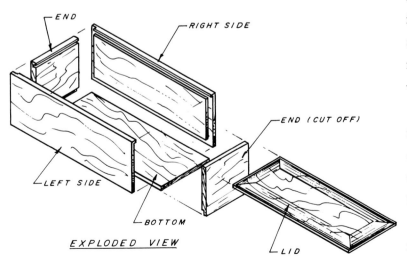

EXPLODED VIEW

 END
RIGHT SIDE
END (CUT OFF)
LEFT SIDE
BOTTOM
LID

1. Carefully study the plans; the construction is somewhat unusual. Note how everything is cut from one piece of wood. The candle box pictured and shown in the plans is made from one board ⅜ x 6¼ x 66 inches. As noted, there will be almost no waste, with some allowance for saw kerf thickness.

Carefully cut the lid from the board. Take care to cut each part to size, keeping the edges and corners square (90°). You can cut the bottom at this time, but you might want to cut and fit the bottom to the assembly later.

On the remaining piece, cut a dado to create a notch ³⁄₁₆ inch wide x ³⁄₁₆ inch deep and ⅜ inch down from the top edge, as shown in the end

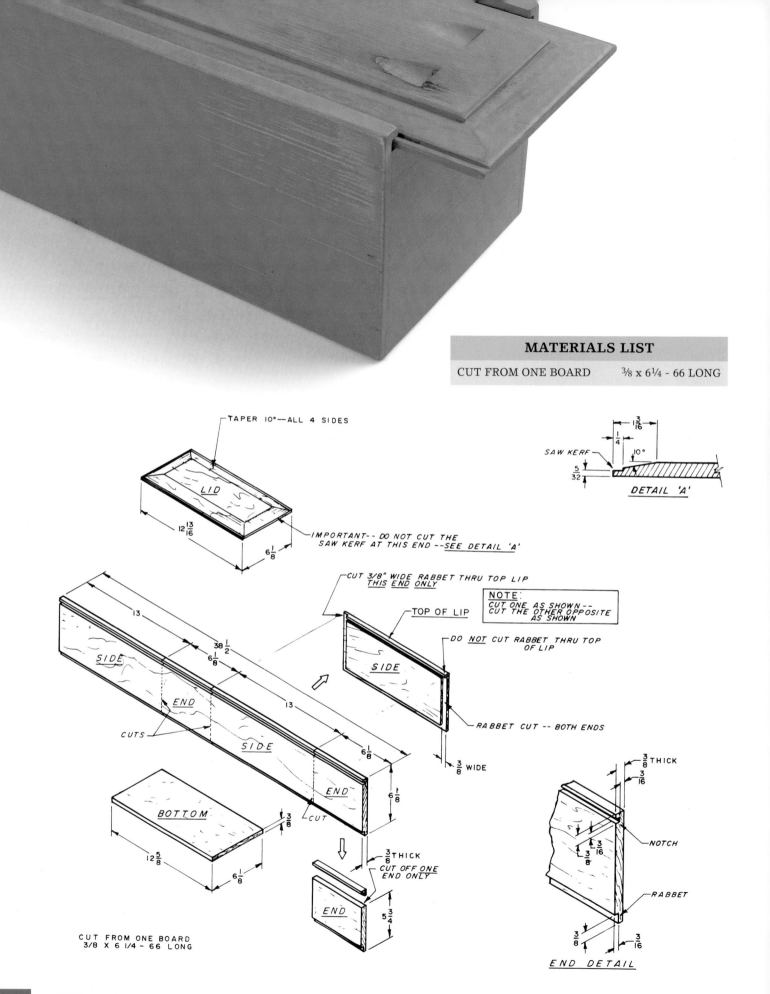

MATERIALS LIST

CUT FROM ONE BOARD	$\frac{3}{8}$ x $6\frac{1}{4}$ - 66 LONG

TAPER 10°—ALL 4 SIDES

LID

$12\frac{13}{16}$

$6\frac{1}{8}$

IMPORTANT-- DO NOT CUT THE SAW KERF AT THIS END --SEE DETAIL 'A'

SAW KERF

$\frac{3}{16}$

$\frac{1}{4}$

10°

$\frac{5}{32}$

DETAIL 'A'

CUT 3/8" WIDE RABBET THRU TOP LIP
THIS END ONLY

TOP OF LIP

NOTE:
CUT ONE AS SHOWN --
CUT THE OTHER OPPOSITE
AS SHOWN

SIDE

DO NOT CUT RABBET THRU TOP
OF LIP

13

$38\frac{1}{2}$

$6\frac{1}{8}$

SIDE

END

CUTS

SIDE

13

$6\frac{1}{8}$

RABBET CUT -- BOTH ENDS

$\frac{3}{8}$ WIDE

END

$6\frac{1}{8}$

BOTTOM

$\frac{3}{8}$

CUT

$12\frac{5}{8}$

$6\frac{1}{8}$

$\frac{3}{8}$ THICK
CUT OFF ONE
END ONLY

END

$5\frac{3}{4}$

CUT FROM ONE BOARD
3/8 X 6 1/4 - 66 LONG

$\frac{3}{8}$ THICK

$\frac{3}{16}$

$\frac{3}{16}$

$\frac{3}{8}$

NOTCH

RABBET

$\frac{3}{8}$

$\frac{3}{16}$

END DETAIL

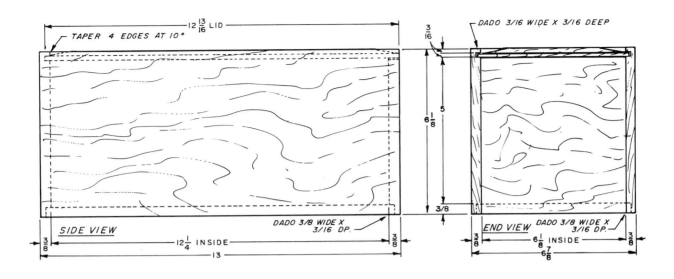

detail. Make a rabbet cut along the bottom edge $\frac{3}{8}$ inch wide x $\frac{3}{16}$ inch deep, as shown in the end detail.

Lightly sand all surfaces and edges with medium sandpaper to remove any burrs and all tool marks. Take care to keep all edges square and sharp at this time.

2. Cut the sides and ends from the board as shown, according to the given dimensions. Cut another $\frac{3}{8}$-inch-wide x $\frac{3}{16}$-inch-deep rabbet along the ends of the side pieces, taking care not to cut through the upper lip on one end as shown. It is important that you make a matched pair of sides—that is, a right-hand side and a left-hand side. On one of the ends, cut off a $\frac{3}{8}$-inch-thick piece from the top edge to allow the lid to pass over and out as shown.

Resand all over with fine-grit sandpaper, still keeping all edges sharp. Make the 10° bevel cuts on the four edges of the lid, as shown in detail A. Fit the lid to the notch in the box assembly.

3. After all pieces have been carefully made, dry-fit all of the parts—that is, put the complete project together without glue or nails to check for accuracy and good-fitting joints. If anything needs refitting, now is the time to correct it.

4. Once all of the parts fit together correctly, assemble the project, keeping everything square as you go. Check that all fits are tight. I usually glue the pieces together as well as fasten them with small square-cut nails. Be sure to drill small pilot holes for the nails so the wood will not split. Check that the lid slides loosely, especially if you are going to paint your box.

5. Finish to suit, following the general finishing instructions in the introduction. This project can be stained or painted. If you paint your box, do not get any paint inside the notch for the lid, and try to put the paint on lightly along the area of the lid where it fits into the notch.

Colonial Wall Shelf

This Colonial shelf uses a cyma curve—a curve that turns back on itself—at the top and bottom. It has graceful lines. In laying out the sides, locate the compass swing points, set the compass at the given radius, and draw the outer shape.

1. Lay out the shape of part 1. Transfer the pattern to the wood, and cut out the piece. It is a good idea to tape or tack the two sides together when cutting and sanding so that both sides will be exactly the same size and shape. Sand all edges.

2. Cut the two shelves and brace to size. Make the ⅛-inch-radius bead in the braces (parts 4 and 5).

3. (Optional.) Cut the plate groove, if you wish, approximately ¼ – ⅜ inch wide, and about ⅛ inch deep.

4. Glue and nail the shelf together. Check that it is square.

5. This project is usually stained, but it could be painted to blend into any room setting.

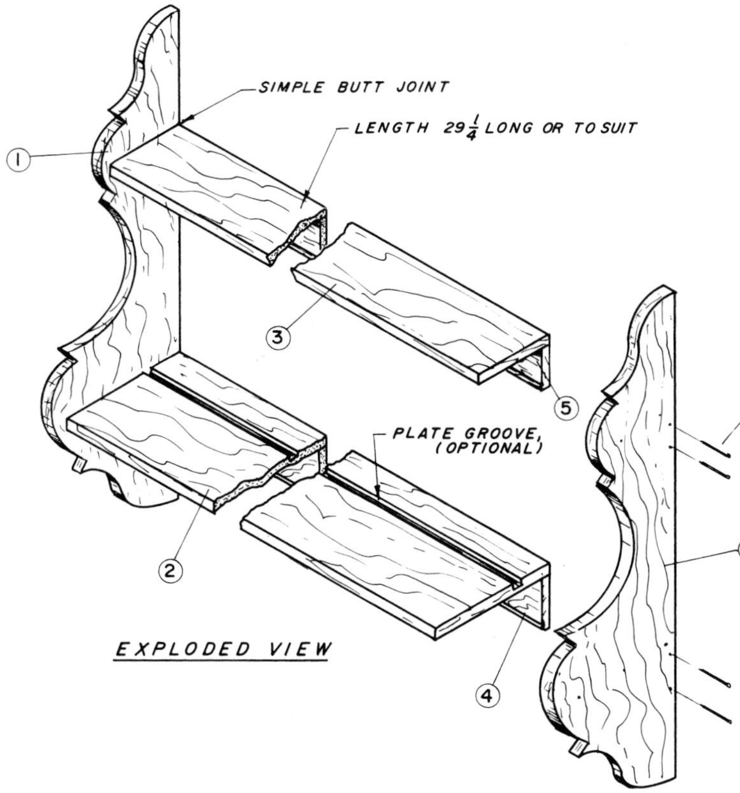
SIMPLE BUTT JOINT
LENGTH 29 1/4 LONG OR TO SUIT
PLATE GROOVE, (OPTIONAL)
1
2
3
4
5
6

EXPLODED VIEW

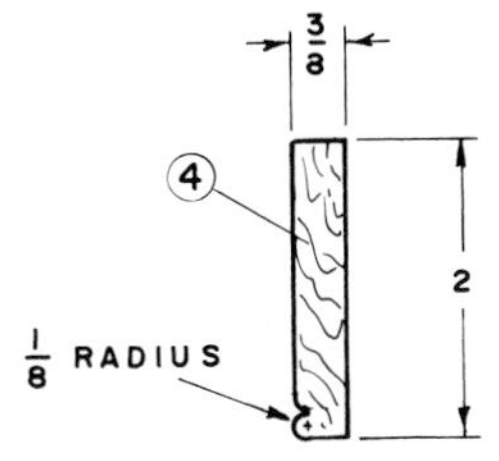
3/8
4
2
1/8 RADIUS

DETAIL 'A'

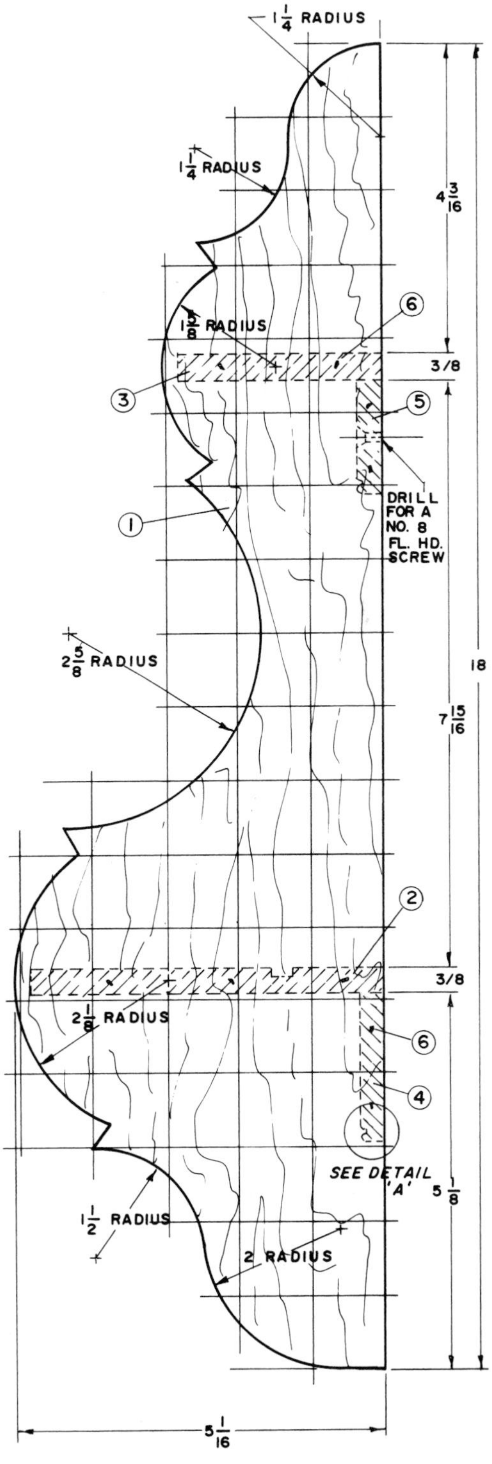
1 1/4 RADIUS
1 1/4 RADIUS
1 5/8 RADIUS
2 5/8 RADIUS
2 1/8 RADIUS
1 1/2 RADIUS
2 RADIUS
4 3/16
3/8
7 15/16
3/8
5 1/8
18
5 1/16
DRILL FOR A NO. 8 FL. HD. SCREW
SEE DETAIL 'A'
1
2
3
4
5
6

SIDE VIEW

MATERIALS LIST

NO.	NAME	SIZE	REQ'D.
1	SIDE	3/8 x 5 1/16 – 18 LONG	2
2	SHELF – LOWER	3/8 x 4 7/8 – 29 1/4 LONG	1
3	SHELF – UPPER	3/8 x 2 13/16 – 29 1/4 LONG	1
4	BRACE – LOWER	3/8 x 2 – 29 1/4 LONG	1
5	BRACE – UPPER	3/8 x 1 1/2 – 29 1/4 LONG	1
6	SQUARE – CUT NAIL	6 d	18

Milking Stool

This is an exact copy of an antique milking stool that I found in Antrim, New Hampshire. This sturdy little stool was so unusual I just had to draw up the plans. The original was made of maple and had worn-off paint from many years of hard use. This stool would have been used in the days when farmers actually milked their cows by hand.

1. Because of the delicate, long legs, this project must be made of a hardwood for sufficient strength. Cut all of the pieces to size. Carefully lay out the oval for the top using the 5-inch radius and 10-inch radius, as shown in the top view. Cut out the top and sand around the edges. Using a ¼-inch cove cutter with a ball-bearing follower, cut the cove around the top surface of the stool top.

2. Lay out the legs using a 1-inch grid, as shown. I taped all four legs together when I cut and sanded them so that all four would be exactly the same size and shape. Be sure to make the top of the legs exactly as shown. The unique angle, at the top of each leg, is designed to fit and lock into the support for added strength.

The support also must be laid out and cut exactly as shown, especially the 25° notch designed to lock in and give the legs strength and support. Locate, drill, and countersink for all screws in all of the pieces, as shown. Dry-fit all of the pieces. Check that the legs fit up and into the support notches. Make any adjustments as necessary. Glue and screw all of the pieces together.

3. The stool should be primed and painted as you desire. This project is perfect for rosemaling or tole painting. You might want to sand the edges slightly to reflect the wear of all those years of milking.

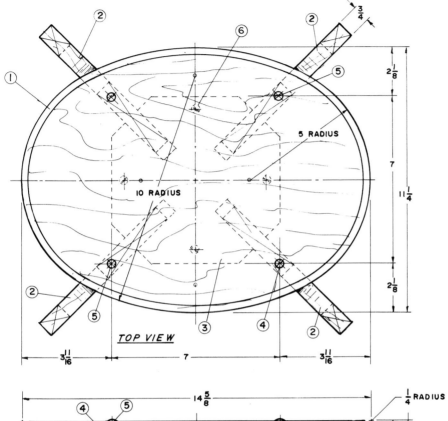

TOP VIEW

① ②

2⅛

7

11¼

2⅛

5 RADIUS

10 RADIUS

3 11/16   7   3 11/16

⑥ ⑤ ③ ④

¾

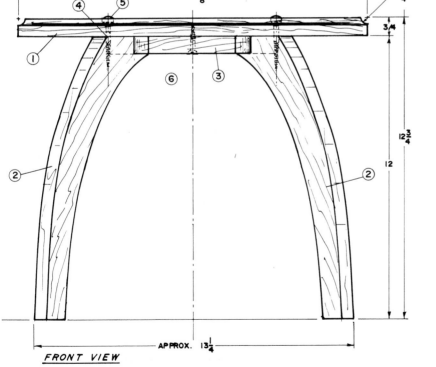

14⅝

¼ RADIUS

¾

12¾

12

APPROX. 13¼

FRONT VIEW

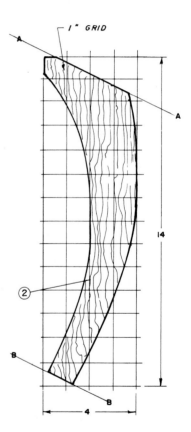

1" GRID

A —— A

14

②

B —— B

4

NOTE: SURFACE 'A' MUST BE
PARALLEL TO SURFACE 'B'

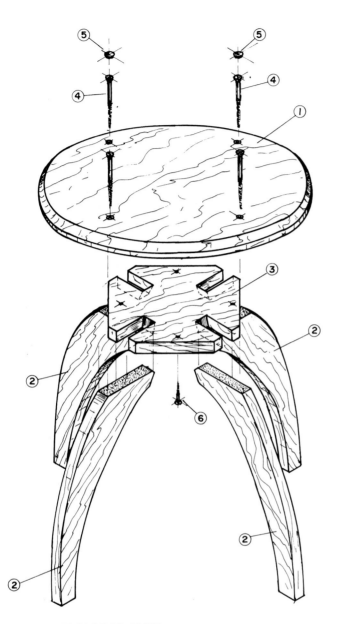

EXPLODED VIEW

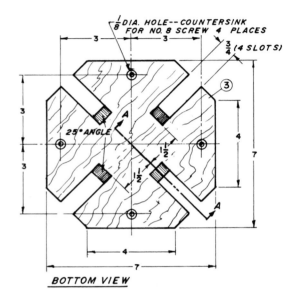

⅛ DIA. HOLE--COUNTERSINK
FOR NO. 8 SCREW 4 PLACES

¾ (4 SLOTS)

25° ANGLE

BOTTOM VIEW

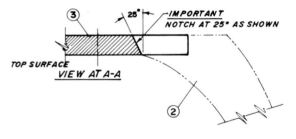

25°

IMPORTANT
NOTCH AT 25° AS SHOWN

TOP SURFACE

VIEW AT A-A

\multicolumn{4}{c}{**MATERIALS LIST**}			
NO.	**NAME**	**SIZE**	**REQ'D.**
1	TOP	¾ x 11¼ – 14⅝ LONG	1
2	LEG	¾ x 4 – 14 LONG	4
3	SUPPORT	¾ - 7 SQUARE	1
4	SCREW – FL. HD.	NO. 8 - 2½ LONG	4
5	PLUG	TO SUIT	4
6	SCREW – FL. HD.	NO. 8 - 1¼ LONG	4

Country Silver Tray

This is a replica of an antique tray for holding silver. I can't understand why silver trays aren't as popular today as they were 150 years ago. They are still very handy and show off silverware to good advantage.

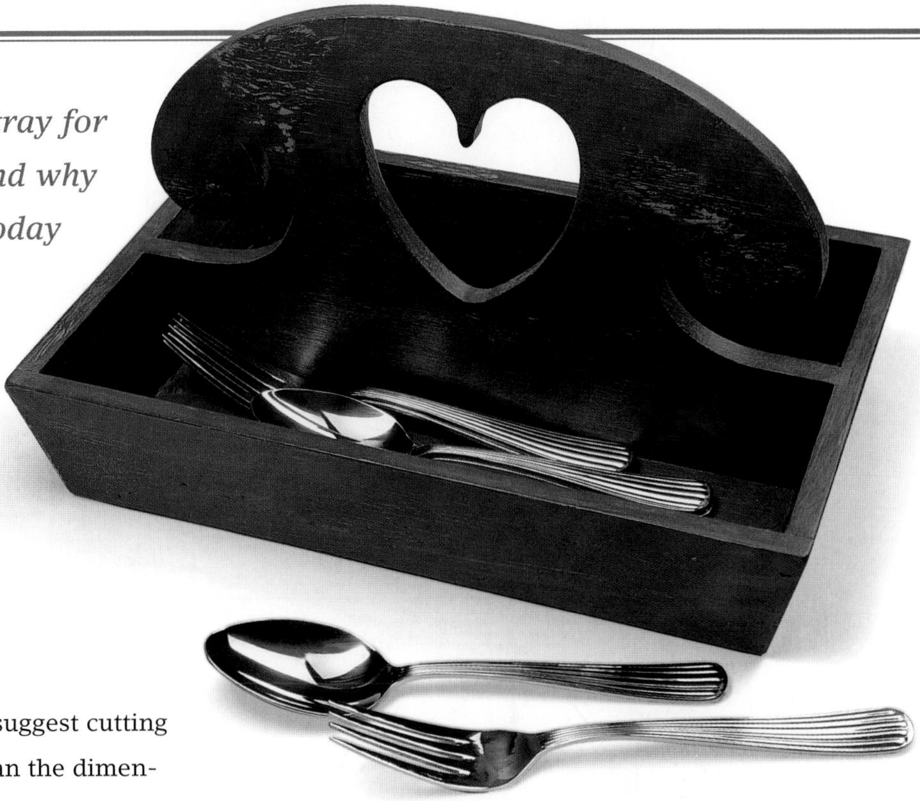

1. Select the stock and cut the parts. I suggest cutting all the parts ½ inch longer and wider than the dimensions given in the Materials List and then cutting them to size as assembly progresses.

2. Cut the joints. Because the sides of this tray slope, the corners are compound miters, and the bottom and top of each must be beveled. Cut the compound miters first.

Tilt the blade on your table saw to 80¼°, and set the miter gauge at 44¼°. Cut a sample joint and check to make sure it meets at 90° without gaps. Adjust as necessary and cut the joints on the long and short sides (parts 1 and 2). Cut each side to length when you cut the second miter on it. Dry-fit all four sides to make sure that they meet tightly and at 90°.

Rip a 10° bevel along the top and bottom of the sides, as shown in the side section. Cut the sides to width when cutting the second bevel.

Rout a dado in the center of the short sides to house the handle. The dado is ⅜ inch wide x 3/16 inch deep and stops ⅜ inch from the bottom edge.

MATERIALS LIST

NO.	NAME	SIZE	REQ'D.
1	LONG SIDE	⅜ x 2¼ – 11¾ LONG	2
2	SHORT SIDE	⅜ x 2¼ – 6½ LONG	2
3	BOTTOM	⅜ x 5¾ – 11 LONG	1
4	HANDLE	⅜ x 6⅞ – 12 LONG	1
5	NAIL – SQ. CUT	1 LONG	24

3. Assemble the tray. Clamping a piece with sloping sides can be difficult. Try this: Put a long strip of masking tape on the bench, sticky side up. Lay a side on part of the tape, outside face down. Tape the adjoining side to it so that the corners of the miters are in contact along their entire length. Repeat this process for the neighboring corners. When you are done, all four sides should be taped together in one long strip. Put glue in the joints, and fold the corners to form the box. Clamp with heavy-duty rubber bands and check for squareness.

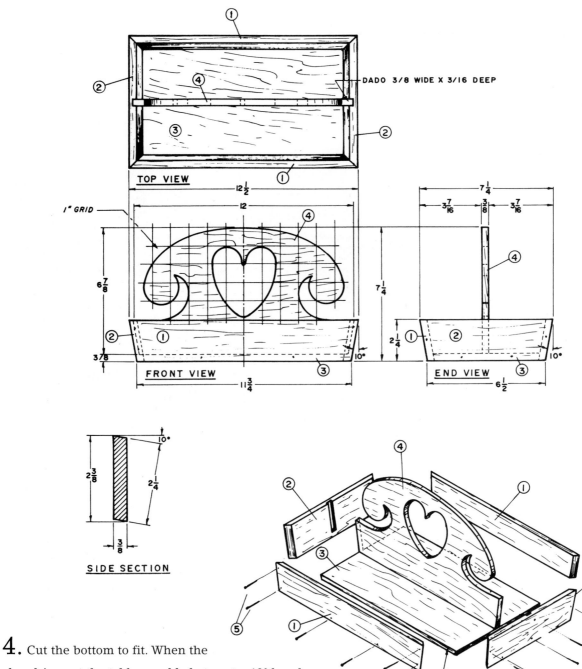

DADO 3/8 WIDE X 3/16 DEEP

TOP VIEW

12½

1" GRID

12

6⅞

7¼

3⅞

FRONT VIEW

11¾

10°

7¼

3⁷⁄₁₆   3/8   3⁷⁄₁₆

2¼

10°

END VIEW

6½

2⅜

2¼

10°

3/8

SIDE SECTION

CUT BOTTOM ③ TO FIT

EXPLODED VIEW

4. Cut the bottom to fit. When the glue dries, set the table-saw blade to cut a 10° bevel, and cut the bottom (part 3) to fit snugly between the sides and ends. Glue it in place. Reinforce all of the joints with square-cut nails (part 5).

5. Make a paper pattern, and cut the handle. Before you cut the scroll work on the handle (part 4), cut it to fit in the dadoes. Measure the distance between the dadoes at the bottom of the box. Set the miter gauge to 80°, and cut the board so the narrowest part will fit this dimension. Trim as necessary.

When the handle fits correctly in the box, cut the scroll work. Make a paper pattern by drawing a grid with 1-inch squares, and enlarge the drawing of the handle onto it. Transfer the enlargement to the wood. Cut the scroll work with a jigsaw or coping saw.

6. Apply finish. Sand the tray and paint it. The original was painted blue-gray.

Sewing Box with Drawers

Here's a project for anyone who sews a lot or knows someone who does. It's a takeoff of an original, antique sewing box with an interesting design, as there are no drawer dividers. All you can see are the three drawer fronts. The one pictured here is made out of red oak, but any wood could be used.

1. Cut all the parts to size, and sand all surfaces with fine-grit paper. Make the two notches on the inner surfaces of the end pieces, ½ inch wide x ¼ inch deep. Also cut the ¼-inch-wide x ¼-inch-deep rabbet in the back edge. Be sure to make a left and right-hand pair of ends.

For this project I would suggest you work backwards, that is, make the drawers first and then fit the drawer supports and case around the drawers. Cut the required dadoes and rabbets for the drawers, and assemble the drawers in the manner shown in the exploded view. Be sure all the drawers are exactly square and that all three are exactly the same overall size, 9³⁄₁₆ inches wide x 18 inches long.

I am sure there are many ways to construct the drawer supports and case, but here is how I did it. Add two layers of masking tape to the top and bottom sur-

faces of each assembled drawer. Now tape all three drawers together to form one large drawer unit. To get exact and correct drawer support locations, place the drawer supports into the drawer dadoes. With the drawer supports in the drawer dadoes, apply a little glue to the drawer supports.

With care, temporarily tape the case side to the three drawers in the position it will be when the case is assembled. Carefully push each drawer support 1/4 inch in from the front edge as shown in the right end subassembly. This will give you the exact location on each side for the three drawer supports.

After the glue sets, untape the sides from the drawers. Once you are sure all the drawer supports are positioned correctly, nail them in place using ½-inch-long brads. (This will allow for any expansion.) Add two layers of masking tape along the sides of the drawers, and

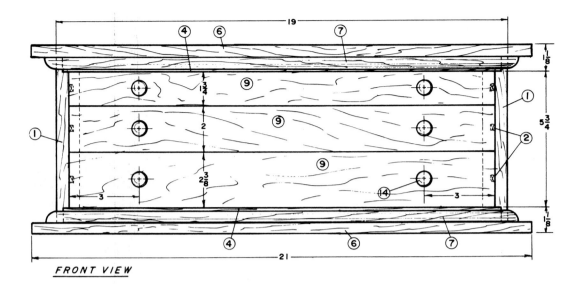

FRONT VIEW

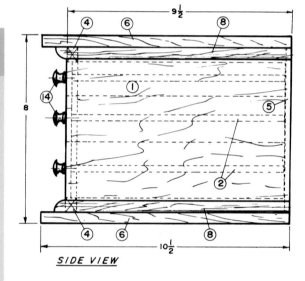

SIDE VIEW

NO.	NAME	SIZE	REQ'D.
MATERIALS LIST			
1	END	½ x 7 – 9½ LONG	2
2	DRAWER SUPPORT	3/16 x ¼ – 9 LONG	6
3	BRAD	½ LONG	18
4	RAIL	½ x 5/8 – 18½ LONG	2
5	BACK	¼ x 7 – 18½ LONG	1
6	TOP/BOTTOM	½ x 10½ – 21 LONG	2
7	MOLDING	½ ROUND – 20 LONG	2
8	MOLDING – END	½ ROUND – 10 LONG	4
		½ x 13/8 – 18 LONG	1
9	DRAWER FRONT	½ x 2 – 18 LONG	1
		½ x 23/8 – 18 LONG	1
		½ x 13/8 – 17½ LONG	1
10	DRAWER BACK	½ x 2 – 17½ LONG	1
		½ x 23/8 – 17½ LONG	1
		½ x 13/8 - 815/16 LONG	2
11	DRAWER SIDE	½ x 2 – 815/16 LONG	2
		½ x 23/8 – 815/16 LONG	2
12	DRAWER BOTTOM	1/8 x 89/16 – 173/8 LONG	3
13	NAIL – FINISH	1 LONG	AS REQ'D.
14	DRAWER PULL	5/8 DIA.	6

build the case around the taped drawers. The two layers of tape will give you a good clearance around each drawer. Adjust the fit of the case pieces, if necessary, so that the case fits snugly around the taped drawers. Glue and nail the assembly together. After the glue sets, remove the drawers and untape everything. Refit the drawers; they should fit nicely with a slight space around each.

Locate the holes for drawer pulls 3 inches in from each end. Stain or paint your sewing box. It will be enjoyed for years to come, and not just for keeping sewing supplies.

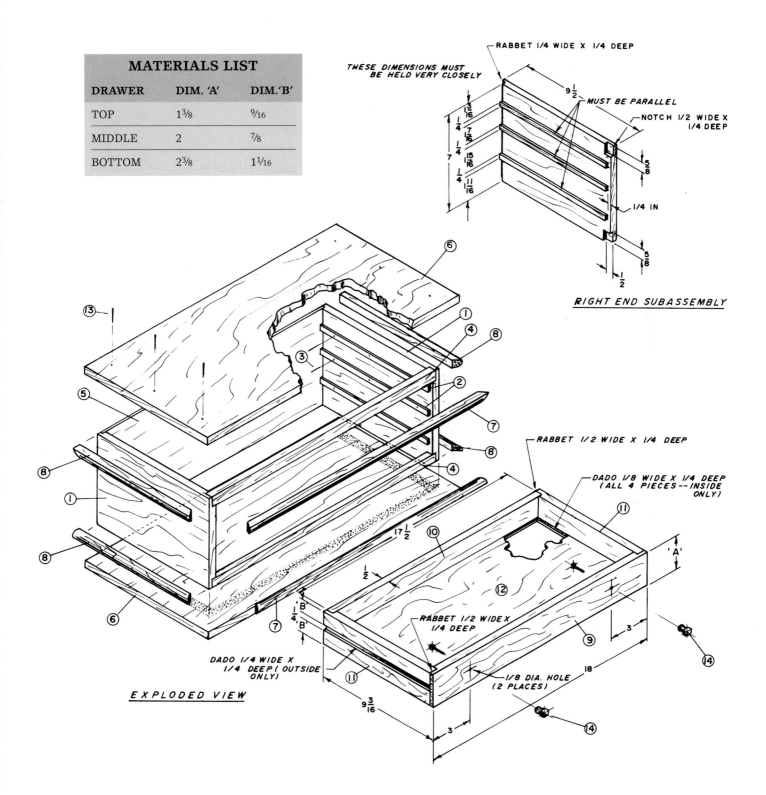

MATERIALS LIST

DRAWER	DIM. 'A'	DIM. 'B'
TOP	1³⁄₈	⁹⁄₁₆
MIDDLE	2	⁷⁄₈
BOTTOM	2³⁄₈	1¹⁄₁₆

RABBET 1/4 WIDE X 1/4 DEEP

THESE DIMENSIONS MUST BE HELD VERY CLOSELY

9½

MUST BE PARALLEL

NOTCH 1/2 WIDE X 1/4 DEEP

3/16

1/4

7/16

1/4

5/16

1/4

11/16

7

5/8

1/4 IN

5/8

1/2

RIGHT END SUBASSEMBLY

RABBET 1/2 WIDE X 1/4 DEEP

DADO 1/8 WIDE X 1/4 DEEP (ALL 4 PIECES -- INSIDE ONLY)

RABBET 1/2 WIDE X 1/4 DEEP

17½

½

'A'

3

18

1/8 DIA. HOLE (2 PLACES)

9³⁄₁₆

3

DADO 1/4 WIDE X 1/4 DEEP (OUTSIDE ONLY)

1/4

'B'

'B'

EXPLODED VIEW

Miniature Blanket Chest

This project is based on a chest made in Pennsylvania around 1820. The original was made of pine and poplar, and it is unusual for its small size. You might use such a box to store jewelry, important papers, or any number of other things. You can still buy hardware very similar to that used on the original.

MATERIALS LIST

NO.	NAME	SIZE	REQ'D.
1	SIDE	$^3/_8$ x $9^1/_2$ – $9^7/_8$ LONG	2
2	FRONT	$^3/_8$ x $9^1/_2$ – $15^1/_4$ LONG	1
3	BACK	$^3/_8$ x $9^1/_2$ – $14^1/_2$ LONG	1
4	BOTTOM	$^3/_8$ x $9^1/_8$ – $14^7/_8$ LONG	2
5	DRAWER GUIDE	$^3/_8$ x 2 – $9^1/_8$ LONG	4
6	LID	$^3/_8$ x $9^{29}/_{32}$ – $15^5/_{16}$ LONG	1
7	LID MOLDING	$^3/_8$ x $^3/_4$ – 40 LONG	1
8	CENTER MOLDING	$^1/_4$ x $^3/_8$ – 40 LONG	1
9	SKIRT	$^3/_8$ x $2^7/_8$ – 40 LONG	1
10	DRAWER FRONT	$^1/_2$ x $2^1/_4$ – 40 LONG	2
11	DRAWER SIDE	$^1/_4$ x 2 – $9^3/_8$ LONG	4
12	DRAWER BACK	$^1/_4$ x 2 – 6 LONG	2
13	DRAWER BOTTOM	$^1/_8$ x 6 – $8^7/_8$ LONG	2
14	HINGE	$^1/_2$ x 2 LONG	2
15	DRAWER PULL	$^3/_4$ WIDE	2
16	NAIL – SQ. CUT	$^3/_4$ LONG	60

1. Select the stock. I used mahogany to make the miniature chest shown in the photograph because that happened to be the only wood I had around at the time. I painted the piece a colonial blue, although the original was painted green. Note that most of the parts must be planed down to a thickness of $^1/_8$ inch. The drawer is made of still-thinner stock. It would be a good idea to make the drawer bottoms out of plywood or hardboard so that they won't push the drawers apart as they expand and contract. Glue up the wider pieces specified in the Materials List, if necessary.

2. Cut the sides (part 1), the front (part 2), back (part 3), and bottoms (part 4) to the sizes given in the Materials List. Everything else will be cut to fit later. The chest has two bottoms: a

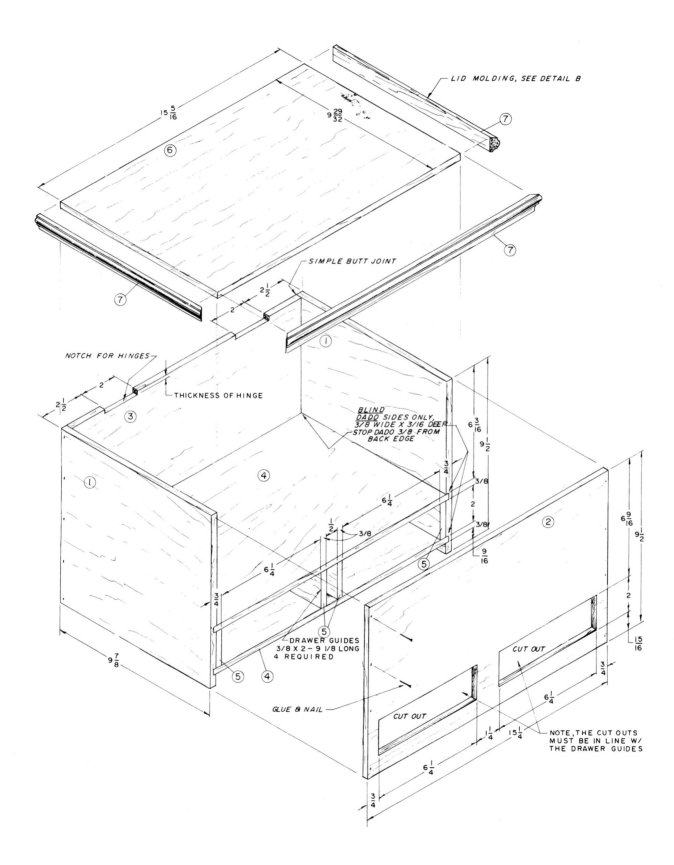

LID MOLDING, SEE DETAIL B

$15\frac{5}{16}$

$9\frac{29}{32}$

⑥

⑦

⑦

⑦

SIMPLE BUTT JOINT

$2\frac{1}{2}$

2

①

NOTCH FOR HINGES

2

$2\frac{1}{2}$

THICKNESS OF HINGE

③

BLIND
DADO SIDES ONLY,
3/8 WIDE X 3/16 DEEP
STOP DADO 3/8 FROM
BACK EDGE

$6\frac{3}{16}$

$9\frac{1}{2}$

$\frac{3}{4}$

3/8

①

④

$6\frac{1}{4}$

2

3/8

②

$6\frac{9}{16}$

$9\frac{1}{2}$

$\frac{1}{2}$

3/8

$\frac{9}{16}$

⑤

$6\frac{1}{4}$

$\frac{3}{4}$

2

$\frac{15}{16}$

⑤

DRAWER GUIDES
3/8 X 2 - 9 1/8 LONG
4 REQUIRED

CUT OUT

$\frac{3}{4}$

⑤

④

$6\frac{1}{4}$

$9\frac{7}{8}$

GLUE & NAIL

CUT OUT

$1\frac{1}{4}$

$15\frac{1}{4}$

NOTE, THE CUT OUTS
MUST BE IN LINE W/
THE DRAWER GUIDES

$6\frac{1}{4}$

$\frac{3}{4}$

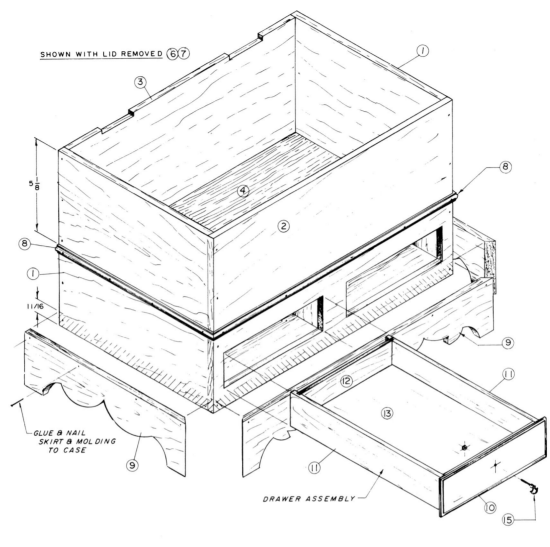

SHOWN WITH LID REMOVED ⑥⑦

$5\frac{1}{8}$

11/16

GLUE & NAIL
SKIRT & MOLDING
TO CASE

DRAWER ASSEMBLY

EXPLODED VIEW

false bottom above the drawers and a second bottom below the drawers. Cut stopped dadoes for each in the sides. These dadoes end ⅜ inch from the back surface.

3. Assemble the case. The case is put together with simple butt joints. Dry-assemble the sides, the back, and both bottoms, as shown in the exploded view. Cut the four drawer guides (part 5) to fit. Note the grain direction. Glue and nail the pieces together.

Make a cutout in the front piece to line up with the openings in the chest. Glue and nail the front panel in place. Sand all surfaces.

4. Attach the lid. The lid (part 6) should be ¹/₃₂ inch longer and wider than the case. Cut it to size based on the actual chest. Notch the back for the hinges (part 14) and temporarily attach them to the lid and case. Check to see that the lid fits well. Check for proper fit again, and then remove all the hardware until after you have applied a finish.

5. Build the drawers. Measure the drawer openings. Actual sizes often vary. Make sure the drawer components (parts 10, 11, 12, and 13) in the Materials List will work. Adjust the sizes as necessary.

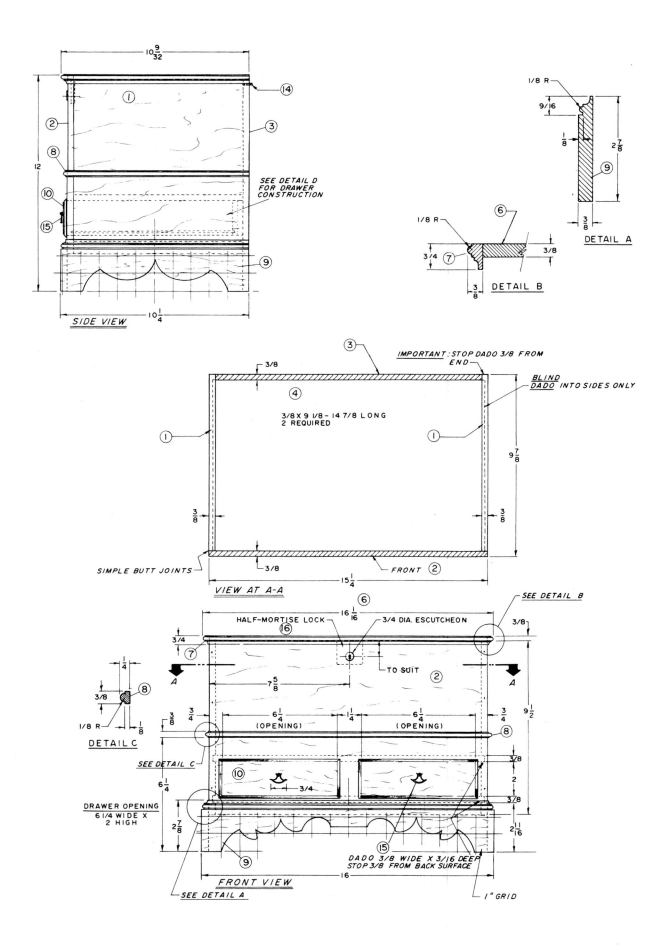

SIDE VIEW

DETAIL A

DETAIL B

DETAIL C

VIEW AT A-A

FRONT VIEW

SEE DETAIL D
FOR DRAWER
CONSTRUCTION

IMPORTANT: STOP DADO 3/8 FROM END

BLIND DADO INTO SIDES ONLY

3/8 X 9 1/8 - 14 7/8 LONG
2 REQUIRED

SIMPLE BUTT JOINTS

FRONT

HALF-MORTISE LOCK

3/4 DIA. ESCUTCHEON

TO SUIT

SEE DETAIL B

(OPENING)

(OPENING)

SEE DETAIL C

DRAWER OPENING
6 1/4 WIDE X
2 HIGH

DADO 3/8 WIDE X 3/16 DEEP
STOP 3/8 FROM BACK SURFACE

SEE DETAIL A

1" GRID

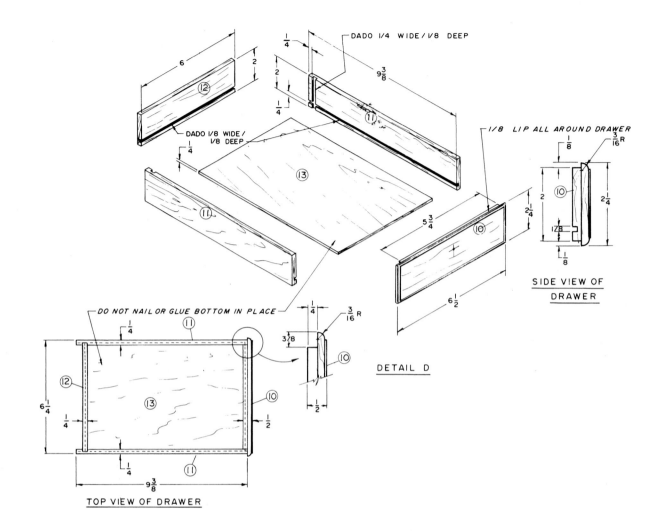

DADO 1/4 WIDE/ 1/8 DEEP

1/8 LIP ALL AROUND DRAWER

DADO 1/8 WIDE/ 1/8 DEEP

SIDE VIEW OF DRAWER

DO NOT NAIL OR GLUE BOTTOM IN PLACE

DETAIL D

TOP VIEW OF DRAWER

Rout or shape a $^3/_{16}$-inch radius on all four sides of each drawer front, as shown in detail D. Rabbet the drawer front, as shown. Look at both the top and side view of the drawers. The rabbets on the top and bottom are different.

Cut dadoes in the sides to accept the back.

Cut grooves in all the parts to receive the drawer bottoms. Dry-assemble the drawer, keeping everything square, and glue and nail it together if you're satisfied with the fit.

Drill for the drawer pulls (part 15) and add them.

6. Attach the skirt and moldings. Shape or rout the moldings and the skirts (parts 7, 8, and 9) to the profile shown in details A, B, and C. Make each an inch or so longer than necessary, and then miter and trim them to fit the chest. Glue and nail each to the chest. To locate the center molding, measure 5$^1/_8$ inches down from the top of the case.

7. Finish the chest. You can try your hand at grain-painting if you want to be true to the original chest, or simply stain and varnish or paint the piece. Finally, add the hinges.

Country Toolbox with Drawer

If your toolbox is like mine, all the small tools you need are always lost in the bottom of the box. I usually have to take out two-thirds of the larger tools to find the smaller one I really need. This toolbox solves that problem. Small tools go in the drawer. I wish I could take the credit for this great idea, but I can't. This is a copy of an old toolbox I saw in an antique shop in southern Maine.

1. Cut all of the pieces to overall size.

2. The center handle will have to be laid out on a 1-inch grid. Lay out the pattern, and transfer it to the wood. Cut out and round the handle area, as shown.

3. Locate and cut the ¾-inch-wide by ¼-inch-deep dadoes in the ends (parts 2 and 3), as shown.

   Note: There will be a small hole in the bottom surface of the dadoes after parts 2, 3, and 4 are assembled. This could be filled or simply left open. It will be seen after assembly.

4. Assemble parts 2, 3, 4, and 5. Add the two sides (part 1) and bottom (part 6). Since this is a toolbox and will get a lot of hard use, I suggest that you glue and nail it together.

5. Make the drawer assembly to fit the opening, as shown. Add the pull, part 12.

6. This project can be either painted, as was the original, or stained.

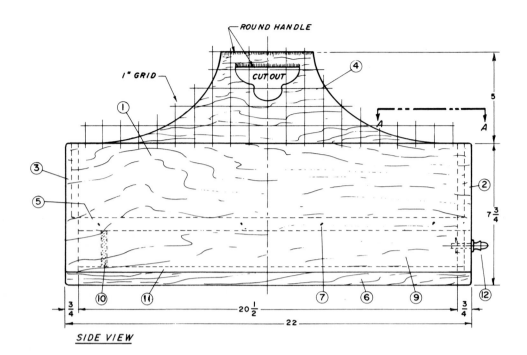

SIDE VIEW

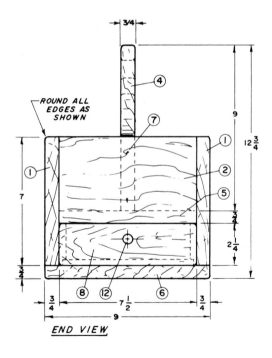

ROUND ALL
EDGES AS
SHOWN

END VIEW

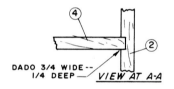

DADO 3/4 WIDE --
1/4 DEEP

VIEW AT A-A

MATERIALS LIST

NO.	NAME	SIZE	REQ'D.
1	SIDE	3/4 x 7 - 22 LONG	1
2	END	3/4 x 4 3/4 - 7 1/2 LONG	1
3	END	3/4 x 7 - 7 1/2 LONG	1
4	CENTER /HANDLE	3/4 x 9 - 21 LONG	1
5	DIVIDER	3/4 x 7 1/2 - 20 1/2 LONG	1
6	BOTTOM	3/4 x 9 - 22 LONG	1
7	NAIL	6d	26
8	FRONT	3/4 x 2 1/4 - 7 1/2 LONG	1
9	SIDE	1/4 x 2 1/4 - 20 7/8 LONG	2
10	BACK	1/4 x 2 - 7 LONG	1
11	BOTTOM	1/4 x 7 - 20 7/8 LONG	1
12	PULL	5/8 DIA.	1

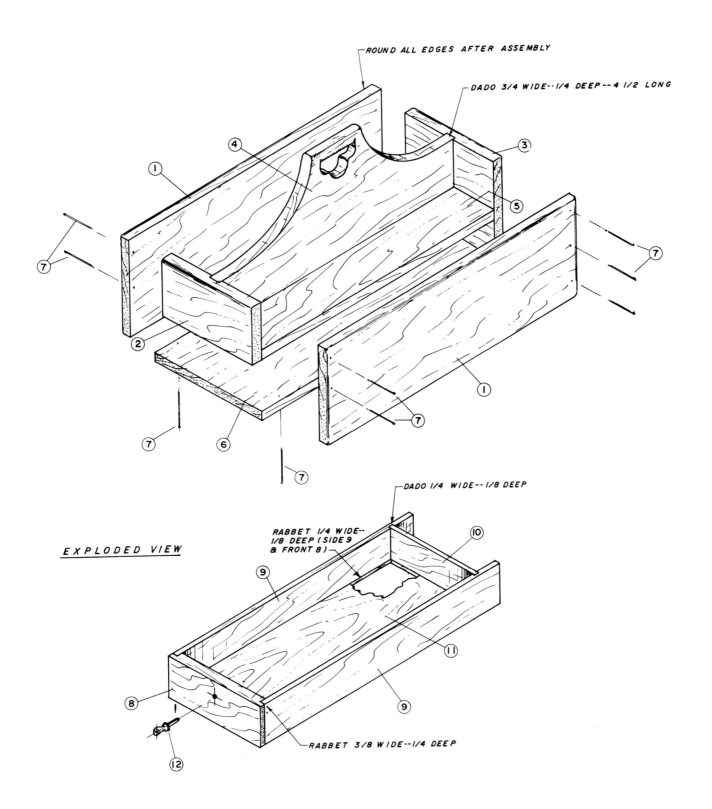

ROUND ALL EDGES AFTER ASSEMBLY

DADO 3/4 WIDE--1/4 DEEP--4 1/2 LONG

EXPLODED VIEW

DADO 1/4 WIDE--1/8 DEEP

RABBET 1/4 WIDE--
1/8 DEEP (SIDE 9
& FRONT 8)

RABBET 3/8 WIDE--1/4 DEEP

Small Child's Blanket Chest

Six-board blanket chests were one of the things the Pilgrims brought to this country from Europe. They were, in effect, their luggage. These wonderful chests came in all shapes and sizes. Most simple ones were painted. Today, if and when we can find an original, it usually has two or three coats of paint on it. Note the wonderful snipe hinges. A very similar snipe can be made from four large cotter pins.

1. Cut all pieces to overall size. If you want a real old look, hand-plane the front and back surfaces slightly to get a wavy effect.

2. Glue and clamp wood for the 13 inch-wide front and back boards (part 2).

3. Lay out and cut the ends (part 1), following the given dimensions. Don't forget to make a notch for the front and back boards.

4. Glue and nail the two ends (part 1) to the front/back (part 2) and bottom (part 3). Check that everything is square. Don't try to hide the nails; most original six-board chests were somewhat crude, and the nails did show.

MATERIALS LIST

NO.	NAME	SIZE	REQ'D.
1	END BOARD	3/4 x 11 – 17¼ LONG	2
2	FRONT/BACK BOARD	3/4 x 13 – 22 LONG	2
3	BOTTOM BOARD	3/4 x 9½ – 20½ LONG	1
4	LID	3/4 x 11½ – 22⅝ LONG	1
5	BATTEN BOARD	3/4 x 1 – 11¼ LONG	2
6	SNIPE HINGE	COTTER PIN – 1¾ LONG	2 PR.
7	SQUARE-CUT NAIL	8 d	42

5. Nail, but do not glue, the batten board (part 5) to the lid (part 4). This allows for expansion of the lid. Place them about 1/16 inch away from the sides of the chest.

6. Using a drill, drill holes at about 45° as shown in the drawing at View at A-A, page 418. Assemble two cotter pins, and place them into the holes, one into the lid and the other into the back board. Temporarily

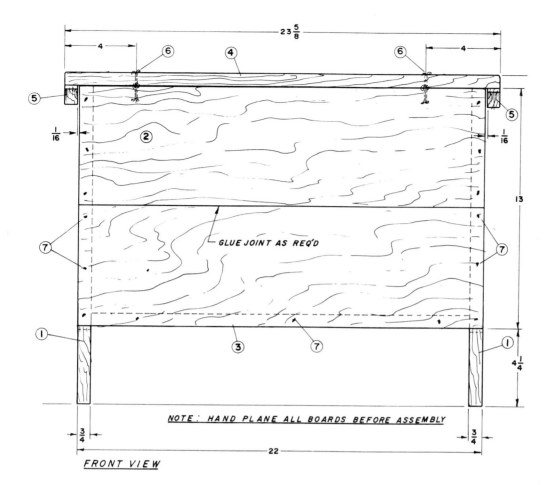

FRONT VIEW

NOTE: HAND PLANE ALL BOARDS BEFORE ASSEMBLY

GLUE JOINT AS REQ'D

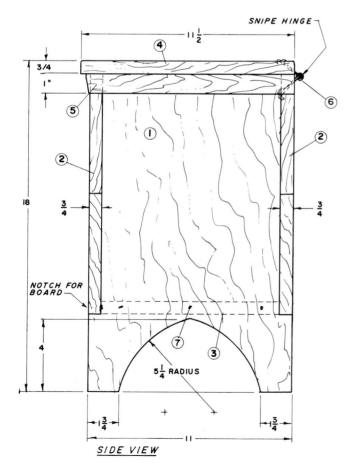

SIDE VIEW

drive them in a little deeper than you think you need, and then with a pair of needle-nose pliers, loop the tips of the cotter pins around and down into the wood. Hammer them down into the wood. This will make a slightly loose fit, but it will look very original. If you don't like snipe hinges, a regular pair of brass butt hinges can be used.

7. Sand all over. Since you want this to look old, round edges where you feel wear would have occurred.

8. Paint or stain to suit. As we like an old-looking blanket chest, we distressed ours and painted it two different colors, one on top of the other. Sand down through the top-coat here and there to show the first color. If you really want it to look old, use a crackle coat, and a top-coat of a black wash.

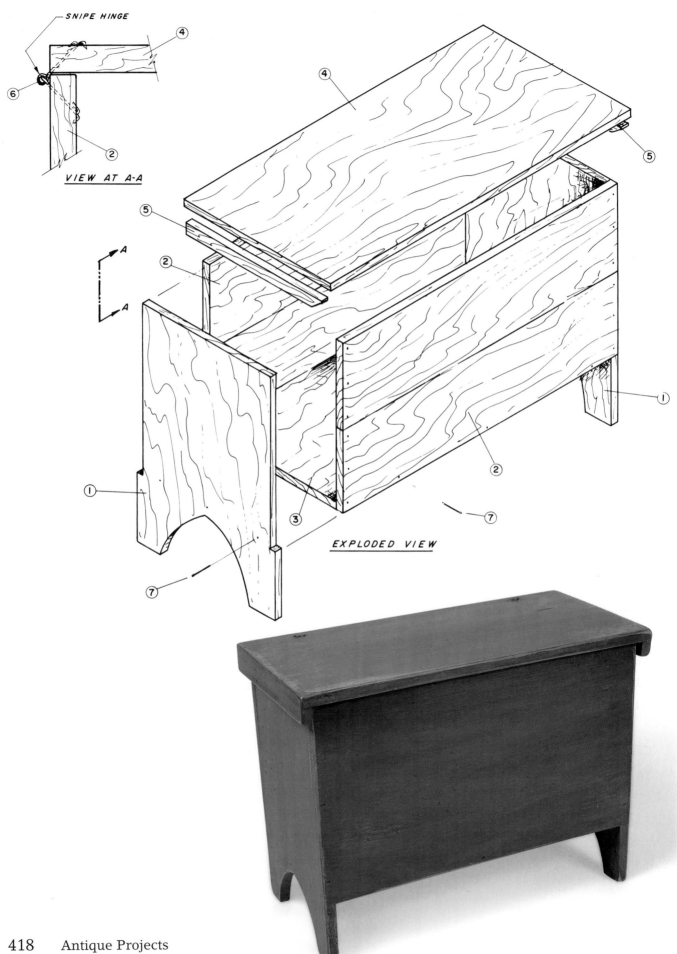

SNIPE HINGE

④

⑥

②

VIEW AT A-A

④

⑤

⑤

②

A

A

①

③

①

②

⑦

EXPLODED VIEW

⑦

Country Bench

This bench is really a plain Jane, but in being so plain, it has tremendous character. Some genuine antique benches, especially Shaker ones, are quite sought after and quite valuable. I hadn't had mine finished four days, and someone wanted to buy it. This is a great project for crackle paint or distressing with at least two layers of color.

1. Study the plans carefully. Note how each part is to be shaped. As you study the plans, try to visualize how you will make each part and how the project will be assembled. Note which parts you will put together first, second, and so on, exactly how you will put it together.

2. Carefully cut all of the parts to size according to the Materials List. Take care to cut all parts to exact size and exactly 90° square. Stop and recheck all dimensions before going on.

   Lightly sand all surfaces and edges with medium sandpaper to remove all tool marks. Take care to keep all edges square and sharp.

3. After all of the pieces have been carefully made, dry-fit the parts; that is, put the complete project together without glue or nails to check for accuracy and good-fitting joints. If anything needs refitting, now is the time to correct it.

MATERIALS LIST			
NO.	NAME	SIZE	REQ'D.
1	END	¾ x 11½ – 17¼ LONG	2
2	SKIRT	¾ x 4¼ – 42 LONG	2
3	INNER BRACE	¾ x 4¼ – 32 LONG	2
4	NAIL – SQ. CUT	1½ LONG	24
5	TOP	¾ x 13¼ – 42 LONG	1

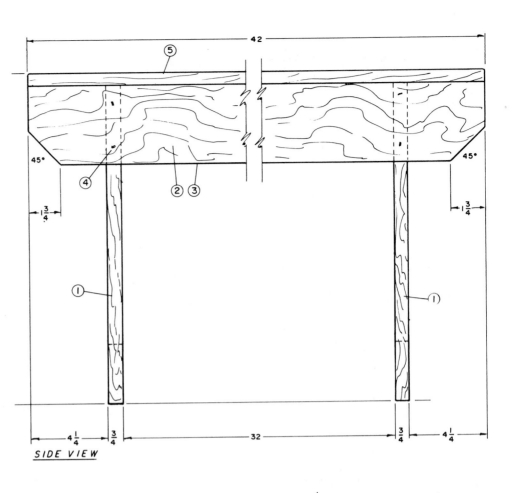

SIDE VIEW

4. Once all of the parts fit together correctly, assemble the project, keeping everything square as you go. Check that all fits are tight.

5. Finish to suit, following the general finishing instructions in the introduction.

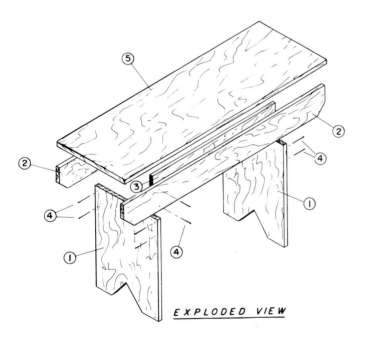

EXPLODED VIEW

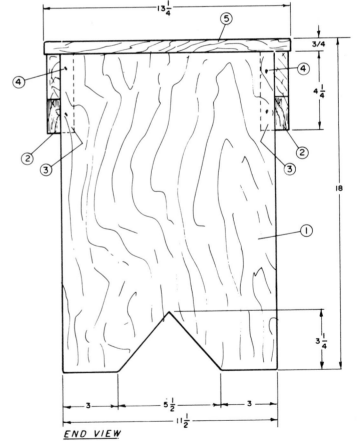

END VIEW

Formal Pipe Box

In the early days of this country, before the Surgeon General's warnings about tobacco, pipe smoking was a popular custom. The pipe box served as a place to store both tobacco and the fragile, long-stemmed clay pipes that were the fashion. Pipe boxes flourished from 1745 until late in the century, but few remain today. Chances are you'll have to go to a museum to see one. It seems that no two pipe boxes were made from the same pattern. They ranged from stocky, crude designs to delicately built containers. Most have an open top compartment for the pipes and a small tobacco drawer below. Cherry, maple, mahogany, and walnut were the most commonly used woods, with an occasional box made out of pine. This project is modeled after a green, painted-pine pipe box made in eastern Massachusetts around 1750. The original can be seen at the Strawberry Banke Museum in Portsmouth, New Hampshire.

Today, a pipe box can be used to store all kinds of small items.

1. Select the stock, and cut the parts. The pipe box is made from five different stock thicknesses. If you can't plane or re-saw the boards yourself, find a mill that can do the work for you. To simplify matters, you can substitute ⅛-inch stock for the 11/32-inch pieces called for here.

Cut the parts to the sizes given in the Materials List.

2. Make a paper pattern, and lay out the curves. Draw a grid with ½-inch squares, and enlarge the curves in the drawing onto it. Transfer the enlarged curves to the wood. Some of the tighter curves will be drilled out rather than cut, so mark the drill centers on the stock, too.

3. Cut the parts to shape. Place one side (part 2) on top of the other, and tape them together. Cut and sand them as a unit so that they will be identical.

Cut the back and front (parts 1 and 3) to shape.

4. Chip-carve the back. The original pipe box has a flower, chip-carved into the back. If you have never tried chip-carving, this is a good beginner's project. If you don't feel like carving the flower, you could simply paint it, or leave it out altogether.

5. Assemble the box. Dry-assemble the parts to check that everything will go together correctly. If necessary, make any adjustments. Glue and nail the sides to the back with ⅞-inch square-cut brads. Glue and nail the front in place, and make sure the box is square. Insert the divider (part 4), and glue it to the front and back. Sand the box, leaving the edges square.

NO.	NAME	SIZE	REQ'D.
	MATERIALS LIST		
1	BACK	11/32 x 6½ – 16⅝ LONG	1
2	SIDE	11/32 x 4 1/32 – 11⅛ LONG	2
3	FRONT	11/32 x 6½ – 6¼ LONG	1
4	DIVIDER	11/32 x 3 11/16 – 5 13/16 LONG	1
5	BOTTOM	⅜ x 4⅝ – 6⅞ LONG	1
6	DRAWER FRONT	9/16 x 2¾ – 6⅛ LONG	1
7	DRAWER SIDE	¼ x 2¾ – 3¾ LONG	2
8	DRAWER BACK	¼ x 2⅜ – 5 11/16 LONG	1
9	DRAWER BOTTOM	3/16 x 3¾ – 5 7/16 LONG	1
10	DRAWER PULL	½ DIA. - 1½ LONG	1
11	PIN	SQ. CUT NAIL TO FIT	1
12	BRAD – SQ. CUT	⅞ LONG	21
13	SCREW - EYE		2

Position the bottom (part 5), and nail it to the box. Note that the scrollwork on the front has a slightly rounded front edge. Use a rasp or sandpaper to get this effect.

6. Make the drawer. The original drawer is dovetailed together. If the prospect of making dovetails intimidates you, build the drawer with rabbet joints instead. Rabbeted drawers weren't at all uncommon on early pipe boxes, so you won't be compromising the authenticity of the project.

Cut the drawer parts to fit the opening.

The heights specified for the drawer sides (part 7) are the same as the height of the drawer opening. Since this won't allow for expansion of the drawer in humid weather, make the drawer height 1/32 inch to 1/16 inch less than the actual drawer opening. The drawer back (part 8) is even narrower so that you can slide the bottom into the completed drawer

Rout the drawer front to the profile shown, with a ¼-inch-radius round-over bit and bearing. The drawer

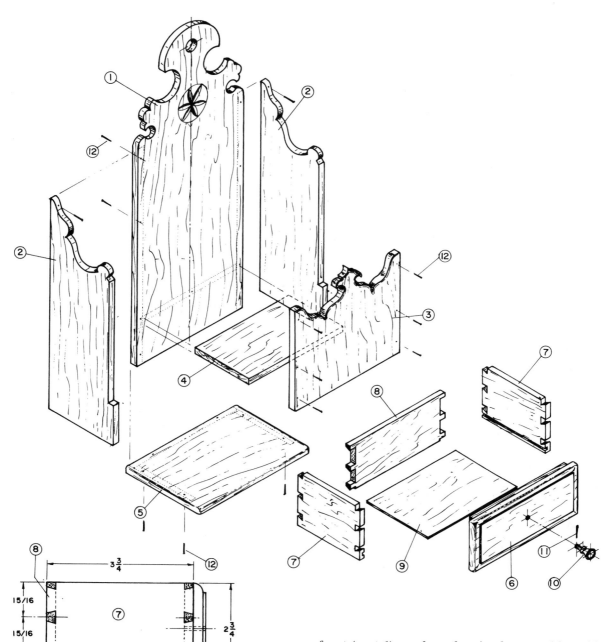

SIDE VIEW DETAIL OF DRAWER DOVETAIL

front (part 6) overlaps the pipe box on either side and has rabbets cut in it to make this possible. Rout a $^3/_{16}$ x $^1/_4$-inch-deep rabbet along the inside left- and right-drawer front edges.

Cut dovetails in the drawer, as shown.

Cut $^3/_{16}$ x $^1/_8$-inch-deep grooves in the drawer front and sides to house the drawer bottom.

Dry-assemble the drawer, starting with the front. Make adjustments as necessary; then glue it up. Slide the bottom in place after assembly. The grain of the bottom runs parallel to the drawer front so that the bottom can expand and contract without pushing against the drawer sides. You can buy a drawer pull (part 10) or turn one, complete with a tenon. Drill a hole for the tenon in the drawer front, and pin it with a square-cut nail (part 11), as shown in the side view of the pipe box.

7. Apply finish. Sand the entire pipe box with very fine sandpaper. Apply a single coat of paint (I used a bayberry kind of green.) and allow it to dry. To suggest the effects of aging, rub the piece all over with 0000 steel wool, wearing away at the edges in particular Apply a coat of paste wax.

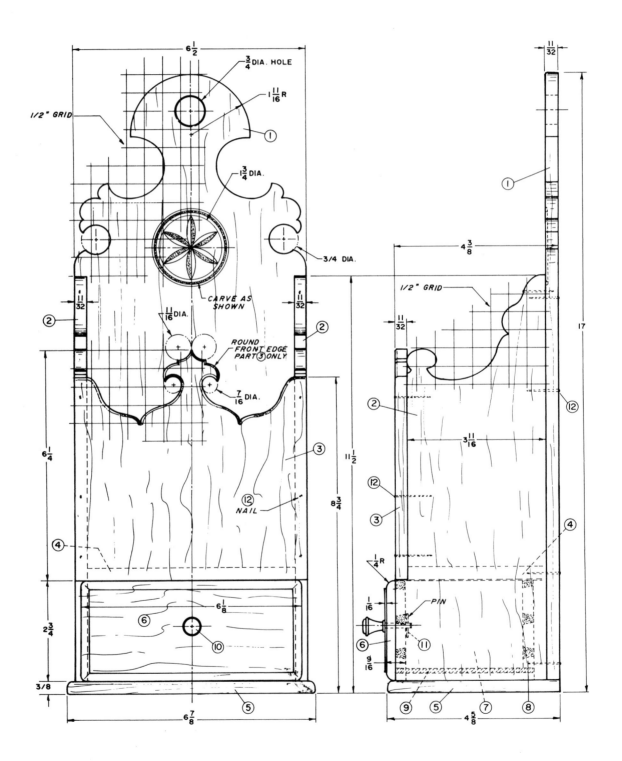

Country Pipe Box

This pipe box makes a great place to store candles, and matches can be stored in the drawer. Or, it could be an outgoing mailbox instead, with stamps in the drawer. You may have some other ideas, such as using it as an attractive place for displaying dried flowers.

1. Make a ½-inch grid on a sheet of heavy paper, and lay out the top portions of the back, front, and sides. Cut all wood to overall size, and then transfer the patterns to the back, front, and side pieces. Cut all of these pieces to exact size following the patterns. Dry-fit all of the parts. Trim as necessary. Glue and nail all pieces together, making sure that all parts are square.

2. The drawer is a simple design, easy to make. Make up the pieces, as shown in the exploded view, to fit the opening of the pipe box. Make the drawer front slightly larger so that it can be trimmed to fit the pipe box exactly. The drawer pull can be turned on a lathe to match the drawing, or a 7/16-inch-diameter commercially made one can be used.

3. Your pipe box should be stained as you desire. If you'd rather not use it for candles or mail, someone could take up pipe smoking! On second thought, why not take up drying flowers; it's healthier!

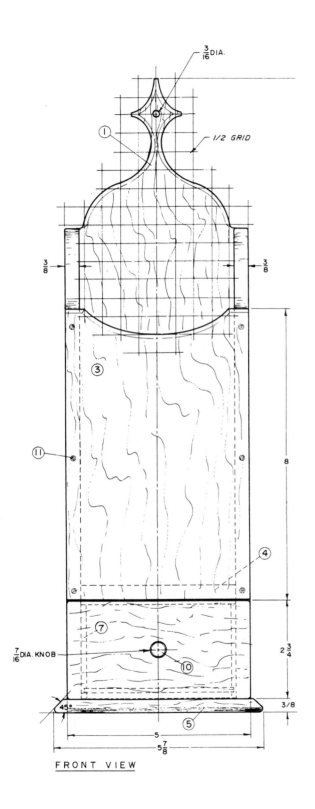

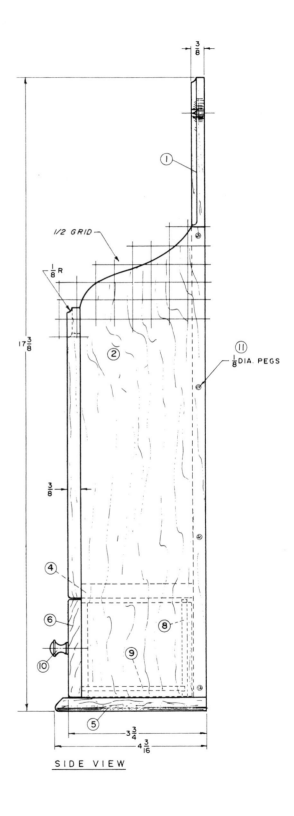

$\frac{3}{16}$DIA.

$\frac{3}{8}$

① ① ①

1/2 GRID

1/2 GRID

$\frac{3}{8}$ $\frac{3}{8}$

$\frac{1}{8}$ R

$\frac{3}{8}$

③

②

8

17$\frac{3}{8}$

⑪   ①   ⑪
$\frac{1}{8}$DIA. PEGS

④

④

⑦

⑥   ⑧

$\frac{7}{16}$DIA. KNOB   ⑩

2$\frac{3}{4}$

⑩   ⑨

45°   3/8

⑤   ⑤

5   3$\frac{3}{4}$

5$\frac{7}{8}$ 4$\frac{3}{16}$

FRONT VIEW   SIDE VIEW

MATERIALS LIST

NO.	NAME	SIZE	REQ'D.
1	BACK BOARD	$\frac{3}{8}$ x $4\frac{1}{4}$ – 17 LONG	1
2	SIDE	$\frac{3}{8}$ x $3\frac{3}{8}$ – $12\frac{7}{8}$ LONG	2
3	FRONT	$\frac{3}{8}$ x 5 – 8 LONG	1
4	DIVIDER	$\frac{3}{8}$ x 3 – $4\frac{1}{4}$ LONG	1
5	BOTTOM	$\frac{3}{8}$ x $4\frac{3}{16}$ – $5\frac{7}{8}$ LONG	1
6	DRAWER FRONT	$\frac{1}{2}$ x $2\frac{3}{4}$ – 5 LONG	1
7	DRAWER SIDE	$\frac{3}{16}$ x $2\frac{3}{4}$ – 3 LONG	2
8	DRAWER BACK	$\frac{3}{16}$ x $2\frac{3}{4}$ – $4\frac{1}{8}$ LONG	1
9	DRAWER BOTTOM	$\frac{1}{8}$ x $2\frac{3}{4}$ – $4\frac{1}{8}$ LONG	1
10	PULL (WOOD)	$\frac{7}{16}$ DIA.	1
11	PEG	$\frac{1}{8}$ DIA. - $\frac{3}{4}$ LONG	18

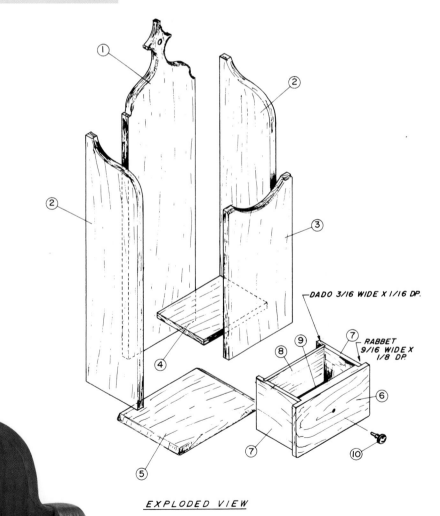

DADO 3/16 WIDE X 1/16 DP.

RABBET 9/16 WIDE X 1/8 DP.

EXPLODED VIEW

Pennsylvania Wall Cupboard

Here is one of the earliest designs in this book. The original is said to have been made around 1725, and it was found in Lancaster, Pennsylvania. The large iron-butterfly hinges and escutcheon plate shown here are true to the antique version.

1. Select the stock and cut the parts of the case. The original cupboard was made from butternut and painted. Cut parts 1 through 10 to the sizes given in the Materials List.

2. Make a paper pattern and cut the parts to shape. Draw a grid with 1-inch squares, and enlarge the profile of the side panel onto it. Transfer the enlargement to the stock. To ensure that both sides (part 2) are identical, tack them together with finishing nails, and cut them out at the same time. Separate them and cut the dadoes and rabbets in the sides, as shown.

Make a pattern for the bottom skirt (part 10), and cut out the skirt. Cut the notch for the drawer opening in the two front boards (part 5), taking care to make both parts identical and all cuts exactly 90°.

3. Assemble the case. Glue and nail the shelves (parts 3 and 4) to the side panels. Nail the back (part 1) and the back support (part 6) in place, keeping everything square.

When the glue dries, nail the bottom skirt and top board (part 9) in place.

4. Make and install the trim. Rout or shape the top moldings (parts 12 and 14) to the profile shown in the drawing. Miter and cut the molding to fit the cabinet. Glue the molding to the front support (part 7), but simply nail the molding to the sides.

5. Cut the door and install the lock. Cut the door (part 11) to fit the opening. Cut and attach the door pull (part 13). The door pull is beveled approximately 15° on the ends and two sides. It overlaps the edge of the door ⅛ inch, as shown, to act as a dust stop.

Mortise the lock (part 22) into the back of the door. Make sure the lock you buy allows a full 1 inch between the door edge and the keyhole; you need the room to install the door pull and escutcheon.

Drill a hole for the door lock in the back of the door, and square off the edges with a chisel to match your lock. Attach the lock and make sure it works.

6. Cut the drawer parts. To work properly, a drawer must be slightly smaller than the opening provided for it in the case. The best way to do it on this drawer is to cut the dadoes and rabbets in the drawer sides first. Put the sides in place in the cabinet, and cut the front and back to give you the proper fit.

This drawer has a raised-panel bottom,

a practice that was common in the eighteenth and early nineteenth centuries. Some drawers were designed so the panel could slip in from the back. Not this one. The panel is held by grooves in the front, back, and both sides.

Cut the grooves to accept the drawer bottom (part 18). On the table saw, cut a raised panel to fit in the grooves. If you don't feel like making a raised panel, you can simply rabbet the edges to create the properly sized lip.

Dry-fit the drawer together. The bottom should fit snugly in the groove. The grooves should allow 1/8

MATERIALS LIST

NO.	NAME	SIZE	REQ'D.
1	BACKBOARD	½ x 14¾ – 25¼ LONG	1
2	SIDE PANEL	¾ x 7¼ – 25¼ LONG	2
3	SHELF	½ x 7¼ – 14¾ LONG	2
4	BOTTOM SHELF	½ x 3½ – 14¾ LONG	1
5	FRONT BOARD	¾ x 3 – 20½ LONG	1
6	BACK SUPPORT	¾ x 1½ – 14 LONG	1
7	FRONT SUPPORT	¾ x 2¼ – 14 LONG	1
8	TRIM	¾ x 2 – 9½ LONG	1
9	TOP BOARD	¾ x 9¾ – 19 LONG	1
10	BOTTOM SKIRT	¾ x 2¼ – 14¾ LONG	1
11	DOOR	¾ x 9½ – 11½ LONG	1
12	TOP MOLDING	¾ x 1½ – 40 LONG	1
13	DOOR PULL	½ x ¾ – 11½ LONG	1
14	BOTTOM MOLDING	½ x 15½ LONG	1
15	DRAWER FACE	¾ x 4¾ – 14¾ LONG	1
16	DRAWER – FRONT/BACK	½ x 4¼ – 13½ LONG	1 EA.
17	DRAWER SIDE	½ x 4¼ – 6¾ LONG	2
18	DRAWER BOTTOM	⅜ x 6¼ – 13½ LONG	1
19	DRAWER PULL	1 DIA. - 2⁷⁄₁₆ LONG	1
20	ESCUTCHEON		1
21	BUTTERFLY HINGE		2
22	HALF-MORTISE LOCK		1
23	NAIL – SQ. CUT	1½ LONG	30
24	BRAD	⅞ LONG	1

inch for the bottom to expand and contract across the grain. Make any necessary adjustments.

7. Assemble the drawer. Glue and nail the face, front, back, and sides (parts 15, 16, 17, and 18) together with the bottom in place. Don't get any glue on the bottom or in the grooves for the bottom.

Screw or nail the drawer face on the drawer. Turn the drawer pull (part 19) on a lathe to a full 1-inch diameter; then use sandpaper to partially flatten the four sides, as shown in the detail. Pin the knob in place with either a 7/8-inch square-cut headless brad or a small wooden peg.

GLUE JOINTS
RABBET 1/2 WIDE X 3/8 DEEP

NOTCH ⑤ FOR DRAWER

NOTE:
DRAWER BOTTOM
SURFACE IS
CHAMFERED
TO FIT 1/4 WIDE
DADO ⑱

DADO 1/2 WIDE X 1/4 DEEP

RABBET 1/2 WIDE X 1/4 DEEP

HALF-
MORTISE
LOCK
㉒

DADO 1/2 WIDE X 3/8 DEEP

RABBET 1/2 WIDE X 3/8 DEEP

DADO PARTS ⑯ ⑰ 1/4 WIDE X
1/4 DEEP -- UP
1/4 FROM BOTTOM EDGE

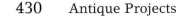

8. Finish the cupboard. You can stain and apply tung oil, or paint the piece to look like the original. To make mine look as old as possible, I painted it off-white, then added a second coat of a traditional shade of blue paint. After the paint dried thoroughly, I carefully sanded through the blue coat here and there to simulate years of use.

9. Hang the door. Because the door hangs on butterfly hinges (part 21) that are nailed in place, you mount the hinges for the first time after applying the finish. Butterfly hinges are nailed in place with cinched nails: The nail is driven all the way through and then bent over from the back.

Nail the escutcheon in place.

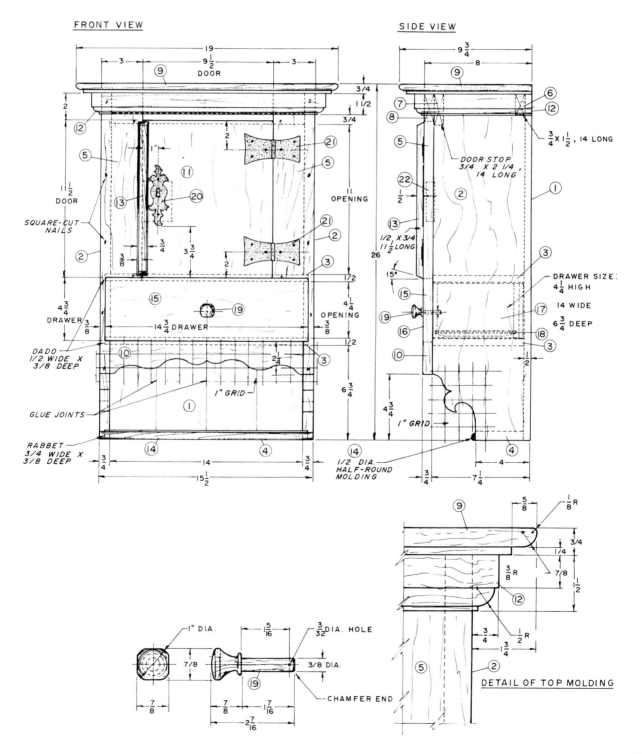

Side Table with Drawer

This design is a little fancier than most side tables, but the lines are so pleasing I couldn't resist it. The canted-drawer assembly is somewhat hard to make, but well worth the effort.

Study the plans carefully. Note how each part is to be shaped. As you study the plans, try to visualize how you will make each part and how the project will be assembled. Note which parts you will put together first, second, and so on, and exactly how you will put them together. The top, aprons, and front trim are irregular in shape and will have to be laid out on a 1-inch grid or laid out to make full-size patterns. Lay out the grids on heavy paper or cardboard, and transfer the shape of each piece to the appropriate grid, point by point. The top pattern can be simply laid out, using a compass and the given dimensions without using the grid.

The top will probably have to be glued up to make the 16-inch-wide piece. Try to match the grain pattern so that the joint will not show. My wife just bought me a biscuit joiner, so I thought I would use it to join the two pieces for the top. It worked great; I don't know how I ever got along without one. If you don't have a biscuit joiner, you might want to use dowels. Many times I have used simple butt joints for something like this; they seem to work okay for me. Sand the top so that it is very smooth.

1. Transfer full-size patterns to the wood, and carefully cut out the pieces. Check all dimensions for accuracy. Sand all over with fine-grit sandpaper, keeping all edges sharp.

Cut the tenons in the aprons and front trim (parts 2 and 3) according to the dimensions given on the plans, and parallel to the ends, as shown.

Carefully cut the remaining parts to size according to the Materials List. Take care to cut all parts to exact size and exactly square (90°). Stop and recheck all dimensions before going on.

Lightly sand all surfaces and edges with medium sandpaper to remove all tool marks. Take care to keep all edges square and sharp.

NO.	NAME	SIZE	REQ'D.
	MATERIALS LIST		
1	LEG	1¼ x 1¼ – 26½ LONG	4
2	APRON	¾ x 5 – 10 LONG	3
3	TRIM FRONT	¾ x 1¾ – 10 LONG	1
4	PIN	¼ DIA. – 1 LONG	14
5	DRAWER – GUIDE	¼ x ¾ – 8½ LONG	4
6	DRAWER – SUPPORT	¾ x ¾ – 9 LONG	2
7	DRAWER FRONT	¾ x 3¼ – 8½ LONG	1
8	DRAWER SIDE	⅜ x 3¼ – 9 LONG	2
9	DRAWER BACK	⅜ x 3¼ – 8¼ LONG	1
10	DRAWER BOTTOM	¼ x 8 1/16 – 8 1/16 LONG	1
11	DRAWER PULL	½ DIA. (BRASS)	1
12	TOP	¾ x 8 – 16 LONG	2
13	SCREW – FL. HD.	NO. 8 – 1¾ LONG	4

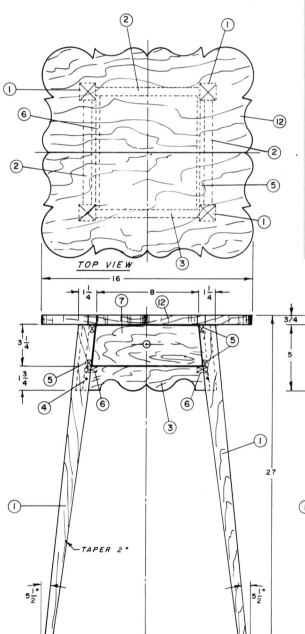

TOP VIEW

FRONT VIEW

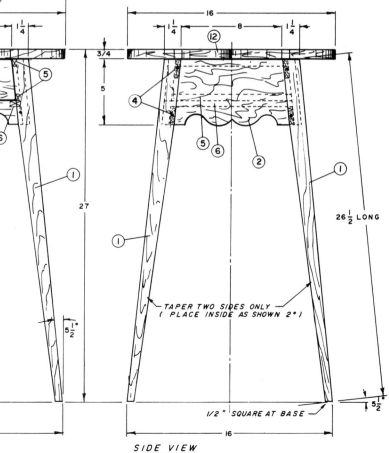

SIDE VIEW

2. I used a taper jig to cut the taper on the legs. If you do not have one, look up how to make a simple jig in a good cabinetmaking book.

Cut the taper for the legs after you locate and cut the ¼-inch-wide by 1¾-inch-long mortises for the aprons (part 2).

After the legs, aprons, and front trim (parts 1, 2, and 3)

have been carefully made, dry-fit the parts. If anything needs refitting, now is the time to correct it. Glue these pieces together using clamps, as needed.

3. After the glue sets, locate and drill ¼-inch-diameter holes, and add the pins (part 4). These pins are actually optional, which I learned by accidentally leaving them out.

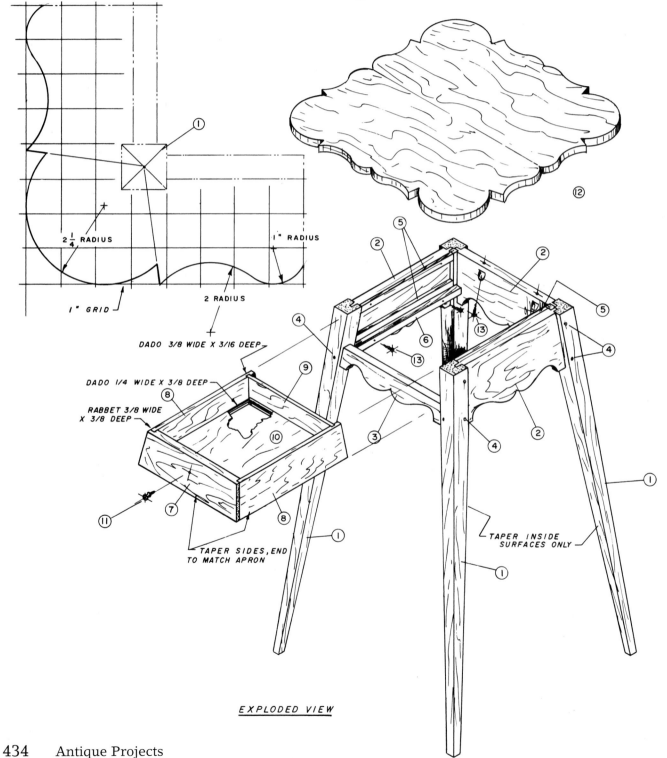

2 ¼ RADIUS

1" RADIUS

1" GRID

2 RADIUS

DADO 3/8 WIDE X 3/16 DEEP

DADO 1/4 WIDE X 3/8 DEEP

RABBET 3/8 WIDE X 3/8 DEEP

TAPER SIDES, END TO MATCH APRON

TAPER INSIDE SURFACES ONLY

EXPLODED VIEW

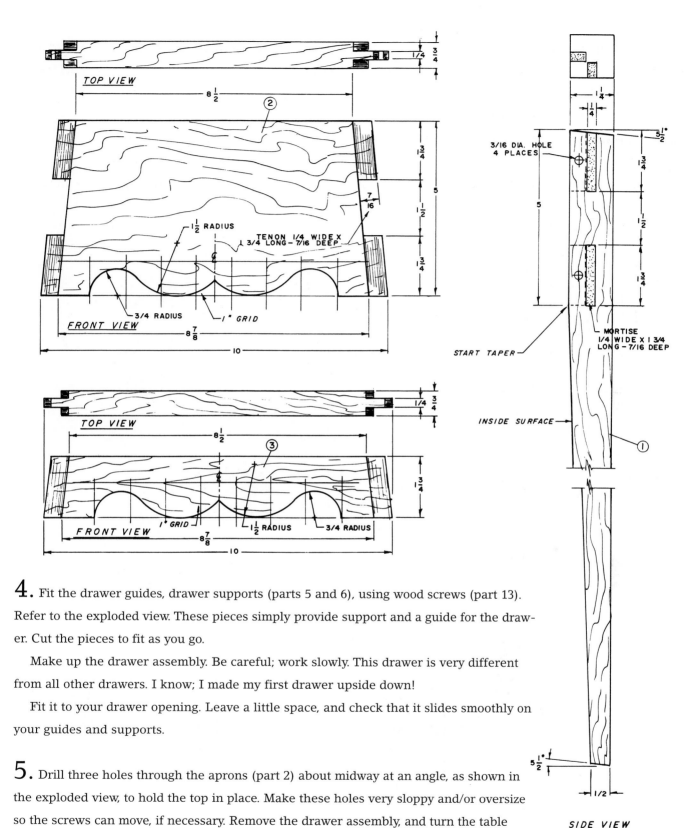

4. Fit the drawer guides, drawer supports (parts 5 and 6), using wood screws (part 13). Refer to the exploded view. These pieces simply provide support and a guide for the drawer. Cut the pieces to fit as you go.

Make up the drawer assembly. Be careful; work slowly. This drawer is very different from all other drawers. I know; I made my first drawer upside down!

Fit it to your drawer opening. Leave a little space, and check that it slides smoothly on your guides and supports.

5. Drill three holes through the aprons (part 2) about midway at an angle, as shown in the exploded view, to hold the top in place. Make these holes very sloppy and/or oversize so the screws can move, if necessary. Remove the drawer assembly, and turn the table upside down to put the three screws in place. Take care not to drill or screw through the top. Do not glue the top in place; let it float, as it will expand and contract.

6. Finish to suit, following the general finishing instructions given in the introduction.

Wall Shelf with Drawers

I first saw the wall shelf I based this one on years ago, before I started writing woodworking books. It was in the Shelburne Museum in Vermont. I really liked it and took a few notes and made a photograph of it. For years, I wanted to make a copy, but I didn't have enough information to correctly build it. While I was researching wall shelves that I had photographed and measured in the past, I came across the old photograph of this one. My interest in it was rekindled, and I went back to the Shelburne Museum to find and measure it. Luckily, it was still there, so here it is! We painted this copy a brick-red color. To make it look old and worn, we distressed it and sanded the edges slightly.

1. Study the plans carefully. Note how each part is to be shaped. As you study the plans, try to visualize how you will make each part, and how the project will be assembled. Note which parts you will put together first, second, and so on, exactly how you will put it together. Except for the drawers, it is rather easy to make. Note that you can use two, three, or four boards (part 9) for the back, according to the widths you have available, or as desired.

The sides (part 1) are irregular in shape and will have to be laid out on a 1-inch grid to make a full-size pattern; only one pattern is needed. Lay out the grid on heavy paper or cardboard, and transfer the shape of the piece to the grid, point by point.

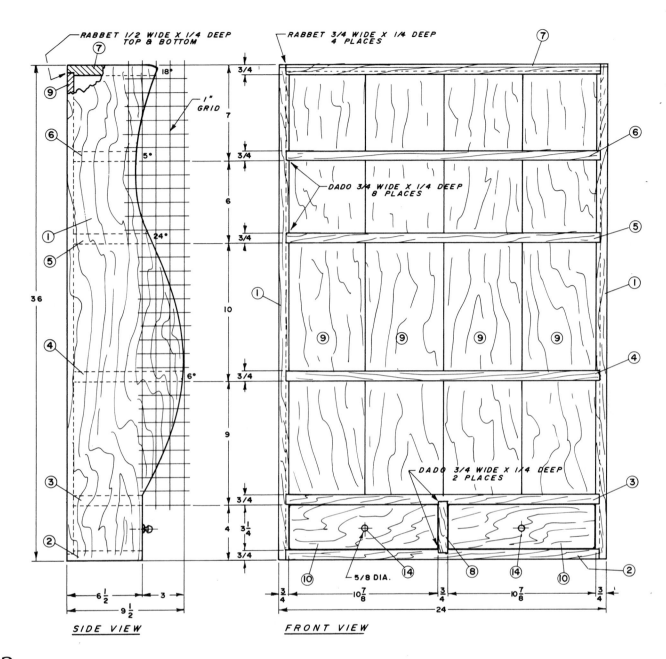

RABBET 1/2 WIDE X 1/4 DEEP
TOP & BOTTOM

RABBET 3/4 WIDE X 1/4 DEEP
4 PLACES

1" GRID

DADO 3/4 WIDE X 1/4 DEEP
8 PLACES

DADO 3/4 WIDE X 1/4 DEEP
2 PLACES

5/8 DIA.

SIDE VIEW

FRONT VIEW

2. Cut the two side boards to the given overall size, according to the Materials List, and carefully locate and make the three dado cuts and two rabbet cuts following the given dimensions. Cut the rabbet along the back edge as shown at this time. Be sure to make one right-hand and one left-hand side.

After the dadoes and rabbets have been cut, tack the two side pieces together; be sure to line up the dado cuts. Transfer the pattern to the wood, and carefully cut out the two sides at the same time. Sand the edges while the sides are still attached to each other. Check all dimensions for accuracy. Resand all over

with fine-grit sandpaper, keeping all edges sharp.

Carefully cut the remaining parts to size according to the materials list. Take care to cut all parts to exact size and exactly square (90°). Stop and recheck all dimensions before going on.

3. If you would like plate grooves in your shelves, now is the time to cut them into the top surface of the shelves. Although not present in the original, a groove ½ inch wide x ¼ inch deep, out 1½ inches from the back edge would make a suitable plate groove for each shelf.

Lightly sand all surfaces and edges with medium

sandpaper to remove all tool marks. Take care to keep all edges square and sharp.

4. After all of the pieces have been carefully made, dry-fit the parts, that is, put the complete project together without glue or nails to check for accuracy and good-fitting joints. If anything needs refitting, now is the time to correct it.

5. Once all of the parts fit together correctly, assemble the project, keeping everything square as you go. Check that all fits are tight.

Fit the drawers to the openings. Use the given dimensions as a guide as your drawer openings may vary slightly. The original drawers had dovetail joints; this one uses simple rabbet joints.

The drawer pulls (part 14) can be either purchased or turned on a lathe, according to the given dimensions for the pull.

6. Finish to suit, following the general finishing instructions in the introduction. The original was painted with two colors, as noted above. If you used a fine hardwood and hate to paint over it, I suggest staining the outside. This will accent the wood and grain pattern. But I would still paint the interior walls.

MATERIALS LIST			
NO.	NAME	SIZE	REQ'D.
1	SIDE	¾ x 9½ – 36 LONG	2
2	SHELF	¾ x 6½ – 23 LONG	1
3	SHELF	¾ x 6 – 23 LONG	1
4	SHELF	¾ x 9 – 23 LONG	1
5	SHELF	¾ x 6⅞ – 23 LONG	1
6	SHELF	¾ x 5⅝ – 23 LONG	1
7	TOP	¾ x 7½ – 23 LONG	1
8	DIVIDER	¾ x 6 – 3¾ LONG	1
9	BACK	½ x 5¾ – 35 LONG	4
10	DRAWER FRONT	½ x 3¼ – 10⅞ LONG	2
11	DRAWER SIDE	⅜ x 3¼ – 5¼ LONG	4
12	DRAWER BACK	⅜ x 3¼ – 10½ LONG	2
13	DRAWER BOTTOM	¼ x 5 – 10½ LONG	2
14	PULL	⅝ DIA. - 1⁹⁄₁₆ LONG	2
15	PIN	TO SUIT	2

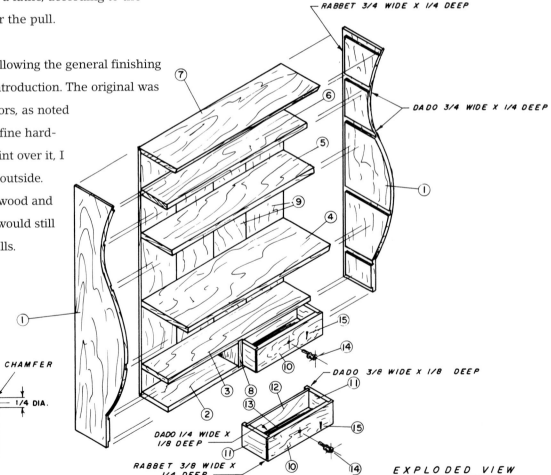

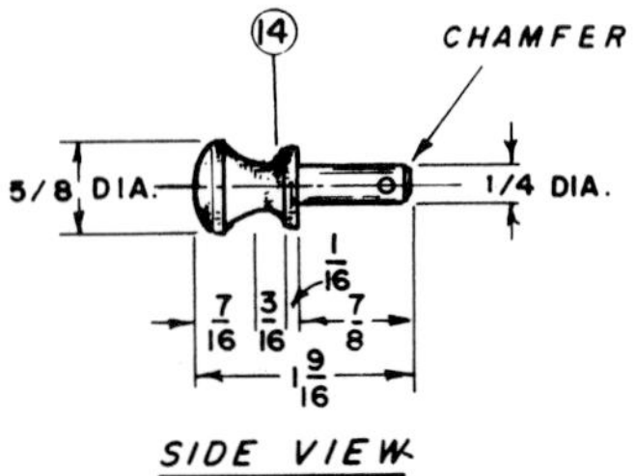

Half-Round Plant Stand

If you visit many antique shops, at least in New England, you will see a few half-round plant stands similar to this one, but most have signs on them: Not For Sale. The dealers use them to display things and do not want to sell them because they are hard to come by. When I realized this, I started making them to sell. They sell very fast here in southern New Hampshire. I can't understand why more people don't make them because they are easy to make and do not require much material.

1. Study the plans carefully. Note how each part is to be shaped. As you study the plans, try to visualize how you will make each part and how the project will be assembled. Note which parts you will put together first, second, and so on, exactly how you

MATERIALS LIST

NO.	NAME	SIZE	REQ'D.
1	LEG	¾ x 7½ – 38¼ LONG	3
2	BOTTOM SHELF		
3	CENTER SHELF	¾ x 18 – 36 LONG	1
4	TOP SHELF		
5	SCREW – FL. HD.	NO. 8 – 1¾ LONG	20

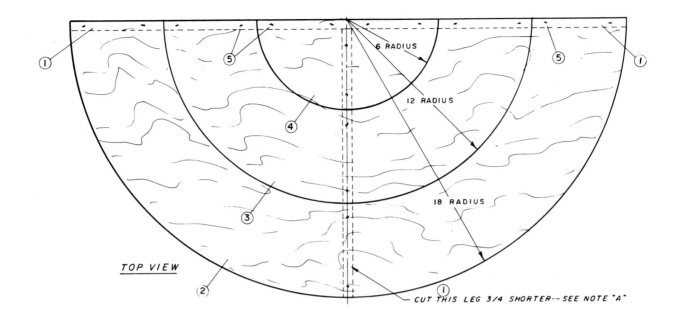

TOP VIEW

6 RADIUS

12 RADIUS

18 RADIUS

① CUT THIS LEG 3/4 SHORTER--SEE NOTE "A"

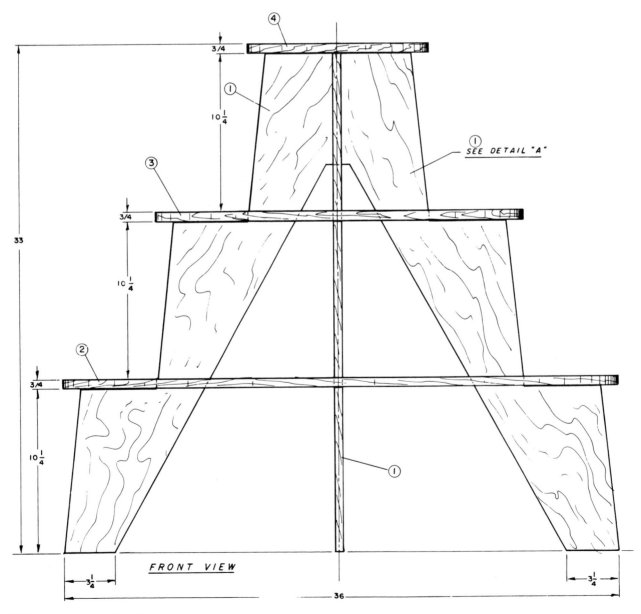

① SEE DETAIL "A"

3/4

10 $\frac{1}{4}$

33

10 $\frac{1}{4}$

10 $\frac{1}{4}$

3 $\frac{1}{4}$

FRONT VIEW

3 $\frac{1}{4}$

36

will put it together. On this project, it is best if you have a helper because holding the three legs and trying to glue and nail the thing is a little awkward alone.

2. You will have to glue up a board ¾ x 18 x 36 inches to make the three shelves (parts 2, 3, and 4). Swing a 6-, 12-, and 18-inch radius with a compass or a string and pencil from the center of the board, and carefully cut out on the lines.

3. Carefully lay out and cut the legs according to the given dimensions. I tacked the three boards together and cut them all at once. This way they are the same exact size and shape. Important: Be sure to keep the 90° angle as noted on the plans. Stop and recheck all dimensions before going on.

4. Lightly sand all surfaces and edges with medium sandpaper to remove all tool marks. Take care to keep all edges square and sharp.

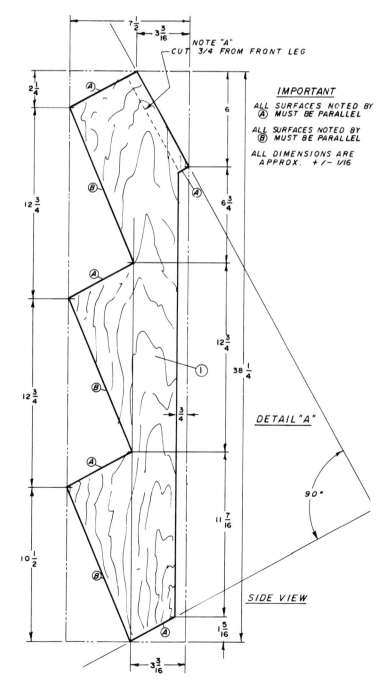

IMPORTANT

ALL SURFACES NOTED BY Ⓐ MUST BE PARALLEL

ALL SURFACES NOTED BY Ⓑ MUST BE PARALLEL

ALL DIMENSIONS ARE APPROX. +/- 1/16

NOTE "A"
CUT 3/4 FROM FRONT LEG

DETAIL "A"

SIDE VIEW

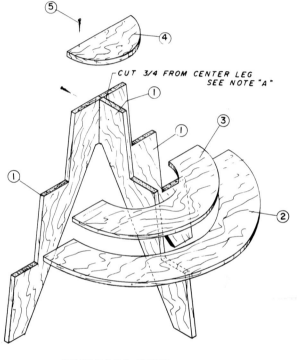

CUT 3/4 FROM CENTER LEG
SEE NOTE "A"

EXPLODED VIEW

Once all of the parts fit together correctly, assemble the project, keeping everything square as you go. Check that all fits are tight.

5. Finish to suit, following the general finishing instructions in the introduction. I have painted some of my plant stands all over, but I found it much faster if I stain the shelves and just paint the legs. Either way, this plant stand will look good.

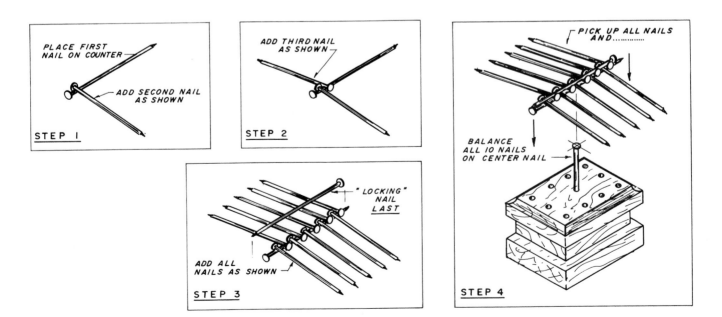

STEP 1
PLACE FIRST NAIL ON COUNTER
ADD SECOND NAIL AS SHOWN

STEP 2
ADD THIRD NAIL AS SHOWN

STEP 3
"LOCKING" NAIL LAST
ADD ALL NAILS AS SHOWN

STEP 4
PICK UP ALL NAILS AND............
BALANCE ALL 10 NAILS ON CENTER NAIL

Metric Conversion Chart

Inches to Millimeters and Centimeters

Inches	Mm	Cm	Inches	Cm	Inches	Cm
1/8	3	0.3	9	22.9	30	76.2
1/4	6	0.6	10	25.4	31	78.7
3/8	10	1.0	11	27.9	32	81.3
1/2	13	1.3	12	30.5	33	83.8
5/8	16	1.6	13	33.0	34	86.4
3/4	19	1.9	14	35.6	35	88.9
7/8	22	2.2	15	38.1	36	91.4
1	25	2.5	16	40.6	37	94.0
1 1/4	32	3.2	17	43.2	38	96.5
1 1/2	38	3.8	18	45.7	39	99.1
1 3/4	44	4.4	19	48.3	40	101.6
2	51	5.1	20	50.8	41	104.1
2 1/2	64	6.4	21	53.3	42	106.7
3	76	7.6	22	55.9	43	109.2
3 1/2	89	8.9	23	58.4	44	111.8
4	102	10.2	24	61.0	45	114.3
4 1/2	114	11.4	25	63.5	46	116.8
5	127	12.7	26	66.0	47	119.4
6	152	15.2	27	68.6	48	121.9
7	178	17.8	28	71.1	49	124.5
8	203	20.3	29	73.7	50	127.0

Index

Acknowledgments

A large book such as this one, with 150 woodworking projects, could not have been done without a lot of assistance. We would like to thank Paige Gilchrist, senior editor at Lark Books, who oversaw the production of the book, and to her dedicated staff. Without their commitment and special efforts, this book would never have been published. And, thanks as well to Deborah Porter-Hayes who photographed two of the larger projects in this book, and last but not least, a special thanks to all of you, the woodworkers who will be using and enjoying this book. It is our sincere wish that you have fun and enjoy making the various projects in this book.

John and Joyce Nelson
Dublin, New Hampshire

A Note About Suppliers

Usually, the supplies you need for making the projects in Lark books can be found at your local craft supply store, discount mart, home improvement center, or retail shop relevant to the topic of the book. Occasionally, however, you may need to buy materials or tools from specialty suppliers. In order to provide you with the most up-to-date information, we have created a listing of suppliers on our Website, which we update on a regular basis. Visit us at www.larkbooks.com, click on "Craft Supply Sources," and then click on the relevant topic. You will find numerous companies listed with their web address and/or mailing address and phone number.